C7 TORREJÓN EL RUBIO II, Ca, p 196
Photo courtesy of F Marco Simón

Symbols and Warriors

SYMBOLS AND WARRIORS

Images of the European Bronze Age

Richard J Harrison

Western Academic & Specialist Press Limited
Bristol, England

Published by Western Academic & Specialist Press Limited
PO Box 40, Westbury on-Trym, Bristol, England
www.waspress.co.uk

ISBN 09535418-7-8

British Library Cataloguing in Publication Data
A catalogue record for this book is available from the British Library.

Typeset in Plantin by Password, Herefordshire.
Printed and bound in the UK by Short Run Press Ltd, Bittern Road, Exeter.

CONTENTS

FIGURES

Acknowledgements

This book was written while on sabbatical study, supported by a University of Bristol Research Scholarship for the academic year 2001–2002, an AHRB award for Research Leave (AN415; APN13343), and help from the British Academy for travel to and within Spain (SG 32402). It was undertaken after I had been the first Head of the new Department of Archaeology at the University of Bristol from 1995–2001.

Writing a book like this is rarely such a single-handed effort as it might seem to the reader and networks of trust and professional sympathy are essential for it to come to fruition. I am conscious of the kindness of many friends and their reservoirs of patience towards me. I owe a great debt of gratitude to my friend Francisco Marco Simón of the Universidad de Zaragoza, who agreed to be co-author of Chapter 6 and who provided digital photographs of over 30 stelae, helped with the critical autopsy of over 40 stelae and located publications that were unobtainable in England. I could not have completed this work without his help. Other friends have generously read drafts and given candid opinions, which I think make a qualitative improvement to the entire work. I am especially grateful to both Teresa Andrés Ruperez of the Universidad de Zaragoza for her sceptical intelligence and influence on the intellectual shape of the book and to Tamar Hodos of the University of Bristol for help with Classical Archaeology, and Volker Heyd also of the University of Bristol, who brought so much of the new work from Germany to my attention and discussed it with me. They have refreshingly different perspectives, but the errors that remain are all mine.

Many colleagues shared new information with me and I am happy to thank Colin Burgess, Dirk Brandherm, Martin Bartelheim, Kristian Kristiansen, Isabel de Luna (Museu de Torres Vedras, Portugal), Fulvia Lo Schiavo, Mark Pearce, Andrew Sherratt, and Nicholas Vella for all the astonishing things they brought to my attention. Dirk Brandherm kindly allowed me to read parts of his forthcoming book on the swords of Spain and Portugal (in press for the Prähistorische Bronzefunde series), and sent me digital photographs of several stelae.

The curators of the Museo Arqueológico Nacional de Madrid, as well as those directing the provincial museums where stelae are held as part of the collections, have been unfailingly helpful in giving access to see the stelae directly, in the cities of Badajoz, Cáceres, Ciudad Real, Córdoba, Sevilla, Toledo (Museo de Santa Cruz) and Zaragoza. Sue Grice, of the University of Bristol, prepared the drawings and figures.

My wife Gloria Moreno López has lived with this book for two years, knows more than anyone else the tribulations that lie behind it, and has been an unfailing support.

Richard J Harrison

Bristol and Zaragoza, 15 January 2003

1

Stelae as windows on the Bronze Age

1.1   Thinking about a world-view

Some 3000 years ago, western Europe was unlike any of the civilised states in the eastern Mediterranean that were its contemporaries and over the 15 centuries until 750 BC, it made its own ideology, history and myths. The beginnings of a self-consciously different European world, centred on the individual person, are detectable from the early third millennium BC and develop fully in the Bronze Age, as an ideal warrior style of living and dying. This new life-style is seen everywhere by the Early Bronze Age (2150 BC) and over the next millennium successive transformations culminate in episodes when paramount chiefs dominated the territory. As the practice of this life-style changed, it was reflected in the grave goods, funerary customs, luxury objects and cult practices. This shared ideology created an identity where common behaviour is expressed through fashions in weaponry, dress ornaments, jewellery, even particular motifs on objects like the water-bird and sun-boat motifs (*Vogel-Sonnen-Barke*), giving tangible expression to the notion of Europe as a continent of linked communities. Shared ideologies and life-style were expressed in many different ways through the second millennium, sometimes using objects or special rituals linked to rivers and bogs, while other practices created a focus around burials and their offerings. In Spain and Portugal, this ideology emerged in a singular manner, taking form as engravings of individual warriors on hundreds of stone memorials called *warrior stelae*.

Intellectual honesty demands that one considers the world-view of the Bronze Age in its own terms, rather than moulded to familiar patterns governed by modern illusions. For this reason, my loyalties lie with Henri Frankfort, who thought that our first duty was to find the unique qualities that define the intellectual shape of a society and make it a valid human entity. Doing this successfully for the prehistoric societies in western Europe demands an engagement with the material world, of pooled and shared experience, whose validity emerges as the contexts of the warrior engravings are understood. So, this account begins from the facts of human actions. The structured form of much of Bronze Age social action is quite obvious and some of it can be interpreted as part of the life-style of the warrior elite.

The essence of Bronze Age Europe lies in the different ways that power was experienced through ritual and ideology, and expressed through practices such as hoarding metal and treasure, constructing individualised landscapes with their cycles of expansion and regressive pastoralism and the local expressions of a dominant warrior life-style.

Everywhere one looks, there are familiar objects, such as swords, axes, brooches and wheeled vehicles, but translated into different meanings. There are selective mechanisms operating at different levels, some on a pan-European scale, others at regional, provincial and small scales, down to parishes or single sites. The pictures on the stelae can help examine them, through inferring the specific meanings expressed in coded form. For this to work convincingly, one must explain how pictures of objects can be the material expression of an ideology of power.

The collection of over 100 unique pictures from Portugal and Spain, engraved on stone slabs and erected as public monuments, recreates part of the world-view of one Bronze Age society. Through a stroke of good fortune, a veritable library of Bronze Age pictures has survived; a gallery of vignettes engraved over 3000 years ago, at the moment when the chiefly societies of Atlantic Europe and the eastern Mediterranean literate civilisations were beginning to know one another directly (figure 1.1).

This book studies an intellectual aspect of that world, particularly the manner in which social values were expressed pictorially in societies without the use of writing. Although very few stelae are found in their original contexts, those that remain where they were erected originally mark a human burial, and it is logical to propose that many originally had a funerary function, or symbolism. The working hypothesis in this book is that they

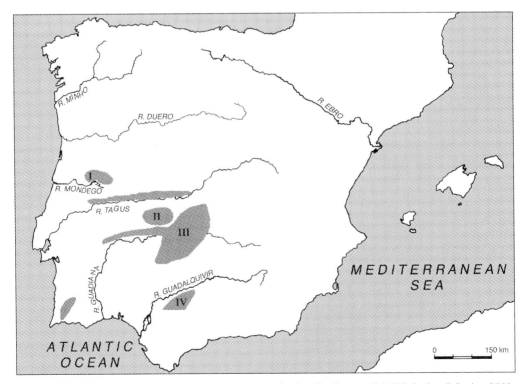

Figure 1.1 *Map of Iberia showing the four main zones of stelae distribution. (Modified after Celestino 2001, Figure 1)*

are multi-vocal monuments, probably derived from grave markers of the sort known from the Early and Middle Bronze Ages in southern Portugal, but which outgrew these limitations. Over time, they came to share common visual references that evolved while they were made. In this way one can better understand why a few are funerary markers, yet others are not; why the symbols grow in number and the compositions become richer over the centuries. Throughout the Final Bronze Age, they seem to have been erected primarily for four overlapping purposes. First, they make a statement of physical possession, marking the landscape as owned by particular individuals who enjoyed all the rights that went with it. Second, they reflect the social status of the owner and his role as protector of his land and its occupiers. Third, they may commemorate the death of an important warrior and perpetuate his memory long after his body has disappeared through exposure, and stand in place of a grave. And finally, it is certain that a few were used to mark graves containing human remains. Evidently, the ownership of the territories of south-west Iberia was strongly contested for several centuries, possibly quite violently, judging by the fortified settlements and the visual importance of weapons on the stelae. That is why the masculine, military and forceful character is emphasised so often and why the symbols have to change over time. These four functions underlie the activity of engraving and erecting stelae and this study will explore the reasons why this was done in the Final Bronze Age and how it was carried out in practice.

The stelae display an ideological code, expressed symbolically in engravings of shields and armed warriors, supported by a panoply of luxurious objects, such as helmets, chariots and rather more mysterious items, perhaps talismans, like mirrors. From these, one can infer that the code has an intellectual vigour as it evolves compositions that culminate in a narrative; some scenes of ritual, hunting or combat, and warriors with animal horns.

Describing and analysing this code provides unique insights into Bronze Age societies. The military aspect and the masculinity of the pictures are explored through specific symbols like shields and toilet articles, which can express other meanings. There is also a hierarchy among the symbols, giving insights into what the world-view might look like. By this means, a description of some intellectual concerns of the Bronze Age is possible and the thought sediments these deposited can be explored systematically. Of course, new discoveries threaten to contradict or reinforce these views; but those are, paradoxically, spurs to analyse the process by which one Bronze Age ideology was created. The task is to explore this world-view through the pictures on stelae and explain how an ideology of power evolved. Once this was in place, it met continual challenges to its authority by enlarging its frames of reference and creating more and more stelae to express them. A parallel intellectual process occurred in Scandinavia at the same time, when a distinctive cosmology and religious expression linked to solar cults arose and expressed itself through an iconography of boats and natural creatures, engraved on bronzes and rock outcrops (Kaul 1998).

1.2   The first stelae in Europe and Iberia

Setting up standing stones and decorating them is an ancient practice in Europe, and the warrior stelae are one group among many. However, before discussing them, it is worth noting some important points about stelae in general, to explain why some hypotheses are stronger than others. Statues and stelae appear in western Europe, the southern Alps and the central Mediterranean from the late fourth millennium BC, closely connected intellectually and physically with the monumental megalithic tombs that dominate the landscapes of that period. Societies identified themselves with founding ancestors, closely linked to home territories, and conceived of their world in these terms. By the third millennium BC, these statues become more elaborate and human in shape, often with geometric decoration and details of costume, ornament and weaponry, that are easy to see; both sexes are present. A trend towards ever more realistic depictions of the human figure culminates around 2600–2200 BC in the southern Alps with the impressive stone figures from Sion (Geneva), the Val d'Aosta and ones in the upper Adige valley. In Iberia, the same process was at work, leading to the stelae and statues carved in many different techniques and styles by the start of the second millennium BC. In these monuments, one can recognise the shift from ancestors, as a group who conferred power upon their descendants, to the display of individuals, who became the principal social actors in the Bronze Age. They establish their ideology and life-style with a new iconography. Recent discoveries make it certain that many stelae formerly believed to be Final Bronze Age in date, are in fact of the later third millennium BC and linked to small megalithic tombs. These are carved on boulders that carry pictures of plump humans, similar to roosting owls, with headdresses and many-stranded necklaces draped over their chests; Spanish archaeologists call them the *Diademadas*. This clears up confusions lasting 60 years, not least because it opens the way to see these sculptures for what they are, distinctive regional traditions of iconography connected to a widespread European custom of venerating ancestors through their tombs. The close association with burials indicates that these are intended to depict ancestors, not gods. The practice of making these stelae spread over the whole of western Iberia. Very probably, many more sculptures were made in wood, or painted on exposed rock faces and have vanished completely. In the second millennium BC in southern Portugal, the dominant persons chose to mark their burials with stone slabs, with axes and weapons carved in relief; these Alemtejo stelae were made between 1800–1300 BC.

Such an historical background explains why stelae were a natural form of sculpture to choose from the Later Neolithic period. There is no working out of any archetypal symbolism here, nor is there any pan-European cult. It is more straightforward than that and one should accept that from time to time societies throughout the world chose the human body as a symbol to express meanings that everyone could understand. What those meanings are differed from place to place. The warrior stelae of the Final Bronze Age were created during the particular historical circumstances between 1250–750 BC and with a political purpose to exalt the status and memory of the leading warriors of the time.

1.3   Stelae as artefacts with pictures

The stelae of south-west Iberia are individual monuments, usually smaller than a man and rarely larger than two metres tall, carved on a single slab of local rock, which was trimmed to shape with a pointed base to set it upright, and a face prepared for carving. On this, a composition of distinct motifs was pecked or incised, probably with pointed metal tools. No more than three are associated with a burial, and nearly all are isolated finds lacking familiar contexts. The oldest compositions have a shield as the main element, flanked by a spear and sword, consistently set out like heraldic emblems. Next, depictions of mirrors, helmets and two wheeled chariots were added. Then a human figure was introduced to the composition, at first on the margin near the central shield motif, but later displacing it as the central element; and at last the shield disappears or is reduced to an inconspicuous size and the composition is entirely dominated by the large human figure, often armed and sometimes located in a narrative scene. Other motifs are introduced, such as secondary human figures, musical instruments, brooches, rings, bows and arrows, combs and tweezers. The latest stelae show more than one human figure and at least three narrate a sequence of events, as if unfolding a story, or the life and funeral of the dead man.

This internal sequence is an evolving code, which can be deduced not only from the associations between motifs and their geographical dispersal, but more importantly, from those which have been re-cut, added to at a later date, corrected, or which have motifs rubbed out. Several stelae are made on Copper Age monoliths shaped originally as huge phalluses; others have been re-used in the later historical periods and have Tartessian and Latin inscriptions cut into them. Thus, many cultural scars were not acquired by chance. Stelae may have been intended to be imperishable statements of power, but rivals and successors to the lands and wealth which gave rise to them refused to accept this and so one finds them all, with one (certain) exception, thrown down or in different locations from those originally intended. Why has only one survived undamaged and in its original location? This cannot be due to chance. The countryside is full of convenient building stone, so why pick out stelae so often for re-use? Questions like this demonstrate the need to understand the processes of creation and rivalry, worked out over centuries. Stelae were carved and erected for at least 350 years and possibly as long as 500 years.

The motifs represent actual objects and human beings, depicted with consistent realism, and are normally easy to recognise. There is no female figure represented and the compositions select only a fraction of the objects available in the Atlantic Bronze Age. Various classifications of them are possible, but since the discovery of the first stelae at the Solana de Cabañas in 1898, everyone has accepted the motifs as representations of human figures and artefacts. One group shows Atlantic Bronze Age swords, as well as long spears, round shields, crested helmets and a range of brooches. A second group depicts objects that originate in the eastern Mediterranean and are not known elsewhere in the Atlantic region. They include handled mirrors, lyres, chariots, combs and perhaps 'tweezers'. This duality lies at the heart of the stelae compositions and is central to understanding them. A third group of motifs are autochthonous and include the various forms of human figure (usually naked), headdresses, dogs, birds, bows and arrows.

Is it helpful to study stelae as pictures? Or, are they physical monuments that happen to bear symbols, based on real objects, whose primary purpose is to communicate a message in a non-literate society? Pictures are representations of something that exists, or has been thought about, and are their visual embodiments, seen through the eyes of their creator, in this case, the eyes of the engraver. They may, or may not, communicate meaning to another observer. However, when different carvers choose an emphatic drawing style for the same objects and assemble them in similar compositions, one can recognise a common intellectual framework that uses symbols to express a meaning understood by more people than just the carver. The pattern of the symbols indicates that there is a message contained within the composition. In the sense therefore, of being able to communicate a reality unambiguously, the pictures do carry meaning, inferred from the symbols in them. The demand to convey this meaning led to the creation of the stelae, in order that a permanent record could be left alone in the landscape, to be recognised by others even if the creators were far away (or dead).

One function of stelae was to record the memory of an individual warrior. A plain standing stone, or a big mound will not do this adequately, since it is impersonal and lacks the imprimatur of the enforcer. This could be the reason that each stela has to bear a picture of a particular owner.

1.4   Aspects of Bronze Age social evolution

It is a puzzle why no early states appeared in Bronze Age Europe, as evolutionary successors to the complex chiefdoms that existed in different regions by 2500 BC. Logically, with the technological opportunities that metal gives for capital accumulation and wealth storage, some social systems should have been able to appropriate and harness its technology for social control as the base for emergent state power. A combination of finance through control of food staples on one hand, or primitive valuables on the other, worked to this effect in the Aegean. But Europe was different. Archaic states never arose and the advanced chiefdoms of 2500 BC were not superseded in social complexity until the historical periods after 700 BC. This means one should consider what social mechanisms allowed this to happen and the processes they represent. One such mechanism may lie in the European preference for a special life-style, focused on the individual warrior and his body, which distinguishes the Bronze Age.

Yet, there are startling discontinuities within regional histories, reflected in the context of familiar artefacts and in the settlements. One therefore finds that similar objects do not necessarily have the same meanings, even in neighbouring areas; they can metamorphose over distance. For example, Herzsprung shields (V-notched) could convey different messages: they may represent an individual warrior in one context, or in another, convey the idea of protection, or represent the universe and the cycle of life and death in the sun's daily path (quite clear in Nordic shields). This may lie behind their varied materials. In Ireland, shields of any kind are rare, yet there are organic and bronze examples; Scandinavia has over 40 bronze shields from rivers and peat bogs, but no organic ones; those in central Europe survive as fragments of scrap metal in hoards; in France, where many shields should be expected, there are none, not even as scrap metal. There are just the three stelae with shields, all from the south. From Portugal and Spain, the 71 shields depicted on stelae are likely to have been made of leather or wood and there are also miniature gold shields from Portugal and votive clay models from Greece. Throughout this period, there is the mutual attraction between the effervescent Late Bronze Age societies of central Europe and the central Mediterranean and the eastern Mediterranean worlds, materialised through a wide range of imports from one area to another. The record extends from raw materials like copper ingots and amber, to weapons, systems of decoration and probably perishable commodities like folding chairs, textiles and slaves. South-western Iberia provides another example of this process at work in a different direction. It lay at the geographical crossroads where two major cultural zones met – the emerging Atlantic Bronze Age industries on a north–south axis and the Mediterranean world, with ideas from the Levant and Cyprus, projected along an east–west axis. In both cases, long-distance links were in place by twelfth century BC, within each zone, which articulated in the areas where stelae were made. Seen in this way, south-western Iberia is at the fulcrum of two huge, independent cultural zones, literally at the heart of the network, and the tribal societies living there mediated cultural values from both worlds. The stelae can be visualised as a political expression of the warrior elite in this receptive geo-political region, open to ideological currents from Europe and from the Mediterranean.

The improvements in absolute and historical dating, due to the accurate tree-ring chronologies, make these contacts intelligible in ways that were poorly understood a generation ago. There are increasingly cogent arguments for the transmission of intellectual stimuli, of ways of thinking about the world in 1200 or 1000 BC, that recognise a system of shared values, which operates in a different dimension from that of objects. Tracing these ideas through an evolving pictorial code should be possible. It should give a broad understanding of the nature of power in south-west Iberia through the evolution of images, the development of a specific iconic expression and the creation of an Atlantic Bronze Age world-view.

2

Between two worlds: the Atlantic and Mediterranean background to the stelae

2.1   The idea of an Atlantic Bronze Age

The concept of an Atlantic Bronze Age is a relatively recent creation, which emerged with real clarity after the pioneering book by Jacques Briard (1965) on the Breton metalwork and a succession of studies in Great Britain, Ireland, France and Iberia, culminating in the catalogues and synthetic accounts of Coffyn (1985) and Ruiz-Gálvez Priego (1986, 1991, 1998) for the regions that directly concern us. It is a convenient shorthand term for describing a cluster of bronze industries and societies flourishing in the later second millennium BC and which drew closer together in the early centuries of the first millennium (Jorge 1998). Some archaeologists, like Cunliffe (2001), think the Atlantic region had a much older sense of a shared identity, forged in the Neolithic and lasting into the Early Middle Ages and that the Later Bronze Age is simply one episode in a long tradition of shared experiences, worked out on the swelling Atlantic seaways. There is a special rhythm to life with marine horizons and the lure of the oceans with their riches and adventure. It is a romantic reconstruction, appealing in many ways, through using comfortable references to historical values. It is unlikely that the same processes are at work over this 7000-year period and there appear to be distinct historical phenomena bringing peoples on the Atlantic shores together. The cyclical regressions and long centuries of isolation between these same communities need explaining, just as much as the expansion stages and their glory moments. The essential strangeness of these societies, or at least those in Bronze Age Iberia, makes it necessary to use a different approach that emphasises the ritual and ideological dimensions of the record.

For this study, the Final Atlantic Bronze Age covers the period from 1250–750 BC and geographically it includes the Atlantic coastlands of Europe, from southern Scotland to the Straits of Gibraltar. Figure 2.1 shows the related cultural provinces at their maximum extension around 1000 BC. Its northern and eastern limits lie in France, clearly marked in the landscape by metalwork hoards and fortified centres to create a cultural and physical boundary with a frontier between it and the central European sphere (Brun 1991). In Iberia it is confined to the western third of the Peninsula and there are substantive Mediterranean links as far as Sardinia. Described in this way, it has the appearance of a cultural block similar to the Nordic one in southern Scandinavia and the Urnfield complex of west central Europe. Materially, it is characterised by idiosyncratic designs of

ATLANTIC BRONZE AGE CULTURAL ZONES
C. 1000 BC

Figure 2.1 *By 1000 BC the Atlantic Bronze Age cultural zone has eleven distinct regional zones, with different metal work, metal alloys, and settlement types. The numbers indicate: 1 Ireland, 2 N Britain, 3 SE England, 4 SW England and Wales, and 5 N Wales. In France the regions are: 6 Brittany, 7 Normandy, and 8 Vendée. In Iberia the regions are: 9 Galicia, 10 Central Portugal, and 11 Extremadura. The stelae occur only in region 11, indicated by heavy stipple*

bronze objects and gold work, especially after 1100 BC. The metalwork is stylistically coherent over very wide areas and strongly emphasises male items. However, metal ornaments (especially ones made of bronze) are scarce and in many regions do not form part of a standardised personal appearance. One archaeologist recently described it in these terms: 'Most strikingly, the bronze industry seems to ignore women (and probably various groups of men) in its products. This is remarkable, especially in comparison with the Urnfield Culture or the Nordic Bronze Age where the fullest skill is often reflected in the production of large richly decorated ornaments and dress fittings' (Sørensen 1998:262).

Another characteristic is the preference for living in small, physically impermanent dwellings, of organic material now wholly perished, that contrasts with the Urnfield village model farther east. There is a great deal of artefact and landscape variety within the regions that comprise it, however, which is a theme discussed in the next chapter.

A defining custom across the whole of Atlantic Europe is the disappearance of formal burial customs in this period, in contrast to the Urnfield practices in central Europe and the central Mediterranean. It is likely that the practice of exposing the human body to the elements and creatures of decay, and allowing every part of it (even the bones) to return to the natural world, replaced the older burial customs of inhumation and cremation. Such practices are known across the world and recur regularly in the prehistoric record. In these cases, the memory of the dead is kept alive through recounting stories and rituals and keeping objects associated with them, or setting up memorials such as stelae.

The long distance exchanges based on amber, metal and finished products became an important form of wealth finance at this time. This is a form of capital accumulation promoted through exchanges of scarce commodities, fostered by socially dominant individuals, in order to promote their status and authority. There is good evidence from Spain and Portugal for links eastwards to the central Mediterranean, especially Sardinia and Sicily, and from those islands onwards to Cyprus and the coast of Syria (Mederos 1996a). The date of the Mycenaean pottery from Montoro (Córdoba) shows these eastern connections were in place by 1300 BC and they were maintained and increased in number and range over time, until the first Phoenician trading posts were established in southern and western Spain and Portugal in the period 850–800 BC. Contacts materialise in the form of eastern objects, or close imitations of them, imported into the Atlantic region, such as a bronze bowl of Syrian or Egyptian type from Berzocana (Badajoz), or the wheeled incense burners from Baiões (Beira Alta, Portugal). Atlantic bronze objects were also exchanged to the east, reciprocating the movement. Thus, one finds elbow fibulae of Spanish design in Cyprus and an articulated roasting spit from a grave in Amathus; Portuguese axes and Atlantic swords are in Sardinian (Monte Sa'Idda) and Sicilian (Castelluccio) hoards after 1000 BC (Giardino 1995, 2000). The best explanation for these sporadic, long distance exchanges is that they are the visible part of chiefly ties, cemented by gifts of exotic items (Mederos 1996b). No doubt many other items were given as presents too, but being made of organic materials, have not survived. Wooden chariots, musical instruments, incense and textiles could all have been gifted as well.

Towards the end of the period, there is a workshop of a bronze smith at the Mediterranean settlement of Peña Negra (Alicante) where he cast Atlantic types of weapons and it seems likely that this is an example of a western craftsman working outside his usual milieu around 900 BC. Therefore, a defining characteristic of the Iberian region of the Atlantic Bronze Age was its eastern linkages. For the time being, it is sufficient to acknowledge the importance of these exchange systems.

Less well understood and much more poorly documented, is the subsistence base. New surveys of Bronze Age settlements suggest that permanent settlements appear by 1100 BC in central Portugal (Baiões and Sta Luzia), but no earlier than 800 BC for southern Galicia. A glimpse of more substantial evidence from Extremadura shows that the region was not only settled and the extensive territory structured around big settlements, but that different landscapes were developed in the Final Bronze Age after 1200 BC (Pavón 1998). The territory was organised systematically and based on natural resources that any dry farming and livestock economy would value, namely fertile soils and water sources. There are diverse settlement types, some on lower ground, others occupying river terraces, hilltops and isolated hills. In the northern part of the region, in the modern province of Cáceres, Final Bronze Age settlements were sited away from the Tagus river, on prominent hills fortified with masonry walls that enclosed areas of over 3 ha. They are sited for control of the landscape and all-round visibility, as well as keeping an eye out for favourable farming soils and probably for tin deposits. To the south in the province of Badajoz, a different settlement pattern emerged, centred on the fertile terraces of the river Guadiana and river crossings. Major sites, occupied from the Final Bronze Age to the present, include the cities of Badajoz and Medellín. Their castles occupy the choicest locations with the oldest settlement traces. Fortified settlements lie at the centre of all the distributions of bronze and gold finds and many of the stelae. There are enough excavated animal bones and charred seeds from the Cerro del Castillo de Alange to prove that a normal range of domestic animals was raised (including horses) and wheat, barley and beans were dry-farmed. This is a standard west European subsistence economy found almost everywhere in the Bronze Age and frankly it would have been unbelievable if modern survey had failed to detect it. So the main settlements can be discovered and perhaps they enjoyed opportunities for stock raising that the savanna woodlands provided. Pavón's work places the stelae in a much richer and more complex socio-economic context than before, so they can be appreciated in a settled landscape and not de-contextualised. It is a great step forward.

A corollary is that it reveals an economic system capable of creating wealth finance for the Bronze Age societies of south-west Iberia. It is perfectly possible that cattle herding became important and part of the strategy of wealth creation. Owning animals confers a degree of mobility and freedom of action that is denied to settled cereal cultivators and

placed in the tenth century, making them contemporary with the hoard from the Ría de Huelva, and that there is a surface find, unconnected with the two deposits, of a Vénat type spearhead with an early eighth century BC radiocarbon date (GrN-7484: 700±120 BC, uncal). The Baiões deposits really characterise the life-style of the elite over several generations in the Final Bronze Age and that is how they should be regarded, rather than as a chronological marker.

The Huelva hoard was dredged from the estuary of the river Odiel over a period of several weeks in February and March 1923, when the harbour was improved. The mechanical dredge had buckets on a continuous chain, bringing sediment to the barge on the surface, where workmen picked out the bronzes, as they happened to see them. Undoubtedly, many pieces were missed and perhaps a few were kept as souvenirs. Later dredging recovered more objects, some of them of Iron Age date like penannular brooches, but these are not certainly associated with the first collection, which is the main Final Bronze Age hoard. There are over 400 objects, mainly weapons, with some brooches, bracelets, belt-hooks and helmets. There are many questions about its manner of deposition that remain unanswered and it is not clear if it was the cargo from a wrecked ship (the preferred functionalist explanation), or if it accumulated as a result of offerings cast into the estuary, at a place that was regarded as sacred (Ruiz-Gálvez Priego 1995). Whatever the case, there are some bronze objects in it that are older than 950 BC and it does not have the appearance of a scrap metal hoard either. An emerging consensus dates it to about 950 BC and it should be of the same period as many of the Baiões bronzes.

The final phase is named after the Monte Sa' Idda hoard in Sardinia, since so much of the metalwork in it originates from Spain and Portugal. In France, the major bronze hoard from Vénat (found in a large clay vase and containing hundreds of pins and scraps of metal for melting into new objects) should be dated to the same period. Vénat is the most reliable closed find of all these major hoards and the only one excavated in such a manner as to guarantee the integrity of its contents (Coffyn 1985).

The first Phoenician trading posts appear on the south-west coast between 850–800 BC and therefore overlap substantially with the Monte Sa' Idda phase (figure 2.2). There are arguments to make the Phoenician trading posts even older, starting just after 900 BC (Mederos 1997). With them we enter into the historical world and the geo-politics of the eastern Mediterranean powers.

Chronologies are still hotly debated and it is possible that, when the dendro-chronology sequence extends finally to the Atlantic coast of Iberia, the earlier dates proposed by Mederos may prove to be correct. If that happens, it will strengthen further the arguments for linkages between the eastern and western Mediterranean societies (known as the 'pre-colonial contacts' since they are older than the first Phoenician contacts [Mederos 1996a, 1996b; 1999; van Dommelen 1998]) and increase their importance in explaining structural changes in the Atlantic Bronze Age. But it would also force a substantial revision of the

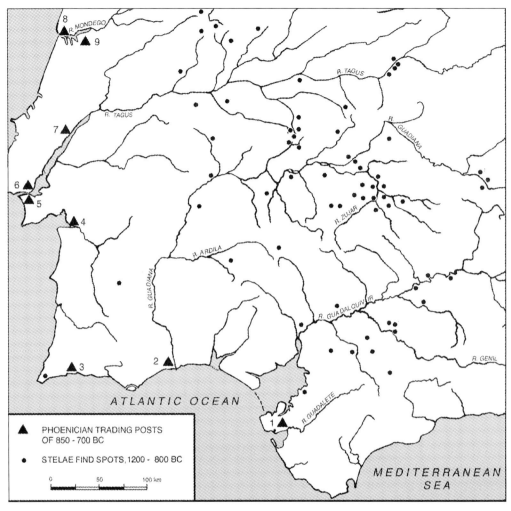

Figure 2.2 *Map of south-west Iberia with the distribution of stelae (black dots) contrasted with the location of the first Phoenician trading posts (triangles) in the ninth-eighth centuries BC. The river estuaries are shown as they would have been around 1000-700 BC. The Phoenician sites are: (1) Castillo de Doña Blanca (2) Castro Marim (3) Rocha Branca (4) Abul (Alcácer do Sal) (5) Quinta do Almaraz (Almada) (6) Lisboa (cathedral cloister) (7) Alcáçova de Santarém (8) Santa Olaia (9) Conímbriga*

historical links in the later second millennium BC and that would require fresh thinking about the cultural mechanisms involved in them.

2.3   Research agendas for the Bronze Age

The vigorous campaign of cultural promotion in 1994–1996, led by the Council of Europe, on the theme of Bronze Age Europe, had some unexpected consequences. Beyond the travelling exhibitions there were seminars, at least one on how political units conceived of themselves and used their material culture to show this identity. Quite a few people imagined the Bronze Age was the taproot of the European identity and hence a source to cherish, since it avoided inconvenient modern labels. However, this is as naïve as it is wrong. Identity is continually created; being a modern European is an active process and one could just as sensibly trace its common roots ('genetic heritage') to the Mesolithic through DNA sequences.

More interesting are innovative studies on a grand scale, kindling fresh interest in matters of ideology, historical dynamics and the nature of prehistoric societies. European archaeologists have rediscovered the fascination for narrative that many had thought vanquished forever. Among the most recent and influential in approach, is the extended study by Kristian Kristiansen (1998), who adapts the core-periphery model and its cycles of cultural expansion and regression (originally developed by Wallerstein [1974] for Europe in the sixteenth century AD). Kristiansen marshals the evidence for repeated episodes of pastoralism in western and central Europe and identifies the ideologies of warrior elites and their codes of conduct, as some of the formative processes accounting for their emergence. In particular, his canvas covers the whole of Europe for 2000 years, letting one see the broad themes that have been obscured among a welter of detail. Anthony Harding's study also ranged widely (2000:418–422), but challenged the core-periphery model on the grounds that it was inappropriate to see the Bronze Age World in modern terms and wrong to divorce political from economic forces. He detected many small cores, each with their own peripheries; and he was notably cool to the idea of cyclical regressions. His thematic approach makes it difficult to discern the important processes at work and in the new era of reliable dates, one can move towards realistic testing of certain propositions. Decidedly ambitious in its west European scope and its approach to the *longue dureé* modelled on that of Ferdinand Braudel, is the study by Marisa Ruiz-Gálvez Priego (1998), strongly committed to the idea of an Atlantic Bronze Age and a pastoral economy. It has a broad view of the Atlantic Bronze Age, but an intermittent and confused approach to ideology. Furthermore, the evidence to define a widespread pastoral economy is tenuous, where not inexistent, and recent work establishes the settlement patterns and extensive systems of animal and crop husbandry for the period. For understanding the social dynamics of chiefdoms, the theoretical rigour and applicability of the models for social power developed by Timothy Earle (1997) are impressive, using comparative anthropological methods and then grounding them firmly in archaeological case studies in Hawaii, Peru and Denmark. His masterly discussion of ideology as a source of power and its materialisation informs the analysis in Chapters 5 and 6.

Looming over all these advances is the shadow of post-modernism, which seeks to deny the validity of making any objective statements about the past, or other cultures. This analysis of the stelae takes the position that visual communication is a social strategy and that compositions make repeated references to Bronze Age warriors, who are empirically identifiable. The final chapter discusses the wider world of the Late Bronze Age and its social values.

2.4   Looking forward

Spanish and Portuguese archaeologists have devoted over 300 publications to stelae in the past half-century and there is no sign of this pace slackening. Martín Almagro Basch published the first good catalogue in 1966; these drawings and large format photographs remain the touchstone for all later work. He included 24 warrior stelae among the 42 he described and he embarked on a detailed typological classification of all the motifs depicted. To Martín Almagro Basch, they were primarily funeral markers erected above the (now vanished) graves of great warriors and were broadly dated to the Final Bronze Age and lasted into the period of first Phoenician contacts. The 1974 supplement to the catalogue continued these views. In 1977 his son, Martín Almagro Gorbea, published more newly discovered stelae, often very briefly described or illustrated and placed them firmly in the context of the Final Bronze Age of south-west Spain, when the precursors to the Orientalising Tartessian elites of the eighth and seventh centuries BC were emerging. Further discoveries were published singly or in small groups throughout the 1980s. After a period of neglect and fashionable criticism, it seems that Almagro Basch's views contain an important element of truth about the function of stelae, namely that they are inextricably linked to the funerary world of the Bronze Age. They do not identify graves as such, but they do mark the memory of a dead individual, in a context where the body is not the chief focus, so that graves were effectively dispensed with. Without a body there is no need for a grave. However, stelae form an ideological bridge between the dead and the living, made through the image that conserves the memory of the dead man. It is this memory that is important, not the body, which was probably exposed and entirely destroyed, which is why we almost never find traces of it.

From 1988 however, we enter into a new stage, with the appearance of major works by Barceló (1988, 1989), Galán (1993) and Celestino Pérez (1990, 2001), which break with the previous typological debates and alter fundamentally our understanding of these monuments. As we shall refer to their ideas and contributions throughout this study, it is appropriate to sketch the main themes here.

Barceló argued strongly that all the stelae were older than the Phoenician presence in Iberia and were the products of a triangular trade between France, Iberia and Sardinia, hence the mixture of elements depicted. Placing the entire phenomenon into the Final Bronze Age allows it to be understood in a qualitatively different way than if it is conceived as part of the Phoenician impact on the far west, since the connections with the Final Bronze Age in Cyprus, the Aegean and Sardinia are clearly important from the eleventh century BC. These early connections effectively discount the simple model of cultural assimilation under Phoenician influence and force consideration of the true range of Final Bronze Age connections across the Mediterranean. His cluster analysis of motifs grouped the stelae, but failed to show either a clear evolution or a geographical pattern. Galán did the same (1993:43–52). Both results confirmed that clustering techniques were not appropriate for analysing compositions, which follow their own logic. Simply breaking pictures down into a set of elements, all uniformly weighted, will not produce a good seriation, since it denies any value to the obvious sense of composition and balance that the engravers had when they did their work. Furthermore, it ignores the hierarchy of value evident between motifs, from their place in the compositions.

It was Galán who first argued that stelae should be considered as features in a prehistoric landscape and that they were not, in any real sense, marking graves with human remains in them. Placing stelae in their prehistoric landscape allows him to view them spatially and he proposed some functional explanations for the patterns of distribution and the motif compositions. Using a sample of 85 stelae (not all of them warrior stelae, however), Galán found the same patterns as others before him, namely that the older stelae with simple weapon compositions lay in the valley of the Tagus river and the later ones were centred on the river Guadiana, with the most complex of all in the Guadalquivir valley. He recognised an exceptional concentration around the river Zújar, a tributary of the Guadalquivir. He argued for a territorial hierarchy with the stelae as markers of drove roads for livestock and that the differences in composition were due to deliberate expressions of identity, to mark specific neighbours and historically known individuals (Ruiz-Gálvez Priego & Galán 1991). For Galán the whole period of stelae construction was relatively short historically (or so he believed), so he treated them as a contemporary group with no significant evolution. For him, the Final Bronze Age chiefdoms producing stelae were in a transition period between two opposed concepts of space; moving from an open landscape, to territories marked by central places and hill forts. Ideologically, they belonged to the Atlantic world, drawn into contact with the Mediterranean through trading networks reaching to Sardinia and Cyprus. This part of the model suffered a hard blow recently, when fieldwork showed that walled settlements and centrally organised territories existed in south-west Spain from the start of the Final Bronze Age, effectively refuting it (Pavón 1998). But there are other difference between Galan's model and the one offered here. The next chapters present the evidence for an evolution of styles and motifs, and also consider more sympathetically the likelihood that stelae are related to the world of the dead.

With this base, Celestino (2001) embarked on the most thorough study of all. Apart from the illustrated catalogue of all 93 stelae known to him (see Chapter 10 of this volume), Celestino's work presents the detailed arguments for the chronological evolution of the stelae in the Final Bronze Age and exhaustively explores the formal parallels to the motifs depicted. By paying very close attention to the actual stelae and making detailed, direct observations of every one of them, he recognises the importance of altered and re-cut stelae and provides better readings of the motifs. In particular, his interest in the actual technique of engraving and the varied styles, means he could interpret the stelae more accurately than ever before. Many new stelae are published for the first time and corrections made to older figures and accounts. Reading the motifs on the stelae is not easy, or straightforward, and there is room for more than one version of what is actually depicted. Celestino divided south-west Iberia into geographical zones, with a wide outlying area that he called the 'margin', and analysed stelae within each one. This supports the evolutionary perspective and shows that Galan's groups were neither homogeneous, nor distinct social territories.

3

Landscapes with stelae

This chapter considers the physical setting of the landscapes in which stelae are found and makes an assessment of the critical natural resources that would have been available three millennia ago. One has to understand the climatic peculiarities of the Mediterranean, and the way this has affected the historical ecology of the dominant oak pastures that every traveller to south-west Iberia notices. The mechanisms by which stelae have been found over the last 100 years are discussed.

3.1   The landscapes and historical ecology of Extremadura

The first thing to notice is that the Extremadura is geographically distinctive, with an immediately recognisable Mediterranean climate and ecology, but that it is not homogeneous. The relief is dominated by parallel ranges of low mountains trending roughly north-east to south-west, chiefly composed of old, metamorphic rocks, usually granite, schist, Palaeozoic sedimentary rocks and basalt. They have worn down to rolling plateaux, buckled into small mountain ranges by tectonic pressure. Contour maps make the area look deceptively accessible and easy to move over, but in fact movement is harder than it appears, since there are many scarps, faults, sharply eroded features that create barriers within the sierras, as well as drainage networks that vary from shallow water courses forded easily throughout the year, to the older rivers that are often deeply incised, at least for part of their length. The main rivers are the Guadiana and the Tagus, with contrasting aspects and hydraulic behaviour. The Guadiana is sluggish with a low flow of water, rising in the flatlands of La Mancha to the east, which supplies its underground water sources. It meanders across ancient landforms, until it reaches more broken terrain in Portugal and enters a series of defiles and gorges. The Tagus has a much greater flow of water all year round, which comes from mountain catchments in the Sierra de Albarracín and often flows swiftly through deep cuttings and gorges through most of its length. Many substantial tributaries feed it. In human terms, the Guadiana landscape is one easy to move across and with relatively fertile soils in its middle reaches; however the Tagus is a formidable barrier, with few safe crossing points and so deeply incised into its bed that its water cannot be used to water fields on the narrow terraces of alluvium along it. Only in Portugal does its valley open out and the river flow more gently.

The surface geology has weathered into large areas of rather shallow, freely draining soils of acidic type, interspersed with smaller regions of ancient alluvial clay and river terraces, mostly in the Guadiana valley and of Tertiary date. Soil fertility varies considerably over short distances and it is not accurate to think that all the soils are poor and suitable only for pasture or tree crops. In fact, if the farmer does not demand too big a yield, a catch crop of cereals or legumes can be planted over much of the region at altitudes below 600m and in higher parts with gentle relief. All along the Guadalquivir valley, which marks the southernmost area of stelae, the agricultural potential is much higher and the area has long been famed for its cereal, olive and livestock yields. The real limits to farming are imposed more by water scarcity, exacerbated by the free draining soils and a marked summer drought of at least five months, than lack of fertility. Its basic geology of ancient, very hard rocks means that it lacks the large, shallow aquifers found under the plains of La Mancha to the east. A myriad of fissures in the bedrock conduct surface water into small underground reservoirs, many of which are not easily accessible. Consequently, springs are relatively infrequent and wells can be difficult to make; all this means that those river courses with water all the year round, like the Guadiana and the Zújar, are exceptionally important in the summer. There are some rich agricultural areas today, notably the extensive irrigated clay lands known as the Tierra de Barro south of the Guadiana river, around Almendralejo. The standard geography of Iberia by Lautensach (1964) and the regional volumes in the *Gran Atlas de España*, give good modern descriptions. The important features to mention are not so much the details of the mountain chains, the routes through them and patterns of watercourses, nor a detailed account of the agricultural and mineral resources. It is the historical ecology that is important, describing how the present landscapes evolved and then working backwards to the Bronze Age ones. In short, it is best to follow the landscape evaluation of Grove and Rackham (2001) and let them explain the ecological processes that could underlie Bronze Age economic patterns.

The Mediterranean climate is one we think we know more about than we, in fact, do. Years of misinformation, linguistic confusions and inadequate runs of climate data for short periods (often badly recorded) have to be overcome. It is only recently that the generalised and inaccurate topical descriptions of seasonal aridity, degradation of once great forests from a greener Eden and the role of erosion in silting up river mouths, have been challenged by better-informed views. Starting with the climate, the intensity of the annual variations in rainfall is the defining feature, far more important than the total amount received each year. In Extremadura it rains heavily in the autumn and winter, from mid-October to early March. In an average year, taking the mean from a 150 year run of readings, about 400–600 mm of rain will fall in the inland areas, rising to over 900 mm in central Portugal and on land above 800 m high. In the drier parts of eastern Extremadura, less than 500 mm of rain is normal and there are local rain shadows in the lee of steep hills. But these figures hide a fundamental characteristic of Mediterranean rainfall; it sometimes falls in torrents, as a deluge, with anything up to half a year's precipitation in one or two days. A deluge is when at least 200 mm of rain falls in 24 hours, or 50 mm in one hour (Grove & Rackham 2001:30). The worst deluges recorded in the last 200 years, in places like Mt Aigoual in the French Cévennes between 18 and 23 September 1890, when 900 mm of rain fell, release astronomic amounts of water. These violent events may occur only once in two centuries, or at even longer intervals, so they are outside one's normal lifetime experience, or even the lengthy meteorological records of centralised states like France, and for this reason have not been recognised for the important climatic features they are. There are usually smaller deluges to measure, however, and they are characteristic pluvial events of the Mediterranean climate. In south-west Iberia, deluges are rare, but they do occur and are relatively frequent in the Sierra Morena (Grove & Rackham 2001: figure 2.7). They are dramatic agents of erosion, able to change the landscape and its vegetation overnight. Annual rainfall can vary from double the annual mean in wet years, to less than one third in dry ones; years with big variations are commoner than ones with 'average' rainfall. The amount of rain and its distribution in deluges or more gently in downpours, is the critical variable in promoting vegetation growth and on which all livestock and dry farming of cereals depends. Therefore average figures are not helpful in determining how many 'good' years there might be in any decade. Powerful but unpredictable storms are normal in this climate.

Modern climates vary more than one imagines. The Medieval Warm Period (1000–1250 AD) and the Little Ice Age (1450–1850 AD) show how extreme 'ordinary' or 'normal' climate can be. Both had a real impact in the Mediterranean, including Iberia. In the Little Ice Age, there are at least four lengthy periods of well-recorded extreme weather events, with bitter winters, late frosts, deluges, droughts and dust storms (Grove & Rackham 2001:140). There is some correspondence between them and volcanic eruptions and it is certain that the great ones did have a global impact. These produced local famines from failed harvests, plagues afflicting populations previously weakened by malnutrition, floods and in places devastation that lasted for generations; it is a record of destructive events. It seems reasonable that similar periods of severe weather occurred in the past, perhaps bringing an entire lifetime of troubles. These climatic analogies of the last millennium are probably valid for the Final Bronze Age. If that is so, extreme weather events, within an otherwise benign climate, have important consequences for predicting human behaviour. Combined with the erratic rainfall, it makes the Mediterranean climate a testing one for herders and farmers. In turn, they respond with subsistence strategies that provide storage of surplus products in good years to tide them over the lean ones that will surely come; these are as ingenious as they are varied.

In the past 200 years, modern vegetation, particularly woodland cover, has increased very greatly in Extremadura. The field evidence is quite unambiguous, that it is denser, more extensive, more productive (and more demanding of labour until the 1960s) than at almost any other time; this is the pattern throughout the Mediterranean savannas in Liguria, Crete and Greece.

In all the countries we have seen, young trees greatly outnumber middle-aged and old. Sometimes old trees, usually pollards, are scattered among them, proving that savanna preceded forest. In every European Mediterranean country that we know, woodland has increased by natural processes, following abandonment of terrace cultivation, decline of pasturage, or cessation of woodcutting … the evidence amply rebuts the belief that Mediterranean ecosystems are fragile and cannot recover. Quite the contrary: they recover more quickly than in England, though not so exceptionally fast as in eastern North America. (Grove & Rackham 2001:61, 65)

Extremadura carries a distinctive vegetation of wood pasture with oak trees and a low under story of grasses and scrub that at times looks like parkland. It is called a *dehesa* in Spanish and *montado* in Portuguese and is best described by the term savanna. It is a landscape dominated by evergreen species, which seem to have increased throughout the Mediterranean in the Holocene to reach their present dominance in the fifth millennium BC. Grove and Rackham explain this as due to the different behaviours of deciduous oaks and the evergreen ones that replaced them (Grove & Rackham 2001:161). The evergreen holm oaks and prickly-oaks (*Quercus ilex* and *Q rotundifolia*) grow mainly on thin acidic soils and granite, while the creeping-oak or live-oak (*Q coccifera*) thrives even on bare rock (actually in its cracks) (Montoya Oliver 1988a). These oaks are all well adapted to browsing animals and regenerate well. They can tolerate hard grazing for decades. From the fifth millennium BC onwards the climate was drier, reaching its most arid period around 1000 BC. This also favoured the extension of evergreen oaks.

Now, the south-west woodlands are not forests in quite the same sense as the stands of beech and fir make in the Pyrenees, but nor are they are a degraded version of a formerly richer forest. There have never been dense forests in the south-west and the savannas are the original form of native woodland. 'Wood-pastures are seldom well documented: their documents tend to be a record of land use rather than landscape. The student must therefore ask the trees. Wood pasture trees tend to live longer than in woodland: most ancient trees are in savanna and are a record of its history' (Grove & Rackham 2001:194). The trees in the savannas are remarkably even-aged, with few old ones. The trees themselves document two energetic episodes of savanna creation, for the period 1870–1920, with a further expansion in the 1930s, but there is almost no written record of this. The trees seen today, uniformly pruned into low crowns with four big horizontal branches and one tree growing every 15 to 20 m, reflect a style of nineteenth century management. It needed a lot of labour and it is an intensification of medieval practices. The origins of these savannas as managed resources go back at least to the third millennium BC (Stevenson & Harrison 1992; Harrison 1996). Savannas are actually richer habitats than forests and more productive in terms of the wildlife they support and the amount and number of domestic livestock they can feed. Getting reliable figures of savanna productivity, especially in a period when transhumance of livestock was common, is not easy.

Erosion must be assessed in a more rational way, too. It can be beneficial as often as it is destructive and does not necessarily involve great amounts of valuable topsoil being stripped away and lost in river silts. Most of the sediment eroded is subsoil or loose material already available in riverbeds and terraces and is transported to a new resting place. The delta formation and coastal deposits of the rivers Guadalquivir and Guadiana do not coincide with known times of erosion. The growth of the Guadalquivir delta was greatest at the end of the Little Ice Age in the sixteenth and seventeenth centuries AD and is certainly post-Roman. The real reason why these estuaries in south-west Iberia filled with sediment is that there has been tectonic movement, as well as local changes to sea level, including a rise between 1200–900 BC (Grove & Rackham 2001:330, note 7). For the Flandrian period from 3000–1000 BC, geomorphologists can show that the estuaries of the major rivers of the whole of the south-west of Iberia, from the Guadalete in Cádiz to the Mondego in central Portugal, were larger than they are today, penetrating far inland, affording very gentle, tidal shallows in which to fish and travel. Many of these extended hundreds of square kilometres; the Guadalquivir was formerly a huge shallow bay of the Atlantic and smaller bays formed around the Guadalete, Odiel and Sado. Long tidal reaches flooded the estuaries of the Tagus and Mondego, reaching over 70 km upstream from Lisbon and creating dozens of shallow inlets on their margins. They gave easy access to the Extremadura from the coastal areas and meant that there were many safe havens for coastal travellers. They were still prominent landscape features in the ninth century BC when Phoenician trading posts were established on many of them and are shown on the coastline in figures 2.2 (p 16) and 4.2 (p 39).

The lesson to draw from the intensity of modern climate oscillations is that in the Holocene dry phase to 1000 BC, equally abrupt weather changes occurred. As they are uncovered in more detail, this modern climate analogy will become stronger. In human terms, it means that one had to plan for extreme weather events, long droughts as well as deluges. The climate until 1000 BC was drier than today's, then became slightly wetter until about 400 BC, when another dry phase began. The water table would have been higher and there may have been more surface water accessible in ponds and riverbeds. The landscape was forested as a savanna with evergreen oaks, although less extensive than in the nineteenth century AD.

3.2   Subsistence in the savannas: herding systems and pastoralism

Economic resources are cultural appreciations. They change over time. It is not easy to project modern analogies back 3000 years and assert confidently that one knows what were the economic forces behind the Bronze Age societies in Extremadura. This region has the advantage of the largest and richest area of winter pasture in the Mediterranean. Today, the managed oak savannas support the cork and pork economy and a modern settlement pattern of large villages from which workers travel into the countryside. Specialised pastures, seasonal meadows, ash groves for supporting plough oxen and many other highly particular land uses continue (Montoya 1983) and clearly have their roots in older practices going back many centuries where they are described in Gabriel Alonso de Herrera's famous manual, the *Obra de Agricultura*, first published in 1513. In 2003 AD, as this book is written, there is still much transhumance of sheep and lesser numbers of cattle, to take advantage of the winter pastures, before returning to summer grazing in the mountains of León, Cantabria, Soria and Cuenca (Terés et al 1995). Herding and stock raising predominate and have done so since the Middle Ages. It is possible to dry farm cereals and legumes over very wide areas and in the river terraces, to grow olives. The prehistoric economy was characterised by mixed cereal farming, extensive livestock raising in combinations of breeds and animals, and wild plants, fruits and animals were in some cases very significant (Pavón 1998:249). Domesticated olives were not grown until later. What is not known is whether a strong interest in cattle herding transmuted into a pastoral economy in the Bronze Age. One possibility is that it did so, perhaps for short periods of a century or two. After all, there were sharp differences in prehistoric settlement patterns within the region and varied economies would be expected as a natural consequence of this. It could be that practices changed as the climate oscillated in its habitual manner, responding to acute pressures that were local in their effect. The answers will come as direct evidence emerges from seeds and animal bones, isotopic analyses from human skeletons to show the palaeo-diet and good proxy data from environmental indicators like pollen and sediment cores. The Extremadura is especially well suited to pastoral exploitation and there are many subtle and fruitful combinations in which it can be exercised.

In particular, the marked climatic oscillations would be the determining factor in bad times. It would make sense in these circumstances to be able to respond opportunistically by having a broadly based production of cereals and animal products and not be too specialised. One has in mind an economy which would allow the pastoral element, whether composed of cattle, sheep or pigs is immaterial, to expand when conditions made crop production uncertain or impossible. It would not be dominant, necessarily, for more than a few decades, or perhaps a little longer, before changing to a different form, perhaps emphasising hunting wild animals for meat and pelts, or sowing more cereals and pulses. The variations would be worked out at the level of individual farms and herds, to respond to the pressures so unexpectedly or unevenly exerted. Such an opportunistic strategy could work out well in a semi-arid Mediterranean environment.

Productivity figures for modern animal breeds in a pastoral setting are difficult to find. Montoya (1983:79) reckons cattle are the simplest of all livestock to manage and require least attention from the herdsman. Pigs need most attention in the autumn when foraging for acorns; and sheep are intermediate, but need a lot of care at lambing time in January and when they are sheared in April. Productivity is also a difficult concept to quantify, especially with rustic breeds of animals which have the capacity to survive without close supervision in harsh conditions, or which have a useful territorial instinct (notable in some sheep breeds and in the Iberian swine), making them easy to find. These animals keep to a fairly small home range. It will often be the case that what is required is an animal with good survival instincts, rather than a breed that fattens up quickly.

Some breeds of Iberian swine quickly learn the commands of their herders, as well as where their sties are, so they can be led to pastures and return home every night with a minimum of supervision (Parsons 1962). It is widely known that mixing livestock in different combinations is good practice; not only to improve the pastures and savannas by selective browsing, but also to increase milk and meat yields. All livestock, including domestic geese and chickens, feed happily on acorns, which are abundant from September to February. There are accurate modern figures for the productivity of pigs raised in the south-western savannas, however, which were brought to the attention of archaeologists recently (Harrison 1996). Pigs in the savannas of Extremadura need to grow healthy skeletons for a year before they are sent into the woodlands with a herder to fatten up for market. Without this preparation they lack the strength to roam the oak woods. Once the acorns are ripe and begin to fall as mast, the pigs are introduced, eating those on steep and rocky places first, which are easily reached while the pigs are still agile. As they grow, they are taken to flatter ground, the whole process extending for about four or five months, in the *montanera*. A hungry pig would enter the savanna in September weighing about 60 kg and depart five months later in February for the butcher's block, weighing 140 to 150 kg. On average, the conversion rate of acorns into pork is reckoned to be ten to one; in ideal conditions on the coast of Beira, the Portuguese were able to feed 5.3 litres of acorns to pigs, which yielded one kilo of pork; an astonishingly high rate of productivity (Parsons 1962:222). Regular pork yields of 60–70 kg annually for each 1 ha of land are reported from holm-oak savannas, but only 7–20 kg from the less palatable cork-oak savannas (known as *alcornocales*, with *Q suber*) (Montoya 1988b). There are accounts of prodigious acorn production that are the stuff of legend: Smith (1977:157–158) mentions and photographs a single holm oak at St Blas (Algarve), spreading 18 m across and standing alone. It cropped so well, it supported a widow all year round, giving crops of 1200 and 240 litres of acorns in alternate years and there are many other oaks known to yield 100–400 litres of acorns yearly. Yields like this compare favourably with any output from cereals.

Stocking rates are hard to determine precisely and Grove and Rackham state it is usual to have periods of heavy grazing, which some agronomists would call over-stocking, to be followed by relaxed periods when the savanna recovers. They saw little evidence of long term overgrazing damage.

The conclusion is that the modern conditions of climate and landscape were not so dissimilar from those prevailing in the Bronze Age. Consequently, a mixed farming economy with some characteristics of the modern *dehesas*, adapted to a smaller and drier savanna, could have flourished. It would also have had the capacity for surplus production of meat and other animal products and could have been controlled from the strategic fortified settlements (Harrison 1985, 1993; Pavón 1998).

3.3   Metals as raw materials in Extremadura

Metal deposits are often cited as a reason for attracting interest to a particular locality in the Bronze Age. In Extremadura, the main metals accessible to Bronze Age technologies would be alluvial gold from the Tagus river and cassiterite, an oxide of tin that occurs as black grains in alluvial deposits or in quartzite veins running through granite bedrock. Today these metals are found extensively as traces but are not especially abundant and past mining may have exhausted the richer pockets, leaving only the poorer grades now. What is certain is that these two valuable metals were known and used in the Final Bronze Age and that traces of their extracting and smelting may leave no traces whatsoever. Refining alluvial gold panned from river gravels requires little more than a small fire and a clay vessel; and smelting cassiterite to obtain metallic tin is even simpler, since tin melts at 232°C and many cassiterite samples contain up to 80 per cent metallic tin. Tin smelting can be done in a small open fire and will leave no slag behind (Merideth 1998). This ease of extraction and smelting means that traces of ancient metal winning may be invisible and its true extent in the Bronze Age unknown. Merideth located 42 mining sites in Extremadura and central Portugal, most of them for tin, but had little luck in demonstrating that any were certainly exploited in the Bronze Age. The most promising location for a Bronze Age tin mine was the Cerro de San Cristóbal, Logrosán (Cáceres), which had lots of pottery and bronze objects of the Final Bronze Age, as well as rich cassiterite ores on the surface in exposed veins and as elluvial deposits (Merideth 1998:51–66; Rodriguez Diaz et al 2001). The knock-down evidence to prove tin collection and smelting this early would be to recover cassiterite grains stratified in Final Bronze Age strata, or clay crucibles with pure tin residues adhering to them; this is missing at the moment, but San Cristóbal is the most likely site to produce it. Therefore, the argument that tin was an important commodity in the Final Bronze Age depends instead on the facts that several large settlements are near some tin sources in Cáceres (Pavón 1998) and the widespread use of tin alloyed to copper to make a good quality bronze, such as the objects in the Huelva hoard. The conclusion is that tin was very probably an important commodity mined and smelted from 1200 BC onwards.

Copper ores abound in the Sierra Morena, which separates Extremadura from the Guadalquivir valley, and are also known in small deposits in the Montes de Toledo. The mines of the Sierra Morena were certainly flourishing in the Tartessian and Roman periods, as Domergue's surveys and catalogues show, but Bronze Age activity is scarcely documented (Domergue 1988). It would be very unwise to discount copper mining as a significant activity at this time simply because there is little information about it; one good excavation of a mining and smelting establishment could revolutionise our understanding, as has happened recently with the discovery of a Copper Age metallurgical site at Cabezo Juré (Huelva). This discovery enabled Francisco Nocete (2001) to propose a social model for third millennium BC metal production and distribution that included the whole of south-west Iberia and accounted for the emergence, and eventual collapse, of centralised political elites. One should expect surprises once detailed surveys begin.

3.4   Finding the stelae

Stelae are found in south-west Iberia, in the modern Spanish regions of Extremadura and Western Andalusia, and in the neighbouring Portuguese provinces of Beira Baixa, Estremadura and the Alemtejo (figure 4.1 p 38). There are outlying examples further to the east, following the river Tagus as far as the province of Toledo and the most distant ones are at Luna in Zaragoza and the three in southern France. The actual distribution today is an artefact of the manner in which they have been discovered and discovery is governed by a host of different pressures and independent agents. Almost no stelae have been recovered in the course of archaeological field projects and excavations; they are the fruit of casual discoveries made by farm workers, shepherds, local antiquarians, landowners with an eye for unusual objects on their property and, in some cases, they have been recovered by museum curators who have journeyed to the quieter parts of their collecting areas to investigate reports of discoveries. In other cases, local people have known them, but news only reached the authorities decades later. This happened to the ones from Las Herencias I (C25) and Aldeanueva de San Bartolomé (C28). There are cases like the stela from Setefilla (C71) being discovered after an excavation in 1926–1927, published, lost, found again by the municipal swimming pool of Lora del Río in 1973 and finally transported to the relative safety of the provincial museum; this is an entertaining story recounted with some relish by Aubet (1997). Others are known to have existed but since been lost (C52 Valdetorres II, C63 Almendralejo, C69 Toya), or which vanished from sight (one hopes only for a short time) when their legal owners abruptly decided to exercise their rights and take them back into their possession (C62 Herrera del Duque). In the case of the stela Écija V (C78) it was probably stolen while propped up against the estate wall.

There are stelae re-used as convenient building stones on account of their large size and smooth faces, for filling in rutted farm tracks to level the surface and others made into a comfortable seat outside a village house. Still others have been hammered into smaller pieces for building stone, or covered with cement and set into a wall as a lintel; inconvenient ones were added to piles of stones from cleared fields. There is no way of knowing how many others were used like this and have been lost from view, awaiting the chance moment of their future discovery.

These histories are not so different from those concerning other classes of artefact, such as Roman antiquities or recognisable metalwork and coins and serve to remind archaeologists how greatly they depend upon simple chance. This means that the factors that have gone into the creation of the stelae sample and influenced its make-up, may have very little connection with the actual or ancient pattern of their distribution. The distributions may have been badly distorted by chance actions and until systematic landscape surveys are conducted on at least some of the areas where they seem commonest, there is no means of determining what the original density of stelae really was, in any area. Even the extent of their true distribution is unknown.

However, if one looks at the places where stelae have been found in the last 10 years and compares them with the distribution of those already known (~80), one sees that not only is the overall area of distribution expanding significantly, but the density of the finds in the core areas around the Sierra Morena and river Guadiana is also growing. The most interesting thing is that they are being discovered in areas where they were previously not known; the finds from the provinces of Toledo, Ciudad Real, Málaga and Cádiz have expanded the known area of stelae use quite considerably. It is also the case that casual discoveries continue at the rate of eight every decade and have been running at this figure for the last 30 years. This is quite important, since it coincides with two modern social phenomena that must affect their recovery rate. The first of these is the rural demography of south-west Iberia, which reached a peak in absolute population numbers and density of rural settlement in the decades of the 1930s and 1940s, only to fall precipitously from the 1960s. Today it is a fraction of what it was then and is falling still. Furthermore, the mechanisation of farming, the changes in the practices of herding and savanna management, have meant there are far fewer people actually walking over the landscape than before and looking closely at the surface of the land and its plants. With the passing of the generation of people who farmed and herded the land in the older ways, walking behind horse drawn ploughs, manually stripping the cork oaks and pruning their branches, charcoal burning and herding the Iberian swine, a great fund of intimate, small-scale geographical and contextual knowledge will disappear. So it is very likely that the number of chance discoveries made by country people, until now the main source of new finds, will fall sharply. On many modern estates, hunting wild boar, partridge and doves is the main activity, but one does not expect hunters to find lots of stelae while they are out shooting; their attention is elsewhere and their gaze turned to the sky. The second feature is a positive one to balance the negative and that is the increasing number of archaeological excavations in the area and the greater efficiency in artefact recovery and documentation by the museum authorities. This means that the social mechanisms governing the recovery practices today are different than they were and one should expect significant changes to, and knowledge of, stelae densities and distributions. Perhaps they will balance one another. It is very likely that the area of known stelae use will expand and that new concentrations of them will be found.

It is also probable that eventually examples in their original contexts will be found and that they may be very different from what is expected. One cannot be sure that the present pattern reflects the ancient one, even at a very general scale. However, there is no alternative but to use it.

The outstanding features of the stelae distribution can be grasped from figure 4.2 (p 39). The catalogues of Galán and Celestino show they are commonest along the middle courses of the Tagus and Guadiana rivers and the lower Guadalquivir, with a concentration around the river Zújar. Local clusters have been found in many places such as Écija, Valencia de Alcántara, or El Viso and some may be related to hilltop settlements overlooking them; they are mostly unexcavated. Equally clear is the lack of stelae in the lowlands of Huelva and in the Alemtejo; there are almost none within 100 km of the coast, either in metal rich areas like Huelva, or fertile agricultural ones like the Algarve or the coastlands of Portuguese Estremadura and Beira Alta. Nor are there any examples along the Mediterranean shores of Andalusia. There is an apparent eastward limit marked by the middle Guadalquivir. New discoveries in the Montes de Toledo and in Ciudad Real continue to expand the distribution into the western areas of the southern Meseta. The outliers are surprisingly far away from the main body of finds; Toya (C69) in Jaén is the only one from Upper Andalusia; Luna (C93) in Zaragoza has a fine stela that is a good 450 km north of the nearest one and those at Substantion (C90) and Buoux (C91, C92) in France are almost 700 km to the north east. There is a case for excluding these peripheral examples on the grounds that their features are so distinct from the main body of warrior stelae that they are unrelated to them. However, they share the basic composition with the shield motif and other specific Final Bronze Age motifs, so are included in the sample.

This distribution, with all the chance elements that go into its composition, is congruent with other geographical and cultural patterns of Bronze Age material. It was Galán (1993:31–41) who explicitly recognised that the find places of most stelae contained important information about their original location, despite the fact that most had been moved. He noted that they were so heavy and bulky that it was improbable that they had been moved very far from where they were originally erected (figure 3.1).

How many stelae were originally erected in the Final Bronze Age? This is not such an empty question as it may first seem, since, if one can arrive at a reasonable estimate, it will help to evaluate their roles as ideological statements and as possible markers in the landscape. All the warrior stelae, except one, have been recognised after 1898, a recovery rate of 99 in 103 years; before that they were unknown, or perhaps one should say, they were not recorded by antiquarians or local informants before the late nineteenth century. This is also the time when the savanna landscapes were renewed and intensively managed for producing cork and pork and the period of maximum population density in rural Extremadura. The present rate of discoveries is running at approximately eight new stelae every 10 years, which shows that it has not slackened and that many remain to be found.

Figure 3.1   The stela C48 from Magacela (Badajoz) is the average size, at 1.43m tall. (Photograph courtesy of the Museo Arqueológico Nacional, Madrid)

They survive even as building stones and road making material (modern 're-contextualisation'). These figures suggest that about 5–10 per cent of those that are still in the ground have been recovered; this in turn represents perhaps half of those that were originally engraved. These calculations suggest that there were once between 1000 and 2000 stelae erected by the end of the Final Bronze Age. If these are anywhere near the original figures, they suggest that they were created steadily over generations and that clusters are likely to be found in the future. This large number also fits in with the idea that they were created for an essential commemorative purpose.

3.5   Stelae in the ancient landscape

By now it is clear that distinctive evergreen oak savanna was widespread from the middle Holocene and that under suitable systems of animal herding and mixed farming, it could give food surpluses, spectacular on occasions. It was a landscape that needed to be managed in an extensive mode, to take full advantage of its winter pasture and abundant acorns in the autumn.

Galán (1993:28–30, 36–37) refreshed an old idea when he determined that many stelae were located in places where medieval drove roads passed by (called *cañadas*, *veredas* and *cordeles* in Spanish, in descending order of their size and importance), linking areas of seasonal pasture. Sometimes these extended northwards for hundreds of kilometres, right up to the summer pastures in the Montes de León in the northern Meseta, while in other cases they were short, local routes for moving stock to fresh forage. They form a dense network of interconnecting paths and are mostly well-known routes, documented in detail. Other places where stelae were found commanded different aspects of the landscape, such as the routes that allowed the best movement through the broken terrain, on foot or horseback, with animals or light-wheeled vehicles. In particular, low passes and river crossings were likely to have stelae nearby. The best examples were those crossing points on the main

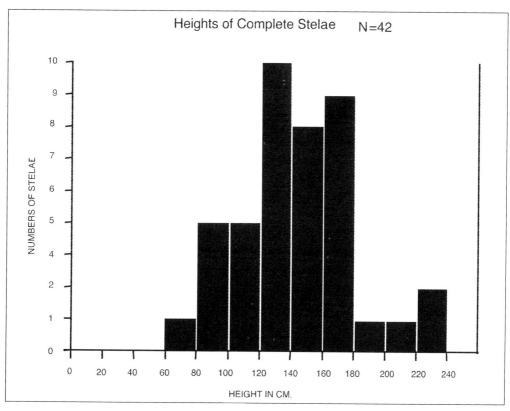

Figure 3.2 *Graph to show heights of complete stelae*

rivers such as the Tagus and Guadalquivir, where their waters run swiftly through deeply cut terraces with steep banks and gorges, making them formidable barriers. They are hard to cross and dangerous through most of the year. There were also stelae placed to command wide views or panoramas. All this suggested they were carefully sited to command particular aspects of the landscape, which was conceptualised at the local level, as well as the larger regional one. Interpreting this as an owned landscape, Galán proposed it was marked out into smaller possessions through the stelae and that this process of territorial definition was a consequence of the expanding exchange networks linking the south-west to the Mediterranean and Atlantic trading spheres.

The merit of this analogy is that it sees the Bronze Age landscape as something actively owned and conceived and that the process of making a particular landscape took form through being named and signposted by permanent monuments, open to view by everyone. So at a general level it has explanatory potential. But significantly, it is untested for its predictive strength. That is, no one has shown that by using it and examining particular passes, drove roads, fords and high points, more stelae can be located. It does not allow us to search purposefully for new monuments. The discoveries made in the last 10 years and mentioned earlier, as well as Pavón's demonstration that a permanent territorial structure with large settlements existed, do not bear out Galán's model. In fact, it was Celestino (2001) who commented on the underlying weaknesses, when he explained that the landscape is so full of significant places that it is impossible to know, really, why one was chosen and another dozen of equal prominence ignored. One can push this a lot further and say that there is really no limit to the number of potentially significant places in the landscape, given its extension and literally innumerable viewpoints, river crossings, hillocks and short cuts. For all the ones Galán selects, others are equally prominent. They are also qualitatively different, in that a major river crossing really is a bottleneck on a well-travelled route, known far and wide, so that it is unlikely to have the same significance as a low hillock or viewpoint. Without detailed cartographic studies of local topography, where the claims for landscape significance have to be tested (but which have not been published), this line of enquiry is at a dead end.

The argument of visibility in the landscape is also flawed. In a savanna, evergreen trees and undergrowth combine with the natural impediments to limit the view, concealing stelae from sight even when they are close by. It is true that unless one knows beforehand where to find a stela, it can be very hard to locate; in these conditions it can take many years to learn the details of even a small landscape. Most of the engravings are so shallow they cannot be seen from more than a few metres away, even with the sunlight glancing on them at a low angle. And even the biggest one from Fuente de Cantos (C85) is only 2.31 m tall; and a lot shorter when set upright in the ground. Most are much smaller than a grown man and if one plots the heights of all the intact ones in Galán's catalogue, their median height is only 140–150 cm (figure 3.2). As visual markers, or 'attention seeking devices' in the words of Colin Renfrew, they lack the fundamental quality of being properly visible, easy to see and making an immediate impact on the viewer. They do not call for attention very loudly. Not one is enhanced by a mound, an avenue, platform or other man-made feature. Frankly, they are modest in size and execution and do not get larger or better over time. The landscape criteria governing their placement seem too vague and ambiguous, too easy to contest and duplicate, to be primary factors in choosing the places to erect them. There must be other, more important and compelling factors influencing the choice of place that we do not know.

Equally reasonable would be to say that the sites were selected as places where the body of the dead warrior was exposed to the elements until it disappeared, or for their historical associations with a contemporary event, a myth, song, fight, heroic deed, pledge of loyalty or friendship, sight of an omen, a notable feast, or even a storm and they were memorialised in this way. Historical contingencies cannot be excluded. The list is almost endless. For that reason, stelae cannot be monuments primarily intended to 'sign the landscape' and express ownership of it, nor are they simple signposts of drove routes. This seems a critical point and indicates that stelae had other purposes; ones that can be deduced by examining their motifs and compositions over time. The ideological function appears to be more important than the actual landscape setting. This is explored in the next chapters.

Finally, the recent discovery of at least 10 fortified settlements, around which single finds of bronzes, gold treasures and stelae cluster, shows where the people depicted on the stelae actually lived. It is these important settlements, exercising ownership of the land-scape through their territorial organisation of it, which probably determined where many stelae should be erected.

4

Observing pictures, motifs and compositions

This chapter presents the stelae as artefacts, following Sebastian Celestino's (2001) detailed account of their development and replacing the previous schemes of Almagro Gorbea and Galán. This marks a big step forward since it permits an analysis of cultural process within a concrete historical setting. The stelae that have been re-cut, or engraved on more than one occasion, are especially interesting since they hold the key to the evolution of the series, as well as giving a key to unlock the puzzle of explaining how materialising an ideology can meet challenges to its authority. This will be discussed in Chapter 5. Re-cutting and re-using stelae in specific contexts occurs in other European countries and in earlier periods too, in fact wherever stelae have been made, and it is recognised as part of the definite period of ritual time when they were important (Barfield 1995:14–15). At Sion (Geneva) there is a famous stela of the Copper Age that was re-cut twice, then re-used for a third time in closing the entrance to a collective tomb (Gallay & Chaix 1984: Vol 2, doc 48). So one must keep an open mind and not expect them all to be single, frozen historical moments. They were artefacts regarded actively.

Composing a long-lived iconography needs a viable code, a selection of suitable motifs to express it. This was done with quite simple means, producing compositions whose pictorial content we can read at different levels. The discussion begins with the simplest level, classifying motifs into object groups.

4.1   Stelae groups and distributions

The idea of treating stelae first as geographical clusters, then looking for evolving compositions within them, was first developed by Celestino. For the first time a clear pattern in the series emerges without recourse to cluster analysis of motifs and independent of the exact find spot, or context. He describes four geographical zones (see table 4.1) (Celestino 2001:44–45) (figure 1.1, see p 2).

Table 4.1 Geographical zones of stelae clusters (after Celestino 2001:44-45)

Zone	Find spot
I	Sierra de Gata
II	Tagus valley-Sierra de Montánchez
III	Guadiana valley and its tributary, the Zújar river valley
IV	Guadalquivir valley

The other stelae are considered marginal, but new discoveries may lead to more zones being defined. Within the zones the distribution of stelae is not homogeneous, but the groupings do account for over 90 per cent of the examples and the zones do have a geographical coherence, based on large rivers and their catchments. The distribution maps of all Final Bronze Age materials, not just stelae, indicate beyond any doubt that lands were chosen for settlement predominantly for their farming potential and there are clusters of stelae around major settlements. A good example is the settlement of Sierra de Alijares (Robledillo de Trujillo) that covers almost 3 ha and has five stelae near it, at Ibahernando, Santa Ana, Zarza de Montánchez, Almoharín and Robledillo de Trujillo; similar stelae concentrations are known around settlements at Cofre (Valencina de Alcántara) and at San Cristóbal (Logrosán) (Pavón 1998:258).

The largest stelae concentration is in the valley of the river Zújar, a tributary of the Guadiana (see figures 4.1, 4.2 and 4.3). Today the river is dammed and its valley flooded, but until recently, it was notable for two important features. Even in dry years it always had running water in its riverbed, so shepherds and stockmen always sought it out, even though the grazing nearby was only average quality; and it provides the best and most direct route of communication between the Guadalquivir and Guadiana river valleys. These were among the most attractive areas for settlement at the time and it is logical to

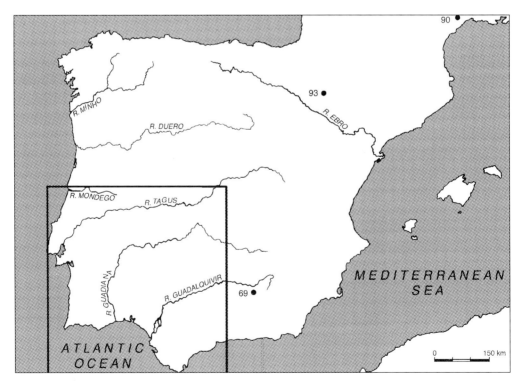

Figure 4.1 *Map of the western Mediterranean showing the area of distribution of stelae. More detail is shown in the inserted box in Figure 4.2. The numbers relate to those used in the catalogue, Chapter 10*

Figure 4.2 *Map of south-west Iberia showing the location of the warrior stelae. The inserted box is expanded in more detail in Figure 4.3. The river estuaries are shown as they would have been around 1000-700 BC. The numbers relate to those used in the catalogue, Chapter 10*

see the many stelae along this route reflecting this fact, rather than as signs of hotly contested tribal territories (Galán 1993).

4.2   Some prehistoric contexts

Since the discovery in 1898 of the first stela of Solana de Cabañas, at least 11 independent observers, among them qualified field archaeologists, have given a first-hand account of a stela in an ancient context and at least eight are prehistoric. This is the place where one needs to listen to the voices of their discoverers, even though some write vaguely and others

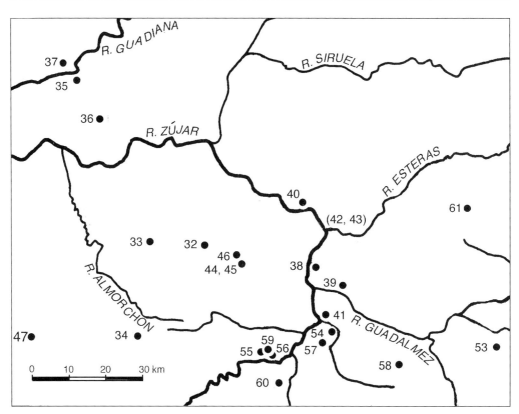

Figure 4.3 *Detailed map of the distribution of stelae in the valley of the river Zújar, a tributary of the Guadiana. The numbers relate to those used in the catalogue, Chapter 10*

describe in too little detail for secure judgements. Some archaeologists, like Almagro Basch (1966:199–201), firmly believed all stelae were grave markers and supported their view with data that others do not accept as reliable today (Galán 1993; Celestino 2001) and which have not been corroborated by any finds since 1966. Almagro Basch's views were undoubtedly coloured by his familiarity with the older (and unrelated) series of stelae in the Alemtejo, now dated to the period 1800–1300 BC, which certainly were used to cover grave cists. However, the arguments in favour of a role as burial markers cannot be dismissed so easily and even if the stelae do not mark graves with a surviving body or a cremation, they may well mark the place where a body was exposed until it disappeared. Formal burial of the body was not common anywhere in the Atlantic Bronze Age and alternative methods of disposal were used, among them exposure. The weight of the data discussed below favours a funerary and commemorative function.

C2 Hernán Pérez. [see picture p 190] Almagro Basch (1972:91, 93) says the fragment of the warrior stela was found piled up loosely with four other stelae, which were of the older anthropomorphic *Diademada* types of the third millennium BC (Bueno-Ramirez 1995). He did not believe that large stone slabs found nearby were from cists marked by stelae and he discounted the circumstantial account of discovery made by one workman. The discovery of a complete and well-preserved *Diademada* stela associated with a cemetery of small megalithic tombs at Arrocerezo, also in Cáceres, makes it even more likely that there was a Copper Age cemetery at Hernán Pérez too, but that the warrior stela was not connected with it (Almagro Basch 1972:112).

C22 Solana de Cabañas. [see picture p 219] The publication in 1898 stated that the stela was found buried under a low mound of loose stones and when it was raised a grave cut into the earth was revealed (Roso de Luna 1898). The grave contained ashes, the impression of some decayed metal and a pot made of yellowish clay. This information was obtained several weeks after the discovery and Celestino (2001:348) doubts its relevance since the real position of the decorated face of the stela was omitted and the pot is of a different type than the ones known for the Final Bronze Age. Almagro Basch (1966:27) believed it did mark a grave and noted Roso de Luna's comment that there were 'light (faint) ashes like a human skeleton' that could well mark the remains of an inhumation. Roso de Luna visited the site of the discovery and also excavated several other promising stone mounds, without finding anything further.

C25 Las Herencias II. [see picture p 222] This stela was found in archaeological excavations in September 1990, in an Iron Age settlement at Arroyo Manzanas on a terrace of the Tagus river. 'The stela had been placed in the interior of buildings made of daub resting on stone footings and of square plan, which correspond, according to the level in which they are found, to cultural material of Cogotas IIb' (Moreno Arrastio 1995:275–276). He continues: 'It was found, offering its engraved face upwards, resting on a fill of clay analogous in texture, colour and hardness to that which we found in other parts of the room. Now, this position was especially resistant to movement' (Moreno Arrastio 1995:279). This is certainly a secondary re-use of the stela as a convenient piece of flat stone for a floor, in a period dating to the fourth–third centuries BC, as the pottery associated with the house shows.

C33 Cabeza del Buey II. [see picture p 236] The stela measures 1.74 m tall and was found upright, completely buried in the ground. Within 20 m were three or four stone circles adjoining one another. Celestino's excavation of this site was fruitless and found no trace of structures or artefacts (Celestino 2001:364–365).

C49 Cancho Roano. [see picture p 257] This is a big stela, 2 m tall, that was found built into the first step that led into the eastern patio of the Iron Age palace of Cancho Roano, firmly embedded between two towers that flank the entrance and which are dated to the fifth century BC (Celestino 2001:387). This is therefore the same type of re-use as Las Herencias II.

C64 Badajoz (Granja de Céspedes). [see picture p 276] The stela was found in 1950, placed above an inhumation burial without grave goods. Almagro Basch (1962, 1966:105–106) was quite clear about the association, writing:

> The stela from the Granja de Céspedes was found with all certainty covering an inhumation burial. It could have been upright and then would have fallen on the body, buried there, crushing it over time, since at the moment of being discovered and the monument recovered, the remains of a body, now very decomposed, were found below it. No other grave good appeared with the bones, the remains of which, conserved in a little box and wrapped in papers, were given to us. They do not have any anthropological value, since they were such scanty fragments, all very broken and decomposed, but one saw they belonged to some long bones and some scraps of cranium, all this, as we said, very decomposed and smashed up.

Celestino (2001:408) thought the records confused and unreliable. He does not explain why he thinks this, but they appear lucid to me.

C69 Toya. [see picture p 283] This stela was properly excavated in 1944 by Mergelina then forgotten, only for a picture of it to be rediscovered by Celestino (2001:414), who quotes the excavator's own words to describe its context.

> ... and at a depth of 1.20 (metres) we found a bed of large smooth cobbles and stones packed into a pit, a metre square and 1.10 (metres) deep, which closely supported a great slab set up on the NE side. This appeared upright ... Once the stone was extracted, we noticed it used to cover the entrance to a cavity and we saw that its interior face showed four badly drawn concentric circles. ... Some other motif below these circles could be detected but was confused and indistinct. The cavity was explored carefully. It formed an almost circular space 1.5 (metres) across by 1.35 deep with a roof in the form of a domed oven. ... (It was a) collective grave in which were made two inhumation burials, then another three later ... The height of the cavity from the base to the roof was 0.80 (metres). Our grave reveals a special interest since it is not abundant in our Peninsula ... it could correspond to the final period of the Bronze Age.

There is no doubt about the stela's context here! The grave goods included two or three small copper or bronze awls.

C71 Setefilla. [see picture p 286] Bonsor and Thouvenot (1928) excavated this famous stela in 1927. The inexperienced student Thouvenot directed the excavations of the tumuli and other flat graves in the cemetery while Bonsor, whose field skills were excellent, was away on other business, so the primary observations about the stela were rudimentary. This is a very great pity. It had been re-used, placed on its side covering a double grave cut into the ground, which contained an inhumation and a cremation of the seventh–sixth century BC. There is no record of grave goods (Aubet 1997). The cemetery had been used continually as a local sacred place since the middle of the second millennium BC and Aubet explains that the re-use of the decorated stela should be seen as a sign of respect paid to an ancient lineage, part of the deliberate cultivation of memory and tradition in that place.

C83 Córdoba II. Celestino (2001:437) [see picture p 304] records first hand accounts that the stela was found 40 cm below ground, decorated face upwards and below it a stain (*mancha*) of black, ashy earth. The stain contained no artefacts. The natural subsoil is reddish gravel and clay, so this discolouration would be quite obvious. It is not clear what this stain was and there is no certainty it was related in any way to the stela.

C87 Figueira. [see picture p 309] Confused accounts of the discovery, with Portuguese archaeologists first stating that it had been found covering a cist grave, were comprehensively refuted later by Viana, Formosinho and Veiga Ferreira and make it impossible to be certain of anything more than the fact that the stela was found upright, with the lower third buried in the ground (Almagro 1966:72). That detail, in itself, is valuable.

C89 Ervidel II. [see picture p 312] Gomes and Monteiro (1977) found this grand stela on the site of an older Middle Bronze Age cist cemetery at the Herdade do Pomar. It was simply lying on the surface, half buried in the topsoil. They could establish no conclusive link for the stela with the older cemetery, but its presence in a burial area strongly suggests there was a continuity of interest and perhaps respect for the earlier burials, as at Setefilla.

C90 Substantion. [see picture p 313] Inside the Iron Age *oppidum* of Substantion, at a depth of 1.10 m, in a heap of stones, pottery and ashes, the excavator found the stela, apparently discarded and no longer in its original position (Soutou 1962:30). These tantalising remarks beg many questions and it is most unfortunate that no plans, photographs or other details were recorded about the find circumstances; not even the pottery was described.

These meagre observations contain almost all the known information about primary contexts. First, it is clear that stelae were originally set upright in the ground, as those from Cabeza del Buey II and Figueira indicate.

Some stelae did mark graves; the stela from Toya certainly marked a tomb. There seems no reason to doubt that human bones were found buried near or under the stelae of Solana de Cabañas and Badajoz, but the precise relationship between the bones and the stelae is not clear and it is not demonstrated that the burials were made at the same time as the stelae were erected. They could be later burials, made at the base of standing stones which later fell over, or both stelae could have been re-used as covering slabs. The description of the pot from Solana de Cabañas supports this, since it is not a Bronze Age type. Almagro Basch's description of the position of the bones below the Badajoz stela does no more than assert there was a burial at the base of the stela; there is no indication that it was of the same date and it could have been later. Only the stela of Toya is definitely linked to the contemporary burials in the sealed chamber behind it and it bears an early, basic composition of a shield motif. There is good evidence for the secondary use of the Bronze Age stela as an Early Iron Age grave slab at Setefilla. A similar respect for funerary tradition is shown by Ervidel II, which was found on the site of an older Bronze Age cist cemetery. This small sample suggests that one function of the stelae was to identify a grave and that four of the five associations with burials are secondary. The fact that so few human remains or grave goods have come to light suggests that these were always slight. But it is important that the only real contextual information points to a function linked to death, burial and commemoration.

Little can be deduced from the contexts of secondary use as building material at Herencias II and Cancho Roano, beyond the obvious point; these stelae are older than the Iron Age buildings in which they are found.

A way forward is indicated by Pavón's (1998) discovery of the Final Bronze Age settlements and the inescapable economic logic behind their placement in the landscape. Much of the other information, such as the location of stelae clusters, burials of gold treasures and chance finds of bronze metalwork, begins to make more sense. As discussed in Chapter 5, chiefdoms (including those in Bronze Age Spain and Portugal) share common organisational principles. Stelae may be isolated monuments, but they can be articulated into a rich social context.

4.3   Evolving pictures on stelae: composition over time

Stelae carry engraved pictures. They are executed on a flat slab of local stone that is usually chipped roughly to an oblong shape, with one surface pecked smooth, or at least its major irregularities reduced, so that the composition can be engraved (there are two stelae made of imported stones, C27 Talavera and C80 Ategua). Often the lower quarter of the slab is left untrimmed, since it would be buried in the ground and not seen. One or two have a human silhouette, like the finely finished one from Luna (C93), now lacking the head and perhaps Baraçal (C4) with its waisted shape and heavy foot, like a torso.

The height of the slabs averages 1.35 m, with the tallest 2.31 m (C85 Fuente de Cantos) and the smallest 0.75 m (C25 Las Herencias I). The prepared surface is engraved in various techniques; Celestino observed that metal chisels and points of different types were used, some with fine points, others with U or V shaped ones of larger size and still others were used to chisel out an area and lower the surface to create more relief, which Celestino calls *rebaje*, or the intaglio technique (Celestino 2001:86–89). There is a sequence in the techniques, starting with ones in Zone I, with firm, deep, incision, which is limited in the detail it can convey. A little later, in Zone II, one sees stelae with the weapons emphasised by having the interior surface of motifs cut away in intaglio (C13 Brozas), increasing the expressiveness of the carving. In Zones III and IV the use of intaglio is generalised on stelae and used for all types of motifs. These differences in engraving are brought out on the stelae drawn in the catalogue (see Chapter 10). Apparently, a single carver engraved each stela, since there is no other way to explain so many idiosyncrasies of technique and composition. The way human figures are depicted, for example, is different on every single stela and the lack of uniformity in technique, the widely different sizes of slab, as well as the practice of re-using older slabs, or re-cutting others, all suggest different engravers. Carving was done by inexperienced part-timers and some were obviously clumsier than others, since they made repeated mistakes in setting out the composition, or in executing the motifs.

Within each zone, stelae can be arranged in a series, whose formal evolution is also chronological. Some of these slabs may never have been set upright, since the symmetrical composition covers the entire surface and leaves no space for a portion to be buried as a foot; it has long been believed for this reason that they were laid flat on the ground, perhaps as covers for cist graves (Almagro Basch 1972; Celestino 2001; Pavón 1998) (examples would be C5 Fóios, C15 Trujillo, C19 Robledillo, C64 Badajoz, C83 Córdoba II). However, there is still no discovery of a stela in context proving this.

Development starts with stelae in Zone I, which have a composition centred on a shield, with a spear above and a sword below. This panoply is found in all four Zones (and variants of it in the Algarve, Aragon and France). The shield dominates the other motifs by being bigger and centrally placed on the stela. To it are added new elements placed in the small spaces around the shield; the first is a mirror, then a brooch, comb and a helmet. This can be seen best in the stelae in Zones I and II and is supported by the Brozas stela, (C13) which has a comb and brooch added to it after the main scene was engraved.

Next, a chariot is added and the first small human figures are placed to one side of the composition, squashed into the edge of the picture in the space left alongside the shield, which is still the dominant motif in the composition. Stelae from Solana de Cabañas (C22) and Torrejón el Rubio I (C6) illustrate this stage and the latter stela has a chariot added to it later on. The next part of the sequence is less clear, in part because of the richness and variety of the motifs. Most schemes agree that the figure of the warrior now replaces the shield in the centre of the composition and over time the warrior grows in size until he dominates the composition pictorially. This can be seen in stelae from Cancho Roano (C49) and Ategua (C80). This stage can be detected also on the stela from Las Herencias I (C25), which started as a shield and sword composition, with the sword re-cut into a human figure and also in C51 Valdetorres I, where a simple stela depicting a shield is re-cut with two armed men over it.

After this, the appearance of a new type of human figure is detectable, wearing prominent horns on its head. This is not is just a horned helmet (as Celestino believes), but rather the appearance for the first time of a new quality in the human figure, giving it the aspect of a powerful, horned animal. Horned figures are always central figures in the composition, never peripheral. They also occur in the more complex compositions of paired human figures, on narrative scenes. This can be seen on the stelae from São Martinho I (C29), El Viso III (C56) and El Viso VI (C59). These types, with warriors as the centre of the composition, are the commonest stelae from the Guadiana and Guadalquivir valleys. For these reasons the horned figures are a historically late development, whose possible meanings are discussed in Chapters 6 and 7.

This is a robust classification with an historical perspective. It combines a geographical element with an evolution of motifs and is supported by internal evidence from re-cutting.

4.4   Changing the picture: stelae transformed by secondary use

This section begins with a personal reflection on human frailty, including the author's. When making direct observations of the stelae in the Museo Arqueológico Nacional in Madrid and the collections in Cáceres and Badajoz, he was astonished to see evidence that stelae were not pictures engraved at one time. Until then, it was not doubted that they were like photographic snapshots, made at one moment, with every motif contemporary, even better than a 'closed find' in terms of contextual reliability. Every one else who had looked at them had believed the same and acted on that belief. There was no hint of anything different by Barceló or Galán, who wrote doctoral theses on these same stelae. It was only chance remarks in short articles by Powell (1976) and Celestino (1990) about two stelae with re-cut motifs that prompted further thought. A closer look at the drawings and photographs in Almagro Basch's book shows that the evidence for this had been published since 1966, but that nobody had recognised it, not even Martín Almagro Basch himself. Did he ever check his draughtsman's work against the originals, one wonders? Why did so many qualified observers miss what is so obvious? It is a classic example of looking at things and seeing what one expected to see, rather than describing accurately what was really engraved. Seeing and observing are not the same. Independently of this experience in 1999 and 2000, Sebastian Celestino (2001:89–91) arrived at the same conclusions and lists eight examples, several of them not published before. The actual total is higher than he gives and they hold the key to understanding many aspects of the iconography and ideology locked in the compositions. However, first the evidence must be presented.

Older stelae in France and Italy also show signs of re-cutting, which has been recognised for many years (Barfield 1995); it also occurs on at least one early second millennium stela from Spain, found at Longroiva (X97) (Almagro Basch 1966). This means re-cutting must take place when the ritual or ideological power of the monument is still in force and that it is an important part of the part of its biography. These are not casual destructive acts, but ones considered and significant.

4.4.1 Re-cutting the entire composition

C9 Torrejón el Rubio IV. [see picture p 200] Celestino (2001) publishes this for the first time (see Chapter 10 of this volume for catalogue entries). It was first engraved with a simple composition of a shield, with spear above and sword below, executed with deep incisions (motifs 1–3) (see also p 53 for discussion of motifs). At a later date (how long afterwards is not known), the scene was overlain by a new composition, featuring an armed warrior holding a mirror in his right hand (motifs 4–7). This overlay the engraved spear and part of it was incorporated into the arm of the warrior. The mirror was evidently difficult to engrave, since it took three attempts to align the handle correctly and the two previous attempts remain, confusing the image (motif 5). The sword at the bottom of the stela was also re-engraved (motif 4), this time changing its alignment. The later engraving is deeper and wider than the first stage. The later mirror is also emphasised using the intaglio technique. This is an exceptionally important stela since it documents the temporal shift from a simple composition of shield and weapons to one centred on the human figure.

C25 Las Herencias I. [see picture p 222] This stela is not easy to study, but the excellent drawing in Fernández Miranda (1987) confirms direct observations that the composition features at least two different periods of engraving. The first one includes the shield, chariot and what was probably a sword (motifs 1–2; 6), all outlined in deep incisions that were later polished and evened out for effect. The second composition changes the sword into a human figure, adding a head by making a deep pit at the tip and engraving arms on each side. The head is carved in intaglio and is the only motif on the stela to use it. The spear, helmet and brooch (motifs 3, 4, and 5) were added; the spear is more lightly incised with finer lines than any other motif. Finally, there are several lightly incised lines and illegible elements that we name as motifs 7–12 and whose date we cannot determine. Motif 9 may be an early, incomplete attempt to draw the chariot wheel. If this reading of the motifs is correct, this stela is also one that began with a basic composition, to be replaced by a later one with a warrior.

C36 Esparragosa de Lares II. [see picture p 241] The first composition is of a poorly executed warrior and some indistinct motifs. These were replaced by a more competent composition of a warrior accompanied by mirror and other motifs. The later engravings are deeply cut. Celestino (2001:369) places the sequence of carving the other way round and sees the deeply cut figure as primary. Whatever the case, it is clearly a stela with two phases of engraving, in different techniques.

C51 Valdetorres I. [see picture p 259] A simple shield motif was later re-cut with a different scene, showing two warriors, one armed and the other with horns, accompanied by a spear, sword and mirror. The mirror is emphasised by intaglio. It shows the same change in composition as Torrejón el Rubio IV.

C67 Aldea del Rey II. [see picture p 281] Only a fragment of a larger scene, it is clear there are two superimposed compositions. The first scene includes a shield and warrior engraved in thin lines (state C p 281)*. The second scene turns the stela upside down and engraves in deep, coarse strokes, an image of a large human figure, possibly with a spear at his side (state D p 281).

C82 Córdoba I. [see picture p 302] A simple composition in the first stage has a shield and spear (and perhaps a sword, now lost) (state B p 302). The second stage was the addition of 32 cup marks, which respected the original motifs (state C p 302).

4.4.2 Stelae with corrections

Making corrections in stone is difficult and usually leaves indelible traces behind, unless the whole surface is cut down and erased. Engravers seem to have had a lot of trouble drawing chariots, either in making them fit the space available, or in placing them correctly for the composition.

C3 Meimão. [see picture p 192] The spearhead has been re-cut to replace an original large spearhead with a smaller, stubbier one.

C 22 Solana de Cabañas. [see picture p 219] The chariot actually has two wheels as Powell suggested in 1976 and not four, as appears to be the case. As Celestino explains, the engraver made repeated mistakes in placing the chariot (motif 7) correctly in relation to the other elements in the composition. Our drawing breaks them down for analysis. First, he seems to have cut one wheel to the left, then abandoned that and made another attempt on the right, with a straight line for the chariot body (stage 1). After he abandoned both these positions, he felt more confident and engraved two wheels and an axle in the centre of the space below the shield (stage 2). This, too, was not right since it would not allow the composition to balance, since he lacked space to fit in the chariot box as well as the horses. Finally, on the fourth attempt, he got the position right, but had to include the useless pair of wheels from the first draught (stage 3). This is less the work of an accomplished engraver, than a demonstration of do-it-yourself persistence. Yet, in other respects, this stela is one of the most accomplished in its overall composition, proportion and balance.

---

* States referred to here are illustrated in the catalogue on the pages cited for the stelae.

C32 Cabeza del Buey I. [see picture p 235] The chariot shows an earlier attempt to engrave it beneath the later one (motifs 3a, 3b). It seems the engraver made a mistake and drew two draught poles instead of one and had misplaced the motif, leaving too little space on the rock surface for the horses.

C33 Cabeza del Buey II. [see picture p 236] An attempt to engrave a chariot on the left hand side near the shield was abandoned while still incomplete (motif 9). The chariot (motif 10) was later added to the side of the stela on a facet that had been prepared for it, allowing more space for it. Celestino (2001:364) thinks the comb (motif 8) may also be later, since it is engraved more finely, with a different chisel than the other motifs.

C37 Navalvillar de Pela. [see picture p 242] The shield has an incomplete fourth circle inside it (motif 1) and could be the result of the engraver not finishing the motif, or be the result of changing his mind once he saw that the shield was too small for the size of the stela and needed a larger diameter.

C48 Magacela. [see picture p 255] The outer ring of the shield (motif 6) was adjusted to preserve its symmetry. The first, inaccurate engraving is clearly visible.

C65 Olivenza. [see picture p 278] The chariot at the foot of the human figure was wrongly placed (motif 6), since it interfered with the legs of the warrior. It was engraved again to the left hand corner of the stela. The lines of the first drawing were used to depict a bow and arrow (motif 9), the axle becoming the bowstring and the draught pole the arrow. It is a messy picture and hard to discern. It is also possible that the motif (16) in the lower right is a first attempt to draw the shield, which was later engraved above it (motif 1); the two motifs overlap one another. It is possible that some of the cup marks are later additions.

C77 Écija IV. [see picture p 294] It appears that the design of the sword hilt (motif 4) has been changed, with two different ones overlapping.

4.4.3 Additional motifs on stelae

These are motifs added later. They are recognisable by their different engraving technique (often with a different pointed tool, which leaves distinct traces visible under low magnification) and by the awkward placement within the composition. They seem cramped, or sometimes distorted, motifs.

C6 Torrejón el Rubio I. [see picture p 195] The chariot at the bottom is incised with light shallow lines (motif 7), quite different from the strong, deep cutting of all the other motifs. It is also placed so low down that, if the slab were set upright, it would be buried in the earth and invisible.

C13 Brozas. [see picture p 206] The comb (motif 4) is incised with very thin, fine lines, quite different from the deep engraving and intaglio used to depict the other motifs. Its vertical edge takes advantage of a deep natural crack in the rock. The brooch (motif 3) may also be a later addition and is incised deeply.

C57 El Viso IV. [see picture p 267] The scene is centred on a warrior and later has a smaller human figure added on a side facet (motif 6), in a position secondary to the main composition.

C59 El Viso VI. [see picture p 269] The sword is incomplete and may have been added later (motif 3).

C70 Carmona. [see picture p 285] A small, secondary human figure was added below the chariot (motif 7), engraved in a different technique from the rest of the motifs. Celestino (2001: 415) believes it is a later addition.

4.4.4   Stelae with erasures

C44 Zarza Capilla I. [see picture p 251] The bow and arrow (motif 10) have been pecked away extensively, leaving a confused motif.

4.4.5   Defacement

C10 Valencia de Alcántara I. [see picture p 202] The fragment has been heavily pock-marked all over its decorated surface, with small, deep cup marks, from which spring short, deeply incised lines in groups of three, as if to energise them (state B). These cannot be due to erosion, nor caused by damage from modern iron farming tools. The effect is to leave the original composition visible, but clearly ruined by this pocking.

4.4.6   Re-use of Copper Age monuments

Two examples are spectacular demonstrations of a male identity. It is significant that more are not known and indicates that the warrior's gender was sufficiently obvious in the motif code not to need a giant phallus for emphasis.

C27 Talavera de la Reina. [see picture p 227] A stone menhir shaped like a phallus, with a human face carved on the glans. On the body below is the Final Bronze Age engraving, with a horned and armed warrior surrounded by his weapons and chariot.

C30 São Martinho II. [see picture p 232] This is a large, perfectly shaped menhir in the shape of a phallus, with a hunting scene engraved on it in the Final Bronze Age.

C90 Substantion. [see picture p 313] This impressive stela was originally a Late Copper Age memorial with geometric patterns on at least three faces and its main face was cut away and re-engraved in the Final Bronze Age.

4.4.7 *Re-use as tombstones with later inscriptions*

C16 Ibahernando. [see picture p 210] A large example of an early stela, with a Latin funerary inscription cut over the spear and shield motifs. This inscription clearly ignores the previous use of the stone, unlike Chillón.

C61 Chillón. [see picture p 272] The stelae was re-used in Roman times and a Latin inscription cut below the original motifs, but respecting them sufficiently to leave them visible.

C86 Capote. [see picture p 308] A cut down stela, re-used as a tombstone, with two Tartessian inscriptions of about 700–600 BC added to it (motifs 6–7). Each inscription is by a different engraver.

4.4.8 *Other additions*

C28 Aldeanueva de San Bartolomé. [see picture p 229] This has an inscription in sixteenth century AD letters, reading JESUS J. J (motif 8).

The picture that emerges from this list is that 27 out of a total of 103 warrior stelae were modified after their creation; this does not include any of the secondary uses to which some were put, as flooring slabs in Iron Age buildings, or as a step in the palace-sanctuary at Cancho Roano. The modifications vary from small changes to complete re-working, so the intentions may vary also. The historical inscriptions should, perhaps, be discounted too. Most of these changes have nothing at all to do with bungled engraving. Even completed compositions were 'topped up', 'completed' or 'improved', with a motif added (or more rarely rubbed out) and in the most drastic cases, they were repossessed by others and appropriated. The intention behind the acts is apparent, but to identify its motivation is more difficult. It occurred repeatedly in the late Copper Age, Bronze Age, in the Tartessian period and in Roman times. Many stelae conveyed messages that other people, not always their creators, wanted to appropriate. Fortunately, they did so in ways that one can recognise. The rate of re-contextualisation, to use the jargon for this activity, needs an explanation; it is likely that here one can actually see the process of materialising ideology and how challenges to its authority were met.

The second conclusion is that the re-cuttings and additions of motifs prove there is a chronological succession to the iconography. There can no longer be any doubt about that. The dynamic formulae are exactly what is expected when individuals struggle to present their essential values and chose to do so by modifying the iconic language.

4.5   Making an iconic language of power: motifs and thematic compositions

The motifs depict Bronze Age artefacts. They represent real objects of bronze and organic material, birds and animals, human beings dead and alive and humans wearing animal horns on their heads. It is a recognisable material world converted to pictures and the objects can be identified without great difficulty. The objects chosen are solid and realistic things and there are no flights of fancy, such as using obvious monsters, or hybrid animal-human forms, or shapes of mysterious 'abstract' objects. There is nothing veiled here; there are no ambiguities in the choice of objects or their placing in the composition. It is a familiar world where every thing is depicted with the maximum clarity, as if the engraver was worried that the viewer would be in doubt about the thing drawn, or even is bold enough to think it was something else and imagines an alternative. If this is true, then one can detect the aim of the engraver through the choice of style; in this case, to get the maximum clarity of expression to force the viewer to make the one interpretation that was intended and no other. For this to work, motifs are selected with the intention of creating regular associations that a viewer will recognise. Over time, the choice of motifs changes and a process of enrichment of the composition begins, first with objects only, then with human beings. Towards the end of the process, stelae composition is again simplified to concentrate on the human figure, or horned being. Nearly every stela carries a structured composition, following a few rules. Ideally, one should be able to see these principles at work in all the complete stelae, but in fact must recognise some ambiguities due to the engraver's lack of skill, poor preservation of the carving, a stone of the wrong shape or quality to decorate, or even the possibility that some engravers were 'off message' and carved the wrong elements, or omitted important ones by accident. An idealised model has to leave room for some incompetence.

The stela itself is the physical boundary for the composition. It is clear to everyone exactly where the edge of the picture is and what motifs are included. At the first level of visualisation, every motif can be recognised as an object and the whole scene (normally containing from three to eight elements) grasped quickly. Its meaning is straightforward and the composition is as simple and direct as the engravers could make it. The second level lies deeper and consists of recognising the cultural references to which the objects allude; this is a subject explored in the next chapters. Previewing them briefly, one sees masculine values expressed through the weapons and armour (warriors); the ornaments indicate prestige through dress and the horned figures assimilate the power of great animals by appropriating their horns. But fundamental to all the compositions, from the simplest to the most complex, is the statement that a single person is commemorated. An individual warrior makes his mark, his demand to live in the memory after death, and the stela materialises it. It is for this reason the evolution of the compositions is so important, as well as the re-use of stelae, since they document the social process of exercising power and defeating rival claimants to it. This process lies at the heart of the ideological expression. Stelae are powerful by virtue of being erected. In the process, the motifs become a simple iconic language of power.

4.6   Motifs and objects

At least 35 classes of object are depicted. Celestino (2001) builds upon previous studies and describes them exhaustively. Fortunately, there is a large measure of scholarly agreement and the linkage from the motifs to known object classes is controversial only occasionally. The motifs were not drawn with modern classifications in mind, so in many cases one cannot classify an object further than to say it is a sword, or a dagger, or a helmet. Much classification is reliable, but the important thing is to recognise the essence of the object rather than its specific detail. Carving fine detail in stone, on an irregular surface, was often impossible, so a stylised shape of outline and volume was created and its position within the composition kept fairly consistent, to allow the viewer to identify it. At times this gives a cartoon-like quality to the composition.

The insistence of the engravers in keeping all motifs separate from one another means that they are drawn in accurate outline but out of natural scale, giving an odd emphasis to smaller objects like brooches or mirrors and making big objects, like chariots, look like toys. Chariots are always shown in a different perspective from other objects, from a vertical position, with the wheels and horses laid out flat on their sides. This visual distortion is a deliberate convention affecting the composition. Ignoring scale in this manner creates visual emphasis and introduces a note of drama into quite small scenes. The naïve quality should not mislead one into thinking that Bronze Age viewers saw the composition in this way, since it is probable that in their frame of reference they could read the iconic language directly.

4.6.1   *Arms*

SHIELD

This is the most common motif on the warrior stelae and defines the series more than any other element; 71 stelae have one. When drawn as the central element of the composition, it is always the largest motif, bigger even than the chariots and warriors near it. The apparent paradox of why there are 73 shields from Iberia yet no trace of any metal ones, not even a rivet, is easily resolved; they depict leather or wooden shields like the one from Clonbrin in Ireland, which is identical to the motif carved on the C13 Brozas stela, even down to the decorative rivets set in pairs and triplets.

SWORD

These are the chief weapons, usually depicted carefully, with their organic handles and scabbards. Some are drawn life size, others not. The early ones are engraved outlines and later ones have the interior cut away, in the intaglio technique. Swords with leaf-shaped blades on stelae C4 Baraçal and C16 Ibahernando, and a parallel-sided sword on C5 Fóios, date from the twelfth century BC at the latest. The later class of Carp's Tongue sword is also recognisable on stelae C28 Aldeanueva de San Bartolomé, C66 Aldea del Rey I and C81 Pedro Abad. They were in use in the eleventh–tenth centuries BC. Many swords are so crudely drawn they are impossible to classify further.

SPEAR

A large thrusting spear is a motif on most of the stelae, shown with a big leaf shaped point and a shaft the length of a man. Flame-shaped spearheads on C22 Solana de Cabañas and C89 Ervidel II seem similar to the British ones known from the Hío and Huelva hoards. No real detail is depicted on the others. Three have a metal butt (C48 Magacela, C51 Valdetorres I and C83 Córdoba II).

DAGGER

Relatively few are shown and only the Carp's Tongue type on C66 Aldea del Rey I is at all clear. C81 Pedro Abad may depict a sheathed dagger (motif 6) next to the sword.

BOW AND ARROW

It is depicted at least 10 times, in the simplest manner.

HELMET

This is shown on at least seven stelae and takes the form of a pointed cap, perhaps undecorated, but embellished with fins and crests on stelae C12 Valencia de Alcántara III, C17 Santa Ana de Trujillo and C21 Zarza de Montánchez. The horned figures may be wearing horned helmets, as Almagro (1966) and Celestino (2001) think, but could also be humans depicted with a dramatic animal characteristic. Bronze fragments of at least one crested helmet are known from the Huelva hoard, but no horned helmet or headdress has been found in Iberia. The nearest examples are bronze models of warriors with horned caps from Sardinia.

BODY ARMOUR (CORSLET OR CUIRASS)

On the C80 Ategua stela the warrior has an elaborately decorated cuirass, which is unique. There is a decorated one from San Antonio de Calaceite (Teruel), found in an Early Iron

Age burial, probably of the seventh century BC. The nearest ones of Late Bronze Age date are those from Marmesses, in northern France.

CHARIOT

At least 22 are depicted. They are all two wheeled vehicles drawn by two horses (sometimes shown as stallions, with their sex marked). The body of the chariot always has two protruding handles at the back and is usually connected to the horses by a single draught pole. Spokes are shown on some wheels. Chariots must have been known as working vehicles in Iberia at this time, since there are bronze terret rings (for guiding the long reins into the charioteers' hands) in the hoards from Cabezo de Araya and Huelva, of tenth century date.

4.6.2 Ornaments of dress and for the body

MIRROR

There are at least 38 (and perhaps up to 42 in total), mostly engraved and emphasised with the intaglio technique. There is some variation in the decoration of their handles, but for the most part they are very similar to each other, with a round or oval face and short handle. At least 14 have decorated handles with balls or knobs on them. They are not objects yet known to exist in the west European Bronze Age and only one handle (tentatively identified from Baiões) has been found in Iberia. However, they are found in hoards of the Final Bronze Age in Sardinia and are well known in the eastern Mediterranean and Egypt.

COMB

At least 21 combs are depicted. They vary considerably in shape, but are all fairly small. There is an ivory comb from the Final Bronze tomb of the Roça do Casal do Meio of the tenth century and a fancier gold one in the Galician hoard from Caldas de Reis.

RAZOR

This can be difficult to recognise, but one may be engraved on C40 Capilla III. Simple bronze ones are known from the hoard of Huerta de Árriba in Burgos.

TWEEZERS

These are even harder to recognise than razors. No example is unambiguous, but the motifs on the stelae of C25 Las Herencias I and C89 Ervidel II may be tweezers; Celestino identifies two others on C67 Aldea del Rey II and C76 Écija III, which seem doubtful to me. Bronze tweezers are in both graves in the tomb of Roça do Casal do Meio, associated with an ivory comb, of tenth century date.

BROOCH

About 17 stelae have a brooch, but many are not easy to see. Well-engraved examples show a simple arc fibula (C12 Valencia de Alcántara III), the common elbow fibula (C13 Brozas) and one antennae fibula (C7 Torrejón El Rubio II). Bronze examples of all these types are well known in Iberia and in Sardinia and Sicily. They span the period from twelfth–ninth centuries.

EARRING

These are clearest on stelae C38 Capilla I, C54 El Viso I, C65 Olivenza and C80 Ategua.

FINGER RING

This is a rare object, but one is on the hand of the figure from C65 Olivenza. A ring is known from the tomb of Roça do Casal do Meio.

BRACELET OR ARM RING

Also a rare object, but seen clearly on the warrior's arm on C80 Ategua.

GARMENT

Identifying dress on any figure is difficult. The figure from C62 Herrera del Duque may be wearing a short kilt. The figures on C44 Zarza Capilla I and C65 Olivenza wear what look like protective leggings, perhaps in the style of cowboy chaps.

MUSICAL INSTRUMENT

At least five stringed instruments like a lyre are well drawn. The clearest one is on C93 Luna, which is especially elaborate. They are known only in the Aegean and eastern Mediterranean.

WEIGHTS (GROUP OF FIVE DOTS)

These were first recognised as a motif by Celestino (2001:181–185). There are clear examples on as many as 12 stelae, notably C34 Cabeza del Buey III, C35, C36 Esparragosa de Lares I and II, C37 Navalvillar de Pela, C44 Zarza Capilla I, C47 Benquerencia de la Serena, C48 Magacela, C53 Alamillo, C65 Olivenza, C70 Carmona, C81 Pedro Abad (uncertain), C85 Fuente de Cantos. Celestino suggests they are a set of weights, symbolising the commercial interests of the warrior and his monopoly on the knowledge of it.

SINGLE DOT

This is a restricted motif on at least 10 stelae, clearly shown on C27 Talavera (motif 6, possibly), C33 Cabeza del Buey II (motif 4), C46 Zarza Capilla III (motif 6), C52 Valdetorres II (motif 2), C67 Aldea del Rey II (motif 6), C76 Écija III, C80 Ategua (motif 5), C81 Pedro Abad (motifs 6 and 9), C85 Fuente de Cantos (motif 4) and C89 Ervidel II (motif 5).

RANDOM DOTS OR PIT MARKS

These occur clearly on four stelae, without apparent order; C10 Valencia de Alcántara I, C28 Aldeanueva de San Bartolomé, C65 Olivenza and C82 Córdoba I.

4.6.3   Human figures

These are the commonest motif after the shield and sword. They can be classified by formal attributes and will be discussed further in the next chapter.

PRIMARY HUMAN FIGURE

Fifty-two stelae have a single human figure as a feature of the composition and on 34 stelae the figure is the central element in the composition. No two are the same and they vary from one another in every particular.

SECONDARY HUMAN FIGURE

These occur on eight stelae, always in peripheral positions in the composition. Sometimes that is shown in horizontal position, in contrast to the vertical posture of the warrior. They are C36 Esparragosa de Lares II, C57 El Viso IV, C70 Carmona, C72 Burguillos, C80 Ategua, C81 Pedro Abad, C86 Capote and C89 Ervidel II.

SMALL HUMAN FIGURES IN A GROUP

These are found on three stelae, C46 Zarza Capilla III, C68 Aldea del Rey III, C80 Ategua and form part of a narrative.

HUMAN FIGURE WITH HORNS

They are clearly distinct from all other human figures. There are at least 16 examples with very large, prominent horns that spring directly from the head. No horned headdress or helmet is known from Iberia. They may represent 'heroes'.

HUMAN FIGURE WITH A DIADEM

These are the *Diademadas*, distinct from the other figures and wear a special headdress.

They are found on stelae C7 Torrejón el Rubio II, C38 Capilla I, C58 El Viso V, C60 Belalcázar, and perhaps on C45 Zarza Capilla II. The central figure in the paired scene in El Viso III is not wearing a diadem. No diadems have been found in south-west Europe.

PAIRED HUMAN FIGURES

These are probably narrative scenes and occur on C29 São Martinho I, C51 Valdetorres I, C53 Alamillo, C56 El Viso III, C59 El Viso VI and C73 Los Palacios. They usually include one or more horned figures.

4.6.4 Animals

DOG

It is found on eight stelae: C 28 Aldeanueva, C30 São Martinho II (this has two dogs, one attacking a deer from behind, the other with the hunter), C33 Cabeza del Buey II, C54 El Viso I, C59 El Viso VI, C78 Écija V, C80 Ategua (with at least two and possibly three dogs in different parts of the composition) and C89 Ervidel II.

DEER

A deer is being hunted on stela C30 São Martinho II.

BIRD

There are three large birds on C30 São Martinho II (or are they stylised trees?).

4.6.5 Unique motifs

WATER BIRD

On C90 Substantion (motifs 12, 13). Celestino indicates they are a mirror and a brooch, but the photographs published by Soutou clearly show they are water birds.

SPOKED WHEEL

There are three on C90 Substantion (motifs 8–10).

QUIVER (?)

On C30 Sao Martinho II (motif 5); C40 Capilla III (motif 2).

BELT BUCKLE

On the human figure with diadem, C7 Torrejón el Rubio II.

BLANKET OR CARPET (?)

On C80 Ategua (motif 12).

4.7   A warrior code of abstractions

The initial hypothesis is that these motifs (figure 4.4) are a structured code, defining the image and status of a warrior (Wason 1994). The discussion begins from the idea that the stelae primarily serve to commemorate the memory of a dead warrior, even if they do not actually mark his burial place or physical remains. To perform this role, the composition would need to refer to the warrior's high social rank as seen in his mirror, lyre and chariot, his fighting prowess depicted in the weapons and armour and perhaps his special dress and grooming through the brooches and combs. A few late stelae may narrate the story of the warrior as hunter, in a duel, or travelling to another world. As the compositions develop historically, the motifs are updated to match the fashions in sword design, or made more complex by the addition of the figure of the warrior himself. None of them shows a recognisable personality, but they are all individual warriors.

Similar ideas of rank and status were shared throughout the Later Bronze Age in western and central Europe, although they are expressed in varied ways through burials, hoards and artefacts. For example, the class of elite warriors in south-western Germany is found in 3–8 per cent of the Urnfield cemeteries, defined by their separate burials, wearing swords and usually accompanied by one or two human sacrifices (Sperber 1999). The graves in the warrior cemetery at Neckarsulm indicate that an aristocracy of sword-wearers transmitted its inherited status over generations and were also physically bigger and taller than others (Neth 2001); Sperber calls this group the '*Schwertträgeradel*'. Men and women can be found in the same elite cemeteries and the women wore enormous bronze ornaments on their dresses and legs. Taste changed often among these warrior elites, so there is a period in the late fourteenth–thirteenth century BC when wagon graves were favoured, then between 1090–1000 BC sword graves disappear in this region, only to reappear by 880 BC, this time with wagon graves. Still other sword wearers had bronze drinking cups, and even complete services, buried with them.

To the east of this group, in North Tyrol, Bavaria and Salzburg, warrior graves are much commoner than in the west (between a third and 40 per cent of all cemeteries have a sword wearer). These warriors confirmed their status with quite different grave customs and not only are there none of the human sacrifices that are found in the west, but the cemeteries are used for many centuries; the one at Volders (North Tyrol) has an uninterrupted sequence of elite warrior graves for over 500 years (Sperber 1999).

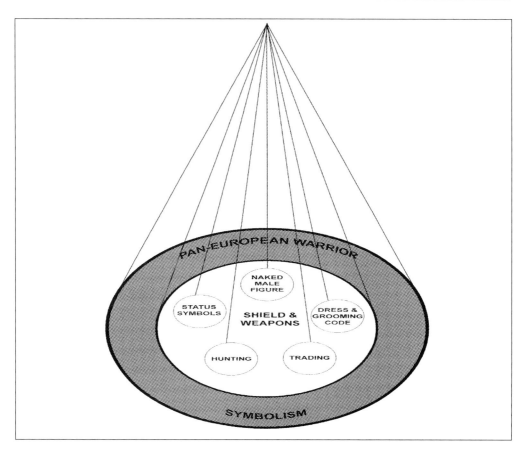

Figure 4.4 *A model of the pan-European warrior symbolism can be expressed in three levels of abstraction. The lowest levels are the five inner circles of status symbols and dress code; the intermediate level is that of the shield and weapons; the highest level of abstraction is the general symbolism, shown in darker texture*

Evidently, European warrior elites conceived of their own codes to assert status and these change quickly. A similar process operated in Portugal and Spain. Therefore, it seems reasonable to expect that the same themes of male and female identity, status display, dress codes, grooming habits (razors and combs), feasting services and so on, were used to express these social values. Some pan-European themes are expressed on the stelae and others are ignored. There is really no way to prove that the excluded themes were thought about in the way proposed here, but it seems likely that they were. It is a problem of representation familiar in other guises when a sample of grave goods is studied and the question is raised as to how representative they are of the wider social world (Pader 1982).

The prevailing ideology is that of the pan-European warrior symbolism, expressing the notion of an elite social status. In Portugal and Spain this is defined specifically by the motifs of a spear, sword and shield. Gathered into this could be five secondary themes, expressed through objects such as grooming equipment, hunting gear and perhaps motifs connected with trade or entrepreneurial activity, although this is more hypothetical than the others suggested. A possible configuration of these themes is shown in the diagram in figure 4.4.

Even as abstractions, these are relatively easy ideas to communicate. They are explicit and public and, probably more important than either, they are permanent statements. This is quite different from the way similar values of masculinity and status are shown elsewhere in the Atlantic Bronze Age, where stelae were never erected, nor formal burials made for warriors.

4.8   Areas of elite social activity not included on the stelae

Many of these issues have not been raised before, nor debated in this context, but they reach into the heart of the social agenda mentioned in Chapter 2 and the structural qualities of openness and closure, inclusion and exclusion, that preoccupied Kristiansen. They also bear upon the different social levels at which the themes and iconic motifs operated. It is intriguing to see how many areas of Atlantic Bronze Age social activity are not included and where the principle of social closure operated. Exploring the hypothesis elaborated earlier, three principal themes can be suggested and within them six subsidiary ones. All are connected to high status artefacts elsewhere in Atlantic Europe and the Urnfield area. The choice of these themes arises from comparing the subject matter on the stelae with the artefact inventory from the same area and by making comparisons within the wider European record. These are visualised as domains with subsidiary themes, in the diagrams in figure 4.5.

The first, and perhaps most important, theme is that of the domain related to the female gender. A thorough search of all the stelae does not reveal a single overtly female motif or sign. The human figures very rarely carry any overt sexual identity (there are only two exceptions, where the penis is shown on the male protagonists on the C89 Ervidel II and C80 Ategua stelae); and there is no example of any secondary female characteristic. Within this broad category are secondary themes of dress and jewellery. The golden jewellery circulating in Extremadura at this time is believed to belong to high-ranking women since some torcs (like the one from Sintra, Portugal) are too small to have been worn by men; it would surely be worthy enough to depict on account of that status, should the wish have existed. The engravers could depict small ornaments when they chose (earrings, bronze brooches and perhaps tweezers). So the principle of the intrinsic value of an object is not active here. The Atlantic Bronze Age is quite different in this respect from the Urnfields in central Europe, or in Italy, where female elite status is directly linked to that of warriors through single burials of females in the warrior cemeteries, the use of specifically female grave goods for them and the practice of female human sacrifice with elite warriors. All of

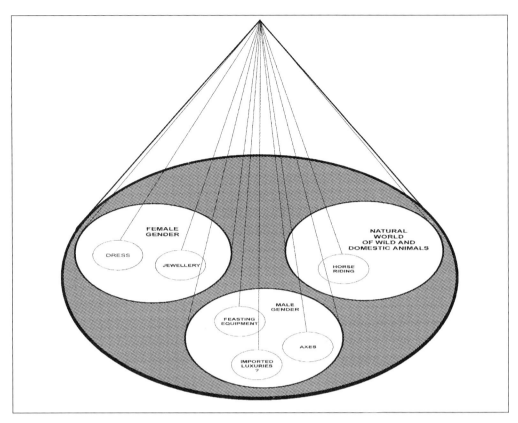

Figure 4.5 *A model which visualises areas of elite activity that are known in the Later Bronze Age, but which are not included in the stelae. There are three levels of abstraction for these domains. The innermost one shows concrete areas such as axes and horse riding; the intermediate level groups them into gender and the natural world; the highest level of abstraction (darker tone) is the world of undifferentiated Bronze Age symbolism*

these female status positions can be seen in the graves in the Landau-Wollmesheim cemetery (Sperber 1999:614 and notes 29–30). There is also a larger range of specifically female artefacts than in the Atlantic Bronze Age, which may reflect a higher status for women.

Within the male domain, three contemporary activities can be recognised that find no echo in the warrior stelae. The first of these concerns feasting equipment. There are no motifs of objects connected with eating and drinking, that was so important in the northern parts of Iberia at this time and which is known, from the presence of bronze roasting spits, to have been practised in Extremadura. Feasting equipment is recognisable as small bronze bowls for drinking and large bronze cauldrons, such as the ones found in the twelfth century hoard at Hío, Pontevedra (Gerloff 1986). The bigger cauldrons easily held 40 litres or more of liquid, but one can only guess what they contained; perhaps meat broth, boiled meat from special cuts, or even heroically large amounts of stimulating drink. Linked to this imposing bronze metalwork are the articulated meat hooks up to 60 cm long, including the masterpiece in the Baiões hoard, which was cast by the lost wax method to achieve the deep decoration, then chased and finished off by attaching loose rings. These were among the grander bronze objects produced in Europe and their manufacture required the highest skills of casting and smithing (Armbruster 1998, 2001).

A second class of objects reflecting social status is the bronzework that was previously highly regarded, such as axes. Axes are emblems of status from the Middle Bronze Age in Portugal and stelae are often engraved with swords on those used as grave markers between 1800–1300 BC. The number of bronze axe hoards increases in the ninth–eighth centuries BC in Portugal and Galicia and the bronze production must be measured in tons of axes every year. The axe was one of the great and lasting symbols through Neolithic and Early Bronze Age Europe and depositing axes singly or, in hoards, was a significant ritual activity. Richard Bradley (1990) explains it in convincing terms as possessing the spirit of the landscape and the axe as the prime tool of land clearance and domestication of the forest into arable or grazing land. The axe came to symbolise man's control of the landscape. In much of the Nordic area, Italy and in eastern Europe, the metal axe was a pre-eminent symbol for men of rank right down to the eighth century.

Another circumscribed area of artefacts that were probably used by men is the group of east Mediterranean objects, of which many were known in central Europe from the sixteenth century BC (Harding 1984; Schauer 1983, 1984) and from the eleventh century in the far west. Foremost among these are the wheeled cauldrons, like the miniature ones in the Baiões hoard, probably used as incense burners, which originate in Syria in the thirteenth–twelfth centuries BC and are carried westwards by Cypriot commerce to Sardinia and from there to Iberia (Mederos & Harrison 1996). Also lacking are any of the torch holders, ivory objects, boxes, seal-stones, or small pieces of furniture such as folding chairs. Instead, what originates in the central and eastern Mediterranean is the eclectic choice of the lyre, mirror and Mycenaean chariot.

A third important conceptual domain is that of the natural world, the one that Ian Hodder (1990) defined as the *agrios*, an untamed place of forest, wild animals and male activities (which he contrasted to the domestic world of women, conceived around the house and agricultural activities). The only domestic animals depicted on stelae are a few hunting dogs and the pairs of chariot horses and just two examples of male deer. The iconography apparently excludes the natural world of animals from any significant protagonism. Especially striking is that there is not one image showing a rider astride a horse. It is not clear if horse riding was practised in Extremadura much before 700 BC, but horses were ridden elsewhere in Spain well before this, from the later third millennium BC. In later iconography in Iberia, after 600 BC, the horseman (*jinete*) becomes one of the commonest icons, used everywhere as a symbol of masculine prowess. Nowhere are there any flocks of sheep or herds of cattle and one should ignore the legendary story of the herds of

Geryon, killed by Herakles as one of his labours and set in Tartessian lands, since it is of oriental origin, displaced to a western source by later Greek writers. Equally notable is the absence of any wild animals, even the fierce ones hunted for trophies like brown bear, wolf, wild boar or lynx. The world-view chosen for depiction on the stelae is man-made and completely centred on the male, with no conceptual room for the natural world beyond it. Other Later Bronze Age societies used images of this natural domain extensively, as the rock engravings from Scandinavia and the Val Camonica (north-west Italy) show.

These observations suggest strongly that social closure took place at more than one level. Levels are the social spheres in which exchanges took place, alliances formed and nurtured, the particular settings in which female roles were recognised and the contexts inhabited by lesser members of society such as children, young men, unmarried women, widows and other dependants. The feasting level is reserved for an internationally connected elite, since the objects connected with it are not only valuable and ostentatious, but ones that are found right across north-west Europe. Feasting, and the exclusive rituals attached to it, was prominent in Ireland and Britain, as shown by the early appearance of cauldrons and flesh hooks; the same artefacts are found less frequently in France and north-west Iberia, but from an equally early date. Each area in the Atlantic sphere had a variant on the feasting ritual, so there are more cauldrons (over 70 and which last until a late period) in Ireland than Britain, while France and Iberia developed big bronze roasting spits; those in Extremadura are long skewers, distinguishable from those with movable spikes from north-west Iberia and France. This equipment is usually recovered from hoards deposited ritually.

The female gold jewellery (especially neck torcs) also belongs to the elite international sphere, since it is widespread in Iberia and shares geometric decorations with Irish and Breton ornaments. There are functionally similar, but stylistically distinct, gold torcs in Ireland and Britain; this implies a picture of Atlantic social connectivity similar to that for the bronze feasting kit, linked to alliance formation.

The level at which bronze axes, or metal for re-cycling, was circulating is more regional. The regional patterning of axes with particular decoration and the differences between the practices of hoarding between north-west Iberia (lots of hoards, mainly of axes), Extremadura (which has very few hoards of axes), western France and Brittany with their riverine hoards and ritual foci, sets them apart from the feasting kit. Hoard contexts, as well as composition, vary greatly between regions of Atlantic Europe where the practice was contemporary.

At what level can the idea of the natural domain operate, the place where untamed animals and great herds of prize cattle roam? If pastoralism became locally dominant in western Iberia, even for a short time, and followed the trajectory of other pastoral episodes in Bronze Age Europe, it ought to be an elite phenomenon. This would be reinforced if long treks were made to distant pastures, so the scale of individual systems could be large.

This is a domain where non-elite groups can flourish; children as herders, young men in their age grades, the setting for raiding and little acts of bravado, or perhaps trophy hunting. None of this penetrates to the most local levels, particularly those in the domestic sphere, which remains opaque.

The natural world is important in another sense, since it was the obvious frame of reference both ideologically and ecologically in the Early Bronze Age of north-west Spain and Portugal. Thinking about symbols through the use of animals is ancient, cross-cultural behaviour. It is an obvious way of describing certain values and kinds of human experience and for making unmistakable visual references to them. Carving animal pictures on flat rocks was a way of marking out the landscape, and deer and horses figure in hundreds of compositions. The carvings relate to general features of the Galician ecology rather than the frequency of granite outcrops suitable to decorate. Richard Bradley (1997:176) explains that sites concentrate near productive land and mark the routes leading between good seasonal grazing lands. In these compositions stags and horses (Bradley is uncertain about the horse identification) complement the images of bronze weapons to express an ideology of masculinity and aggression, in this case, closely associated to territorial claims and social position. The stags outnumber other animals by at least 15:1 and no domestic animal is recognisable anywhere. Bradley concluded that mobile populations used petroglyphs to lay claim to the natural resources nearby.

So there is evidence that alternative Bronze Age world-views were known and developed, based on imagery of natural places populated by wild beasts and domestic creatures. One voice from the code on the stelae comes across strongly; this is a world of humans, where the only animals are servile creatures like dogs, or ones subdued in harnesses like chariot horses. There is no room here for spirited animals acting independently of their masters, or of wild creatures able to challenge the warrior for strength and ferocity. The single deer being hunted is about to be killed. The whole measure of the world depicted on the stelae is man and his manufactured objects. Perhaps this is to be expected, in a visual code that originated in burial markers and was conceived as a part of the pan-European ideal of the warrior.

The key to reading the motif code is the evolving compositions. This historical process puts into our hands an instrument for discussing the materialisation of power, expressed in the pictorial composition.

5

Recognising ideologies: social strategies in the Bronze Age

5.1   The character of chiefdoms

In the Final Bronze Age, societies organised as chiefdoms flourished in Spain and Portugal. These are social formations varying considerably in size and political complexity, which usually act as autonomous units and have a formal independence from one another. Anthropologists like to talk of chiefdoms as being simple, complex or so large and elaborate that they reach a new category called archaic states. They range in size from tiny polities of a few hundred adults to ones that command the labour of tens of thousands; but whatever their size, they share common features. Foremost among these are the hierarchical social organisations in which those at the social apex are distinguished sharply by dress and possessions from other people and in whom are vested special powers that are expressed at moments when rituals or ceremonies are enacted. Typically, one finds that individuals at the apex are usually closely related to one another and often reside in separate communities. It is the nature of chiefdoms that those at the apex are more privileged than the rest of the population and extract surplus for their own consumption through the exercise of power in various ways; these are the recognisable political strategies of exploitation (Renfrew 1982). It is to gain an abundance of the good things of life and exercise power that stimulates men to be chiefs, not a desire to be fair-minded managers or disinterested go-betweens to the gods.

Chiefdoms in south-west Spain would have been at the smaller and perhaps simpler end of the spectrum of evolutionary social complexity, if for no other reason than the small size of their populations and their relatively modest dwellings and central places. Nevertheless, these settlements contain the political heart of the chiefdom and control lesser communities in the region. Some comments have to be hypothetical given the gaps in current knowledge, but there is enough to show that the social formations were at this general level, as was the case throughout the rest of Atlantic Europe. Although the signs of chiefly power can be proposed in theory, based on ethnographic analogies, it is likely that there was no single pathway to success in creating a chiefly entourage. On the ground, it would be ideal to take into account the particular historical conditions that prevailed in Bronze Age chiefdoms, but the reality is that it is precisely these conditions that are the most elusive. For that reason, many theories of chiefdoms have emphasised the ecological constraints that govern their productive capacity, since these have been relatively amenable to study with archaeological methods. As a result, chiefdoms have been defined first in economic terms, with the political motivation obscured since it was considered inaccessible to archaeological investigation. However, Earle (1997) is clear that the heart of a tribal chiefdom is a political construction, a formation that is created deliberately for the benefit of an elite group. He proposes that it arises from manipulative social strategies. For this to be convincing, one has to be clear about the methods used to identify political motives and distinguish them from others, such as a combination of natural resources, favourable communications on natural routes, or climate changes. In chapter 3.2, the natural resources and landscapes of south-west Iberia were discussed in cultural terms, indeed actually called cultural perceptions, for these reasons.

Population pressure, often described in stark demographic terms and amplified by restricted natural resources, is another popular explanation for the emergence of chiefdoms. The argument runs that natural resources (especially fertile land) are strictly limited and physically circumscribed; population increase is a natural state of affairs in food producing societies; this leads to increasing strains on resources as there are more mouths to feed; social friction rises inexorably until it becomes intolerable. At that point, leaders (the future chiefs) emerge, as opportunistic managers with a taste for power, which, once gained is never lost. In this process warfare in all its forms becomes the engine of social change and the means by which the competing leaders eliminate rivals. This model of social evolution by Robert Carneiro became well known in the 1970s as his Circumscription Theory (Carneiro 1970). Since it was proposed, a lot more fieldwork has been done, especially on landscape survey and on the best means to reconstruct prehistoric economies. There is clear evidence now that the rise of a chiefdom does not depend primarily upon the internal pressures of population size or density pushing a group towards a more marked social hierarchy. Populations grow and decline erratically in the European Bronze Age in local cycles that are not connected to a generalised pattern of economic progress, nor indeed are they connected, as far as one can see, to any other obvious pattern, not even climate change on the scale discussed in Chapter 3. The dynamics behind population movements are constantly shifting and the keys to understanding them lay in the specific political processes that chiefdoms chose to follow (Kristiansen 1998); this reverses the evolutionary argument and has important consequences. One is that decision making by identifiable individuals returns to the centre of the stage as a prime mover of cultural changes, with all the unpredictable results that flow from it. For a long time, archaeological theory emphasised the role of the social group, or paid attention to a historical process, rather than recognising the leadership that talented individuals can exercise. Current trends in theory now recognise the importance of historical contingency, which may be better at explaining the rise of chiefdoms in some places than broad models of social evolution. In Bronze Age Europe there are local cycles of expansion and regression, often over a short time (perhaps 150–200 years) and usually not synchronised over wide areas. Erratic cycling is one of the hallmarks of chiefdoms, unstable and short-lived as so many were (Frankenstein & Rowlands 1978). To cite only one example, several distinct expansion cycles are documented in Spain in the second millennium BC for Aragon and Catalonia, the northern Meseta and north-west Spain, among others (Harrison 1994).

Chiefdoms share general characteristics of behaviour and organisation and the definitions proposed by Timothy Earle (1997) help one to understand the networks of social power that they used. His discussion is followed here. The first and most notorious of these is their political instability, already mentioned. Chiefdoms are organised on the principle of kinship, the idea that blood linkages (or ones purporting to be based on blood affinity) between the ruling families entitle them to the status they enjoy. But excluding disappointed family members, or meeting the challenges of others who aspire to the same status, means that there are continual threats to the position of the chiefs; these often take the form of warfare in one form or another.

> Chiefdoms are continually at war and war is a critical element in chiefly power strategies. The power of force rips at the social fabric, the institutions of society. To be effective as a power of centrality, coercive force must itself be controlled, a difficult task that is achieved by binding the military with economic and ideological tethers. (Earle 1997:106)

Fighting is endemic. Most chiefly families have great difficulty in retaining power for more than a few generations before losing it to usurpers. Despite the varied strategies developed by chiefs to retain power, using combinations of force, ideology and economic strength, many Bronze Age chiefdoms probably lasted little more than the lifetimes of their founders, as suggested by the accounts of modern chiefdoms. The burials of the Early Bronze Age, when these data relating to personal status are at their most abundant for study, contain too many 'chiefs' for them all to have been successful for long. Competition between them must have arisen from the time they first appeared and the record of it is left behind as bronze weaponry, forts and style changes in ornaments in Bronze Age Europe.

Another characteristic of chiefdoms is the manner in which positions of social leadership are generalised. A bundle of rights and privileges, even claims to divine status, were bound up in the person of the chief. In concrete terms, this means that they would exercise power as military leaders, they claim the right to a religious prerogative in conducting exclusive rites and ceremonies and in many cases they claim divine status and expect the same treatment as gods; this leads to the theocratic quality of many of the historically documented chiefdoms in Polynesia or Africa. Chiefs may administer the exchanges for luxury products and have an effective 'trading monopoly' within their community, and in many pastoral chiefdoms they own all the livestock. Such a combination of powers may exist even in complex chiefdoms with many tens of thousands of subjects, undiluted by delegation. What does this mean in practice? Any one of these roles would keep a chief busy and to monitor all of them means that a chief has to be active and visible; it is a 'hands-on role' requiring constant alertness in the exercise of all the powers and privileges claimed. The moment these are neglected, rivals appear and their challenges have to be met. The generalised role has the advantage that no tactics for self-promotion are excluded, but it has the corresponding weakness that in order to be effective the ordinary chief would have to be exceptionally competent. All real power is concentrated in the hands and voice of one person, nearly always a man. Although this could be delegated, that could be dangerous unless closely supervised. Altogether, this job specification seems a tall order and ineffective chiefs would not last long, so a self-selecting mechanism for prowess, or at least energy, would be in place.

For these reasons, chiefs needed to be pragmatic, with a social network through which they could exercise their powers. Ideally, this would be consensual, but in reality a lot would depend on the threat of force to ensure compliance, an uncertain and often ineffective mechanism. In the long run, Earle suggests that chiefs were interested in other sources of power, such as ideology.

5.2   Social networks and sources of power in chiefdoms

The classic studies explaining how social power is made legitimate are those of Max Weber. Leadership confers tangible benefits that make it worth the struggle for dominance and prestige, and in all societies there are individuals who seek their own political advantage. Weber identified four sources of power, which Earle (1991, 1997) described as (1) social relationships (including kinship), (2) economic power and control of production and exchange, (3) military might, (4) ideology, a code of social order which 'establishes an authority structure'. One could call the last three exchange, warfare, ritual, and of these, the power derived from production and exchange is the strongest and restricts access to the others. The manner in which these sources created contrasting dynamics over time is what interests us in this section. In Atlantic Iberia all of these strategies were used between 1250–750 BC and they overlap in time, if not in physical space.

Exchange in an economy only a little above subsistence level, which is what all the west European Bronze Age ones were, should be seen as an activity intended to finance the political activities of the chiefs conducting it. Without surplus resources the chiefs cannot exercise their trade monopolies, nor reward their followers for good behaviour and loyalty. So the problem for chiefs is first, how to get a surplus into their control and second, how to retain it. Earle makes the standard distinction, between staple finance and wealth finance. By staple finance he means a tax in staple products like cereal, livestock, metals or salt, or extracted in labour on a large project or building, with a property system in place to make it work. Systems of land ownership capable of doing this probably did not exist in

Late Bronze Age Iberia, nor in most of Europe. Wealth finance is the alternative system that was chosen and is 'the use of objects (primitive valuables, prestige goods, or money) as political currencies to compensate people within ruling institutions'. Earle continues:

> I argue that control over the ideology of social ranking rested on control over the system of wealth finance. Wealth finance has a major advantage over staple finance. Its highly valued objects are easily transported over considerable distances and can be used to exert long-distance control over people. The centralised distribution of wealth allows surpluses to be accumulated centrally. (Earle 1997:73–74)

This seems clear enough; once the high value objects are identified, the scale and dimensions of the system will become apparent.

Earle discussed the specific case of the emergence of the Early Bronze Age chiefdoms in Thy (Jutland, Denmark) and discussed their pastoral economy; 'animal herding lowers the carrying capacity of a region and makes no sense in the logic of the subsistence economy. Its increase most probably resulted from the use of animals as a source of movable wealth within a prestige-goods exchange system' (Earle 1997:65). He goes on to say:

> The primary advantage of cattle ... would have been the ease with which they could have been managed and owned as currency in the political economy. An animal is a convenient unit of ownership and production. In herding chiefdoms, the preponderance of animals is owned by the local chief, who lends them out to individual households for their subsistence in return for support. Herding economies are thus comparatively easy to control in one sense; each animal, although not highly productive, is, like an individual field, naturally defined and clearly marked as a unit of subsistence production and ownership. To be an effective source of wealth, cattle would have been traded regionally for the storable wealth of prestige objects. (Earle 1997:100)

As it happens, this scenario could be adapted to the conditions of the live-oak savannas, just as well as maritime Denmark. So cattle herding could have been one source of local wealth finance in south-west Iberia, although it is probable there were other elements too, such as collecting tin ore and perhaps alluvial gold. Nor can slave raiding be excluded. However, the present evidence for large-scale cattle herding in south-west Iberia is largely circumstantial, based on tiny samples of animal bones (Cardoso 1996).

With these elements there is enough material to start up and maintain long distance exchange networks for luxuries unobtainable locally; such items would be the Near Eastern bronze bowl from Berzocana with a massive gold torc inside it, the wheeled incense burners from Baiões of Cypriot inspiration and probably the first two-wheeled chariots, given the technical accomplishments needed from wheelwrights and joiners to make such a display vehicle. The list of Mediterranean exchanges would widen considerably if one includes perishable materials such as textiles or wild animal products like furs, or arcane ritual knowledge transmitted through music and poems accompanied by a lyre. A similar list could be drawn up for exchanges with the Atlantic regions in the form of feasting gear, ingot and axe hoards, weapon designs and female gold work. To flourish, these systems need to be open to novelties from afar, but sufficiently self-confident to be able to assimilate them selectively in a process of re-contextualisation. It is characterised by a 'repetitive dialectic between maintaining regional traditions and interacting across their boundaries, between sharing international value systems and re-contextualising them locally and regionally, between openness and closure' (Kristiansen 1998:56). Objects acquire value by virtue of their strangeness and rarity as much as through their crafts-manship and when worn out, those made of bronze could be melted down and made into new valuables. The crucial point in appreciating a system of wealth finance is that the size of its exchange networks is far bigger than any Bronze Age chiefdom, so that the system is more than the sum of its parts. Apparently, the links between chiefs rarely extended beyond their immediate neighbours, all of whom seem to have had territories about 30 km wide, so a series of independent cells was set up, with the result that no chief would know the full extent of the system, but could participate in it. This would resolve the apparent paradox of far-flung and complicated trading systems being created by unstable, belliger-ent and small-scale polities like chiefdoms. The exchanges were vital for the survival of the political elites.

Coercion is a common source of chiefly power. Warfare is apparent from the beginning of the period, shown by the prominence of bronze swords in hoards and in ritual deposits and weapons are the oldest and most obvious symbols on the stelae. Weapons are the pri-mary evidence for warfare until fortified hilltop settlements appear around 900 BC in central Portugal. Studies of the edge wear and damage to bronze swords in Denmark, Hungary and Ireland prove they were weapons used for attack and parrying the blows of other swordsmen, so the aggression was real, not symbolic. The other weapon favoured throughout Bronze Age Europe was the thrusting spear. Like swords, they survive in their thousands and the variations in size and shape are due to more than the mere development of better weapons or different fighting styles and techniques. The normative ideas of what the Final Bronze Age sword and spear should look like are changed in subtle ways to cre-ate objects that identify a particular group, with the shape and style of the piece as a marker (Sperber 1999).

Ritual is the third source of social power, made evident in the practice of hoarding bronze and gold metalwork. This is a complicated matter to describe briefly, but prestige goods were produced in metal and then consumed or destroyed by the act of burial, usual-ly in the earth, but also in the waters of flowing rivers, estuaries and in places prominent in the landscape like river fords and mountain passes. There are cycles of deposition of metalwork, even within the short period of the Final Atlantic Bronze Age, when periods of abundance alternate with scarcity (a point mentioned in the previous section). Some, but not all, hoards were ritual deposits in Iberia. There are changes in the social geography, too, as hoards in the Final Bronze Age in Iberia shift from one region to another, with the latest ones concentrating in central Portugal. It is notable that hoarding bronze work (for whatever purpose) was never common behaviour in the area where stelae are found. Very few true hoards are known in Extremadura and their scarcity must reflect different attitudes to metal consumption in these neighbouring areas, especially in the period 950–750 BC at the end of the Final Bronze Age. Hoarding metalwork and erecting stelae were taking place at the same time in central Portugal and neighbouring Extremadura and the same weapons are buried in hoards and carved on the stelae, but they are complementary and exclusive uses of the same status symbol: the bronze sword.

Another way of reading this distinction between hoarding and stelae is to see them as different abstractions of essentially similar ideas, which were intended to make chiefly power legitimate:

> The isolation of this shared construction – in comparison with other cultural elements in these societies – is of essential importance in understanding both the Bronze Age warrior ideologies generally and its local form within western Europe. … The strong focus on weaponry is shared by the whole of the Atlantic Bronze Age; but the additional construction of stelae makes Iberia different. Either an extra dimension is added to the warrior ideology, or their figuration is merely metaphorical. Meanwhile, the stelae's depiction of warriors and their emblems may be an abstraction, they nonetheless embody and humanise this role in a manner that is different in its essence from how weapons (in particular the sword) are assumed to symbolise or signify the warrior in the rest of the Atlantic Bronze Age region. There is a subtle distinction in terms of the level of abstraction at which the male/warrior exists and thus how this figure is experienced. This, furthermore, probably relates differences in ideology and means of empowerment. It is therefore of significance that stelae in addition to their other distinctions were used in the construction of landscape in a manner that is distinctly different from how weaponry could perform – either during their use, or when ritually deposited. The deposition of swords and other weapons uses principles of invisibility and secretness to gain significance. As the weapons disappear from sight they transmute into power. The stelae, in contrast, are visible and permanent in the landscape. While united by their shared reference to male/warrior, weapon deposits and stelae are equally divided by their different presence in people's lives. Such differences question the nature of power within the various Final Bronze Age societies in western Europe – some aspects of ritual life and thus the generation of power and legitimacy, were articulated and practiced very differently across the Atlantic Bronze Age despite the shared references to a 'warrior ideology'. (Sørensen 1998:262)

Not all of this is congruent with the ideas expressed in Chapter 4, explaining the essential funerary connections of the stelae and their commemorative function; and the idea that stelae help to construct the cultural landscape is not demonstrated (Galán 1993).

There is a second expression of ritual power visible in the scenes of horned men on the stelae, representing either deities or warrior 'heroes' consorting with them (it is important to remember that they may not be men wearing horned headdresses or helmets). The physical link between the bronze hoards and horned men on the stelae is the sword, actually worn at the waist by the figures on stelae C27 Talavera de la Reina, C48 Magacela and C65 Olivenza. If some of the horned men were warriors who died and became 'heroes', it should be possible to press the analysis further and explore the impact of east Mediterranean beliefs, developed as part of a broader theology in the later second millennium BC, upon the Bronze Age chiefdoms of south-west Iberia. There is no reason to think the horned figures represent 'The Smiting God' of the Syrian and Hittite civilisations, since his attributes and posture are quite different and these eastern deities almost never wear horns (Petrovic 2001). It is more probable that the horned figures show a warrior empowered with new vigour and force in the after life, with the horns giving him a super-human aspect. Horns are emblems from the natural world of full-grown cattle and bulls and in putting them on the head of a warrior, a statement is made that he possesses these natural qualities of masculinity, bravery and energy, or even that his power is assimilated into the source of his wealth, which lies in the herds of cattle. These are just some of the interpretative possibilities of these ritually powerful scenes. In these cases it would make sense to use the medium of a stela, to show this status long after his death, and retain his presence in the lives of the people he formerly controlled. Stelae used like this construct an image of power and make it permanent, in quite a different manner than depositing bronze swords at a river crossing, or ritually throwing weapons into the water (as may have happened at Huelva).

A third area of powerfully expressed ritual is actually making and setting up the stelae: the materialisation of power.

5.3   Ideology and its visual expression

Ideology is a code of social order. It is a real, created order that is particular to a culture or group at one time and permeates all societies, in one form or another. There can be many competing ideologies in a society at the same time and different groups may claim them exclusively; thus, there may be an ideology based on the female gender, or connected to an economic activity like animal herding, or expressed in myths belonging to kin groups like the chiefs' families. It is grounded in shared knowledge and ranges from quite simple ideas to elaborate theologies of cosmic order; nor need it be true to be believed, or powerful.

> Ideology is evidently a source of power. An ideology, as a view of the world, sets forth an understanding of what is right, what is natural. It contains theories of the

world and of the place of human society and its segments within it. Characteristically, an ideology is founded on principles of a moral and religious order. Things are the way they are because of cosmic laws. (Earle 1997:144)

In chiefdoms it is expressed commonly as a style of decoration of special artefacts, or in ceremonies and cult places, or in the case of the Atlantic Bronze Age, in the form of stelae. In all the known cases, where chiefdoms use ideological codes as part of their strategy for retaining power, they must be converted from a shared belief into something tangible; this conversion process is what anthropologists call 'materialisation' (De Marrais et al 1996:15–16). It makes it possible to control, manipulate and extend ideology beyond the local group. The process takes place at the moment when ideology (broadly defined) takes a concrete form, which can be objects, symbols, pictures, songs, myths and so on. Its aim is to achieve shared values and communicate power to a broader population. In the abstract, this sounds obvious and apparently not very contentious, but do not be deceived by this bland expression. Actually demonstrating the correctness of the inference from an object to a belief is tricky and more so when the societies are prehistoric and there are no informants to ask, or act as a double check against a wrong inference. The explanatory strength of the inference depends crucially upon the context in which the image (or images) is found; this context is provided by the compositions on the stelae, which incorporate 35 different motifs. Each stela is a self-contained composition pecked into stone for permanence and inalterability. It has already been shown that the motifs are only a small selection from a wider cultural world, rich in other expressive possibilities, so it is reasonable to infer that they materialise that same selection and no other. In other words, the specific ideology is placed in its context by the act of composition to define, in this case, a world-view of masculinity and martial qualities. This is the same as Weber's warrior status group, which is best conceived of as a warrior retinue rather than as a chiefly warrior elite, since it is a broadly shared ethic that extends beyond the limits of the chiefly family or clan. Sharing the ideology strengthens it and makes it more acceptable and also reduces the challenges to which it is likely to be exposed.

Ideology is about power and 'Power is linked to the knowledge of power, which must be experiential; in simple terms, power rests on materialised ideologies' (Earle 1997:144). The first statement rather skirts around the question and makes everything depend on individual experience, which is not knowable. This is not the way forward. If the second statement is true, then one should be able to see how ideas are communicated in a material form.

The stelae are the materialisation of a chiefly ideology. Their compositions have a symbolic content, which is expressed in the particular motifs engraved on the standing stones. By choosing certain motifs, a message is created that is made permanent and communicated widely, to everyone who looks at it. A central theme in this message is the confident assertion that there is a specific life-style that a warrior should follow and that this is not just a matter of carrying a shield and sword and knowing how to fight skilfully. This life-style goes much further than that and is stated with dramatic simplicity by using the naked human figure in over 70 compositions. The human figure becomes the defining icon through its heavy-handed insistence on the uniqueness of each warrior. That is why it becomes the dominant motif in all the later compositions, since the growth of the size and visual force of the body matches the increasing power of the warrior and his retinue. There is deliberate ostentation in depicting personal consumables (weapons, brooches for clothing, lyres, chariots) that repeats the abstraction of manliness in different forms and registers.

As discussed in Chapter 4.3, the stelae have a unique historical sequence embedded in them, which we can discern through the practices of re-cutting and by adding motifs later on, to compositions that were originally simpler. As the subject matter evolves from weapons to prestigious objects, the human figure is introduced and gradually displaces all other elements in the composition to become the central figure. At the end of the sequence, the horned figures appear and there are narratives and ritual scenes involving deities or warriors immortalised as 'heroes'. This evolution of compositions actually is the process of materialisation; and this particular (and historical) sequence of changing beliefs, not the act of pecking out the designs, constitutes the social reality of the Final Bronze Age.

This reality is broader than a behavioural strategy to accumulate power by a few individuals; it is a shared process that was consensual among the elite group as a whole, with the intention of participating in a common experience. The occasional need to re-cut stelae and obliterate shield emblems with more complex scenes with human figures at the centre (as in C51 Valdetorres I) proves this. Furthermore, the stelae altered in this way are a warning not to think that one or two were singled out especially for this treatment; in varying degrees the practice of re-cutting and amending compositions affected one stela in seven and is spread geographically over the whole of the south-west. The very act of changing the symbols in the Final Bronze Age must have been one sanctioned by the elite; it is not credible that clandestine stelae-peckers would do their work in secret, on a public monument.

Chiefs had to face up to another problem inherent in the process of materialising their ideology, which is this: how can the elite, who commanded the stelae to be set up in the first place, be sure that the ideas and meanings are not going to be subverted by their rivals? If one is a Bronze Age warrior, how does one stop a competitor from challenging the validity of the claims to power and masculinity made in a stela? Characteristically, post-processual archaeologists put the question like this:

How does a materialised ideology achieve a shared status? How is normativeness attained? De Marrais et al are wrong to think that the control of materials can lead to the control of ideologies. One of the most distinctive attributes of material symbols is that they become distant from their producer or 'author'. Through time and space it becomes notoriously difficult to control other readings and interpretations of the same monument or artefact. It is not enough to control materials: the meanings too have to be maintained in the face of alternative and contested interpretations. How is normativeness constructed and maintained? (Hodder 1996, 58)

Setting aside the jargon of deconstruction for a moment, the answer is not hard to find. The stelae are erected over a period of at least 350 years, possibly 500 years and in that time they evolve. The challenge to authority is met by evolving the code, by changing its content through non-stop ideological upgrading of the composition until it finally makes claims for 'heroic' status in the horned figures and narratives of power in stelae like C89 Ervidel II and C80 Ategua, which appear at the end of the sequence 900–800 BC. The number of motifs increases at the same time. The oldest stelae are austere compositions with just three motifs; this form is widespread in all four geographical zones. The stelae erected afterwards rapidly acquire first the mirror (C1 San Martín de Trevejo, C14 Alburquerque) and soon afterwards helmets, combs and brooches appear (C12 Valencia de Alcántara III, C13 Brozas, C50 Quintana de la Serena), then the chariot is added (two stelae, C10 & C11 Valencia de Alcántara I-II). Now the broad historical process is known, and with it the approximate visual content to be expected at each stage, it becomes clearer why the later additions of motifs are so important to the individual stela. The challenge to the authority of the Brozas stela (C13) was met by engraving an elaborate comb on the monument, to make sure the fullest complement of motifs had been included; on C6 Torrejón el Rubio I a chariot was carefully engraved into the stone later. Possibly the comb was added later on the C33 Cabeza del Buey II stela.

Further dialogue between the memory of the dead, their heirs and competitors is evident in the re-engravings on C9 Torrejón el Rubio IV and C51 Valdetorres I, which transform simple shield and sword stelae into warrior-based compositions. This act is materialising the change from a warrior panoply to figurative compositions. On the C67 Aldea del Rey II stela (which is actually a small fragment) the stone is turned upside down to cancel out the first composition and another at twice the scale replaces the first warrior scene. In fact, in each case it would have been easier to find another stone slab free of engravings and start the compositions from a fresh surface, so that the visual message would not be blurred by the previous motifs showing through into the later ones, apparently spoiling their visual impact; but this was not done. Defacing the previous composition was more important and it needed to be visibly over-ridden, even if it meant the later message was technically confused. From these stelae, the viewer would draw the lesson not from the motifs, but from the act of re-cutting itself. In effect, it would be like the *damnatio memoriae* practised on the images of the Pharaoh Akhenaten, or in later Roman times.

Other owners added small human figures to make the composition more forceful, as in C57 El Viso IV and C70 Carmona, where they are placed in positions of secondary importance, or obvious inferiority, by being shown one third or one quarter the size of the main figure. Here the message is not that the lesser figures are inconspicuous, but that they are palpably inferior. Big figures are invariably more important than little ones. Size does matter; Bronze Age viewers knew that. Then there are chiefly families who appropriate for themselves monuments already a thousand years old and probably respected for that reason, like the man-sized phalluses of C27 Talavera and C30 São Martinho II. Perhaps they needed to make an overwhelming statement of gender empowerment in this way, or refer to symbols of fertility and procreation, which are otherwise ignored in the symbolic code.

All the time this was going on, the chiefs made every effort to keep up with changing fashions in dress and weapons, so motifs of brooches evolve from archaic bow shapes to elbow fibulae and finally into the antennae type. Mirrors become fancier, with elaborate handles on the later ones, and hunting dogs appear on a few pictures. There is a typological evolution in the swords, from those with parallel-sided blades and simple hilts like C5 Fóios, to leaf-shaped-blades and eventually to the Carp's Tongue swords with their large handles and prominent pommels. The latter sword shapes overlap in time, as hoards like Huelva show. It appears that sword typology is less clearly depicted than the style changes in other artefacts, despite many swords being depicted at life size on some stelae (C5 Fóios) and that the reason for this is that swords are shown with their organic handles and sheaths. For archaeologists, only the bronze blade actually survives to classify, hence the discrepancy between what a Bronze Age and a modern observer will see in a sword. Nevertheless, this steady, long-term historical process of motif change seems to be the active, vigilant process of materialisation. The creators of the stelae met the challenges to their claims to power and status by enriching the code and maintaining that quality of 'normativeness' in the artefacts. This may well be the reason for the choice of the cartoon-like simplicity of the outline drawing conventions that were chosen, to steer clear of ambiguity and force the observer to see what the creator intended to depict. If this is a correct reading, it provides a functional argument in support of the engravers' choice.

More than that, it reveals what the idea of 'normativeness' meant for the Bronze Age observer, which is this; details of shape, size, decoration and manufactured quality of all the objects mattered a great deal and were like modern designer labels on luxury products, a guarantee of the object's authenticity. The intention was to depict real objects so they could be recognised immediately. No *simulacra* would do; duds or copies were not acceptable and by keeping real objects of metal in circulation, a normative standard was maintained of what the chief's mirror or sword should be. The same applied to the wooden chariots, musical instruments, or sets of accurate weights. This accounts for the need to relate the motifs to real objects, to authenticate the message depicted through the code. Even the repetitive act of erecting a new stela can be seen as a way to maintain normative control; and hence the significance of the estimate in Chapter 2 suggesting that between one and two thousand stelae were erected in the Final Bronze Age. Setting up stelae was an active historical process in building power.

Not every chief's memory was respected. There are examples where the validity of the ideology was successfully contested and refuted. Leaving aside the problems of the bodily removal of stelae from the original places of erection and the secondary uses at a much later date, there are examples of defacement, at least one dating to the Bronze Age. This is the C10 Valencia de Alcántara I stela with multiple cup marks 'energised' by three lines. Every part of it is damaged and all the motifs slighted. The simple stela from Córdoba I (C82) may have had 32 cup marks added and while they confuse the original composition, the cup marks do not actually damage the motifs, which remain legible. It is hard to know if this is intentional defacement. Perhaps not exactly defaced, but not much respected either, is the stela from Capote (C86), which was physically cut down to a smaller size, inverted and two short inscriptions in the Tartessian script were added to the blank area that was originally the foot; they date from 700–600 BC, not long after the stela was originally created. This is an act of re-appropriation.

However, this process seems to have been more active early on in the development of the basic stela. Overwhelmingly, the stelae with a human figure in the centre were not defaced, or re-cut; there are just two cases where this happened. It is the older ones with the warrior panoply that are attacked in this way. Why should this be? What is it in the use of the human figure that stops later re-cutting? Or to go further, one can ask why were these assertive stelae not challenged ideologically? The argument must backtrack for a moment and recall the importance of the human figure for asserting the warrior's personal individuality, his uniqueness compared with everyone else and his adherence to the shared ideology of his group. It is possible that the pattern is significant; that respect was actually shown to the memory of the individual depicted for a period after the need to do so had gone. There are several possible reasons for this: one could be that their descendants had acquired much greater status and no longer needed these primitive displays to assert it; another could be that the geographical foci of economic power had shifted to the coastal lands and the Guadalquivir valley and areas formerly important became backwaters; a third reason could be that many stelae were actually 'killed' and their authority nullified by being buried shallowly, or pulled down from their original vertical positions and that this physical act was enough to desecrate them. There are several stelae in contexts that would fit this reconstruction. Particular historical events may have played a role too and thorough destruction of a hated memorial may have obliterated it entirely. It would not be so hard for a few men with boulders to shatter a stela into unrecognisable pieces. In the more complex chiefdoms of the eighth–seventh centuries BC, new codes of display arose, among them the return to fashion of burials for people of all social conditions, not just warrior retinues. The human body was used now in a different way than in the Atlantic Final Bronze Age; it was no longer stereotyped in an abstract public memorial, but ideologically transformed through burial or cremation. So in this historical reading, the last warrior stelae were left undamaged because their ideology became obsolete and impotent.

The conclusion is that the key to understanding how a chiefly life-style was maintained in the Final Bronze Age lies in the symbolic changes in the ideological code.

Reading the codes: symbols and meanings

(Written in collaboration with Francisco Marco Simón)

6.1   Context and meaning

It is important to establish an adequate methodology for studying the codes on the stelae and explain why it is possible to identify objective grounds for interpreting their meanings.

Recently, the archaeologist Robert Layton assessed the claims of the postmodernists by reviewing the history of communication and believes the solution lies in seeing it as a social strategy. While it is impossible to recover the semantic content of meaning in cultures long past, it certainly is possible to recover the social strategy because there are references made to objects or agents that we can recognise today. There is a wider discourse outside the narrow one embedded in the message itself. When these references are repeated to form a pattern that can be correlated with contexts, then: 'archaeology can escape from the closed worlds of postmodernist theory' (Layton 2001:29). He accepts the idea that, despite correlating styles and contexts, these systems will be empty of semiotic content and that original meaning can only be discovered when members of the tradition that created it can speak about it to the observer. Clearly, this is an almost impossible condition for the Final Bronze Age, but nevertheless we can answer the question of how to recognise signification in other cultures. There is a crucial difference between hard postmodernism (Derrida 1976, 1978) and softer versions of it (Foucault 1972; Eco 1990). The softer ones accept the possibilities of references to objects and in effect open the way to engaging with the real world.

This engagement occurs when one tries to imagine the project in which the other person is participating (Layton 2001:30). He establishes two types of reference, a broader one of general discourse and the more defined one of objects or animals or human beings. The broader discourse can be based on existing notions of what a landscape is (with Bronze Age settlements, central places with fortifications, stelae and treasure hoards), or a life-style expressed in the notion of a warrior's physical beauty and the aesthetic values essential to its maintenance, or accepting the conventions of depicting humans. It is essentially a controlled usage of ideas, with a recognisable authorship. The narrower one of objects, such as swords or chariots, ideally ought to be communicated through speech from Bronze Age informants. Since this is obviously absurd, one has to accept that certain physical interlocutors are valid and competent and reject others as lacking that status. In the case of stelae, this validity would be established by textual readings from Levantine sources (for example, texts from Late Bronze Age Ugarit referring to chariots and warrior heroes), or the closed contexts of actual objects like swords in hoards such as Hío and brooches in deposits like Huelva. This is how one can uncover the social strategies behind the stelae codes and explain the historical changes in them. Since they are multi-vocal, their meanings will change and some will remain undecipherable.

Such comparisons are not an indulgence, but an essential tool to assert the specificity and difference inherent in the stelae. A sensitive passage by Ricardo Olmos conveys the importance of iconography as the creator of meanings, and not a mere reproduction of reality, when he discusses Iberian sculpture and imagery:

> I believe that the ancient world used not to represent the commonplace. That which was irrelevant and simply factual had no place in the figurative composition. The image is not a simple projection, substituting for reality, nor even a symbolic representation, but rather more of its essence. For this reason I am emboldened to suggest that the image could come to be converted into the source, as a model of reality itself (Olmos 1996:31).

Another fruitful approach to analysing the meaning within a code is by considering how comparison, or analogy, works in practice. The difficulties of establishing valid comparisons between elements of societies widely separated in space and time are well known. There are real problems in understanding or translating the categories that other societies use when treating their dead members and making these intelligible today. For that reason, comparative social anthropologists have split into two broad factions: those who champion the emic approach, using the terms and concepts of the societies they investigate; and the etic approach, which recognises the impossibility of using the emic analysis, since the interlocutors are dead or the culture extinct and instead creates new categories for analysis in the modern context. Barbara Ward reasoned that: 'There is no reason why anyone attempting an outsider's analysis of another culture – or his own as if from the outside – should not erect whatever categories seem to him to be the most useful'. Nevertheless, 'If one is to interpret the native insiders' understanding of their own culture one must try to comprehend – and use – their categories, not impose one's own' (Ward 1979:36). It is evident that to understand the Bronze Age stelae one cannot use the emic approach and, given the complete absence of written accounts concerning them, not helped by the meagre gleanings from the archaeological contexts, that the etic approach has to be followed, closely adapted to the historical realities of the late second millennium BC. The way forward is to build what Dan Sperber calls 'interpretative generalisations', which are not, properly speaking, models capable of empirical testing, but which are instruments that are logically possible (Sperber 1982).

It is here that the comparative method becomes desirable and essential. It is especially powerful with cultures close in time and space, such as the Aegean-Canaanite world, or the Archaic Greek societies, from which there is written information, as well as iconographic materials of every type. However, it is necessary to make good use of comparison, avoiding the mechanical transposition of similar elements to reconstruct a genealogy of institutions on the basis of homologies and through a forced unity derived from stereotypes, determined by modern perceptions. Comparisons of ancient religions, fertility cults and mother goddesses lead nowhere. Contrary to what is widely believed, the comparison of similar structures does not usually answer the questions posed. The 'true' comparison is a prudent method of working, and to make analogies is to reflect upon one particular culture through aspects of another and inspired by homologous contexts, to stimulate the ideas and questions through which a place or ritual can be explored. In other words, to compare is to construct the object of study.

This comparison is not only convenient, but also necessary, once structural similarities have been established. A valid comparative method has to go beyond cataloguing similarities between different cultures, as if they were a hidden essence. What is required is that it should highlight that which is specific, and the nature of the difference, and for this reason, the comparative method should be a point of departure for the discussion, not its conclusion.

> It is axiomatic that comparison is never a matter of identity. Comparison requires the acceptance of the difference as the grounds of its being interesting and a methodical manipulation of that difference to achieve some stated cognitive end. The questions of comparison are questions of judgement with respect to the difference: What differences are to be maintained in the interests of comparative enquiry? What differences can be defensively relaxed and relativised in light of the intellectual tasks at hand? (Smith 1987:14).

From these positions, it is clear that comparison aims to distinguish phenomena and realities of a certain complexity. It does not attempt to establish an identity between different things, which in the real world never existed, but instead develops its first principle, that historical contexts must be respected.

These are the methodological bases used in this study of the Bronze Age stelae. They permit the comparison between the information contained in the stelae and other types of documentation that, although distant in time and space, are frankly interesting insofar as they illuminate aspects of Bronze Age society and belief.

6.2   Compositions and motif groups

This section presents the compositions chronologically, discussing the central elements of each iconographical stage. The term 'composition' is value-laden, but it does help to describe the way in which the engraver arranged the components of his scene; that is, behind the formal choice of motifs lays the idea of a structure that he wishes to share with the viewers. So, when Anthony Snodgrass discusses composition in Greek art and literature of the Iron Age, specifically referring to the Homeric stories, he takes pains to explain why this is a prime condition in order to understand them. Greek art also compresses time into a single frame in order to represent it, a point he insisted upon as central to Greek ideas of what composition should include (Snodgrass 1998:151–163; Whitley 1995:47–53). Composition is the essential intellectual step that connects the iconographic elements of things that do not exist in the world of nature, like shields and horned men, and gathers them together so they convey a message, while allowing the viewer to make up their own stories about them. Later on, more motifs and human figures may have guided viewers towards remembering more complex stories or myths, or ones relating to a specific, named person. But the Greek understanding of composition is more complex than anything shown on the stelae, with the exception of three narrative scenes.

The sequence was established in Chapter 4 and develops the idea that stelae bear formal compositions which express successive ideological changes. These changes overlapped one another in time and it is probable that once the process of ideological development was set in motion, most stelae would be decorated in the latest fashion. That is, there would be a short time lag between the creation of the most recent ideological position and its reception by a particular chieftain, so the sequence will appear as a continuum. This could reflect a real situation, where ideology was actively constructed and contested, in the Final Bronze Age. The process is likely to have been an uneven one historically; it is unknown if there was a long period of stability, followed by rapid ideological change, or if the entire sequence was regular. The first suggestion is more likely than the second, given the lack of clarity in the typological definition of the leading artefacts and the overlapping compositions and their re-cuttings. As a result it is to be expected that there will be a long period of basic compositions, followed by elaboration and rapid evolution into figurative scenes. The sequence will therefore be asymmetrical, with quick development compressed into the final phase (figure 6.1).

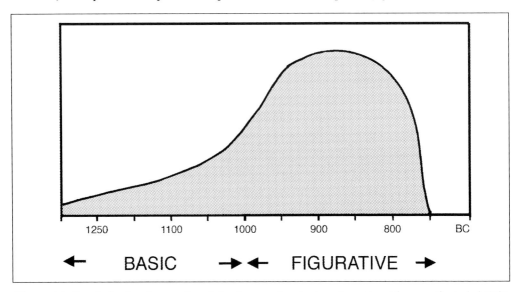

Figure 6.1 *Graph showing the growth and development from basic to figurative stelae over the period 1250-750 BC*

A generation ago, Gomes and Monteiro (1977:198–99) used a sociological model to interpret this sequence. They saw an opposition between the basic stelae and the rest and used the terms *emblematic* and *commemorative*, stressing that there were two different aesthetic structures behind these compositions; one based on objects (weapons), the other centred on the individual human figure. They interpreted this as a shift from a simple code where the status of a warrior was depicted emblematically, to a one where a dead person was memorialised and perhaps conceived as a hero. A shift in intellectual categories, one that reflected fundamental differences in intellectual outlook, lies at the heart of it. Despite its attractions, this binary scheme runs into difficulties since semiologists assign rather different meanings to the terms *emblematic* and *commemorative* and using them provokes confusion. Equally importantly, we know of twice as many stelae in 2002 as were published in 1977 and among them are compositions that establish a single sequence from the simple weapon designs to the elaborate pictures with figures. This is convincing at several analytical levels and refutes the dichotomy between two sharply defined groups. Furthermore, although Gomes and Monteiro recognised some re-cut stelae, they failed to build this information into their model to demonstrate an historical sequence; they simply assumed it, because of the morphological variety of the stelae. All of this means that the model of aesthetic and ideological duality cannot be sustained and should be replaced with one that sees the entire group as evolving a single code of values over many centuries. It is quite true that the compositions change their aesthetic content and for that reason it is useful to coin the terms 'basic' and 'figurative' as general descriptions for groups of stelae at the beginning and end of the process. However, these terms do not imply any ideological opposition between the early and later carvings, nor an evolution to a 'stronger' code, since it is a single code that is expressed throughout, culminating in the narrative scenes at the end of the process.

It is permissible to suggest meanings for the motif groups because this period has historical reference points, which can be traced into the eastern Mediterranean. This applies to the whole of the Final Bronze Age in the western Mediterranean, which was in contact with the Aegean, Cyprus and the Levant from at least 1300 BC, through intermediaries on Sardinia and Sicily and interaction intensified sharply after 1050/950 BC (Mederos 1996a, 1999). It is legitimate to discuss shared systems of values expressed in similar symbols throughout this area and draw upon written historical sources to suggest particular meanings (Treherne 1995). This is a different ideological world from that of the Copper Age two millennia earlier, which lacks these links to the east and whose symbolism is consequently harder to decipher (D'Anna et al 1995; Mezzena 1998). One should not forget that the south-west of Europe was in contact with a literate world in the eastern Mediterranean and on the periphery, if not the margin, of its geo-political systems.

The following analyses discuss only the complete stelae, since fragments of compositions are, in most cases, impossible to reconstruct accurately.

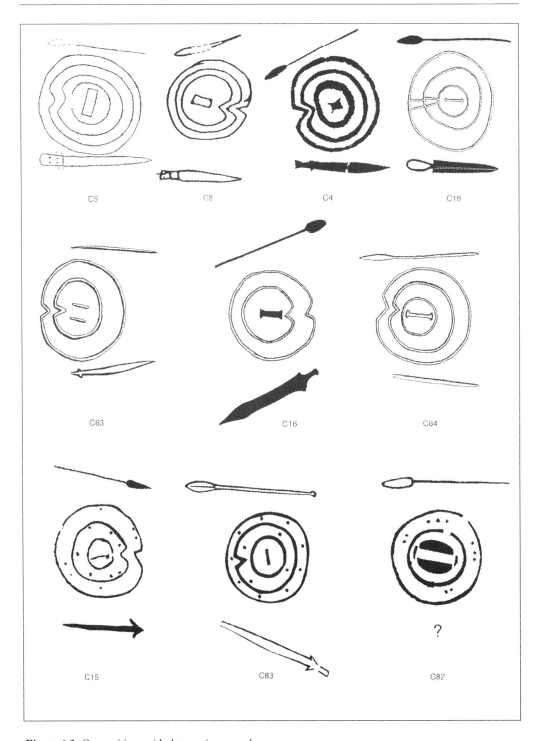

Figure 6.2 *Compositions with the warrior panoply*

6.2.1 The evolution of the warrior panoply

The basic composition consists of a large shield placed centrally, with a spear aligned horizontally above and a sword horizontal below it. The composition is symmetrical and balanced. There is no individual identity expressed in it; the nature of basic codes is that they identify groups, in which shared values are expressed on behalf of the whole social section, in this case the warriors. As compositions become more elaborate, with motifs added, that of the individual warrior gradually replaces the generic identity of the warrior group or retinue, but he is still invisible, without human form. It is as if a ghost in human shape lies behind the composition, only to be identified through the position of the motifs on the rock surface. In this metonymic code the body is not shown, material things represent the transparent warrior and the shield symbolises the protection that the warrior extended to his whole group.

Its evolution into a body-centred code took place in the period after 1100 BC, in the area of the middle Tagus and Guadiana valleys in Zones II and III. The metamorphosis from naked warrior to horned figure is clearer in the Guadiana valley (Zone III) and especially the Guadalquivir valley (Zone IV) and may date after 1000 BC. However, the depictions of figures with outstretched arms and animated silhouette are found on the geographical periphery of the main distribution: C87 Figueira, C89 Ervidel II, C65 Olivenza and C27 Talavera. There are none from the areas of dense stelae concentration in the middle Guadiana and Guadalquivir valleys, where they might be expected.

The final monuments show narratives (C46 Zarza Capilla III, C80 Ategua and perhaps C68 Aldea del Rey III), where for the first time a diachronic sequence is used (Leach 1976).

WARRIOR PANOPLY WITH SPEAR, SWORD AND SHIELD

The basic composition of three arms survives on 10 complete stelae, all very similar to one another: C4 Baraçal, C5 Fóios, C9 Torrejón el Rubio IV (first stage), C15 Trujillo, C16 Ibahernando, C19 Robledillo de Trujillo, C63 Almendralejo, C64 Badajoz, C82 Córdoba I and C83 II (figure 6.2): Toya (C69) is probably of this type too, but the drawing is incomplete. A circular V-notched shield occupies the centre of each one, usually with a spear and sword placed horizontally above and below it, in a symmetrical arrangement. The swords vary in shape and technique of engraving, but this group includes the oldest designs with Rosnoën swords and the leaf-shaped blades that disappeared by 1050/1000 BC. The spears are not informative and are simply depicted. Since some compositions occupy the entire surface of the stone, leaving no room for part of it to be buried in the ground to set the slab upright, it is possible that some stelae were used as grave markers and laid flat on the ground. However, none have ever been found like this, so the idea is just a guess. More obviously, it is clear that some very early stelae like the ones from Baraçal and Ibahernando were intended as vertical monuments since they have the lower half of the stone free of motifs and perfectly adapted as a footing and the Toya stela actually closed the entrance to an underground tomb. Once the shield is established as the dominant motif, in size and centrality, it retains its position for several hundred years as the defining object of a warrior stela.

The bronze sword is the first metal object in prehistoric Europe to be designed specifically for killing a human being (Osgood & Monks 2000). As such, its symbolism is terrific and its association with the adult male reinforces the centrality of weaponry to the lifestyle of the individual. This imagery is linked later on to the (naked) human body, in the figurative compositions, but is not more powerful for that.

Clearly, in these readings of the symbols, the basic compositions have a potentially greater depth of meaning than is at first apparent. Not just the choice of symbols, but the decision to display them openly, indicates an ideological commitment to publishing the core of the code, stating that it is absolutely essential to see it to understand the message.

WARRIOR PANOPLY WITH ONE ADDED MOTIF

There are two motifs added as individual items to the basic composition, without any other accompaniment. These are the mirror (C1 San Martín de Trevejo and C14 Alburquerque) and the lyre (C93 Luna figure 6.3). In compositional terms, they precede the adoption of the full panoply,

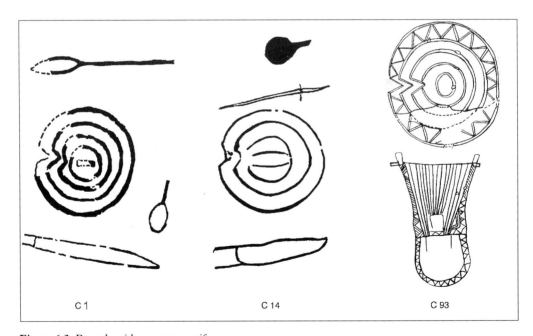

C 1   C 14   C 93

Figure 6.3 *Panoply with one extra motif*

which includes the helmet, bow and arrow, chariot with horses, brooch and comb. They are added as objects without any reference to each other at this stage and represent different functions: the mirror may be a talisman or relate to the special physical appearance of a warrior; the lyre may be a symbol of his knowledge of song and myth. Both can be taken to represent esoteric knowledge that was only to be obtained from other worlds and which was exceptional and extraordinary, beyond that familiarly experienced. This special knowledge resided in the experience of the human image and a specific aesthetic reflected in the mirror, or in the oral knowledge the lyre would represent. Clearly, these are culturally meaningful categories to the viewer; and neither is connected to weaponry. As far as one can tell, these motifs are essentially Mediterranean, for real mirrors and lyres are found in the Aegean and central Mediterranean. It must be historically important that the first additions to the basic composition come from this direction, rather than the Atlantic and it is possible that, since they have come from a great distance, their symbolic potency was enhanced. They are tangible contacts with distant and exotic worlds and exploring those far-off places was expected from the leaders and warrior heroes (Helms 1988).

WARRIOR PANOPLY WITH TWO OR MORE MOTIFS ADDED

The first stelae to have two added elements (figure 6.4) are C17 Santa Ana with brooch and helmet and C13 Brozas with brooch and mirror. At a later moment, the comb was added in a different engraving technique. The two motifs of the horse-drawn chariot and the bow and arrow are added after the others, as seen on the stelae C6 Torrejón el Rubio I and C50 Quintana de la

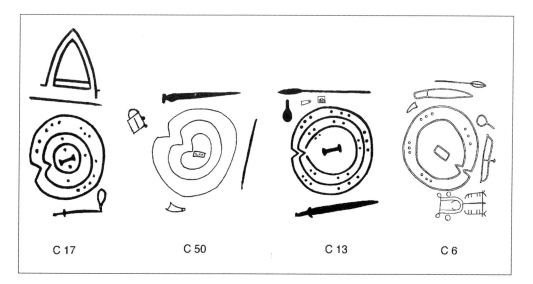

C 17   C 50   C 13   C 6

Figure 6.4 Panoply with two or more motifs added

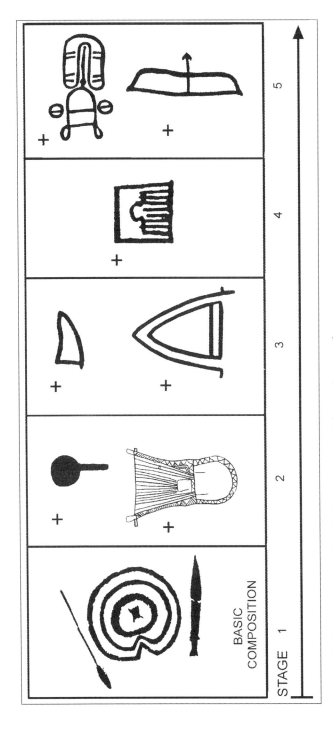

Figure 6.5 Diagram showing the evolutionary sequence of the warrior panoply

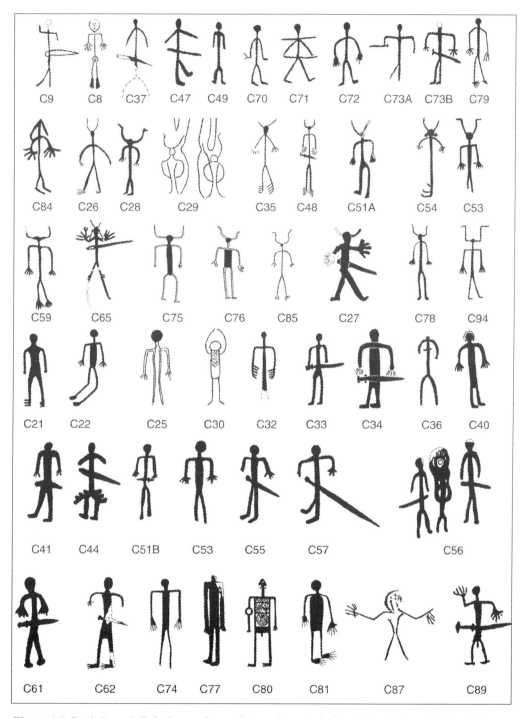

Figure 6.6 Depictions of all the human figures that are the central element in a stela composition. They are scaled to the same size for comparison

Serena. The seriation gives the following sequence of objects being added to build up the final panoply:

1	Mirror and lyre	3	Comb
2	Brooch and helmet	4	Chariot and bow & arrow.

From this sequence on figure 6.5, one can infer that the warrior panoply was conceived one item at a time and was not introduced as a package of elements. This has important explanatory potential. It indicates that the ideology evolved in piecemeal fashion, but that once formed it was quickly contextualised and expressed systematically with these elements. These Bronze Age objects must have been known originally as separate items, with particular frames of reference for each one, so the mirror was probably introduced for its own qualities (perhaps magical); and the same can be said for the musical instrument. The brooch and helmet are items associated together in the Huelva hoard and both have functional and practical uses, the brooch to fasten a cape of fine cloth and the helmet as a display item. These two elements are probably of Atlantic origin, although both have a widespread distribution across the central Mediterranean and the brooches reach Cyprus and the Levant (Megiddo). That leaves the comb, which is an item of either adornment, or more likely a toilet article, closely associated with the aesthetic appearance of the warrior. Combs are known from across Spain and Portugal, as well as the eastern Mediterranean, from the third millennium BC. Last in this sequence are the arrival of martial and hunting symbols in the form of the chariot and the bow and arrow. The chariot is an artefact strongly associated with the elite warriors in the Levant (Ugarit), Egypt and the Aegean from at least 1700 BC and should be an idea borrowed from those regions.

From the modern point of view, the order in which the objects are added seems odd, inasmuch as one would expect the brooch and helmet to be added before the mirror and lyre; this sequence may be a consequence of the small size of the sample and could change with future discoveries. Nevertheless, it is an impressive list of luxury items to assemble and its obvious eclecticism from the very wide range of manufactured goods on display in eastern societies, such as Sicily or Sardinia to name the two closest ones in the central Mediterranean, suggests purposeful choices were made. All of these objects amplify the ideological claims to special status and importance. This ought to mark a significant ideological change in the elite's self-perception.

6.2.2 Figurative compositions with warriors

Figurative compositions (figures 6.6–6.8) are those with a human figure as the centrepiece, to whom are related all the other elements and motifs. In them, the figure eventually displaces the shield as the central motif and in the ideologically mature stela, the careful arrangement of the weapons and ornaments around the naked human body shows the hierarchy of values. The human image is the central symbol; it embodies in a durable form the fundamental (but wholly arbitrary) cultural principles of the group who erected the monument. These principles are expressed precisely through the artistic convention which shows the human body as a separate image from almost every other artefact or animal in the composition, with the exception of the sword. Over 95 per cent of the motifs have no physical contact with the human form, even though in real life they must have been handled and touched frequently and been in intimate contact with living flesh. (There is one clear excep-

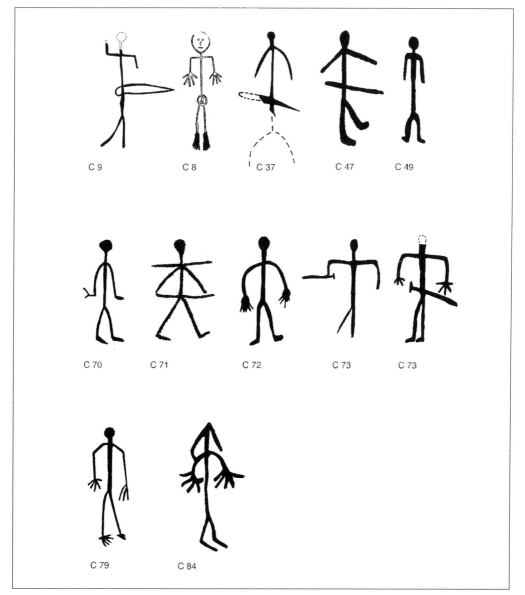

Figure 6.7 *Depictions of all the human figures that are the central element in a stela composition, drawn as stick figures. They are scaled to the same size for comparison*

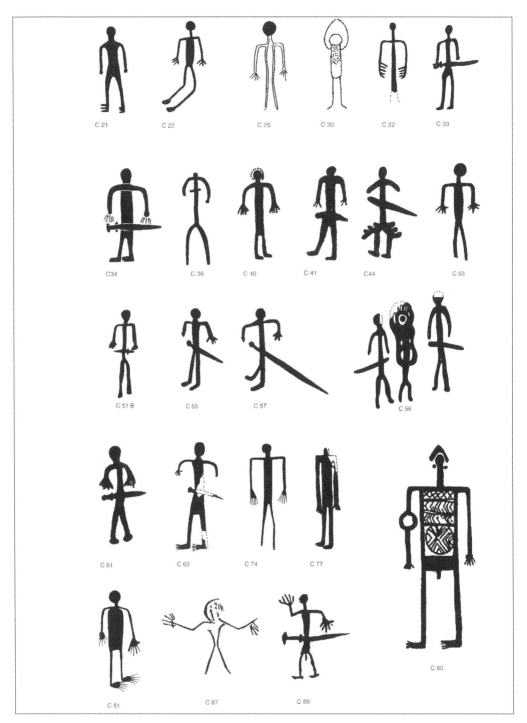

Figure 6.8 *Depictions of all the human figures that are the central element in a stela composition, drawn to give volume to the human body. They are scaled to the same size for comparison, except C80, which is drawn larger to show the interior detail*

tion to this scheme, which is the Ategua stela, C80. Here the main figure is armoured and wears an arm ring.) So whom do these figures represent? The most logical answer is that they are warriors and some of them were perhaps chiefs. Detaching the body from any other motif shows it is exceptional and recognises its unique character and self-consciousness. The body is being treated as an object as well as an individual, although the figures are too schematic to convey many individual qualities. Most face the viewer and are not shown in profile. The human figure is conceived to be looking at the viewer, engaging him (or her) directly, choos-

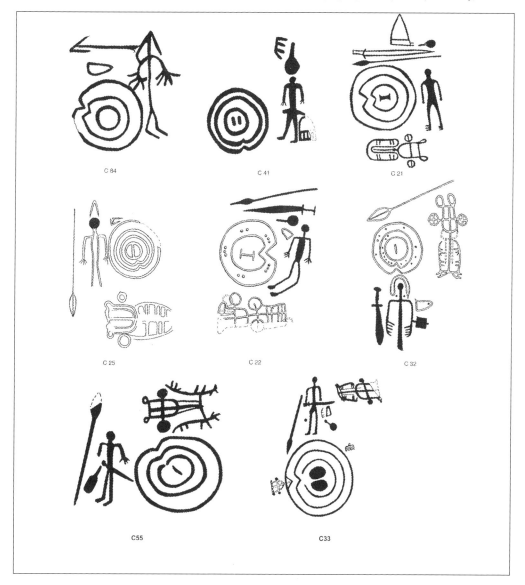

Figure 6.9 *Early figurative compositions with the human figure introduced as a secondary motif to the shield. Stage I*

ing a posture that we habitually use to express a challenge, or in speaking face to face. (In the iconography of the Iberian and Celtic world after 400 BC for example, the direct gaze characterised a divinity, expressing in this way the personal involvement of the deity with the onlooker.) The engraver does not need to depict facial features to show that the figure observes the viewer, almost as if gazing at them. Even small figures exude a feeling of menace (like the Écija ones C74, C77); figures on C89 Ervidel II and C65 Olivenza are active, one striding to the left, the other with legs apart and arms outstretched, fingers individually detailed to show the grasping power of the hands. The detail of the fingers and open hands

Figure 6.10 *Early figurative compositions with the human figure and shield equally prominent. Stage I*

is important, since it is clearly intended to show the physical ability of the figure to grasp the weapons around him, repeated on 20 or more figures.

The sequence of figurative compositions can be arranged into four stages, with the first one showing the warrior figure in a secondary place, usually close to the main motif, which is still the shield (figures 6.9 and 6.10). These marginal figures are drawn quite large, even at this initial stage of their introduction to the arrangement. In stage II the human figure displaces the shield and becomes the central motif. One group has simple figures (figure 6.11) and another group has similar compositions, but with the figure of a horned man (figure 6.12). Eventually, in stage III there are compositions with no shield at all, with the focus entirely on the naked warrior (figure 6.13). Probably the group of *Diademadas* should belong to Stage III as well, since the compositions lack shields and weapons, which are the core of the warrior panoply (figure 6.14). It is not entirely certain that the *Diademada* stelae really belong to the warrior series at all, despite being their contemporaries. Finally, there are four groups that seem contemporary in Stage IV, with compositions displaying more than one figure. Although the shield survives in some pictures (figure 6.15), the dynamism of the composition shifts from the warrior panoply to the interplay between two or more human figures. These are compositions with two figures arranged in a hierarchy, or perhaps a war scene (figure 6.15). There are paired scenes where one figure is horned and they have no shields (figure 6.16); the individuals with horns as their attributes could be 'heroes' in a broad sense. There is a unique scene with a ceremonial triad from El Viso III (figure 6.17) and last of all narratives scenes (figure 6.18). The shield retains its protagonism in Stages I and II, in equilibrium with the figure, which reinforces the importance of the shield as the central element in the whole series. In Stage III the shield largely disappears and by Stage IV human figures dominate completely.

This hypothetical sequence deliberately offers an historical series for testing and in some respects it reproduces the scheme suggested for the evolution of the warrior panoply. Compositions evolve and show an intellectual growth, as motifs are added, or the importance of the human figure is altered and then increased. It is a process that is driven by the realisation that, once created, the composition could be varied expressively.

How could one know this sequence is valid and not invented by tidy-minded anthropologists? The best way to answer this question is to see what would be the case if all the monuments with human figures were contemporary. The Bronze Age world is one with strong status differences between neighbours separated by only a day's walk from one another. Some will express their power and warrior-hood in the old way; others decide to use the images of the human body to promote themselves in this place, right now. They have risen above the rest of the brotherhood and command a force of men, not just their own strength. The code is aggressively male, used by a society with a warrior ethos. It is likely that all the major categories of artefacts were known and available in all the regions where stelae were erected (Chapter 7 and also Ruiz-Gálvez Priego 1998). Given these conditions, the growth of a warrior code would make it impossible for competitors to survive very long using only basic compositions. Once the figures

Figure 6.11 *Figurative compositions with the human figure as the central motif, but still with the shield. Stage II*

appear and the human body becomes the chief medium of signification among the motifs, social meaning is grafted on to it that cannot be removed easily. The physical body of the warrior is now presented in frontal view, to materialise in the same way as the swords, shields and mirrors, with the intention of creating a person-hood whom the viewer will recognise. In a real sense, using the human body as an image asserts that it is the memory of the dead man that sustains his physicality, rather than a burial where his body and bones lie. Everyone not only had to compete, but succeed in order to survive as a recognised warrior; the code served to enforce the ideological drive towards chiefly power. This means that only the latest stelae would be ideologically potent and active and that earlier ones would be ignored or slighted; this may be the reason so few remain in their 'original' contexts, or still standing upright. This would be logical,

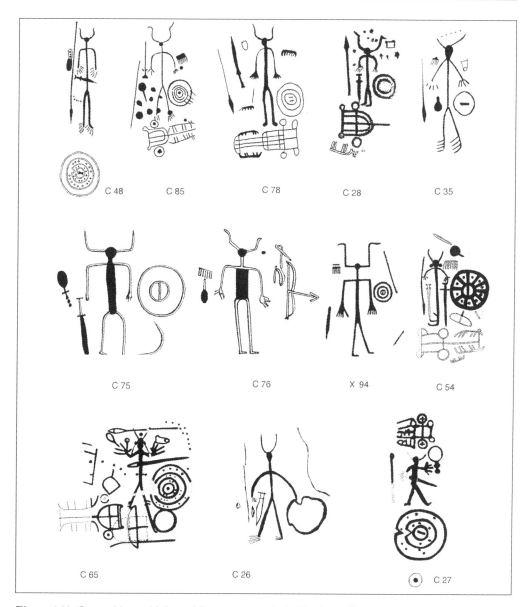

Figure 6.12 Compositions with horned figures, most with shields. Stage II

if stelae are multi-vocal monuments, one of whose tasks is to represent the dead body of a warrior whose corpse has disappeared through exposure. It is also in accord with the coded ideals of a warrior life-style, expressed in a bodily aesthetic (Treherne 1995).

Using all the complete stelae, the scaled compositions are arranged in sequence and show how the theoretical development of 'ideal compositions' can be worked out in reality. Note that three of the four zones participated; after the precocious development of basic stelae in Zone I

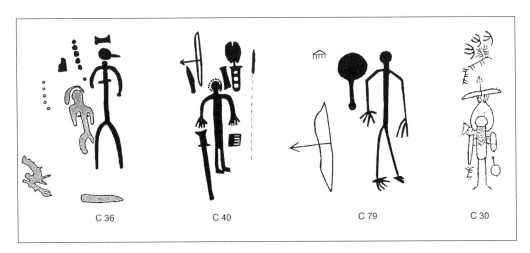

Figure 6.13 *Compositions with the human figure as the central motif, without any shield. Stage III*

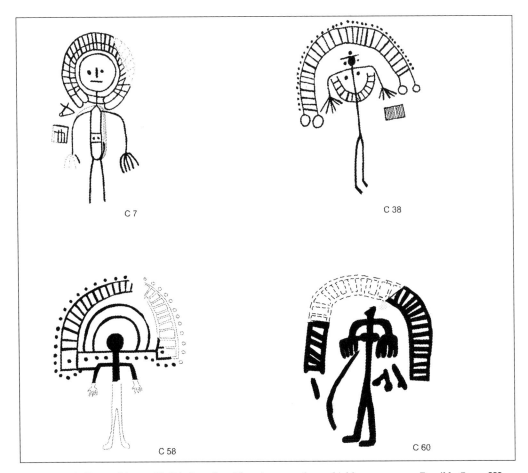

Figure 6.14 *Compositions with Diademadas. Note that none have shields or weapons. Possibly Stage III*

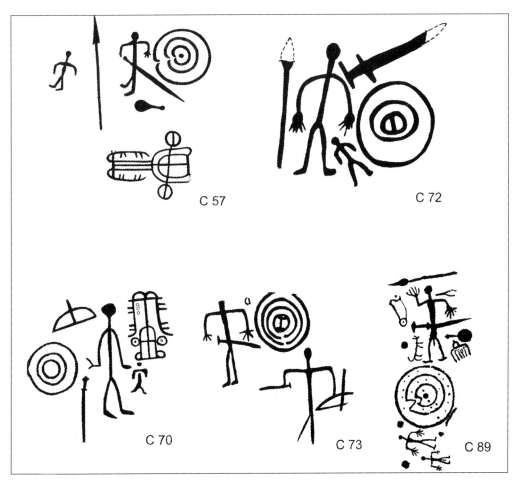

Figure 6.15 *Compositions with paired figures showing a hierarchy, or perhaps a war scene. Note they all have the shield present. Stage IV*

(Sierra de Gata), later changes covered Zones II–IV equally, with the arguable exception of some late stelae being erected in Zone IV, the Guadalquivir valley. This is important since it shows that the whole of the south-west was socially interconnected.

Stage I Human figures introduced as marginal motifs
Zarza de Montánchez, Solana de Cabañas, Las Herencias I, Cabeza del Buey I and II, Capilla IV, El Viso II, Almargen (figure 6.9).

Stage I Human figures sharing equal prominence with the shield
Cabeza del Buey III, Chillón, Herrera del Duque, Setefilla, Pedro Abad (figure 6.10).

Stage II Human figures as central motifs
Torrejón el Rubio III, Zarza Capilla I, Cancho Roano, Écija I and IV (figure 6.11).

Stage III Horned figures as central motifs, usually with the shield
Las Herencias II, Talavera, Aldeanueva, São Martinho I, Esparragosa de Lares I, Magacela, El Viso I, Olivenza, Écija II, III and V, Fuente de Cantos, El Coronil (figure 6.12).

Stage III Human figures as central motifs without the shield
São Martinho II, Esparragosa de Lares II, Capilla III, Montemolín (figure 6.13).

Stage III *Diademadas*, headdresses and hair coiffures
Torrejón el Rubio II, Capilla I, El Viso V, Belalcázar and perhaps X95 Lantejuela (not shown) (figure 6.14).

Stage IV Paired figures in a hierarchy
El Viso IV, Carmona, Burguillos, Los Palacios, Ervidel II (figure 6.15).

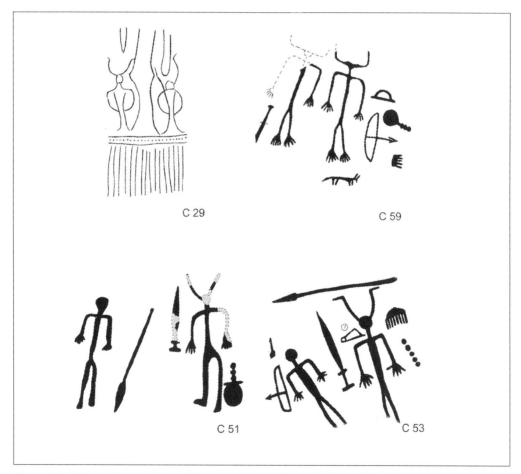

Figure 6.16 *Compositions with paired figures, one or more horned, without shields. Stage IV*

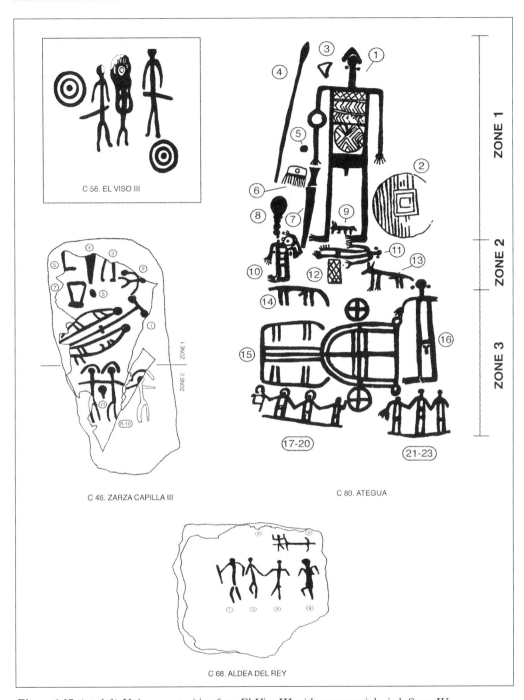

Figure 6.17 *(top left) Unique composition from El Viso III with a ceremonial triad. Stage IV*

Figure 6.18 *Three figurative compositions, which carry a narrative in two or three scenes. They may show events or myths in the life of a 'hero'. Stage IV*

Stage IV Paired figures, one horned, without shields
São Martinho I, Valdetorres I, Alamillo, El Viso VI (figure 6.16).

Stage IV Ceremonial triad
El Viso III (figure 6.17).

Stage IV Narrative scenes
Zarza Capilla III, Ategua and possibly Aldea del Rey III (figure 6.18).

6.3   The coded meanings behind the symbols

This section considers the questions as to why certain objects were chosen and what their particular meaning for the viewer was intended to be. To do this, one needs to pay attention not only to the way the motif was placed in the composition, but also the wider frame of reference that was available in contemporary Bronze Age Europe. The choice of symbols followed strict conventions, fixed to particular values held in common by most of the Mediterranean societies. The symbols of social power, royal attributes, divine qualities and dress codes developed in this way, making direct reference to these values and linking them firmly to the wider world. There is no mysterious, unique code on the stelae to be deciphered here, like a lost language. Rather, it is one version of many codes that were created at this time in Europe, as a means of expressing the status and authority of men engaged in fierce social competition who were prepared to use force when required.

One place to start is the point where there is an abrupt symbolic shift and work backwards from it. The difference between the subject matter on the stelae and the grave goods in the succeeding Early Iron Age (after 750 BC), suggests that the older stelae functioned like surrogate graves, standing in for the bodies that had disappeared through exposure to the elements and in this way returned to the natural world. Once the body has been wholly consumed, the memory and deeds of the individual are preserved through the permanent record of the stelae and perhaps through songs, music, oral genealogies and objects kept as heirlooms. In this setting, objects could become the repositories of memories and events, outliving their owners but immortalising their deeds.

In the Tartessian period after 750 BC, entirely new objects appear in graves and furthermore, the human body was retained, usually as cremated bones. Shields and mirrors are rarely found as grave offerings, nor are musical instruments; and chariots are scarce, too (Torres Ortiz 1999). This symbolic shift in the ideological projection of the elite is deliberate, since these classes of status objects did not disappear from the real world after 750 BC. On the other hand, personal ornaments and especially dress fittings like brooches, buckles, appliqués and studs, small knives and toilet boxes, become important objects among grave goods, marking a real change in ritual emphasis from the older customs.

6.3.1 The shield device

The shield device is the first symbol of the warrior in his *persona* of protector of his dependants and his land. It is the most forceful element in the oldest compositions and must mark the beginning of the code that spread quickly from the Sierra de Gata in Extremadura to most of south-west Iberia. It is also the major unifying symbol in the entire series, yielding its protagonism only in Stage IV. Why is the shield so important for so long in Spain and Portugal? The shield does not threaten other warriors, but it signals the warrior's function as that of a protector and can be considered a metaphor of the warrior protecting his dependants and the land where they live; and by dominating the composition on so many stelae, it also dominates their meaning. In this respect it is curious to observe that many engraved shields show the handle clearly and this can only mean that the shield is depicted as if the viewer were looking at it from the inside. However, it is likely that the shield as a motif or object had more than one meaning and that it would not necessarily carry the same ideological significance everywhere in Europe.

Once rapiers developed as offensive weapons in the sixteenth century BC and the slashing swords in the fourteenth century, some defence from them in combat became essential and it is highly probable that the idea of making simple round or oval shields occurred to many fighters. The ones in the Aegean, for example, seem to belong to a separate series to those that developed elsewhere in Europe. For that reason, it is probable that shields have multiple origins and that the first ones would be of leather and wood, which have only survived in special circumstances. Afterwards, shields of thin bronze appear in central Europe in the thirteenth century BC and a little later in Britain and north-west Europe. These were delicate, unable to withstand a single blow from a weapon and all were destined for ritual consumption in hoards and bogs. None comes from a grave, nor do any seem to have a link with the world of the dead, or even of individual warriors, as do the shields on the Portuguese and Spanish stelae. Certainly, there are important differences in function and context between the Iberian organic shields that were part of a visible panoply and the metal symbol shields of Britain and north-west Europe, invisible forever below the waters of mere and stream, where only a few people would know of their exact location. There are profound differences between the role of the shield depicted on the stelae, as a protective symbol of the warrior in his social *persona*, copied from a functional object, and the delicate metal ones consumed ritually in hoards placed in bogs and rivers. These practices started early and continued for many centuries in the Atlantic world. It is also remarkable that no metal shields are known in France, yet bronze helmets are well represented in French hoards; it appears that different pieces of armour were selected for ritual display and consecration, according to local rules.

Shield symbolism, seen in the miniature gold shields from the Portuguese hoards from Outeiro da Cabeça (Torres Vedras) and Fortios (Portalegre) (see figure 7.8 p 133), survives into the eighth century. These are sets of over 30 buttons to be sewn as ornaments on to shirts or capes and each hoard may represent one set for a garment.

In Archaic Greece, five miniature shields of clay of Herzsprung type were found at the shrine of Hera on the island of Samos and fragments of one in bronze sheet. There are a few larger metal ones in the sanctuaries of Delphi (one), perhaps the Cave of Idaean Zeus on Crete (one) and at Idalion and Palaeopaphos on Cyprus. These are probably symbols of highly prized western objects that were deposited in these international island-sanctuaries. By the time they were deposited, Greeks fought in hoplite armies with much larger round shields, not as individual warriors.

In central Europe, the round shield becomes subsumed into a different symbol, the sun. The shield is round, with concentric rings and a big central boss and lacks the U or V notch that defines the Herzsprung type. This symbol is used repeatedly in bands of ornamentation on the extraordinary conical gold hats from France (Avanton, Vienne) and Germany (Ezelsdorf and Schifferstadt) (Menghin 1999; Springer 1999) and also on the spiked gold cap from Leiro (La Coruña). These are prime examples of ritual regalia and the largest one from Ezelsdorf-Buch is an astonishing 88 cm tall and weighs 350 g. Several friezes are composed entirely of embossed shield motifs (or suns, if one prefers that term), as well as a band of eight-spoked wheels (Schauer 1986). Precisely this combination of shield ornament and spoked wheels is found on the Substantion stela (C90), which also has two water birds. This is genuinely important, since it shows a materialised ideology of shields and wheels being expressed at the regional level through different materials and in quite distinct contexts; indeed, they are antithetical in the categories we just mentioned. But most of all, the specific symbolism was regional in its expression. The active re-contextualisation of similar objects is characteristic of the Bronze Age elites.

Shield-imagery is also closely bound up with certain cults and funerary practices in the Mycenaean and Minoan civilisations and miniature round and figure-of eight shields decorated ivory boxes and jewels (Laffineur 1999). The round shield endures until historical times in Archaic Greece, celebrated in the literary theme of the cosmic symbolism of the 'shield of Achilles' (Atchity 1977; Fittschen 1973; Taplin 1980).

6.3.2   *Arms make the man: the masculine/warrior code represented by spear and sword*

The spear and sword are inseparable elements in the basic compositions and retain their symbolic potency for centuries. The spear is shown usually in two positions; horizontally above the shield, in the position where it can be grasped quickly and thrown; or upright next to the warrior, within reach of his hand. A conceptual difference may lie behind these positions. The older idea shows the spear ready for use, above the shield, while some later compositions with warrior figures have vertical spears, some pointing down, others upwards. The first idea may conceive of the spear as a weapon only; in the second it may have become a symbol of real possession of the land where the stela stands.

The swords show similar dichotomies. Early swords in the simple compositions are usually placed horizontally below the shield and like the spear, are ready for use. Many are naked and a few may be sheathed. Later compositions with figures portray the sword more subtly, sometimes it is worn at the waist, other times within reach of the warrior, at right or left hand, point upwards or downwards, as the engraver elected to show it. Now, swords are never depicted slung on baldrics, as was the custom on the older Middle Bronze Age slabs from the Alemtejo, or on the example X96 Preixana, but are always worn at the waist, on a belt. Only once do warriors actually brandish a sword (C73 Los Palacios).

This difference between the naked and a sheathed weapon is not a chance stylistic convention, but is a conceptual difference between a weapon ready for use instantly and one out of harm's way, equally potent but with a latent threat. Furthermore, the sheathed weapon is under control on 18 of the 19 figures shown wearing a sword. There is a clear difference between the sword as a naked symbol and the sheathed weapon worn by the warrior, that corresponds broadly to a chronological evolution; the naked weapons are usually shown on the basic stelae of the early types, whereas the sheathed ones are worn by figures that occur on the figurative stelae, which are later in date. This evolution of the motif's symbolism is matched in others, such as the displacement of the shield from its central role and the emergence of the human figure as a dominating element in the composition.

Swords never become the dominant motifs in any composition, yet they are an indispensable symbol of the warrior's physical prowess, of his ability to use force. Since swords are pre-eminently weapons for fighting other humans, their message of violent retribution, possibly death, is plain. Equally, they are masculine symbols and on occasion, figures wearing outsize swords appear to have giant phalluses.

6.3.3 The face of death: mirrors as talismans

The motifs identified as mirrors are usually placed on the earlier stelae in a position that implies there is an invisible hand of a warrior holding them (C14 Alburquerque), while later ones with the human figure make this explicit (C74–C76 Écija I–III) and on C9 Torrejón el Rubio IV the warrior is actually holding the mirror in his right hand; in C51 Valdetorres I and C27 Talavera, the horned figure has a sword in the right hand and a mirror at his left.

Richard Gregory's words in *Mirrors in mind* (1996:x) carry us into a world of perception and illusions and it is this quality of ambiguous images that is essential for understanding the significance of Bronze Age mirrors, not the fact they are status objects or double as toilet items. No doubt they had these functions, too. Their importance actually lies in the illusions they create.

> Mirrors have always been seen as magical. With our present understanding they
> remain puzzling and evocative. … Mirrors seem hardly to exist, apart from what

they reflect … How much and how we learn of ourselves from our mirror image is just one of the puzzles. Very different is the puzzle of 'mirror-writing' – everything reversed right-left, yet not upside down. Puzzling in its turn is why such a simple and universally experienced phenomenon is, for almost everyone, so hard to explain. Here there is astonishing confusion in the literature of optics, perception, physics and philosophy,

Gregory continues:

… Mirrors reflect ancient questions of what exists 'objectively' and what we create 'subjectively', by perceiving and thinking. So we are led to some curious questions of physics and psychology and where they meet in perception and understanding. Mirrors present the opposite of blindness – sight without touch. As the mirror world is not checked by touch, or any of the other senses, it is less than a complete copy of the world we call reality. But it is also more, for our visual imagination is not constrained by counter evidence. So, long before recorded history, reflections provided visual evidence of ghosts and demons drowned in still water, or buried in glassy rock … Very likely it was mirror images that suggested minds and souls separate from our bodies. No doubt, mirrors inspired the possessive *Doppelgänger* of horror.

These remarks penetrate the confusing reflections that we cannot touch and which are disembodied images of ourselves. Precisely these qualities of illusion and ambiguity make the mirror a potent object for casting spells, for scrying the future and defeating the power of the evil eye by deflecting its gaze.

Understanding these qualities of the reflected image help us appreciate just how mysterious and at times truly frightening, a mirror could be. Mirrors allow one to see what it is otherwise impossible to see, one's own face and the eye that is doing the seeing. 'In seeing your face in the mirror, you know yourself as others know you: face-to-face, in an exchange of glances. Access to the self is gained through the external projection of that self, through being objectified' (Vernant 1991:142). He continues, saying that mirrors can counter the perils of the eye – 'a face-to-face ordeal with its exchange of looks and the inevitable reciprocity of seeing and being seen'. (Vernant 1991:147) In the Greek legends of Perseus and the Gorgon Medusa, the mirror can transform the living into the dead by controlling the power of radiation from Medusa's eyes. Gregory gives another reading to this when he says: 'It is a strange quirk of biology that without mirrors we cannot see our faces; for it is facial expressions that give the game away for reading minds' (Gregory 1996: ix). There are Classical Etruscan mirrors with the Perseus and Medusa stories actually depicted on them (Anlen & Padiou 1989:388–389).

These remarks indicate something of the talismanic power that a fine mirror could have, a handsome, shiny disc of shimmering metal, mounted on an elaborate handle, able to defeat the evil eye of one's enemy when held up before his gaze. However, the depths of the fearful world of the soul seen in the reflected human images, fashioned by a completely natural phenomenon such as a still pool or mirror, are unfathomable. The modern writings of Jorge Luis Borges have explored notions of personal identity and time and the contradictions that arise between the uniqueness of identity and the passing of time; for Borges, uniqueness was embedded in vitality and mirrors were hateful things to him because they multiplied reality and stole away one's uniqueness (Borges 1953). The idea is that the mirror can steal the soul through capturing it in a ghostly reflection, rob the personality of the one looking into it and weaken him to the point of death; death occurs when the soul flees the body. What would be more logical than for a warrior to protect his own soul by keeping a mirror in his possession?

The way mirrors and their images were understood changes with the centuries. In antiquity, Plato and Aristotle, like the other ancient philosophers, were certain that the visible image, whether in a mirror or not, originates from physical contact by means of rays that emanated from an object and imprinted themselves in the eye. Following this logic, it becomes understandable that the Basilisk or Gorgon could be killed by its own poisonous stare, reflected back by a mirror.

Joining the idea that images are physically real is the notion of the double, or the *Doppelgänger*, widespread in folklore and myth. Otto Rank analysed the archaic beliefs in the double, such as those seen in reflections in pools of water or as shadows, and interpreted them as the first material expressions of the human soul (Rank 1914). The double was born from the division of the self (the split between reality and its identical image) and emerges when the personal relationship is missing or deliberately falsified.

> Its mission was to protect man from death, for this exact replica of himself was gifted with a real and immortal life, which assured him of survival in the future after the disappearance of his body. But at the same time that the double serves as a guarantor of immortality, it reminds man endlessly of his fate, a spectre of death that never leaves him. Promise of death and force of life: this ambivalent cachet marks most manifestations of the double … (Melchior-Bonnet 2001:256).

These passages provide possible explanations for the mirror as a motif of choice in the Final Bronze Age, locating the images within specific world-views. The first two are perhaps closer to the cosmo-vision prevailing in the Mediterranean in the later second millennium BC, since they offer powerful readings that could be incorporated into the world of emerging chiefdoms. In particular, the idea that a mirror could serve as a protection for the soul, through guarding it as a double and keeping it safely locked inside an object, would make it especially suitable as a symbol for a stela commemorating the power and status of a departed warrior. If immortality could be assured in this way, then the warrior would have no reason to fear death and would be able to exercise power like the gods or heroes, or perhaps choose to pass it on to his heirs and legitimate descendants. It is not by chance that the very first motif to be added to the basic composition is the mirror, the symbol of immortality and life force.

Another property a mirror has is the ability to catch light and reflect it as a brilliant flash visible for several kilometres. Who as a child has not played for hours with a mirror on a bright day? It is an instrument that confers an apparently supernatural power to its owner, brings the sun and its glowing rays into his hand, to be directed at will wherever he wishes it to fall. Distance does not dim it. In its superhuman dimensions the beam of light can travel farther than any weapon, it is silent but can outreach the sound of the loudest shout and speed faster than any living thing, faster even than thought. Shining the beam on the eyes can blind in seconds; a destructive power utterly different from the beneficent light and warmth of the sun in its familiar guise. Control of a flashing beam of sunlight in the glare of day perfectly demonstrates the warrior's power to call the natural force of the sun to his aid; even the natural world obeys his will. No other artefact can control the rays of the sun. Only the warrior with the mirror has these powers.

As a symbol of occult power and demonstrably magical properties, a mirror has few equals. Like a fine sword or helmet, its creation is the work of master bronzesmiths, since casting a perfect disc, free of imperfections or pits on the surface, in bronze with a high tin content and polishing it properly to get a precise image, is beyond the talents and skills of an ordinary bronze worker. These mirrors were technically hard to imitate and this difficulty of reproduction would ensure that those who possessed them would not fear imitations by rivals or people of lesser status. That is how their rarity value was guarded.

6.3.4 *Music and oral culture*

With the clear depictions of at least five lyres, perhaps more if indistinct motifs are included, one has to ask what musical instruments are doing on warrior stelae? Of all the surprising objects to include, these must be among the least expected, because they are objects that are completely unknown in Atlantic Europe and force one to look at the eastern Mediterranean civilisations to find adequate parallels for them. There is no doubt they are of Final Bronze Age date; in the case of the Luna stela (C93), the lyre is a Bronze Age Aegean type which was current in the period 1300–1150 BC. Why should warriors who flourish weapons also wish to add a lyre to their panoply?

The answer to this question lies deep in the roots of how chiefs behaved in the Final Bronze Age and to what social values they aspired. Mary Helms' pioneering work and comparative anthropological studies show that physical distance added value to an object, or to intangible knowledge regarded as esoteric and rare, so that artefacts which were commonplace in their homelands became highly valued far away; and the same process of transformation through re-contextualisation would operate on knowledge, such as songs, incantations, charms, stories, perhaps even the type of musical scale and harmonic system (Helms 1988). So, musical instruments would be visual evidence of this process being enacted in south-west Iberia. It would not be necessary for the chiefs themselves to be musicians and singers, but only to control closely those people who were. In such cases, the value of the song lay in its complexity and exclusivity and in the knowledge (perhaps spurious, but believed nonetheless) that it was remembered exactly as it had been learned, to guarantee its authenticity. Perhaps they were sung in foreign tongues, adding to their mystery. The instruments may well have been imported too, from the eastern Mediterranean (the Aegean, Cyprus and the Levantine coast are all equally likely areas for this direct contact).

6.3.5   'The warriors' beauty': life-style ideals expressed through toilet articles and hair coiffures

The 'warriors' beauty' is an ideal at the centre of Bronze Age life-styles. It is the idea that a specific way of living, behaving and dressing defines a warrior and, by extension, sets him apart from the rest of his society and from other males who may be younger, weaker, senile or excluded from this group altogether due to a servile status. The key features of male beauty that show he participates in this life-style are conventions that define the specific personhood and mark his individuality in life, as in death. Life and death share the same style and codes of behaviour and beauty and are rooted in the body when living and its remains (or the memory of it) when it is dead. Paul Treherne (1995) brings German scholarship to the English readership and explains how deep is the commitment to this ideal, which is not a charade, nor devoid of emotional content. It is a deeply serious undertaking and a warrior expresses his commitment to it, in life by dress and behaviour and in death by making his body the centrepiece of a symbolic system in a grave, surrounded by possessions that materialise it explicitly. The stelae compositions show many elements of such a life-style and function metaphorically exactly like a burial, showing the warrior (or his main emblems) surrounded by those objects that are necessary for his grooming and personal beauty. Remember that this is an active process and it does not end with death, since the possessions and the memories kept alive through visits to the grave, sightings of the stelae pictures and handling the possessions and heirlooms that are imbued with personal qualities, all refresh the ideal of a beautiful life.

Living in a special style is associated with certain forms of personal grooming. Hair and fingernails are freighted with symbolic meaning in most societies, for they grow throughout life yet can be cut off painlessly and are truly physical parts of the body that can be detached. They are ambiguous in that they grow continuously, yet are dead but not corrupt, like flesh or bodily fluids. It is also widely accepted that hair is specially associated with the self, the individual person from whose head it grows and in some way it conserves the physical essence of that personhood (Treherne 1995:125–127, with full references). Cut hair is commonly thought to contain part of the vitality of its owner.

Nearly all the figures appear clean-shaven, with no facial hair depicted, and nude. The few warriors who do have beards are all Early Bronze Age in date like the one from Longroiva (X97) and he also wears a long tunic. His beard reaches his breast, trimmed horizontally and perhaps combed and waxed into vertical locks, like the Assyrian beards, or the one worn by another culture hero famed for his hair, Samson. One can assume that the fashion in the Final Bronze Age was for a shaven face. Hair may have been plucked, but the tweezers to do it are very rare artefacts, as are bronze razors for a close shave.

A couple of stelae may show plaited locks of hair drawn back from the face, but in general there is no sign of how hair was treated, unless the *Diademadas* are accepted as pictures of them. More informative are the combs shown in many shapes and forms and which existed in precious materials like gold and ivory. These ought to be the symbol for grooming hair into a special style. At the very least, they show the importance of hair and perhaps coiffures, to the warriors' life-style. Practical care of the hair, perhaps in daily rituals, would powerfully express an aesthetic life-style.

Beyond the toilet articles are the ornaments and dress distinctions which set off the human body and confer a specific identity to it. The frequent engravings of brooches may also be a visual shorthand reference for the viewer to imagine the warrior wearing a special garment. Some figures wore tunics, possibly a skirt in a couple of cases, but most are nude. The fashion for warriors being clean-shaven and naked is also seen in other regions of Europe, notably Scandinavia.

Finally, there are 41 or 42 mirrors, which may also have doubled as toilet articles. Obviously of eastern origin and usually connected with important individuals, they are an outstanding example of an object appropriated as a symbol by the south-west Iberian warriors and one which could almost be said to define them specially, since no other Atlantic Bronze Age men asserted their life-style quite like this. Perhaps their intention was to be different from all other warrior elites?

6.3.6   *Chariots: The essence of speed, or metaphysical transport to an afterlife?*

A chariot is the essence of speed; that is what distinguishes it from any other vehicle. Powell captures something of its elegance, saying a chariot is

> … a light vehicle mounted on a pair of spoked wheels, normally drawn by two matched horses and designed to carry no load other than its human occupants. The chariot might convey only one man: a warrior, huntsman or racing driver, but more usually it contained two; its lord, whatever his immediate purpose and a charioteer whose special skill lay in this service. (Powell 1963:153)

From the warrior's point of view, a chariot is a fine thing to own. Mounted in it, he is physically above all the infantry, functioning at a different level from ordinary soldiers and psychologically elevated. He can grandstand, can move faster than anyone else and wherever he goes his prestige is unchallenged; what a splendid symbol of supremacy a chariot is, for war, hunting or travel. No wonder they were depicted so many times.

Nor could his competitors easily acquire a chariot or make a copy; they are the pinnacles of the wheelwright's achievements, using skills that take years to learn. Even the raw materials are choice and require time to collect and season. Making a chariot to rival those of the elite, to challenge their material possession of such a treasure, was impossible unless one belonged to the same social group. Chariots were supreme as symbols of status.

Such vehicles were known as far away as the southern slopes of the Urals in Russia by 2000 BC and may have originated there. By 1700 BC they had spread across the Near East, the Aegean and Egypt and about 20 were depicted on the Bronze Age rock engravings at Frännarp (Southern Sweden) (Thrane 1990; Coles 2002) and on slabs in the Kivik tomb in Sweden (probably of Period IV, according to Verlaecket 1993). There is a line of argument, influential among Indo-European linguists but not popular among modern archaeologists who work with material culture, that the Indo-European expansion westwards was closely bound up with the chariot, to the point that many encapsulated the idea as *ubi equus, ibi patria* (Polomé 1997:261). Unfortunately for this theory, the origin and use of the chariot in the Bronze Age was quite varied from one society and civilisation to another and there is no good case to make for it being spread by a single cultural process, or mechanism, or linguistic group (Raulwing 2000). More relevant is the way in which the image of the chariot was captured as an ideological symbol in the Near East and Aegean.

In Mesopotamia, deities had chariots that they used in their journeys and battles and often the divinity is depicted standing next to a chariot, especially the Storm God Ishkur/Adad. Certain texts recount how a divinity watched over, or intervened, in mortal combats. In other texts of the seventh century BC the deity Bunene appears as the chariot-driver and son of Utu, the solar divinity who travelled across the heaven each day in his chariot and at night into the 'depths of the firmament' (Black & Green 1992). The Ugaritic texts from Syria frequently refer to the god Baal as the 'chariot-driver of the clouds' (*rkb<rpt*), a common epithet of the god found often in the mythologies and only matched by the even more popular name 'the victorious one' (*aliyn b<l*). The Greek religious system created a similar role for the chariot, as a mark of rank among the divinities, with the most important Gods (Zeus, Hera, Poseidon) in chariots while the others went on foot, exactly as the Black-Figure vase painter Sophilos showed them in his picture of the betrothal of Thetis and Peleus (Laurens & Lissarrague 1992).

Bronze Age Greeks painted chariots being used in other ways. A use in religious or funerary ceremonies is documented particularly for the Dual chariot. There are also hints of a legendary or mythological context: deities, for example, riding in chariots may be seen in some representations with supernatural or unusual draught teams (Littauer & Crouwel

1979:147). In Late Geometric Greece (800–700 BC) chariots were often painted on the funerary pottery; it is disputed whether these scenes provide a heroic ambience for the dead person, or if they show real chariots used in a funeral procession. Other possible uses are in races at funeral games and as an essential part of the cortège for a Greek aristocrat.

The prevailing consensus of opinion is that they were exceptional objects of status and prestige, as their association with divinities indicates, and that they were used in processions and cult practices. These two roles were common all over Europe for chariots, as well as four wheeled wagons throughout the Later Bronze Age from 1250 BC and they show that the idea behind the chariot depictions was to make the chief's power evident. It is not clear if it was a metaphysical vehicle to transport the spirit to another place. This agrees with the conclusions of a study of Etruscan chariots, which overlap in time with the later wagon burials and must be understood as emblems of social class, not as vehicles for a 'journey to the beyond'. Höckmann (1982:151–152) doubts that such an idea ever existed in Greek or Etruscan thought.

6.3.7 Heroes

Heroes emerge as a category of personages in the later third millennium BC in the area of modern Syria. An ancient tradition is attested at the city of Ebla, where there is an heroic cult of the ancestors in a type of mausoleum from around 2400 BC. This is quite distinct from the traditions in Mesopotamia, much more theocratic in its social structures, where heroes do not appear until the Epic of Gilgamesh was written around 2000 BC. The poem of Aqhatu and Danilu, written in the second millennium BC by scribes living in a city near the Syrian coast, shows in an exemplary manner the mechanism by which a category of heroes emerges (Merlo & Xella 2001). This poem describes how a dead man is transformed into a member of a group called the *Rapiuma*, who are a body of heroes in the underworld composed of kings, warriors and other locally famous people, whose purpose is to help the living members of their society through the gifts of fertility and procreation, healing and cures and responses to questions posed by the oracles of the living. The group is venerated by the living so that their benevolence is maintained and not allowed to decay, provoking the heroes to brood and persecute the living. The *Rapiuma* travel in warriors' chariots moving quickly across the territory and they visit threshing floors and plantations of crops and trees. Although dead, they remain in their graves and associate in family groups. Their name translates as 'Saviours' or 'Curators/Protectors' (*rpu/rpum*). These dead are special beings, who have reached their status in the *Rapiuma* after a ritual of exaltation following their death. Once elevated, the heroes appear as protectors of the city and its reigning dynasty, assuring its stability and continuity, with the ability to bestow peace and health, although still conserving their warrior nature, which is repeatedly demonstrated by their journeys in their war chariots. Their very name is an attribute of splendour, power, leadership and the ability to rule.

All this is documented for the city of Ugarit on the Syrian coast in the late second millennium BC, where a distinctive form of ancestor cult flourished. Central to it was the selection of special personalities from the general historical record of that time and their elevation to the status of heroes after their death, in ceremonies of translation. Given the strong links between Cyprus and Ugarit and those between Cyprus and the Aegean and central Mediterranean from 1200 BC, it is possible that this concept of heroes became widely known. Certainly, the antiquity of the texts shows they precede the more tentative cults of the elite dead in the Mycenaean world.

Following the fundamental analysis of hero cults and their origins (Brelich 1960:381), the characteristics defining a category of heroes are as follows: (1) they form an open category distinct from that of deities, but share some special powers and prerogatives with them; (2) unlike the gods, the heroes had lived mortal lives and experienced death (with very few exceptions); (3) they form a particular category of ancestors and share the prerogatives as well as the nature of the dead (hence the importance of the grave cult to maintain these privileges); (4) they manifest an incredible variety of personalities and functions; (5) they act as patrons and protectors (especially of their city), guarantee a wide range of enterprises and are equally capable of unleashing disasters. Brelich goes on to explain how these ideas were understood by the Greeks centuries later and reappear in the Archaic Period. A growing consensus in Greek archaeology converges in important particulars (Morris 1992; Whitley 2001). It is now widely admitted that the Mycenaeans practised a cult dedicated to a special category of dead personages and that it seems to relate to an elite social category. It is in embryonic form separate from the normal anonymous grave cults and still without any clear evidence of a hero cult. There are few physical structures related to it and the offerings are modest. Several centuries later, a true and intense hero cult emerges in the Archaic Period of the early eighth century, with its roots lying in the Dark Age and probably reaching back to the Mycenaean world (Antonaccio 1995; Whitley 1997). Even discounting Nilsson's optimistic arguments for continuity of cult practice from Mycenaean kingdoms through to the Dark Ages, it is equally true that there are no obvious ruptures. There is also general agreement that that the hero cult is not simply the veneration of ancestors. Its emergence is closely bound up with the rise of the *polis* and the Greek city-state; they are two parts of the same historical process. Erwin Rohde was not far off the mark when he proposed that, at least originally, the heroes were ancestors rooted to their territory. In this respect, the function of the hero and indeed the structure of a *heroön*, went far beyond that of a grave or funerary memorial (Cirio 2001).

The persistence of the Bronze Age stelae in Iberia could be understood within this framework of ancestor cults developing into heroic ones, if one thinks of a single, original funerary purpose evolving into a multiple one over time, giving rise to the pluri-vocality discussed in Chapter 4. From this perspective, they would be monuments to chiefs that intentionally accentuate their warrior-hood, serving the double function of marking the territory they would defend and stating their legitimacy to do so by asserting their ancestral privilege as a member of the warrior group. This is how the Greek city-states conceived of their own heroes, and the double character of protector and ancestor that characterises 'national' heroes in the Levant or Greece is paralleled in a similar duality in the divine sphere, as the examples of Melkart and Mars show. For larger social groups, such as the tribe or national community (*ethnos*), there is an argument that what really mattered was the control of time, rather than occupying territory (Morgan 1991). According to this theory, the legitimate owners of a territory came by that right through their descent from a particular person or group, and it is this use of a particular local history to claim rights through association with heroes that appears in the hero cults of Menelaus or Helen in Sparta, for example. Applying this principle to the stelae could explain why so few are actually linked to graves or used as the focus for burials later on.

Throughout the Indo-European speaking cultures, the notion of the epic hero reverberates and although Georges Dumézil's compendious studies are remembered today in rather the same light as Sir James Frazer's work on religion, they capture an intelligible thought-world that arises from particular cultural structures (Scott Littleton 1982). The idea of the hero has been degraded progressively from that of a demi-god, to a man distinguished by extraordinary acts in war and at last to a man who has marks of great pride or nobility. The key in many comparative studies of the epic hero in history and poetry lies in recognising the peculiar aggression that he shows; war and fighting are absolutely central to his life. These deep springs of violence and danger tap into psychological patterns and probably social pressures, producing what Max Weber would call a charismatic leader. The notion of heroism has many distinct strands in Greek thought, held together through the powerful images of death and fear of oblivion, but these are shared in other epic traditions too. Quite specific traits define the hero: he is a unique and isolated figure, whose arm is strong and deadly; he is devoted to combat, which he actively seeks out; he is detached from ordinary social space and so is shown to be tremendously swift, able to cross time or distance between worlds; and he is a very dangerous person in society and is therefore much better detached from it and sent away on a quest where he cannot harm ordinary mortals (Miller 2000:163–164). Apart from these qualities, a hero bears weapons that become his symbols, so the sword, shield and body armour define him as a glittering persona. True heroes often have two swords (rarely shown on stelae, but depicted clearly on C54 El Viso I), emblems of their extraordinary force and integrity.

Heroic stories from Celtic Ireland express themes that emphasise the protective role of the warrior, even after his death. There are legends which recount how the pagan Celtic heroes gave orders that after their death they should be buried standing upright, fully armed, on a prominent hill where they could face their enemy, awaiting the moment of resurrection when they would fight again and by this means continue to protect their people (Velasco López 1999). The story of king Loegaire, son of Niall and lord of Tara, of the Uí

Neill clan, sworn enemy of the men of Leinster, embodies all these elements; the literary sources stretch back into the fifth century AD, to the Life of Saint Patrick (*Bethu Phátraic*) and the *Lebor na hUidre* (Stokes 1987). The persistence of this theme is of great significance, as it dramatically expresses the double role of the hero as protector and ancestor.

Now, on the stelae there are traits that could be interpreted in a similar way, that were intended to refer to a mythological world and provide a visual reference for the hero's precocity and superhuman strength. Looking carefully at the horned figures (figure 6.12), it seems some are not wearing helmets with horns, but are actually human figures with horns emerging from their heads. One hypothesis is that they represent heroes, human beings with super-human attributes, in this case the horns of a great ox or bull, to characterise their status and separate them from all the other human figures depicted elsewhere. Choosing horns to identify heroes has an obvious logic to it. The choice of cattle horns links several areas of activity and cultural choice into one convenient symbol; there is the economic value of the animal; its great size and strength; its link with the domestic herds as well as the world of wild animals; and perhaps a sexual symbol of male potency. All this (and more) could be read at a glance from the horns. A related iconography is found on contemporary Sardinian bronze figurines of horned warriors and so-called 'warrior demons' represented as human figures with four eyes, four arms and multiple shields and weapons.

Of all the examples given in this short discussion, it appears that the most persuasive structural correspondence to the figures and objects depicted on the later stelae lies in the Syrian poem of Aqhatu and Danilu. It encapsulates the process by which heroes emerge and, most importantly, it explains why objects such as the chariot, shields and swords were selected and why the personality of the warrior as protagonist should figure so prominently. These are precisely the elements depicted on the stelae and it should not be forgotten that their compositions were assembled piecemeal over many years. The historical sequence of the compositions would suggest that the idea of the warrior with 'divine' claims, in his dual roles as protector and ancestor, was known around 1000 BC in southwest Iberia.

6.3.8 Diademadas

The four stelae with figures wearing headdresses (figure 6.14) are puzzling. One (C7 Torrejón el Rubio II) apparently wears a large headdress, since it is tied beneath his chin; the other three could perfectly well be figures beneath a structure, perhaps a bower of vegetation, or a cave, for instance. The scale of their 'headdresses' completely dwarfs the human figure beneath it and cannot be matched to any known artefact. These stelae are also distinguished in that they have neither shield nor weapons and they can only be linked to the full warrior series by the brooch and comb on the stela from Torrejón el Rubio

II. It is possible they are unconnected with the rest of the group, since their iconography is so distinct.

6.3.9 Horned figures and paired scenes

In several monuments, horned figures appear. They bear a trait (animal horns) that is quite familiar and found in very varied cultural settings, one charged with metaphor and symbolism; or to paraphrase Lévy-Strauss, animals are good to think with symbolically. As is well known, the duality and contrast between the animal mind and human mind are essential elements that characterise the discourse of occidental identity which took place in the Greek world (Sorabji 1993). The use of animal horns, especially those from cattle, is culturally significant (Rice 1998).

The crown with horns appears in Mesopotamia as the distinctive sign of a divinity and as an isolated emblem it represents the divinity, often placed on an altar, from the Kassite epoch to the Achemaenian period. As the emblem of divine status it represents the supreme deity in the pantheon (Black & Green 1992:102–103). In a similar fashion, the representations of the 'bull-man', a hybrid figure with a human head and chest, but with horns and the lower body and feet of the bull, are known from the Early Dynastic Period in the third millennium BC, linked to the solar divinity Shamash (Utu) in the Old Babylonian and Kassite epochs and later on as a protector demon (Black & Green 1992:48). It is logical that the horns, the essential emblem of divine status, should become the characteristic sign of divine royalty; the best-known example of this iconography is the early Sumerian stela of Naram-Sin, king of Agade (2291–2255 BC), commemorating his victory over the Lullubi (Lloyd 1984: fig 96). Apart from Mesopotamia, horns are known as a symbol of a divinity from various Mediterranean and Levantine contexts, sometimes as a variety of zoomorphic *taurismo* used for storm gods (based on the symbolic correspondence between the bull's roar and the rumble of thunder), of which familiar examples are Teshub of the Hurrites and Hittites, Baal of the Caananites, Zeus of the Greeks and Dolichenus of Commagene. All are dynamic individuals in their respective pantheons.

Although they are part of an Egyptian temple, the eight relief scenes of the war with the Sea Peoples, carved on the north wall of the Ramesseum at Medinet Habu by order of Ramesses III in 1190/1176 BC, depict a great naval battle at the western mouth of the Nile and portray enemy soldiers with horned helmets. These are often identified with the Shekelesh, a people who may have come from Sardinia (Barnett 1975).

Some horned figures appear on the stelae paired with a normal warrior (figure 6.16), although one has two horned figures (C29 São Martino II). Symbolic pairing is also widespread in the Mediterranean. On Crete, horns appear as important symbols only after the start of the Palace Period (MM II), frequently placed in pairs on altars and in sanctuaries, as in the Shrine of the Double Axes in Knossos. This iconographic variant could reflect a twin divinity, an idea widely disseminated in Indo-European myth and iconography

(Puhvel 1987:284–290). In southern Scandinavia, twin horned figures appear seated and holding axes (Grevensvaenge figurines from Zealand), in what seems to be another expression of this idea (Kossack 1999:177). It is characteristic of ideas relating to twins that they are believed to rupture the natural order through their inherent ambiguity (arising from the idea that a divinity has a one-to-one relationship with a mortal, which is undermined by identical twins). Twins are also widely related in ritual and belief to other areas of power, such as fertility and abundance. At the level of a hypothesis, it may be that twinning horned figures shares these ideas, of doubling their power and abundance.

Transferring these general ideas to the stelae compositions on figures 6.15 to 6.18 suggests that few, if any, scenes can be recognised as depicting divinities. The scene that is most likely to represent a variant of the theme of the 'divine twins' is that from São Martinho (C29) with its paired horned figures. The other paired scenes appear to show male figures, with a certain hierarchy between them such as one with a diadem, enveloped in a voluminous garment (C56 El Viso III) (figure 6.17). This stela is also the best example of a public event, or ceremony, being used to create a symbolic association. On stela C72 from Burguillos, the big standing figure could be the victor in a combat over the (dead) enemy, shown as a small figure lying at an oblique angle next to his feet (figure 6.15). Eminent personalities may be represented in stelae C51 and C53 (figure 6.16); they may represent men for whom a 'heroic' status was intended. Other stelae show a dominant figure accompanied by a lesser one, perhaps an attendant or page (C57 El Viso IV, C70 Carmona, C80 Ategua and C81 Pedro Abad) and they may also be depictions of 'heroic' warriors. Different and richer in the information they contain are the narrative scenes on C46 Zarza Capilla III and C80 Ategua (figure 6.18), where complex celebrations of death include the following identifiable elements: (1) the victory over the enemy whose corpse lies on the ground; (2) the symbolic departure of the funerary chariot; (3) the funerary dance (which also appears on C68 Aldea del Rey III (Bendala Galán 1977; Castelo Ruano 1990) (figure 6.18). Bendala Galán suggested that the Ategua scene may actually follow the pattern of the Archaic Greek 'prothesis' and his view is a valid comparison.

6.3.10 The historical memory of stelae

The concept of historical memory (*kulturelle Gedächtnis*) is really very interesting in respect of the stelae (Assmann 1992; Rowlands 1993). In recent years the analytical separation introduced by Jack Goody, between literate and non-literate societies, has been replaced by a more profound understanding of the different ways that codified ritual provides a structure of memory, since it is structured memory which is used in cultural transmission. The ritual replaces the need for a written text and provides a vehicle for the ideas represented in its performance, or display of its distinctive motifs. Whitehouse (1992) proposed a distinction between 'inscribing' and 'incorporating' practices. The persuasiveness and enduring impact of incorporating practices depends on iconic symbolism and their power lies in their capacity to assault the senses. The conservative transmission of cultural form is particularly likely when people are exposed constantly to highly visible examples of material objects, invested with credible authority. This could be operating in the case of the south-west Iberian stelae, which for centuries maintained basic motifs like the shield and sword and it could well account for the careful choice of motifs described in Chapter 4 (Izquierdo & Arasa 1999).

In the far north of Portugal and the neighbouring Spanish province of Orense, there are about 30 granite statues of warriors of the Late Iron Age. They depict fully dressed and armed warriors standing rigidly to attention, gazing impassively. These are the 'Lusitanian Warriors', wearing a short tunic, arms pressed to their sides, some with a short sword or dagger. Their most characteristic element, however, besides the neck torcs and arm rings, is the small, round shield slung low over their abdomen. Although their precise date is unknown, it is likely to be from the late second century BC, when the hill forts of the region were populated at their greatest extent (Tranoy 1988) and which fits well with the classical descriptions of the arms borne by Lusitanian fighters. Diodorus (5, 34) and Strabo (3, 3, 6) describe similar armament carried by Lusitanian warriors when they fought the Romans led by D Iunius Brutus in the campaign of Gallaecia about 137 BC. The meaning of these statues is much discussed, but Tranoy thinks that they do not depict a known chief or notable warrior, but are a collective expression by the community living in the hill fort who affirm their strength through this figure of an anonymous warrior; but he admits they could also be heroic ancestors, or even deities identified with the clan chiefs.

Despite these uncertainties in interpretation, two concrete elements are of especial interest. In the first place, the shield is the central motif on all the statues, which would seem to indicate that their role was to protect the entire community, which is the same function explicitly recognised on the older warrior stelae and within their range of multi-functional attributes, that goes back to their origin in funerary monuments in the second millennium BC. For this reason, it is worth remembering that the shield appears as a main motif on the coins minted by P Carisius on the occasion of the Asturian-Cantabrian wars in 26–25 BC. Above all, the position of the statues at the entrance to the hill fort (a good example is Monte Mozinho) reinforces their protective symbolism for those living inside the defences.

In the second place, four of the statues have a Latin inscription carved on them, either on the tunic or over the shield. These are from the Castro de Rubias (Orense), S Paio de Meixedo (Viana do Castelo) (this one mentions a person called *L Sestius Corocaurus*, which is a Latinised form of an indigenous name), S Julião (Vila Verde) and Santa Comba (Refojos de Basto), the last one mentioning that the authors of the monument were some *artifices Calubrigenses et Abianis(enses?)*. These four statues show the persistence of the memory of these figures and the deliberate use of an older form of monument. They do not appear to be older statues re-used with Latin inscriptions added to them, and are therefore functionally distinct from the stelae which had funerary inscriptions added to them centuries after they were made. From the beginning of the Empire, and for a period afterwards, the *Principes* (probably the local aristocrats) were among the most important agents in the process of Romanisation, who by this means not only showed their integration into the new power structures through the use of Latin epigraphy, but also that they continued to erect statues of heroic personages, inspired by their ancestral tradition. In doing this, they perpetuated the memory and function that the indigenous society had ascribed to these statues and through Romanising them, they made them serve as new vehicles for their own self-representation, reinforcing their aristocratic status. The paradox is that this was done through traditional symbolic codes, not Roman fashions.

7

Materialising the motifs as Bronze Age artefacts

7.1   Archaeological data for ideological motifs

In this chapter evidence linking the motifs on the stelae to the physical world of real objects is presented. At one level, their materialisation is not problematic, since most categories can be recognised unambiguously, but deeper down one recognises the complexity of the contextual information and how many of the objects come from contexts where special rules were applied to their burial. Nevertheless, there is a good correlation between the objects engraved as motifs and their actual representatives, which overcomes one of the principal problems in analyses of this type, which is correctly identifying the depictions. There is now a large measure of agreement on what objects are depicted and it seems that earlier writers were mistaken when they saw belt buckles instead of combs, and four wheeled carts where there are only two-wheeled chariots with big handles at the back of the platform. Added to this is a surprising result that comes from listing all the motifs, which is that there are large numbers of mirrors, combs and chariots, while objects like lyres and helmets are less exceptional than previously thought. Enlarging the number of warrior stelae from 24 examples known to Martín Almagro Basch in 1966, to 94 available in the catalogue in 2002, has not led to a four-fold increase in the type of objects depicted. Quite the contrary; new discoveries reinforce the range of motifs already known, while at the same time removing many ambiguous readings on famous stelae, like C22 Solana de Cabañas or C10, C12 Valencia de Alcántara I and III. So one can see the variety of real objects inspiring the Bronze Age engravers, whereas before there were too few examples to resolve problems of depiction, or to reconstruct accurately those confused readings which arose when a composition survived as a fragment. The capricious nature of archaeological discovery and the haphazard processes affecting the survival of individual stelae, seem to have evened themselves out to produce the existing sample. If the rough calculations are correct that between 1000 and 2000 warrior stelae originally existed (explained in chapter 3.4), it is likely that the great majority of them would duplicate the compositions and motifs already known and probably few new categories of object would enter the repertoire.

One effect these data have on the analyses is that, for the first time, one can appreciate realistically just how widespread some objects were, since it was previously believed that mirrors and combs were scarce depictions, probably of rare objects. Another effect is to support the chronological sequence of basic compositions proposed in chapter 6.2, building up the warrior panoply one item at a time, rather than as a package of elements. If future discoveries support this suggestion, they will strengthen the argument that the stelae chart a process of ideological expansion and reinforce the idea that they are multi-vocal monuments. The increase in sample size greatly improves motif recognition.

7.2   Shields

Shields (figures 7.1–7.4) are the commonest motif, controlling the compositions of at least half the stelae. With more than 70 shields depicted, the south-west Iberian group is the most numerous of any in Europe, followed at some distance by the group of more than 32 bronze shields from the British Isles, then the ones from the Nordic area. The design of a round shield is functionally simple and probably arose in more than one area, as the practice of fighting with rapiers and stabbing swords spread in the early second millennium. There are three classes of shields on the stelae:

Class I: Round shield with a V-notch (Herzsprung type)
- IA rectangular handle (figure 7.1)
- IB rectangular handle and decorative bosses (figure 7.2)
- IC no handle shown (figure 7.3).

Class II: Round shield with no V-notch (figure 7.4)
- IIA rectangular handle
- IIB rectangular handle and decorative bosses (one example known of this type)
- IIC no handle shown.

Class III: Round shield decorated with a full-field design (figure 7.4).

This typology gives priority to Class I with the V-notch (Herzsprung type), although to date no one has been able to explain satisfactorily why a round shield needs such a feature and what functional use (or symbolic meaning) it has. Perhaps it shows which way the shield should be held, or helped keep it symmetrical when the leather was moulded to a circular shape. It is a curious, common characteristic of shields in all materials, wood, leather and bronze and the clay votives from the Aegean. There are 46 Class I shields on the stelae.

   Shields in Classes I and II vary in their decoration, form of handle and the number of concentric rings, but stick to a canonical shape and model of what a shield should look like. Class III shields are rare and each carries unique decoration. Many subdivisions can be made, but more important than the classification minutiae is the fact that the three classes chart an historical development, with the Class I shields the oldest and clearly associated with the earliest stelae. Among these are the ones decorated with many bosses, arranged singly, in pairs or in sets of three. The Class II and III shields are later, do not have decorative bosses (except for the unique example of C82) and were in use until the early eighth century BC.

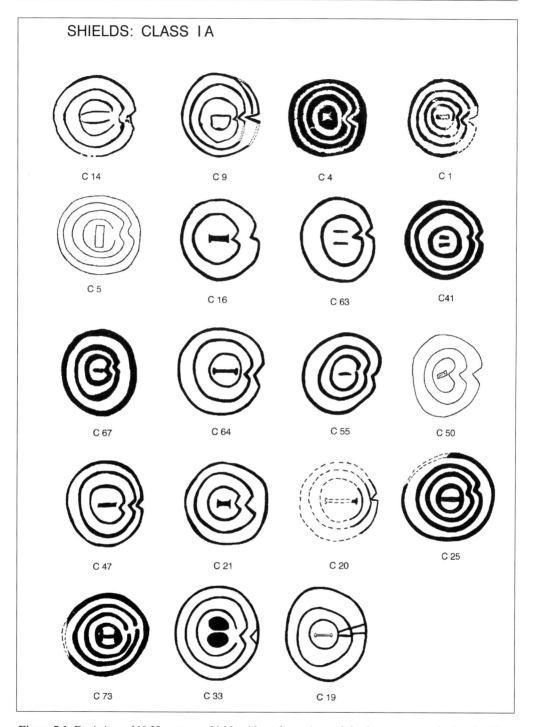

SHIELDS: CLASS I A

C 14   C 9   C 4   C 1

C 5

C 16   C 63   C41

C 67   C 64   C 55   C 50

C 47   C 21   C 20   C 25

C 73   C 33   C 19

Figure 7.1 Depictions of 19 Herzsprung shields without decoration and that have a rectangular handle (Class IA). Shield C4 is engraved in relief. They are scaled to the same size for comparison

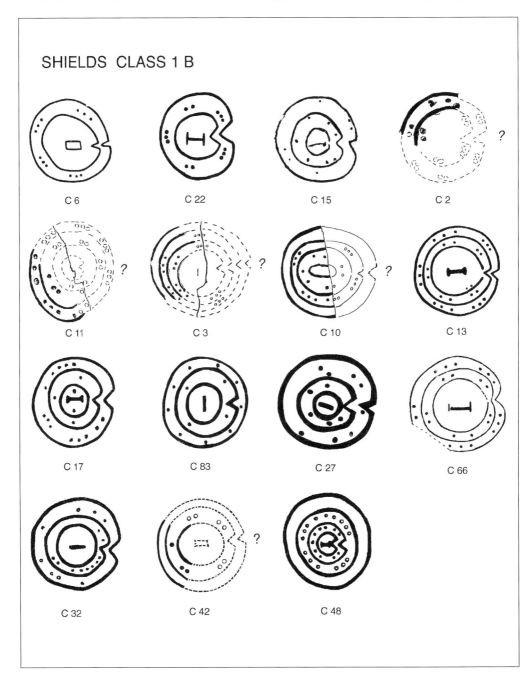

Figure 7.2 *Depictions of 15 Herzsprung shields, decorated with large rivets and having a rectangular handle (Class IB). They are scaled to the same size for comparison. Reconstructions are indicated with a broken line*

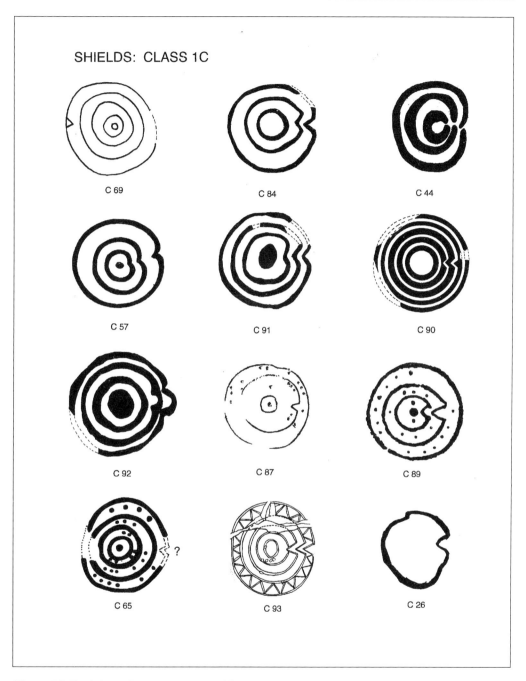

SHIELDS: CLASS 1C

C 69   C 84   C 44

C 57   C 91   C 90

C 92   C 87   C 89

C 65   C 93   C 26

Figure 7.3 *Depictions of 12 Herzsprung shields with a round central boss and no handle shown (Class IC). They are scaled to the same size for comparison*

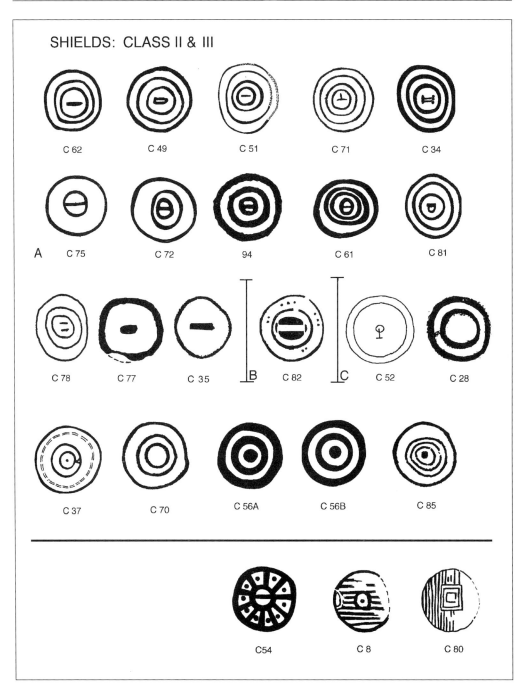

SHIELDS: CLASS II & III

C 62   C 49   C 51   C 71   C 34

A   C 75   C 72   94   C 61   C 81

C 78   C 77   C 35   B   C 82   C   C 52   C 28

C 37   C 70   C 56A   C 56B   C 85

C54   C 8   C 80

Figure 7.4 *Depictions of 21 round shields with no notches (Class II). Class IIA shields have a rectangular handle and are at the top; the one Class IIB shield is C82. The Class IIC shields have a round central boss and no handle. Class III shields with unique overall decoration occupy the bottom row. They are scaled to the same size for comparison*

7.2.1 Herzsprung shields (Class I)

There are 46 examples of the type known as the Herzsprung shield (figures 7.1–7.3; 7.5), named after the hoard of two bronze shields found in 1844 at Ostprignitz, in northern Germany, which contained the first continental examples to be studied systematically (Sprockhoff 1930:10). This round shield, with concentric ribs and a V-notch cut into one or more of them, is one of the most widespread and long-lived artefact types of the Bronze Age, with examples found in Greece, Cyprus and Iberia, as well as northern Europe (Coles 1962: fig 1; Schauer 1980; Gräslund 1967; Eogan 1990). Its extended chronology covers the period from the fourteenth–seventh centuries BC. There is a variant with one or more U shaped notches, largely confined to Scandinavia and unknown in Iberia.

Round leather Herzsprung shields with the V-notch existed by the middle of the second millennium BC, shown by the radiocarbon determinations on two wooden moulds for making them. One was found at Kilmahamogue (Co Antrim) and has a calibrated date of 1950–1540 BC (OxA–2429; 34470 ± 70 BP); and the other comes from Cloonlara (Co Mayo) and has a calibrated date range of 1380–1020 BC (OxA–3228; 3150 ± 90 BP), both at two standard deviations (Hedges et al 1991, 1993). These dates are scientifically acceptable. The leather shields from these moulds would both have V-notches, between three to five concentric circles for decoration and a big central boss; exactly like Class IA and IC shields from Baraçal(C4) or Substantion (C90).

Figure 7.5 *Photograph of the inner and outer faces of the leather shield from Clonbrin, Ireland. (Photograph courtesy of the National Museum of Ireland, Dublin)*

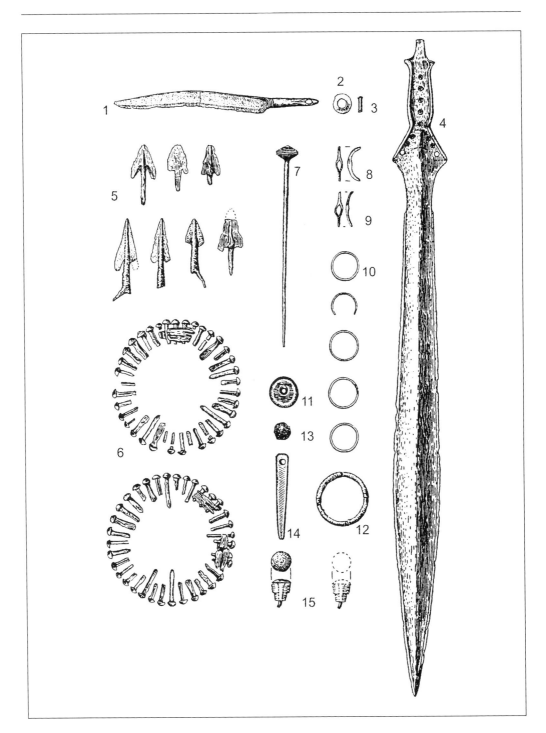

Figure 7.6 *Organic shield from Grave 1, in the cemetery of Landau-Wollmesheim (Germany). The shield is represented by the decorative bronze rivets (No 6). (After Sperber 1999, Abb 6)*

Here the remarkable likeness between the embossed leather shield found in a peat bog at Clonbrin in Ireland and the V-notched shields on the stelae like Brozas (C13) and Solana de Cabañas (C22), must be mentioned (first discussed by Hencken in 1950 and followed later by Coles 1962; Almagro 1966; Waddell 1998). The Clonbrin shield was found in 1909 at a depth of nine feet below the peat. It is made of leather, probably from an ox-shoulder, and has a thickness of about 5–6 mm, with a leather capping laced on to the surface of the boss. On the back the handle is a separate piece of leather, also laced into position (photograph of inner and outer faces in figure 7.5). The engravings must depict real leather shields very similar to it. If this is so, then it is in order to see the V-notched shields as an invention of the Atlantic armourers responding to the need to protect their warriors in rapier and sword duels, as Celestino (2001) and Cunliffe (2001) explain.

Another early organic shield came from the single warrior burial at Hagenau (Regenstauf, Kr Regensburg) and had been placed at the foot of the burial and decorated with no fewer than 43 bronze bosses; 13 small ones and 30 of large size. It could have been a Herzsprung type. It is accurately dated by the bronze sword and pin to a period just before 1300 BC (Boos 1999). Another probable shield of wood, decorated with 69 bronze rivets, is well documented from a sword-wearer's grave at Landau-Wollmesheim (Rheinpfalz), with spearheads and a leaf shaped bronze sword of Erbenheim type (Ha A2 date, or twelfth century BC) (figure 7.6). This grave contained a male and female burial, following the local elite burial customs (Sperber 1999: Abb 6). These examples show that organic shields were widely known in western Europe by the third quarter of the second millennium BC, before most warrior stelae were erected.

The bronze shields and votive miniatures of clay found in the Aegean develop from these organic, western prototypes and ought to be the latest ones in the series; quite possibly they were trophies from the 'barbaric' west, offered to classical gods on the island sanctuary of Hera at Samos (Cunliffe 2001:286). The distribution maps of Herzsprung shields (and engravings of them) have been used to argue for contacts between the eastern Mediterranean and Atlantic Europe for many years (Hencken 1950:297) and it is now probable that the type originated in Iberia or Ireland by 1250 BC and the distinctive design spread later to the Greek and Cypriot city-states and to the Nordic region (figure 7.7).

7.2.2 Round shields (Classes II & III)

There are 24 depictions of round shields on the stelae (figure 7.4). Most of these are on chronologically later monuments, especially ones with human figures, horned men and paired scenes.

The round decorated bronze shields have a different distribution (and almost certainly a different history of use), lasting throughout the period 1250–800 BC in northern, western and central Europe (Schauer 1980). These are the only kind found in the British

Isles, where there are no Herzsprung shields. The oldest one is a bronze shield fragment with repoussé decoration of concentric circles and bosses from the hoard of scrap metal from Nyírtura (Hungary) that is well dated to about 1300/1250 BC with its Peschiera-type

Figure 7.7 *Distribution map of the Herzsprung shields across Europe and the Mediterranean. Herzsprung (top) and regional (bottom). (Modified after Gräslund 1967)*

dagger and Patay (1968) discusses metal shield scraps from three other hoards of the same date in the Carpathian basin. This supports Stuart Needham's arguments for a similar date for the Nipperweise class of shields of Nordic type and really makes the important point that armour, whether functional or for display, was widespread by 1250 BC and shared similar characteristics (Needham 1979).

Miniature round shields exist in Portugal, in two hoards of gold jewellery, but have escaped much comment until now; 30 gold ones come from the Outeiro da Cabeça treasure (Torres Vedras), with concentric circles of repoussé decoration on the outer face, a twisted wire rim to maintain rigidity and neat handles at the back to attach them to a thin fabric. Another hoard from Fortios (Portalegre) had 38 similar shield buttons (Pingel 1992:298 and Taf 103/12) (figure 7.8). These hoards date around the eighth century BC because the miniatures shields are related to the Atlantic Final Bronze Age gold-work,

Figure 7.8 Gold buttons in the form of miniature shields, from the Portuguese treasures found at Fortios (top) and the Outeiro da Cabeça (bottom). The shields are the symmetrical Class II types with four concentric rings, or three rings with bosses. (Photograph courtesy of V Pingel; drawings courtesy of the Museu Municipal de Torres Vedras)

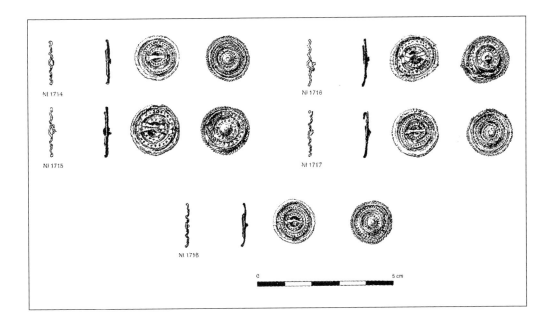

especially to examples from Ireland. George Eogan's illustrated catalogue of Irish gold-work of Atlantic traditions shows that the motif of a boss with four tight concentric circles is often used, on small gold boxes, on disc-mounts from gorgets and is also the chief element in the well-known sunflower pins (Eogan 1994). Ultimately, this motif and its symbolic charge originates in central Europe in the twelfth/eleventh century BC (Schauer 1986) and is one of the many elements incorporated into the Atlantic Bronze Age from that direction.

Many contemporary bronze figurines from Sardinia of warriors and supernatural beings (also called the 'warrior demons'), carry round shields, but in every case they are small round ones with profuse decoration like the Class III shields. There are no Herzsprung shields, or indeed any with concentric decoration, or bosses; this is remarkable, because there are well-attested finds of Atlantic swords and axes in bronze hoards and sanctuary deposits on Sardinia. They are probably made of organic materials.

The conclusion is that organic round shields are an integral Atlantic component of the warrior panoply and the Herzsprung type probably developed in Iberia and Ireland and spread eastwards from the ninth century BC.

7.3   Swords

Thirty-seven swords (figure 7.9) are depicted as separate motifs, with another 19 worn at the waist by male figures. Since swords are numerous artefacts and have been closely studied across Europe since the early nineteenth century, considerable effort has been expended in trying to match the existing classifications to the weapon shapes on the stelae, with mixed fortunes. This is an object like the brooch, which is easier to recognise than to classify and this scheme makes no attempt at close definition of such imprecise drawings. Celestino (2001:102–108) is surely correct in recognising a general evolution from the leaf-shaped swords, depicted as outlines, to those with large hilts and pommels that look like the Carp's Tongue swords of the tenth–ninth centuries BC. This discussion benefits from comments from Dirk Brandherm and relates to his forthcoming *Prähistorische Bronzefunde* volume on swords in Spain and Portugal. The scheme has four broad groups, which trace an historical development:

- *Group A*. Motifs are drawn as outlines only, most of which are found on the simple stelae in Zone I and are therefore the oldest.
- *Group B*. Motifs depicting leaf-shaped swords with rounded hilts.
- *Group C*. Motifs with pronounced cruciform hilts and pommels (that is, sword hilts shaped like a cross), but a variety of blade shapes.
- *Group D*. Motifs showing swords sheathed, or types drawn too schematically to be able to classify.

The dating of all the swords falls into the period 1260–750 BC, the majority of them belong

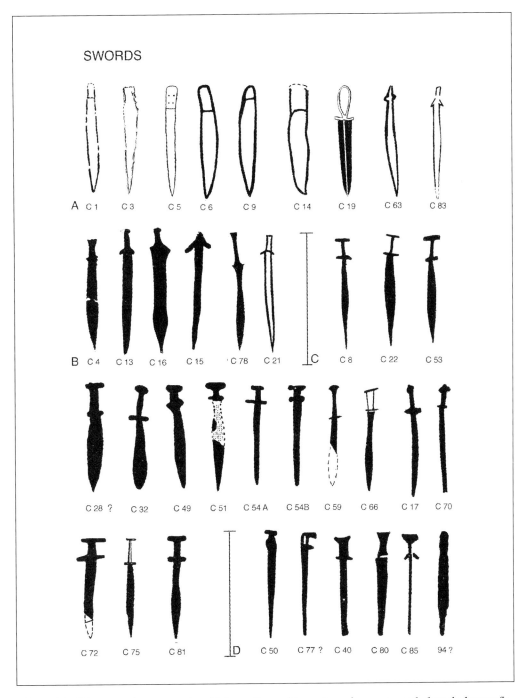

SWORDS

A   C 1   C 3   C 5   C 6   C 9   C 14   C 19   C 63   C 83

B   C 4   C 13   C 16   C 15   'C 78   C 21   ]C   C 8   C 22   C 53

C 28 ?   C 32   C 49   C 51   C 54 A   C 54B   C 59   C 66   C 17   C 70

C 72   C 75   C 81   ]D   C 50   C 77 ?   C 40   C 80   C 85   94 ?

Figure 7.9 *Thirty-seven bronze swords, which are all complete weapons shown separately from the human fig-ures. They are all scaled to the same size for comparison. Groups A to D are general classifications that chart an historical trend from 1260-800 BC*

to the final periods of Huelva and Monte Sa'Idda, from 950–800 BC. The first Atlantic swords are those with parallel-sided blades of Rosnoën type, found on basic stelae like C5 Fóios. There is also a Rosnoën type sword on the first composition on stela C9 Torrejón el Rubio IV which was re-cut and replaced by a leaf-shaped sword, giving a useful internal stratigraphy for the type.

These weapons were superseded by slashing swords with pronounced leaf-shaped blades and examples of the type can be seen on stelae C1 San Martín de Trevejo, C4 Baraçal, C6 Torrejón el Rubio I and it is possible to divide this group according to the blade shape and hilt details, with a developed form showing a hilt of U or V shape such as C13 Brozas, C16 Ibahernando, C15 Trujillo, C63 Almendralejo, C78 Écija V and C83 Córdoba II. Generally, these are similar to continental swords of early Urnfield designs.

The latest swords in the series are the Carp's Tongue forms and examples appear on stelae C54 El Viso I, C75 Écija II, C81 Pedro Abad and C89 Ervidel II. This great class of sword originates in western France in the early tenth century, from where it spread rapidly to south-east England and south-west to Iberia (figure 7.10). Its advantage in fighting lay in its very strong hafting giving a secure grip, a ribbed blade to make it stiff enough for thrusting and a reinforced point which was long enough to pierce between armour and through padded jerkins. Bronze weaponsmiths in Iberia developed the Monte Sa' Idda sword from it, with shorter blades and distinct pommels.

Some swords do not fit this classification very well, such as C53 Alamillo and C66 Aldea del Rey I. It is perhaps easier to see their similarities in terms of the big cruciform hilts, with pronounced guards and large pommels, than in the shape of the blade. The Alconetar type, with solid metal hilts, is probably depicted on C17 Santa Ana, C70 Carmona and less securely, also on C85 Fuente de Cantos. The sword on C77 Écija IV may have been re-cut, producing its unique shape.

Most swords are shown naked, drawn out of their scabbards; this is in contrast to the manner in which swords were depicted on older stelae in the Middle Bronze Age, since the ones from Preixana, San Juan de Negrilhos, Pedrereinha and Assento show the sword clearly sheathed and suspended on a belt, or baldric (Almagro Basch 1966, 1974).

The conclusion is that there were many different types of sword in favour and in use in the western Mediterranean, that have not yet been found, or which have not survived into the archaeological record. The list is surprisingly varied; there is the ribbed sword with a big ring handle C19; C32 has a grossly expanded blade; C59 has a thin, elongated handle; C77 with a rapier-like profile and its handle is probably re-cut with two different designs superimposed; and finally the stiletto-like weapon on C85. Some of these may be eastern designs, or even unique weapons. It is also clear that the modern classification of existing blades does not bear much resemblance to the features that attracted the Bronze Age engraver, since he invariably makes the handles and sheaths prominent and on some stelae he drew the weapon at full size, as if he had placed one flat on the stone and traced an outline around it.

Remarkably, the commonest shape of sword, with the cruciform handle (Monte Sa'Idda

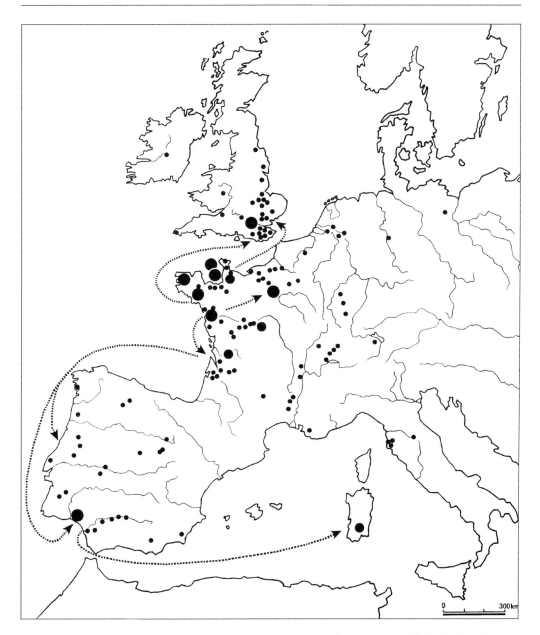

Figure 7.10 *Map showing the distribution of Carp's Tongue swords in Europe. (Modified after Briard 1965)*

type), is a type rarely found in Spain and Portugal, but does occur in Sardinia (figure 7.11). If that reflects a true situation in the past, then one should think through the production processes of bronze swords in a new light and see them, perhaps only in certain periods, as rather rare objects made one at a time for their warrior owners, rather than as run-of-the-mill weapons produced to a standard form. Indeed, it is instructive to look closely at the swords in the largest hoard from Spain, that dredged from the river Odiel at Huelva; although many are of the same Carp's Tongue type, they vary in subtle details, weight and length (Almagro Basch 1940; Ruiz-Gálvez Priego 1995). So do the swords from the hoard of Monte Sa'Idda in Sardinia, which were probably made in southern or western Iberia and traded eastwards (Burgess 2001; Giardino 1995).

Why should there be such a discrepancy between the kinds of swords depicted and those that survive? One possible answer is that only the swords ritually deposited in rivers, or lost in shipwrecks, have survived in any numbers from south-west Europe and that most have been re-contextualised through the process of intensive recycling of old weapons into new artefacts. Another is that perhaps there were relatively few swords in Iberia in the Bronze Age and that the standardised patterns achieved by the bronzesmiths in western France or Ireland for their warrior patrons were the exception, due to intense demand over shorter periods of time. Whatever the reasons may be, it is the case that an apparently uniform object like a bronze sword may have been valued differently according to the region and time in which it was circulating and that these subtle distinctions are reflected in the manner in which the weapon was depicted on the stelae.

7.4   Crested helmets

Crested helmets (figure 7.12) enjoyed a long period of use, and the first bronze one is known from the ritual offerings in the hoard at Piller (Nordtirol, Austria) dating to the end of the Middle Bronze Age, in the fourteenth century BC (Period Bz C2 [Egg & Tomedi 2002]). It is a round cap decorated with a solar motif, with a preposterously large crest flaring above it, edged with little bosses in repoussé. On the wider European scene, helmets are prestigious bronze artefacts made in a variety of styles from the fifthteenth or fourteenth century BC, made possible by mastering the techniques of sheet bronze working that derive from the Aegean world. Therefore, it is not so surprising to see the helmet as an early motif added to the warrior panoply of the basic compositions.

There are as many as 11 helmets shown as separate motifs or worn by the warrior. The object near the head of the warrior (motif 5) on the C22 Solana de Cabañas stela may be a simple helmet, or a brooch, or even a drinking cup; another like it is on the C34 Cabeza del Buey III stela. Strictly speaking, only three helmets – C12, C17 and C21 – bear enough detail to show the original shape. They are conical, with horizontal fins that stick out from the crest, to increase the size and stature of its wearer. These crested helmets are known from two examples from the Huelva deposit in Spain and from two north Portuguese finds, one a small hoard at Vila Cova de Perrinho and a hilltop settlement at Avelas (Coffyn 1985:171). Helmets from France are better preserved, as in the spectacular votive deposit of nine complete bronze helmets from Bernières d'Ailly (Calvados) found in 1832. These were

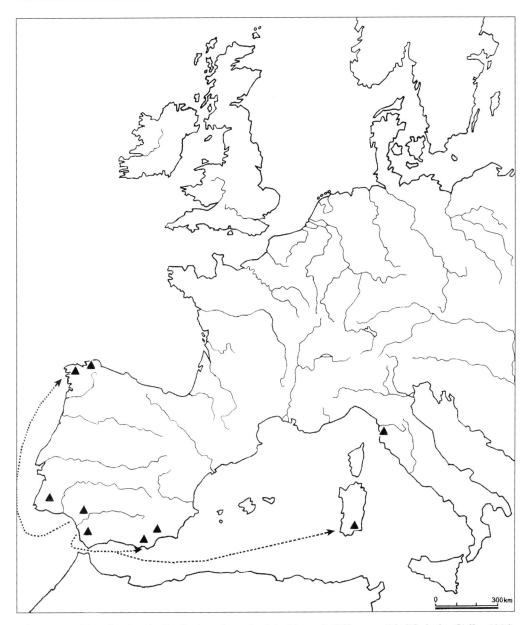

Figure 7.11 *Map showing the distribution of swords of the Monte Sa'Idda type. (Modified after Coffyn 1985)*

buried in three groups of three, placed inside one another and may have been associated with an axe, two spears and a pair of bracelets (Hencken 1971:66–74). All of them match the stelae motifs and agree in date too, belonging to the tenth–ninth centuries BC.

The only examples known from England comprise some rivets and bronze sheet recov-

HELMETS

C 12   C 17   C 21   C 22   C 34

C 32   C 46   C 71   C 84

C 25   C 80

Figure 7.12 Depictions of helmet motifs. In row A, the first three are crested helmets with fins; the last two may be plain bell shapes. Row B depicts six figures wearing helmets and row C shows schematic helmets of pointed shape above the warriors' heads

ered from the massive ritual alignment of timbers at Flag Fen outside Peterborough (Pryor 1991, Plate 91). It is likely they are imported armour from northern France, where they are much commoner and where there is no doubt that some were used as votive offerings; very few ever finished up as scrap pieces in hoards like Vénat.

Those in Italy are later in date and true masterpieces of the bronzesmiths' craft, with multiple repoussé designs and exaggerated crests. They are mainly from graves of high status men in the Villanovan cemeteries at Tarquinia and Vei. There can be no doubt from these contexts that they were symbols of rank for the wealthiest section of the elite. This practice of elite burial is like that of the Aegean and is distinct from the rest of Europe.

Are there any horned helmets as Celestino (2001) and many others think; and if not, what are they? If one examines the 16 stelae on figure 7.13, it is apparent that in most cases the horns emerge directly from the side or top of the head of the human figure. This is clear despite the lack of precision in the engraving. In 13 of the 16 cases, the horns turn through an angle to gain width and emphasis and many have a second twist at the tips. Nothing would have been easier for the engraver to depict than a horned helmet, had he wished to do so, using the conventions already established; marking a triangle above the figures' head, with the horns attached to it, would have carried off the trick visually with no ambiguity. But no figure is shown like this. Nearly every one has horns sprouting directly from the head, not from a headdress or a helmet. The two possible exceptions are the figures C27 Talavera and C65 Olivenza where a headdress with attached horns might be shown; but the detail is very hard to determine. Horns do not necessarily have any connection with helmets, a view reinforced by Hencken's brusque comment on the ubiquity of the taste for adding horns to human figures, when he remarked that: ' … this urge was in fact a very ancient and long-lived one in many places extending from the Upper Palaeolithic sorcerer of the Trois-Frères to Wagnerian Opera' and he made his point by listing a dozen examples (Hencken 1971:167–172).

From this perspective, the interest in crested helmets lies in their contexts. Bronze helmets are unknown in Ireland and very rare indeed in Britain or Portugal; yet these are three of the heartlands of the Atlantic Bronze Age, with many accomplished bronzes. In searching for similar objects, the famous pair of helmets from Viksø on Zealand (Denmark) is compared frequently to the motifs on the heads of horned warriors, but this is a misleading analogy. These helmets were found in a peat bog, resting on a wooden platter, as a ritual deposit (Norling-Christensen 1946). Both helmets (they should really be called headdresses) are composite objects, with the embossed shell of the helmet probably made in Carpathian workshops (perhaps in modern Slovakia) and traded northwards to Denmark around 1000 BC. Once there, Nordic bronzesmiths used the skills they were most familiar with and cast the crest and horns separately, then fixed them to the thinner shells. It is not even certain that the embossed metal shells were intended originally as headdresses, since they may have been decorated bowls. The Viksø helmets belong entirely to the central European and Nordic bronze working traditions. Nearly all the helmets from western and northern Europe come from rivers or wet places where they were placed intentionally as offerings, while those in central and eastern Europe are commonly found

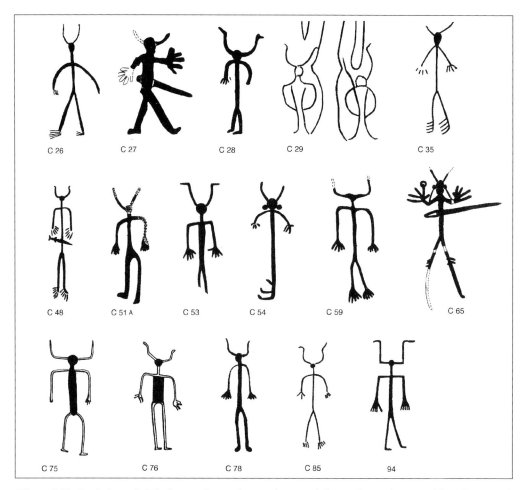

Figure 7.13 *Depictions of all the human figures that are the central element in a stela composition, drawn with horns attached to their heads. They are scaled to the same size for comparison*

as scrap metal in hoards waiting to be melted again. Such different attitudes to the context of valuable objects suggest profound divergences in the function and symbolism of helmets between the east and west of Europe.

In this respect, the south-west Iberian chiefs' cultural behaviour with regard to helmets is western or Atlantic, congruent with their attitudes to the shields, discussed earlier. This is significant, since the parallels to be explored for the horned headdresses, or indeed the horned figures, do not lie in the west at all, but rather in Sardinia and to a lesser degree, in the eastern Mediterranean and Cyprus. This suggests that the horned elements are not fixed to helmets, but are perhaps special attributes that identify some warriors as 'heroes'.

7.5   Horned figures

No horned headgear is known from Iberia, nor indeed from any Atlantic Bronze Age context. There is just one little wooden carving of a horned figure from the burial cave of Es Mussol (Menorca), which is of the Late Bronze Age (Risch et al 2001, Abb 63). However, from the island of Sardinia come over a thousand bronze figurines (at least 700 now published), among them 20 statuettes of human figures with horns. This is the largest single group of objects that are, at least formally, similar to the horned warriors. Finds from sanctuaries, sacred springs and the *Nuraghi* themselves show that such warrior figurines began to be made from the eleventh–tenth centuries BC (Fadda & Lo Schiavo 1992; Lo Schiavo 1999). The horns vary in size and prominence. Obviously some are part of a soft cap, or attached to a metal helmet and worn by men with bodies of natural proportions and shape; others are not and in the case of the 'warrior demons' (monstrous beings with double pairs of arms, eyes, shields and daggers), they are integral symbols of these mythical or divine beings. About five per cent of all warrior statuettes are of this mythical category (Webster 1996:202). On some figures the knobbed horns can be so large as to form one quarter or even one third of the height of the entire figurine, sweeping upwards to heighten the statuette. There is general agreement that the figurines depict real armour and weapons accurately and show an exceptional variety of forms and types. The far-reaching connections between the central and eastern Mediterranean, at least in warfare, are most striking (Stary 1991). But close examination of these figurines fails to produce any that are really similar to the stelae motifs and none that is identical. An illusion of similarity has been created, not a demonstration of it. The figurines with horns emerging directly from the head are the warrior demons like those from Abini (Lilliu 1966, Nos 104, 105, 259); and there are no examples where the horns take on the huge spreading forms like those depicted on the stelae shown on figure 7.13.

The larger-than-life-size stone statues from Monte Prama are further evidence of the interest of Sardinian society in using cattle horns as symbols of male empowerment. At least eight warriors survive among a collection of 25 sculptures, including 17 bare-chested boxers, and models of many Nuraghic fortresses and towers. In iconographic terms, they are exact counterparts of miniature bronze figurines from Abini and their carved details show how the design derives from metalworking techniques. One well-preserved head shows a warrior wearing a horned and crested helmet reaching back to cover the neck.

Monte Prama has a collection of over 2000 sculptural fragments recovered from a rubbish dump, which lay on top of a cemetery of single graves that went out of use by about 625 BC. The relationship between the graves and sculptures is not known, but it is possible that an older *heroön* (a structure known from Archaic Greek contexts, with warrior burials underneath) with the stone warriors existed here from the eleventh–ninth centuries BC and that after its abandonment, a cemetery was established in the same place. The sculptures would have stood on a low wall, visible in the open air, like other Bronze Age shrines and cult areas in Sardinia. When the *heroön* was demolished (perhaps as late as the fourth century BC), the fragments were used to level the area and bury the cemetery too (Lo Schiavo 1997:427). This proposal fully respects the stratigraphy (Tronchetti 1986:49).

The interesting feature of Monte Prama is that a unique iconographic form was chosen to celebrate claims by a few families to high social status and that its main sign was its size and public display. It manipulates the human figure and emphasises men and a physical display of aggression (boxing) or arms. Perhaps the boxers were performing in sacred games. Size is their defining element, closely imitating bronze miniatures of the eleventh–ninth centuries BC from Abini. Other Sardinian communities continued to use small bronze figurines for their rituals.

This has moved away from the matter of the horned warriors on the stelae. But it is an example of how a specific iconographic form emerged quickly and how it utilised existing motifs and symbols to make objects that struck observers with one message, immediately. Given what is known about the prevailing ideologies and religious practices in Sardinia, it is likely that the men depicted were not divinities but prominent aristocrats, perhaps with designs on a sacred kingship or 'heroic' status. At this ideological level, there is a structural similarity between the Monte Prama statues and the human figures on the stelae, since both assert political authority and control any new tastes and customs that may arrive from 'outside' their own territories.

7.6   Other weapons

Forty spears (figure 7.14) are depicted, but their simplicity reveals few details of interest. Most had relatively small points, which the engravers have not differentiated, except for the ogival outlines of C22 and C89. The shafts on C48, C51 and C83 are fitted with a bronze spear butt like those found in the Huelva hoard. The spears are arranged according to the type of composition to which they belong. Their symbolic importance, derived from the place they occupy in each stela composition, was apparently more important to the engraver than any particular detail. There is no means of distinguishing the unusual British types of spearhead.

Eleven bows and arrows (figure 7.15) are depicted in the same simple manner as the spears. The bronze arrowheads, which tipped their missiles, are very common artefacts throughout Spain and Portugal.

7.7   Chariots

The 24 stelae with chariots (figure 7.16) show the same type of vehicle drawn with identical conventions. It is depicted as if viewed from above, but the wheels and horses are shown in a different perspective, which is a side view. Combined, these give the special quality to the motif; it is a widespread convention where the artist wished to depict a complex object and is not peculiar to the stelae. All the vehicles are two wheeled chariots, with a square body that has low side panels, which end in large hoops or handles. These help the chari- oteer or warrior jump onto the platform and give him a secure handhold, avoiding a sharp tilt of the vehicle's body as his weight lands inside. A draught pole runs from below the chariot proper to the two draught animals, which must surely be horses and which are apparently harnessed, or yoked at the neck, to the pole. Despite a widespread belief to the

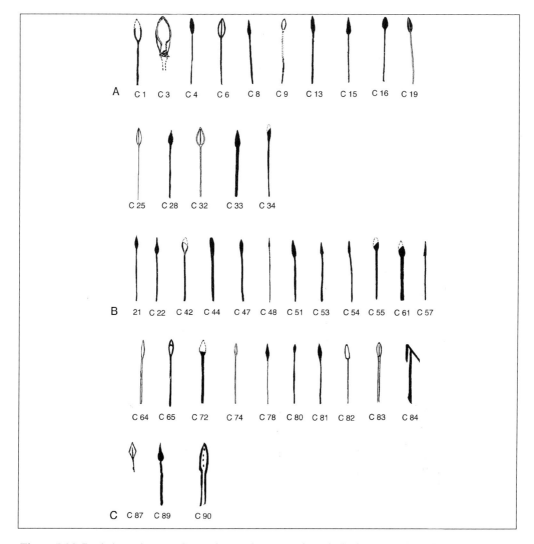

Figure 7.14 Depictions of spears. Group A comprises spears from the basic compositions. Group B comprises spears from the figurative compositions. Group C comprises unique spear shapes. Spears C48, C51 and C83 have rounded butts

contrary, yoking at the neck does not restrict the horses' capacity to run fast and pull strongly and practical demonstrations prove it is not inefficient harnessing (Spruyette 1977). Reins are sometimes shown. A few horses are clearly stallions, but most have no sex shown. The wheels are four-spoked, although artistic convention shows some of them without spokes.

They could be nippy vehicles with an impressive turn of speed; galloping horses easily

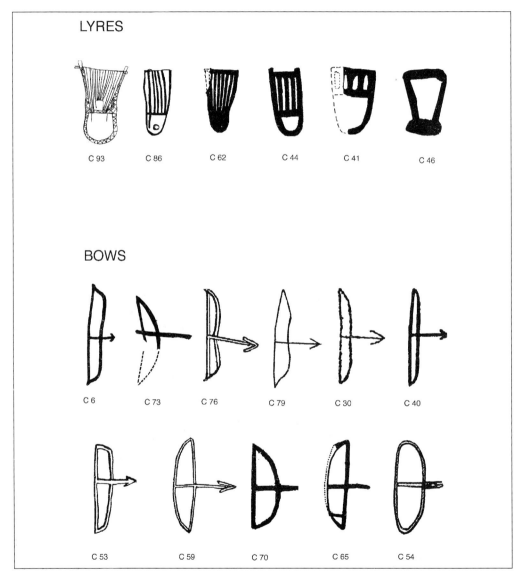

Figure 7.15 *Eleven depictions of the bow and arrow scaled to the same size for comparison (lower rows). Six depictions of musical instruments (upper row). The one from C93 (Luna, Zaragoza) is shown enlarged to appreciate the decoration; the others are scaled to the same size for comparison*

reach speeds of 38 km per hour. A pair of strong ponies could take a chariot 50–60 km in a day with time to spare, or a return journey of 30 km each way (Piggott 1983:89). Finding a matched pair of horses, or ponies, is not easy and if they are unequal in size, strength or character, the charioteer will be in difficulties. Well-trained horses, and indeed a culture in

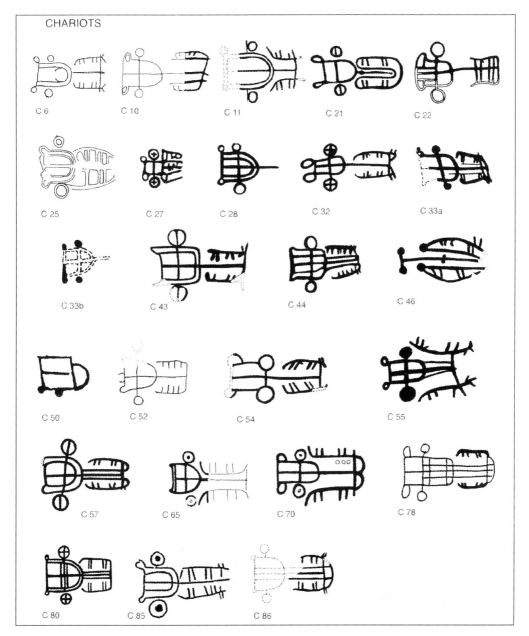

CHARIOTS

C 6   C 10   C 11   C 21   C 22

C 25   C 27   C 28   C 32   C 33a

C 33b   C 43   C 44   C 46

C 50   C 52   C 54   C 55

C 57   C 65   C 70   C 78

C 80   C 85   C 86

Figure 7.16 *Depictions of 24 chariots scaled to the same size for comparison. They are arranged in numerical order, as in the stelae catalogue. There are two attempts to draw a chariot on stela C33*

which fine animals were trained and accustomed to the discipline of a harness, are essential and quite as costly to obtain, as are the wheelwright's skills in making the chariot. What of the charioteer? He must also be a skilled and courageous man, knowledgeable about horses and, like them, disciplined and trained. Even the warrior carried in the chariot needs practice to mount it when it is moving and make sure he does not tip it over when he jumps in (or out).

Chariots must have been made almost entirely of wood and sinew, partly on account of the tensile qualities of these materials and partly because of the weight (and cost) that metal imposes. Metal is used in chariot fittings, however, and a few of these survive. Terret rings are bronze rings used to separate the reins and avoid nasty tangles and examples are known from the hoards of Huelva and Cabezo de Araya, dated to the tenth century BC and contemporary with the stelae. There are terrets of the eighth century, larger than the Bronze Age ones, from the settlements of Aboloduy, Cástulo and Grave 17 from the cemetery of La Joya in Huelva and after that decorated ones with stylised lotus buds on them of seventh century date come from Úbeda La Vieja (Ferrer Albelda & Mancebo Davalos 1991). This is good enough evidence to prove chariots really existed in southern Spain and Portugal. Evidence for chariots after 700 BC is unambiguous and there are good examples of noble burials in Iberian chamber tombs like Toya and Galera that are discussed by Fernández Miranda and Olmos (1986).

It is likely that Aegean chariots inspired the Bronze Age ones in Iberia (Quesada 1994). One telling detail which supports this are the large looped handles at the rear of the body, common to both; another is the use to which they were put in the Aegean, to carry the warrior to battle, so he could dismount and fight on foot with sword and spear. The Atlantic Bronze Age fighting style was close to the Mycenaean one, as far as one can judge, a matter of individual combat or fights between small groups, not like the armies of thousands deployed in the Near East. The basic design of a chariot, once understood, could be kept for several generations with few changes made to it, as seems to have happened in the Aegean down to the Geometric Period. A late Mycenaean origin would fit the chronology for the Final Bronze Age.

Two wheeled chariots are rare elsewhere in prehistoric Europe until the late Iron Age. The recent discoveries of chariots buried with armed warriors from the Sintashta culture in the south-east of the Ural mountains in Russia changes fundamentally the discussion of their origins. These vehicles had spoked wheels and were drawn by pairs of horses, some of them sacrificed and buried in the same graves as their owners (Anthony 1995). Several radiocarbon determinations from horse skulls from the chariot burial at Krivoe Ozero show they were buried around 2000 BC, making them the oldest true chariots known. This challenges the previously accepted ideas that they are Mediterranean vehicles, whose origins lie in the early second millennium BC, in the area of modern Syria (Littauer & Crouwel 1979:51). If the Sintashta chariots are correctly dated, then it is clear that the

Early Bronze Age societies living in the Urals had contact with northern Syria and that their vehicles were adopted. By 1800 BC a light chariot with spoked wheels drawn by two horses, controlled and harnessed in a new manner, was available. It swept through the Levant and by 1700/1600 BC had become an indispensable weapon of war and was used by the Hyksos chieftains in their assaults on Egypt and figured on the stone stelae that were erected above shaft grave V at Mycenae.

Quite early on, the Near Eastern and Egyptian chariots became mobile platforms for skilled archers, who were trained to fire while moving; many Egyptian temple and tomb paintings show the Pharaohs and military aristocrats hunting game, or riding over defeated enemies on the battlefield. Chariots massed in their thousands and fought with both armies alongside large infantry formations at the celebrated battle of Kadesh between the Hittites and Egyptians in 1286/1280 BC. For many centuries in the Near East, the chariot was valued principally as a military conveyance, fast and prestigious, drawn by trained horses in carefully matched pairs. From 800 BC the Assyrians developed a stronger chariot for their armies, to carry heavily armoured archers and a charioteer.

In the Aegean, chariots of the later Bronze Age (1500–1200 BC) had a different use and, it seems, a different manner of construction. They were heavier than the Egyptian ones and '... served as transport for warriors who fought on the ground, with swords and daggers and, in particular, spears' (Crouwel 1981:145). They were not archers' vantage points. The special features of Aegean chariots, called the Dual Type, were the ' ... curved extensions at the rear sides and the traction system with its pole brace and pole stay'. Using chariots to transport warriors across the battlefield, and whisk them away when they wanted to escape, is described repeatedly in the *Iliad*.

Complete chariots were excavated from the royal graves at Salamis, Cyprus, where Tumulus 79, built in 725–700 BC, had impressive later burials placed in the entrance passage around 700 BC; among the grave goods were four wheeled vehicles, buried in pairs as a chariot and a six- and four-wheeled hearse. All the vehicles were horse drawn: the animals lay next to the draught pole, killed by a great blow and laid to rest in rich harnesses (Karageorghis 1973–1974, Plate IX). Ivory inlays, bronze bosses and decorated panels, rings and other ornaments embellished the harnesses as well as the chariots, so they would have been a gorgeous sight. The splendour and variety of rich furniture with the chariots extended to ivory thrones, an ivory and glass inlaid bed, ivory torch holders, large dinner services of pottery with foods and so on. Salamis Tomb 79 proves that the chariot was not only a funerary vehicle, but a physical symbol of aristocratic standing, as were the other grave goods. This is later in date than the chariot motifs on the stelae, but it finds an echo in Spain in the remarkable Iron Age grave in the cemetery of La Joya (Grave 17), in Huelva, dated to 700–650 BC. This suggests that this is an 'ideal type' of royal burial and that the general idea of what its main elements should be was widely known.

Horseback riding was of very little importance in Bronze Age Greece and the Near East and stands in marked contrast to the high status of chariot driving. It was of little interest to the upper classes and it is clear that chariots with horses precede horse riding in warfare. Crouwel (1992:50) was at pains to explain why this should be, since it seems to go against the common sense view that riding must have preceded horse driving. He thought that there were no good saddles with which to mount a horse; nor were there any horseshoes to protect the soft hooves against the weight of a heavy rider and hard ground; horses have a herd instinct and pull together more strongly than when ridden alone; horses become smelly and sweaty in the heat and this may have deterred close physical contact; chariots let a warrior devote his entire attention to battle and he can carry more and heavier weapons than a single horseman. Horse riders only really come to the fore from the eighth century in Assyria and Greece. Discoveries of horses in Copper and Early Bronze Age settlements in Spain have moved the debate on from this point and it is known that horses can be ridden bareback, controlled with a simple cord fastened to their noses and need no shoeing to ride long distances over Mediterranean ground (Harrison et al 1994). In short, the evidence from Spain indicates that horses were ridden by 2300 BC and quite commonly until 1200 BC, when the first chariots appeared. The interplay between the fashion for chariots and horseback riding is a fascinating topic that can only be touched upon here, but it was Piggott (1983:134) who noted that chariots are never depicted on Iberian pots from the fifth century onwards, yet they are replete with images of horsemen and warriors; a real symbolic contrast with the stelae and their chariots.

Bronze Age chariots are depicted realistically on a large rock surface in Frännarp (Sweden), the engravers following the same artistic conventions (figure 7.17). The details match each other so exactly in terms of spoked wheels, chariot body shapes and paired horses attached to a draught pole that it is very likely they are the same vehicles (Thrane 1990).

Elsewhere in Bronze and Early Iron Age Europe, wheeled vehicles drawn by horses were well known throughout the Urnfield area and used in elite burials; however, they

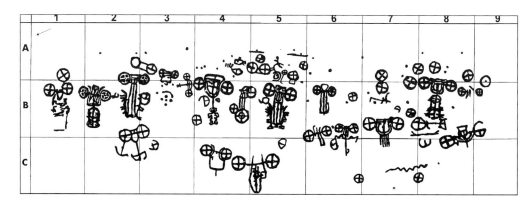

Figure 7.17 Engraved rock panel from Frännarp (Sweden), depicting many chariots. (After Thrane 1990)

were elaborate four wheeled carts, not chariots. At least 242 wagon graves are known from 1300-500 BC. Their construction developed continuously and rapidly incorporated technical innovations from the Near East and Etruria (Pare 1992). The wagons were carefully made, fully functional vehicles, with four-spoked wheels, shod in iron. Their construction required specialised, sedentary craftsmen who would need well-equipped workshops to store and season the timber required. These are not vehicles that could be assembled from green wood by handy carpenters; they needed wheelwrights, men with lathes to turn the wheel hubs and decorative spindles on the wagon-box and a variety of different timbers, sawn and split to close tolerances. Christopher Pare could find no clear evidence of their original function, but could show they were objects of personal status and prestige and that they were used in processions and cult practices. These two roles were common all over Europe.

7.8   Mirrors

The group of 42 mirrors (figure 7.18) is the largest one known for any Bronze Age society in Europe or the Mediterranean, outside Egypt. All mirrors were small enough to be held in the hand and show variation in the design and decoration of their handles. There are five groups:

- *Group A* depicts mirrors of simple form and straight handles which are drawn as outlines
- *Group B* contain more simple mirrors, engraved in the intaglio technique
- *Group C* mirrors have simple knobbed handles
- *Group D* depicts mirrors with fancy handles engraved in the intaglio technique (except C27 and C30)
- *Group E* contains motifs that may be mirrors but are not certainly identified as such.

Metal mirrors are known from the western Mediterranean and in Spain and Portugal they are artefacts of Mediterranean inspiration. The oldest is a handle of open work design from the Portuguese hoard at Baiões, which may belong to a mirror (it was previously identified as part of a large razor), although this is unproven. There are at least five prehistoric bronze mirrors on the Balearic Islands, the most recent being a discovery from the cave of Es Mussol, from where the horned wooden figure was recovered. The object is 174 mm tall and is decorated with thin bands of incised strokes on the back and although its function as a mirror is uncertain, its date to the Final Bronze Age around 1000 BC is secured by radiocarbon determinations (Risch et al 2001:488 and Colour Plate 27). At La Lloseta (Mallorca) a hoard of distinctive bronze ornaments and weapons contained another mirror, with a long handle with a rounded pommel with holes for an organic fitting, perhaps of bone (a good photograph is in Almagro Basch 1940, Lám VII). The hoard can be dated by the metal hilted sword in it and the style of the toothed bracelet, reminiscent of the Estremoz types made in gold and placed in the period ninth–eighth centuries BC. The shape of the La Lloseta mirror with its handle is similar to Archaic Greek bronze examples (Anlen & Padiou 1989:357).

No Bronze Age mirrors are known from western or central Europe and there is not one from any Late Bronze Age Urnfield context.

The two oldest examples in mainland Spain are a small bronze disc from the Orientalising treasure found at Aliseda (Cáceres) in 1920; it is probably from a grave and dates to the eighth–seventh century BC; and the princely grave 17 from La Joya (Huelva), with a bronze mirror mounted on a silver and ivory handle. Like other Phoenician objects of exceptional craftsmanship, they were perhaps imported from Cyprus or Phoenicia.

The Sicilian Bronze Age is rich in both graves and settlement evidence and in the south-east of the island, in the fertile limestone region, the great cemeteries of Pantalica provide some extraordinary objects. They belong to populous chiefdoms with substantial settlements and organised territories. These cemeteries of large, rock-cut tombs were perhaps used until 650 BC and many had been looted completely by the time Paolo Orsi was able to investigate them at the end of the nineteenth century. No Greek material (except for a stray surface find) was found there. He discovered five round bronze mirrors in tombs belonging to the Pantalica I period 1250–1000 BC (see figure 7.19) (Orsi 1899). Like most investigators after him, he assumed they were imports from the Aegean or Cyprus, but it is more likely that most are locally made copies of eastern types, made by well trained bronze smiths (Harding 1984:240; Leighton 1999). The Pantalica tombs are notable for not having Mycenaean pottery in them like those in the eastern part of the island, but they do contain imported Mycenaean bronze weapons. Grave 37 with the mirror also contained a pair of gold earrings and a bow fibula; Leighton thinks it may be a woman's grave (Leighton 1999:178). Mirrors are not found in the later grave goods at Pantalica. We do not know if they were restricted to male burials only.

The Lipari bronze hoard also had a fragment that may be an imported bronze mirror of Aegean origin of the same date as the Pantalica ones (Bernabò Brea & Cavalier 1980, 780, No 283), but its identification seems doubtful and it looks like any other flat bronze scrap. This was a scrap metal hoard weighing 75 kg, buried in a large pot on the acropolis of Lipari, just below a destruction level with heavy burning. It contained many weapon and tool fragments of Thapsos types, as well as pieces of an ox-hide ingot, all ready to be melted into new objects.

On Sardinia, mirrors were always prestige objects and at least four are known. There are fragments of one mirror from a cave-shrine called the Grotta de Pirosu (Su Benatzu-Santadi), along with a bronze tripod and brooches (van Dommelen 1998:75). In the hoard from Costa Nighedda, excavated from inside a round building, were a mirror handle with a tiny bird inside it, another 30 metal items, including a miniature bronze boat, animal heads with exaggerated horns and small daggers (Lo Schiavo 2000:147). Another two are

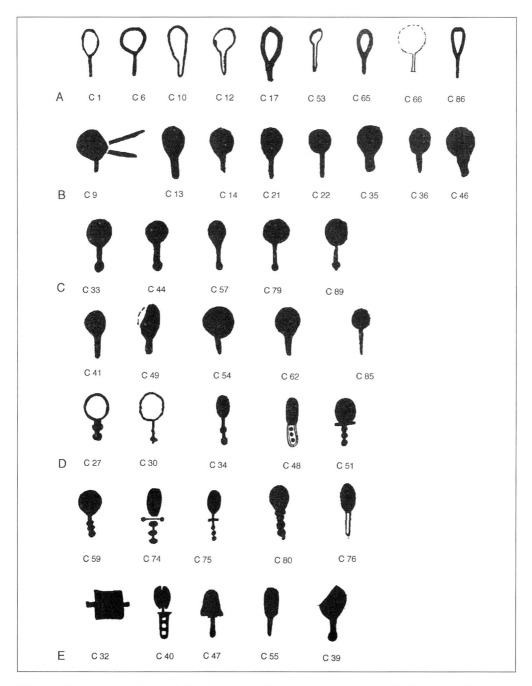

Figure 7.18 *Forty-two mirrors scaled to the same size for comparison and arranged in five groups. The top row (group A) depicts mirrors of simple form and straight handles, which are drawn as outlines. The next three rows (groups B and C) contain more simple mirrors, engraved in the intaglio technique. Group C mirrors have simple knobbed handles. Group D depicts mirrors with fancy handles engraved in the intaglio technique (except C27 and C30). Group E contains motifs that may be mirrors but are not certainly identified as such*

known from Teti (Abini) and Tore (Nuraghe S Pietro) (Lo Schiavo & Manconi 2001, figure 20). These last two have identical handles to that depicted on the stela C40 Capilla I. A lively debate about the date of all this material is gradually resolving into a consensus that it belongs to the eleventh–ninth centuries. Now, these mirrors (except the possible mirror fragment from Lipari, broken for re-melting) are in archaeological contexts that are in some way religious in nature, in metal treasures in special buildings, or cave-shrines. Their rarity and the restricted period of use (or at least the period when they were regard-ed as suitable grave goods), is obvious.

Only in the eastern Mediterranean are there many metal mirrors. This sample, gath-ered to illustrate contextual detail and date, reflects their contemporary high status and relative importance. They are a regular funerary offering in Minoan and Mycenaean graves. The Late Minoan III cemetery at Zafer Papoura outside Knossos had notably rich graves with mirrors and was well published by Sir Arthur Evans almost a hundred years ago. What he found, in the undisturbed and intact tombs, is of the greatest inter-est, since 12 bronze mirrors and two ivory handles for another pair were recovered and of these eight were in their original resting places. From this, it is certain that they

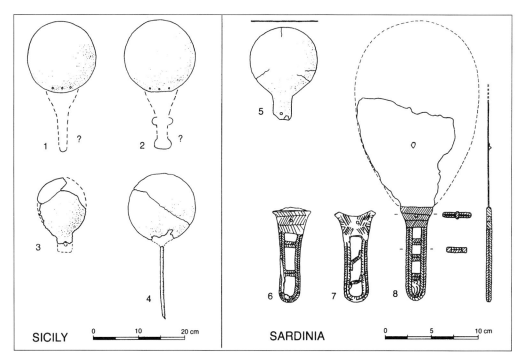

Figure 7.19 Bronze mirrors and handles from Sicily (numbers 1-4) and Sardinia (numbers 5-8). Reconstructed elements are shown by broken lines. The Sicilian mirrors are all from the Pantalica cemetery (Graves 37N, 23N, 140N and 173SO). The Sardinian ones are from Grotta Pirosu Su Benatzu (5), Abini (6), Costa Nighedda (7), and the Nuraghe San Pietro (8). After Lo Schiavo et al 1985, Figure 11; Lo Schiavo & Manconi 2001, Figure 20

accompany both male and female burials and that the mirrors could be placed either by the left shoulder, at the left hand, or at the left foot of the body. The mirrors themselves were all round, of bronze, with two to four holes to attach an organic handle; in at least three cases, ivory handles, sometimes richly decorated with Sphinx motifs, enriched them. They were quite small, around 13 cm in diameter; the biggest one came from the Royal Tomb of Isopata and was 22 cm across. The size matters, since the smaller ones could be held in the hand comfortably, but the Isopata mirror was so heavy it would need a supporting stand. Evans noted that no mirrors were found in the Shaft Graves at Mycenae and he thought they were an Egyptian fashion, introduced into Crete in the Late Minoan II period and flourished after that. The grave goods from Zafer Papoura (except those in the Royal Tomb) are all fourteenth century BC and already in 1904, Evans knew of the Sicilian discoveries by Paolo Orsi and made reference to them (Evans 1905). The burials are among the most important ever recovered in Crete, but the interest lies in the way they confirm the high value of the mirror as a prestige object and show that its placement close to the body is exactly like the positions for the mirror motifs on the stelae.

On the Greek mainland, in Mycenaean contexts after the fourteenth century BC, bronze mirrors are known from several chamber tombs, but the nature of these collective burial vaults makes it hard to be certain which grave goods are associated with a particular burial. It is sufficient to note that round bronze mirrors are known from tombs at Asine and from four others in Prosymna (both in the Argolid). Decorated mirror handles of ivory are also known from contemporary contexts in Cyprus and may well be specially commissioned luxury items, given their 'heroic' subject matter of helmeted warriors fighting a griffin (Krzyszkowska 1992; Schäfer 1958).

Elsewhere, mirrors of bronze are well known sumptuary items in the Levant and Egypt from the early third millennium BC and reach exquisite standards of craftsmanship by the Old Kingdom (Lilyquist 1979). The face of many Egyptian mirrors is slightly concave to make a clearer image with no peripheral distortion, but also one that is smaller; a concave mirror can focus light to a brilliant point. Some have the face coated in silver, tin or gold, for a better reflection and a few were even of solid silver. Mirrors were most commonly associated with ladies of high or royal status and their primary purpose was cosmetic; in the grave they perhaps lit the way of the deceased, conserved their appearance and acted as depositories of the soul. They were not warriors' talismans.

They remain important items as grave goods and as elements of social display right through the classical and Roman periods (Anlen & Padiou 1989). Many hundreds of bronze mirrors are known from the Etruscan civilisation and nearly all were made in the sixth–fourth centuries BC, which is long after the stelae had ceased to be erected (Mayer-Prokop 1967).

Elsewhere, in later Iron Age Europe mirrors are found in culturally specific contexts. They are extremely rare on La Tène sites. Echt illustrates three important bronze mirrors of this period, all from high status graves of the early fifth century BC. He describes a remarkably large bronze mirror from a princess's tomb at Reinheim, with the handle modelled as a human figure with a Celtic headdress (Echt 2000:111–115, Taf 7). There are two more mirrors, but made from iron not bronze, from fifth century BC warrior graves at Arras in Yorkshire, associated with chariots (Stead 1965). They would cast a very dark, sombre reflection of the face, more sinister than the lighter-toned images on a bronze mirror. Note the similar male symbolism employed in the Arras graves and the south-west Iberian stelae, where both have individual warriors, with chariots, horses and mirrors. However, an iron mirror has been found at Wetwang (Yorks) in an intact chariot burial with a woman, so both sexes had access to them (Hill 2002). Mirrors are exceptionally rare, if not absent, in contemporary Iron Age Iberian graves. An important series of Celtic bronze mirrors in the British Isles (the exquisitely decorated ones from Birdlip and Desborough are well known), probably associated with male cremation burials, belongs to the last century BC. In contrast to these western customs, many Scythian graves of both sexes have a mirror placed in them, a practice which imitates the classical Greek use of the mirror and which probably spread from the Greek colony at Olbia. All this serves to show just how culturally specific the burial customs concerning mirrors can be and emphasises the singularity of the practice in south-west Iberia. For this reason, a specific hypothesis is necessary to explain their use and the one most likely to be correct is that which explains mirrors as male talismans, with magical powers of the sort described earlier.

A few of the motifs called mirrors may, as a faint possibility, represent something different (figure 7.18). One is that some are drawn with the handle upright, giving the impression of a small bottle with a long, thin neck, perhaps a flask of perfume or opium (C13 Brozas and C35 Esparragosa de Lares I). Another is their similarity to a striking class of bronze object found in Italy, called a palette, whose use is believed to be to shovel perfume grains on to an incense burner or fire, or to collect the ashes of the dead person from the funeral pyre. Over 50 are known and they are dated to 900–600 BC; many have a blade over 30 cm long and elaborate cast bronze handles (Zuffa 1956–1957). In outline they look remarkably like a mirror. None has been found in a Bronze Age context in Iberia. Two motifs called mirrors may be short daggers in a sheath (C48 Magacela, C74 Écija I).

This short survey shows that mirrors were high status objects in the later second millennium BC in the central Mediterranean and used in ritual rather than domestic contexts. Even on a conservative assessment, the closest examples in date and formal design all belong in the Late and Final Bronze Age, linked to the late Mycenaean and Cypriot trading enterprises (figure 7.20). This early dating is reinforced by the fact that the mirror (and probably the lyre) is the first eastern object to be added to the basic stelae compositions.

7.9   Metrology

It is possible that groups of five small pits, on 12 stelae from Zones II and IV, may represent a set of weights, indicating the entrepreneurial interests of the elite group (Celestino 2001:181–185). His suggestion is supported by chance finds of stone, bronze and lead weights from various contexts and dating from the eighth century BC in Portugal and Spain (García-Bellido 1999), but there is plenty of evidence for standardised systems of weights across Bronze Age Europe, derived from accurately weighing imperishable objects of gold, from identifying scales for weighing and sets of weights from shipwrecks in the east Mediterranean.

Networks of commercial exchange required systems of standard weights. With them it is possible to create comparable units of value and establish the equivalences between them. Once established, it is possible to create commercial exchanges that allow raw materials to be exchanged for finished goods and the first stages of exchange in commodities and of systems of wealth finance. Many different ones arose in the eastern Mediterranean, Mesopotamia and Egypt and recently a universal conversion system for them has been proposed (Pulak 2000; Mederos & Lamberg-Karlovsky 2001). In practice it works by taking the weights in a known system, say talents, shekels and minas from Ugarit, and then determining how they can be divided in whole numbers to match the weight system of Syria, or Egypt. Once the interrelations are established, all the equivalences allow the weights to be used in different combinations and thus to make the conversions from one weight system to another. To make the correlations requires a simple balance and many of these are known from central Europe at this time (Pare 1999). Similar weights systems were known in the Aegean and central Europe, based on fractions of the talent (which weighs 31.440 kg) expressed as fractions such 1/480 or 1/720 and readily demonstrable in the Late Bronze Age gold work (Eiwanger 1989).

Bronze Age goldwork in Spain and Portugal shows three separate weight systems in use simultaneously: the unit of 11.75 g equivalent to the Hittite and Anatolian Shekel, seen in the gold torcs from Sagrajas and Bodonal; the Aegean unit of 65.27 g used in the hoard of gold bowls from Villena; and the Phoenician shekel, with a weight varying between 7.9–7.5 g, which was used in the gold hoard of Caldas de Reis (Ruiz-Gálvez Priego 2000). It is probable that some people in the west knew how to convert between these systems and perhaps guarded the knowledge, along with the weights themselves, as something precious.

This shows that the far west was integrated into the eastern Mediterranean economies, implying that they had shared commercial interests, alongside which moved technology, ideological concepts, symbols and other intangible cultural material, identified as value-added knowledge to be acquired when wanted. This suggests a relatively high level of complexity for the Final Bronze Age, which is congruent with the ideological model being proposed.

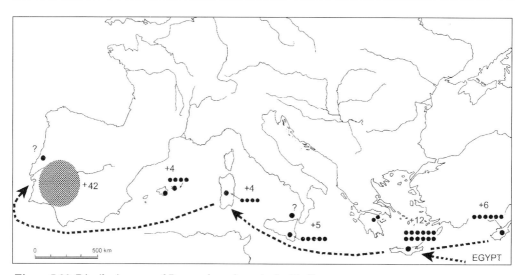

Figure 7.20 Distribution map of Bronze Age mirrors in the Mediterranean

Weights are a good choice to materialise in an ideology of supremacy, as explained in Chapter 5. Without the weights themselves, or knowing the weight multiples of a gold bowl or torc (objects which were elite treasures), it would be extremely difficult to steal this knowledge, which would remain secure in the hands of its owners. A system of weights could therefore be an elite possession, an authentic symbol impossible to counterfeit, perfectly suited to depict on the stelae. It is important to remember that this motif is chronologically late, found only on figurative stelae and restricted to Zones II and IV, along the Zújar river and the middle Guadalquivir valley.

7.10   Lyres and harps

Once musical instruments (figure 7.15) were recognised in 1975, the hunt was on to find eastern Mediterranean sources for them; and depending on one's viewpoint about the antiquity of the stelae, they were identified with Greek Geometric or Phoenician lyres of the period after 800 BC (Bendala 1977; Blázquez Martínez 1983). However, it is obvious from the detail on the best preserved lyre from Luna (C93) that it is a complicated instrument with nine strings for creating sound, anchored on a prominent bridge and another seven cords attached to the sides as decoration, in groups of three and four respectively, fixed directly to the sounding board, which is an impossible position from which to place them under tension to create a note. Only the strings under tension could resonate properly and there are nine in all. The lyre's frame is decorated with zigzags, which represent a binding, or perhaps inlays of wood or ivory. The stela itself is an early one, with a large

V-notched shield as the central motif and the lyre beneath it. It should be among the oldest stelae and date to the period of the thirteenth–twelfth centuries BC.

Alfredo Mederos discussed where such a handsome instrument could have come from, since there are absolutely none like this known anywhere in western or central Europe and he concluded that the best parallels were the lyres made in Minoan Crete or Mycenaean Greece in the period between 1300–1150 BC (Mederos Martín 1996b). This is convincing, all the more so since the lyres known in the later periods are simpler instruments, with about four strings and very small sounding boxes and are in fact small harps, relatively easy to play.

There are at least four other lyres on the stelae, relatively simple constructions with two to six strings and small sounding boxes. In design and outline, admittedly drawn at small scale on the stelae, they find general parallels in the later Greek musical instruments, painted on pottery of the Geometric period (Wegner 1968:figs. 1–3).

7.11   Combs

Twenty-one combs (figure 7.21) are recognisable, but some of them are so schematic and roughly drawn that interpretation has to be tentative. None is a belt buckle, however, which was an old idea of Almagro Basch that is now rejected. The clearest examples of combs are the motifs on stelae C13 Brozas or C80 Ategua, since they have a frame with a perforated handle to set off the implement's teeth. Combs are scarce artefacts anywhere in prehistoric Europe and while once they may have been very common and made of wood or thorns, they rarely survive. The few we can refer to are exceptional ones.

A delicate comb made of boxwood was excavated from the burial cave of Es Càrritx (Menorca). Although less than 80 mm wide, its design with a T-shaped handle and long teeth is a confident and complex one. It was associated with locks of hair, cut from the head and body of the dead and conserved in cylindrical wooden boxes (Risch et al 2001, Taf 105b). The date from radiocarbon determinations is between the eleventh–ninth centuries BC. There is another comb from the male burial in Grave 1 from the Roça do Casal do Meio, made of imported elephant ivory and unique in the Atlantic Bronze Age (Spindler & Veiga Ferreira 1973). Its trapezoidal form is elegant and restrained and it would have been held directly in the hand when used. It should be dated to the tenth century BC. A second ivory comb is reported from the Final Bronze Age settlement of Cerro de la Mora in Granada and a bone one at Lebrija (Celestino 2001:168). Both the ivory combs are made of imported raw materials and may be actual imports themselves; but this is impossible to determine at the moment. A splendid Bronze Age comb in Iberia to mention is one of solid gold, decorated with three arches protruding from the body, recovered among the huge treasure of Caldas de Reis (Pontevedra), now dated to the Early Bronze Age around 1700 BC (Hernando Gonzalo 1989:45). Gold and ivory combs were precious objects. The ivory could be found no closer than the Maghreb (modern Morocco), where elephants still roamed in the first millennium BC and it is a material traditionally reserved for the social elite in the eastern Mediterranean and used to embellish furniture and toilet articles of the highest value. Contacts in the thirteenth–twelfth century BC between Morocco and the Atlantic world are confirmed by the find of a Rosnoën type of bronze sword from Larache, on the Atlantic coast of central Morocco, and it is possible that the elephant ivory may have come from there, rather than the eastern Mediterranean.

In the Aegean there are ivory combs from several Mycenaean sites dated between 1400–1100 BC, which have a formal similarity to the motifs. However, Celestino (like Almagro Gorbea in 1977) believes the comb is a late motif and therefore rejects the possibility of links with this civilisation, but sees it as part of the pre-Phoenician contacts established from 1050 BC. The possibility remains open that the Aegean, or Cypriot, models of ivory combs inspired the ones on the warrior stelae. It is certain that combs are

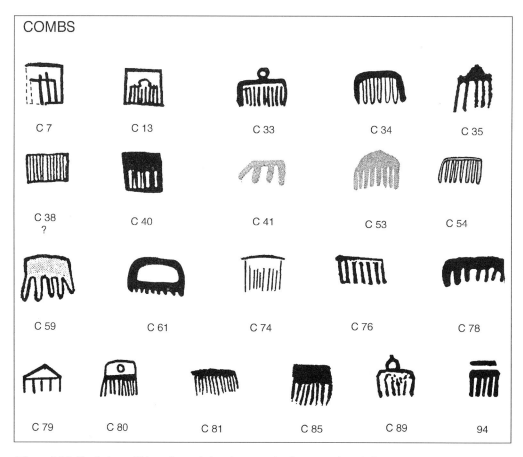

Figure 7.21 *Depictions of 21 combs, scaled to the same size for comparison. It is not certain if C38 is comb or some other object*

commonest on stelae in the Guadalquivir valley and scarce elsewhere, which suggests a relatively late date for them. However, the reality may not be this straightforward, since the ivory comb from the Roça de Casal do Meio in Portugal dates to the tenth century and the addition of a comb to the C13 Brozas stela at an unknown (but probably early) date shows that combs might be early motifs, which later on became popular in the Guadalquivir. In fact, one cannot say with any certainty that the combs are late motifs. Much more important than the date of the motif is its likely symbolism, since the comb is a sign that the warrior was proud of his physical beauty, of which his hair was an essential part, and therefore the comb would represent this notion to the viewer.

7.12   Brooches

Among the smallest objects on the stelae are the brooches, bronze fibulae used to fasten capes or loose garments on the shoulder (figure 7.22). About 17 examples are recognisable, but they are often indistinct, or when clearly engraved, their shape is so simplified that one cannot recognise the type of brooch being depicted. In many cases one can say only that a brooch is depicted and these observations often differ from those who have published the same stelae before. Given this genuine uncertainty, it seems that the energetic determination by Celestino (2001:185–210) to classify and thereby date the brooches is too ambitious, since it assumes a degree of precision in the engravings that only rarely occurs, thereby undermining the typological scheme. There is little agreement on the details of the typology or evolution of the elbow brooches and much confusion arises from grouping heterogeneous material together, that goes back all the way to the first study by Almagro Basch in 1940 and which is repeated by Coffyn in 1985. What one can do is recognise some broad classes and the period when they were in use. Figure 7.22 brings them together in four classes:

- arc fibulae on row A
- elbow fibulae and variants on rows B and C
- antennae fibulae (Torrejón el Rubio II) on row D
- derivations from elbow fibulae on rows E and F.

The earliest brooches are probably the arc fibulae and the big engraving on the C12 Valencia de Alcántara III stela leaves little doubt as to the object's type. This example from an early composition, suggests that brooches, like crested helmets, were known by the twelfth century BC.

Probably as old are the elbow or Cypriot types of the twelfth–eleventh centuries BC, most of them shown with the characteristic sharp angle (the 'elbow') in the bow and a coiled spring in one corner. These details are interesting since the brooches with the off-centre elbow are later types in the series and differ from the symmetrical elbow brooches from the grave find at San Roman de la Hornija (Valladolid) and the Huelva deposit. Given their calibrated radiocarbon dates between 1100–950 BC, these elbow brooches must be later, probably from the eleventh century. No fewer than 21 of the 26 known examples of the specifically Huelva brooches come from Iberia (Mederos 1996a, figure 1).

The two brooches (row F; C65 Olivenza and C89 Ervidel II) with protruding double elbows are later than the others. There is one antennae brooch on (row D) C7 Torrejón el Rubio II that is the latest of all, perhaps of the later eighth century.

These types are all known from bronze originals actually found in the soil of Spain and their derivatives are widely dispersed in southern France, the central Mediterranean, Cyprus and the Aegean, commonly found in tombs and on settlements. Hundreds of

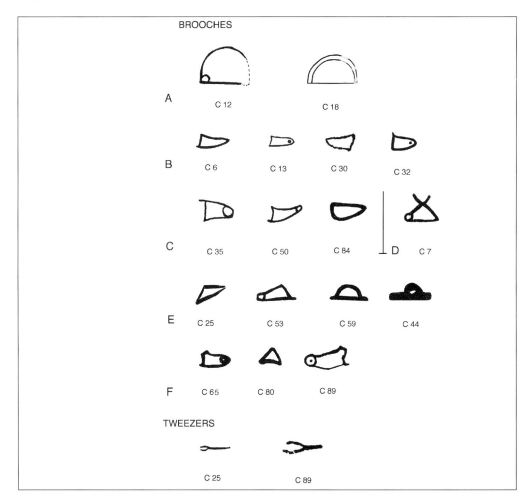

Figure 7.22 Small bronze objects. There are 17 brooches arranged in groups. Row A depicts bow fibulae; rows B and C depict variants of the elbow type fibula and D is the unique horned fibula from Torrejón el Rubio II. Rows E and F depict fibulae that may also be based on elbow models. The bottom line shows two tweezers

brooches are related to these classes and from the tangled typology and confused chronologies that characterise their study, which Celestino explains clearly, certain points emerge. The first is that the oldest forms of the arc and elbow type appear in the Final Bronze Age in Spain by the eleventh century BC and do not have local prototypes. They are probably eastern ideas that reach the far west through contacts in Sicily and Sardinia. Second, numbers and varieties of brooches proliferate enormously in the Iberian Peninsula between the late eleventh–ninth centuries, just as they do on Sicily, and these varieties are probably the ones intended to be depicted on the stelae. Third, Celestino is certainly correct when he observes that local brooches seem to develop at the same time as the round shields replace the Herzsprung (V-notched) shields.

The bigger picture, derived from distribution maps of the various brooch types, shows that fashions for nearly identical dress ornaments spread over great distances (figure 7.23) and linked Iberia, France, the central Mediterranean and east as far as the Levantine shores at Megiddo (Giardino 1995:240–249). It is well known that the oldest brooches (the violin bow types) arise in north-central Europe in the thirteenth century and then spread to the Balkans and the Aegean and that the arc and elbow types develop from them. Fashions in dress are shared all over the western Mediterranean and those brooches arriving in the east are usually in historical contexts of later date than in the west. Future discoveries in Spain may well support this idea, as part of the ebb and flow of exchanges that transferred other western objects discussed earlier (Mederos 1996a:98–101, 112).

7.13   Toilet articles: tweezers and razors

The one motif claimed to be a razor by Celestino on stela C40 Capilla I is more likely to be a mirror, as we have explained earlier (figure 7.18 and see p 246). There are bronze razors from the hoard of Huerta de Árriba in the northern Meseta, but they are unusual finds in the Atlantic Bronze Age in Iberia. Two pairs of tweezers are depicted and there are bronze tweezers from the two graves at the Roça do Casal do Meio. These are also rare objects in Iberia, deriving their importance from what we can infer from them about the customs of shaving and plucking facial (or body) hair. They belong to the figurative stelae compositions.

7.14   Diadems and hair coiffures

Only four stelae depict human figures with diadems above their heads (figure 6.14). Two different objects are depicted in this group. On the stela from Torrejón el Rubio II (C7) is a unique motif, fitting close to the head and tied underneath the chin. It may be a wig, or something similar. On the other three stelae a different 'object' is shown, one that is separate from the figure and many times bigger than the head; it appears to be a semi-circular aureole or headdress, or even a construction. Impressive by their size and complexity, these 'headdresses' share many details, even down to the number and spacing of the compartments that create their design. It may be that they are the functional equivalent of the gold ceremonial hats found in Germany and eastern France and that they are special ceremonial regalia. Given the long tradition of headdresses on Iberian figures, stretching back into the third millennium BC, and their association with small megalithic tombs, it is likely that these figures maintain a truly ancient custom, one peculiar to the Iberian peninsula (Bueno-Ramirez 1995).

Celestino thought these figures wore a diadem and cited the ornaments made of boars' tusk, mounted in bronze settings from eastern France, as examples (Celestino 2001:252–253). Recent excavations have discovered more of these ornaments on the chests of undisturbed inhumation burials and they are all pendants, not diadems (Piette 1998). Therefore, there are no artefacts to which we can relate these motifs. Whatever they may represent, it is not an artefact we can recognise today, nor is it a diadem.

Finally, there are two figures with elaborate hair arrangements on the C38 Capilla I and X95 Lantejuela stelae. These have escaped much comment until now, since they were called diadems or helmets. In fact, they are more likely to be special ways of preparing the hair in plaits or coils, pulled back from the face. From the front they would appear as a series of ridges or dots on the head, which is how they are depicted.

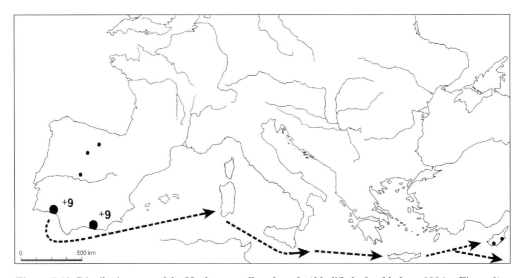

Figure 7.23 *Distribution map of the Huelva type elbow brooch. (Modified after Mederos 1996a: Figure 1)*

8

Placing the Iberian stelae in their European context

8.1   Cultural geography in the Bronze Age

Bronze Age Europe can be divided geographically into areas that share a common cultural tradition expressed in their settlements, artefacts, patterns of hoarding and consuming metal objects and most interesting of all, the common social values. The extension of each area is broadly known (figure 8.1). Regional distinctions and interrelationships are expressed most clearly through the bronze metalwork. The two oldest traditions are in the Aegean and the Carpathian basin, which is sometimes called the Hungarian tradition. Linked to the Hungarian industries are the expansive traditions of the north Alpine region and farther north of them, the bronze industries of the Nordic cultural zone. Together, these three form the core of the Later European Bronze Age, strongly stimulating their neighbours in Atlantic Europe and northern and central Italy. The north Alpine region includes important areas attached to its eastern frontier (the Lausitz culture) and the south-west of France and Catalonia in Spain. There are also distinctive cultural expressions on the Mediterranean islands such as Cyprus and Sardinia and in areas where fieldwork has been less intense, such as the interior of Spain or the Balkans. However, it is apparent that distinctive patterns of behaviour and cultural values emerged in the Carpathian basin by 1700 BC and appear later in central Europe as the Urnfield Tradition, defined by its bronze metalwork and shared practice of cremation burial. In particular, the metalwork and ritual expressed through its manufacture and hoarding, was adopted selectively by the societies living in the Nordic area and along the Atlantic coasts.

By the Late Bronze Age, a lively network of exchanges linked these areas to one another and more importantly, allowed the flow of ideas. Of course, such systems can be traced back for centuries in many regions, but the point is that by the thirteenth century BC the Atlantic region had taken shape and was being drawn more closely into the north Alpine orbit. In this way the common theme of a warrior elite was assimilated by leading Europeans, sharing a panoply of arms and ornaments and probably similar notions of physical beauty. Related cultural practices were developed and shared, including feasting and drinking suites, as well as elaborate ceremonial ornaments (some could be called regalia, without exaggeration) and a shared symbolic imagery (Harrison & Mederos Martín 2000; Sørensen & Thomas 1989). However, there are significant differences. Women enjoyed high status throughout the Hungarian, north Alpine and Nordic zones as shown by their dress fittings and cult objects, but these are missing from the Atlantic tradition, implying that women's status was lower.

Relations with the east Mediterranean world are stronger with south-west Spain than with any other areas of Atlantic Europe, with notable consequences for their history after 750 BC. It seems obvious that different messages are being imparted and received and that they do change with time. It is quite possible to discuss these without slipping into simplifications that gloss this period as one of 'warriors, heroes and gods' and concentrate instead on the shared cognitive elements.

What are the social and geographical scales at which these societies operated? What ideologies would they be likely to share by 1100 BC? A good guide to answering the first question is provided by detailed studies of north Alpine and Nordic metalwork, whose distributions show that organised territories typically covered an area 30–40 square kilometres, or occasionally more and that they were linked by circuits of exchange (and sometimes intermarriage) to their neighbours. These tribal formations ebb and flow repeatedly, at times with dramatic intensity, documenting the concrete histories of their societies. Similar patterns will probably be discovered from central Portugal and south-west Spain, where networks of fortified settlements appear after 1000 BC, articulating the landscape into units of similar size and providing the social focus for its inhabitants (Pavón 1998; Vilaça 1995). Therefore, the social scales look comparable across Europe, with little evidence for larger political groupings such as archaic states, or palatial complexes like the residences of the Mycenaean kings in fourteenth century BC Greece. This modest size corresponds best to tribal organisations, with most people living in villages or dispersed settlements.

Tribal ideologies are often determined by the practical needs of the principal families, who would be their main beneficiaries. These social elites have been studied intensively, with the result that we know quite a lot about the objects they used, their changing tastes and the craftsmen and workshops that produced them. The most obvious examples are the swords (Schauer 1971), shields (Schauer 1980) and bronze armour (Schauer 1978, 1990) and beaten metal vessels (Thrane 1966), to name just a few of the well-studied classes of artefact. Linked to this personal consumption and the patterns of exchange that supplied it, is the distinctive pan-European practice of burying hoards of metal objects. In the Hungarian, north Alpine and Nordic traditions, hoarding occurs sporadically, punctuated by long periods when the practice almost ceased. The chief episodes are the earlier Hallstatt A2/B1 horizons in the eastern Alps, the later Hallstatt B2/B3 hoards in the western Alps and Germany (Furmanek & Horst 1982, 1990) and the contemporary hoards from Scandinavia. These latter peak in Period V, in the ninth–eighth centuries BC (Verlaeckt 2000). In the Atlantic tradition, hoarding reaches a peak at the same time, but shows important variations between lowland England and Germany on one hand (hoards commonest in the eighth century BC) and Galicia, Brittany and south-west France, with the hoard depositions most frequent a century later (Huth 2000, figure 12.7). However, the composition of the hoards varies markedly from one area to another, clearly indicating the

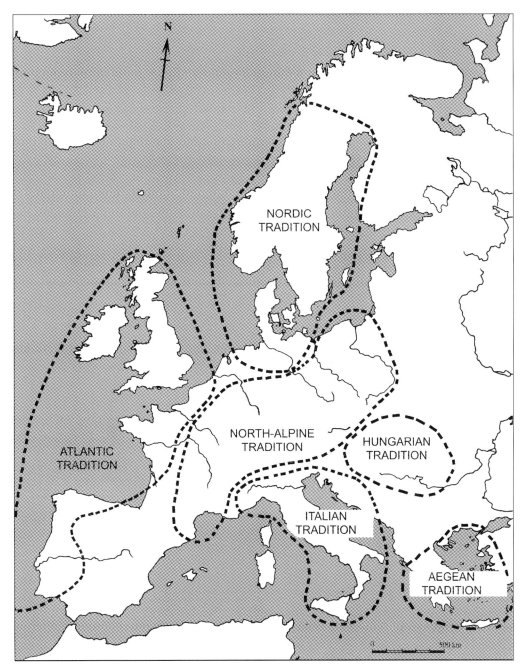

Figure 8.1 *Map of the main regional cultural traditions in Europe from 1200-1000 BC*

ideological autonomy of the societies who were burying the metalwork. Broadly speaking, these episodes alternate with periods when burials prevailed and it is likely that they are ideological alternatives. A variation on this exists in Portugal and Spain, since hoarding characterises some regions but not others, and in the south-west the stelae can be thought of as surrogate burials, using the human image engraved on stone instead of the buried body. Once more the Atlantic tradition is different in that almost no burials are known in any of its provinces from 1250–750 BC. Apparently, the ideological differences were as important as the shared ideas.

8.2   Connections across Europe

The Final Bronze Age of Spain shared many characteristics with the rest of Europe and was always integrated with it. There was, to a considerable degree, a common idiom of power expressed through similar objects and weapons (Kristiansen 1993). Of course, Europe was physically diverse and strongly regionalised, so that the cultural landscapes of the Late Bronze Age have distinctive regional histories, but they can be structured coherently, with the pulses of activity identified in the cycles of expansion and contraction. In part, this is due to the different archaeological sources that are available, with hoards and water finds dominating in some areas, graves in another, waterlogged villages of wooden buildings in the western Alps (from 1060/1050 BC), and the highland landscapes of Dartmoor in England. The stelae from Spain and Portugal provide, at this regional level, a graphic visual example of one warrior aristocracy, documented from its own engraved monuments rather than its artefacts or burials. Individually interesting, these archives gain greatly in explanatory potential when they are considered together and used to supplement one another, through comparison and contrast.

Coordinating these varied sources has never been easy and different scholarly traditions have followed their own paths. Despite that, there is an emerging consensus about some of the social characteristics that define aristocratic behaviour in this period. The selected examples are merely illustrative, but in particular, modern accounts, backed by exciting discoveries in Germany, deserve sharing widely.

It is an error to think that distant regions of Europe were isolated from the main intellectual currents of their times simply because of their physical distance from one another. Many independent strands of evidence show that Europe forged long distance linkages across the seaways, along the Atlantic shores, through the Baltic waters and over all the European landmass, penetrating the Alps and mountains around the Danubian basin with ease (Bouzek 1985). The Scandinavian rock engravings, with hundreds of ships, indicate the number and size of the maritime vessels available (Coles 2001). The Mediterranean was part of this world too, and it is through the long distance voyages made to Cyprus, the Aegean, Sardinia and between Atlantic communities of Ireland or Brittany, that these connections were forged and then kept open. They may have been sporadic and frequently interrupted, but the broad picture is of a continent with an imaginative map of itself that knew, through objects from far away places, that other worlds existed and that they shared values as well as objects (Schauer 1983, 1984, 1985; Sherratt 2000). Since these studies were completed, much has happened.

Stefan Winghart (2002:175) summarised recently some of the spectacular new finds for the decades around 1360 BC from the fortified settlement of Bernstorf (Kr Freising) in Bavaria, dated by dendrochronology. They include regalia of beaten gold sheet (diadem, body ornaments and belt) that probably adorned a wooden image of a deity, for which there are general parallels in the gold ornaments from the Mycenaean shaft graves (however, opinions are divided about the authenticity of two amber beads (perhaps a mask and a seal), inscribed with Linear B signs: see Gebhard & Rieder 2002). This fortified site had wooden walls five metres thick and 1.8 km long, enclosing an area of at least 15 ha (Gebhard 1999). Other signs of eastern Mediterranean contacts can be seen in the remains of at least 16 elegant folding chairs from Denmark and north-west Germany, whose fine workmanship and delicacy identify them as ceremonial pieces, probably inspired by Aegean models (Werner 1987; Thrane 1990). The metal fittings and preserved wooden examples show them to have been exquisite objects. There are even examples of the distinctive ox-hide ingots of copper (traded raw material commonly found in Sardinia, Greece and Cyprus), shown by the four fragments from the hoard of Oberwilfingen (Baden-Württemberg), dated to the Middle Bronze Age period C2 (Primas & Pernicka 1998).

Such discoveries go some way to dispel the rigorously reductive assessment of Anthony Harding in 1984, which found very few authentic documents to link the Aegean and central European worlds in the Bronze Age and judged many to have been over interpreted. The emerging picture restores a missing dimension of elite contacts between the Mycenaean world and the early Urnfields, that had been intuitively suspected as far back as the early 1900s by Oscar Montelius and others, but which had always lacked convincing examples to support it. The site of Bernstorf suggests that many similar fortified elite centres existed in the area and almost certainly had direct links with, and knowledge of, the Greek citadels such as Mycenae, Tiryns and Orchomenos (Bouzek 1985; Winghart 2002).

Other elite objects include early examples of wagon-graves; one ceremonial wagon from Munich-Poing (Upper Bavaria), dated to the early thirteenth century BC, not only contained the vehicle and horse gear, but also symbolic ingot fragments, metal cake and clay nozzles for bellows to heat up a metal furnace (Winghart 1999). These are unmistakeable signs of elite control of metal production and exchange, taken into the grave of the dead chief and which reflect customs followed in the middle Elbe and Oder valleys, where over 20 graves with similar remains are known (Jockenhövel 1990, Abb 10). This idea of connecting the elite directly to the activity of metal production finds a good parallel in Iberia, where sets of weights for measuring commodities, probably tin or other metal, appear on 12 stelae, all of them late examples in the series, dating from the eleventh–ninth centuries

BC. These examples illustrate notions that the warrior elite expected to control metal working and its supply and chose to indicate this in their graves and on their memorials. This is surely part and parcel of the widespread knowledge of Aegean and eastern Mediterranean weight standards that spread across Europe.

Aristocratic control also extended over the fertile grain-growing lands in southern and western Germany, shown symbolically by placing one or two bronze sickles among the grave goods of the sword-wearers (Sperber 1999:609 and note 15). A similar intention to show who really controlled the harvests and owned the land is probably one of the multiple roles performed by erecting warrior stelae in Iberia, giving a regional expression to a widespread type of ownership. Funerary customs (and rituals) were chosen to carry these messages since they linked broad rights of power and possession to one particular man and his family.

Feasting and drinking were other arenas of elite emulation. They figure prominently in high status metalwork from the Atlantic Bronze Age, including Iberia, in the form of bronze cauldrons and various shapes of roasting spits and articulated meat hooks (figures 8.2 and 8.3). In the Atlantic region, distinctive cauldrons were made in each area and the same regionalism is expressed in the designs of the flesh hooks for lifting the boiled meat from the cauldron and in the roasting spits for those regions in Iberia where roasted meat was preferred to the boiled kind. However, in the west there are almost no vessels related to drinking wine, of the sort that characterise the north Alpine and Hungarian areas. In the same wagon grave at Munich-Poing, there is a superb perforated bronze wine strainer, with a complete drinking service of clay bowls. It appears that while feasting and drinking were widespread elite habits, what was actually eaten and drunk, and the artefacts used to present the feast, varied greatly. This is one area of elite behaviour that is not included in the subject matter on the Iberian warrior stelae and is a significant differential mark between this region and other parts of the Atlantic Bronze Age.

8.3   The ideal of the Late Bronze Age warrior

The figure of the armed warrior dominates the European Later Bronze Age. Everywhere he is recognisable through variations on the same theme, as if there was an ideal social type, which was endlessly interpreted and remade to conform to local values and expectations. This was recognised almost half a century ago by Müller-Karpe (1959) in his ground-breaking study of the metalwork north and south of the Alps, and the idea was refined by Schauer (1975), who defined what the weapon suites would have looked like in different regions and how they developed over the period from 1250–750 BC. In the artefact record, weapons, fittings and armour bulk large. There is general agreement that by the early Urnfield period, high status warriors were equipped with sheet bronze armour, probably modelled on that made earlier in the Aegean and captured for us in the image of the plate bronze armour from Dendra (Nauplion, Greece). The weapons were certainly functional and the majority of swords, from all periods and most regions, show signs of being used for cut and thrust combat, with edge damage and re-sharpening visible on their edges (Kristiansen 2002; Osgood & Monks 2000). The spears do not show such obvious traces of use, but there is no reason to doubt that they were also functional weapons, probably for thrusting and stabbing at short range. Many would have been too heavy to throw any distance. Spear designs, like swords, were regional preferences and many British ones ended up in northern France and even Iberia; but their distribution does not closely match that of the other weapons, such as swords or shields (figure 8.4a,b).

This basic fighting equipment was designed for individual combat at close quarters and it is for this reason that armour was developed, at first in leather and later on in bronze. The leather rarely survives, but the pictures of Herzsprung shields from Spain and Portugal and the leather and wooden ones from Ireland, suggest it was once widespread and effective protection (Coles 1962). However, the bronze armour seems to have been functionally distinct. Experiments show that most of it was too delicate to resist a blow from a weapon and that its primary function must have been to display a status or confirm a social role, or to be used in a ceremony, rather than in combat. The evidence from the contexts of bronze armour supports this. Nearly all the metal shields come from hoard or ceremonial contexts in the north Alpine, Nordic and British areas. Shields seem to have been charged with multiple symbolism, as the variety of decorated examples from the Nordic, Alpine and British areas show. Some have birds, solar symbols and multiple ribs, while others carry unique designs. Just as the engravings of the sun boat and its animal familiars on Nordic razors describe the iconography of the Nordic sun cult (Kaul 1998), so could the shields.

Other bronze armour is distributed in a manner that suggests it played a ceremonial and ritual role. Helmets are known throughout the Italian, north Alpine and Hungarian areas; they are rare in Iberia and almost unknown in the British Isles. Body armour also has a distinct distribution, with most pieces coming from hoards and deposits in wet areas from the north Alpine region. Certain patterns emerge. First, there is no complete suite of bronze armour deposited anywhere. The custom and usage was to dedicate a piece (or sometimes two pieces) from the ideal panoply, not the complete set of shield, helmet, cheek pieces, cuirass and greaves. In much of the Atlantic Bronze Age, even single pieces of armour are rare, so that despite the metallic riches represented by axe hoards in northwest Spain, Brittany or Ireland, metal armour is almost never buried there. Another seems to be the reality of armed combat for many warriors. Fighting was in earnest. A third regularity is that individual style in weapons and many other artefacts was specifically created to identify local manufactures and by the same token, express in a material way identity and difference within quite small communities. In these behavioural aspects, the warrior elites of Portugal and Spain were much the same as their contemporaries.

As for the graves of the warrior elite, the sword-wearers, it is time to recognise their

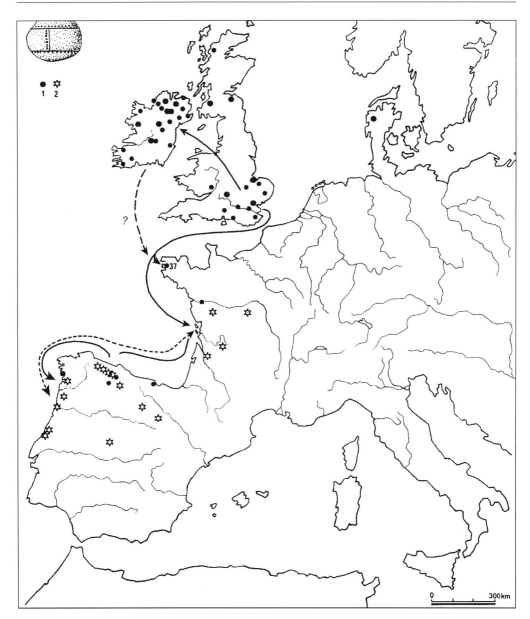

Figure 8.2 *Distribution map of cauldrons for elite feasting in the Atlantic Bronze Age. These examples date between 1200-800 BC. (Modified after Coffyn 1985, Carte 22)*

importance. Although these burials are scarce in the north Alpine area, they are not insignificant. Lothar Sperber's revealing analysis explored the nature and extent of the social variation in these graves, with clear differences between a western area where they were rare (in just 3–8 per cent of cemeteries) and the eastern area, where they occur in

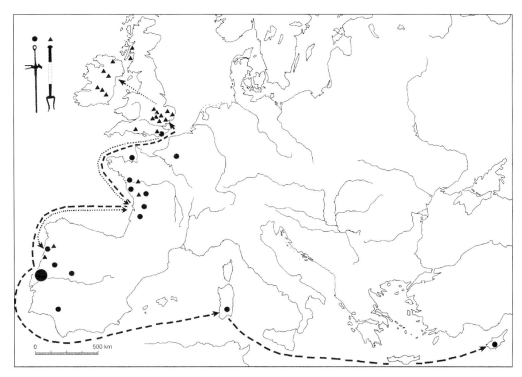

Figure 8.3 *Distribution map of roasting spits (circles) and flesh hooks (triangles), used for elite feasting in the Atlantic Bronze Age. (Modified after Coffyn 1985, Carte 21)*

about 33 per cent of cemeteries (Sperber 1999). In addition, shifting fashions dictate that at some times swords disappeared for almost one and a half centuries, so that swords were actually intermittently buried, even though they continued as symbols of rank. In the east, where the agricultural wealth of the settlements was augmented by control of the abundant production of copper metal from the central Alpine mines, swords were continually buried over a period of 500 years. The custom of burying the elite warrior of each generation is revealed in the cemetery at Volders (North Tyrol), where the graph indicates that for at least 13 generations, successive sword-wearers were honoured in this way (figure 8.5). A closed, self-conscious tradition of old families guarding their privileges, overseeing the rest of the population, can be reconstructed from these graves. More broadly, the rights to power and possessions of this elite were stable, since many cemeteries show centuries of use. As Sperber explains, the north Alpine region was a full landscape, one where possessions increase in importance and land and territory become the essential resource for those in the west, while metal (and probably amber) supplemented those in the east.

The recent excavation, to the best modern standards, of an extraordinary cemetery at Neckarsulm (Kr Heilbronn, Baden-Württemberg) highlights other aspects of the social world of Late Bronze Age warriors of the western group (Neth 2001). The cemetery was fully excavated and contained 33 inhumation burials, with 51 bodies distributed among them. All the bodies were laid out full length, with heads to the south. The graves were placed in neat rows of military precision and respected one another in their regular spacing. Among them were 21 single burials, one grave with five bodies, three graves each with three bodies and eight graves with two bodies; all the deaths in each of the multiple burials

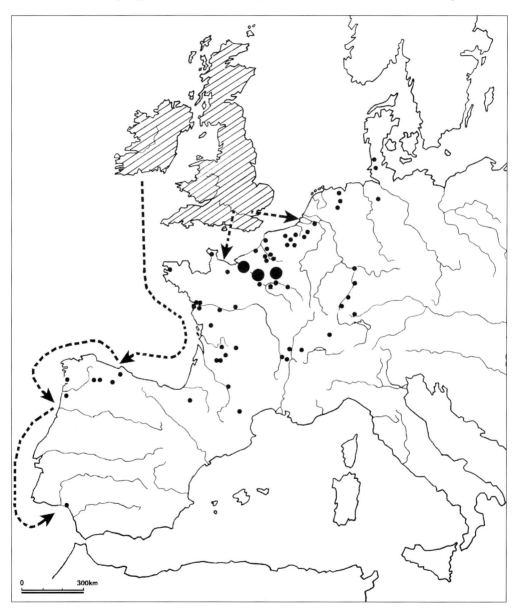

Figure 8.4a *Distribution of bronze socketed spearheads of British types in the Late Bronze Age. (Modified after Coffyn 1985, Carte 17)*

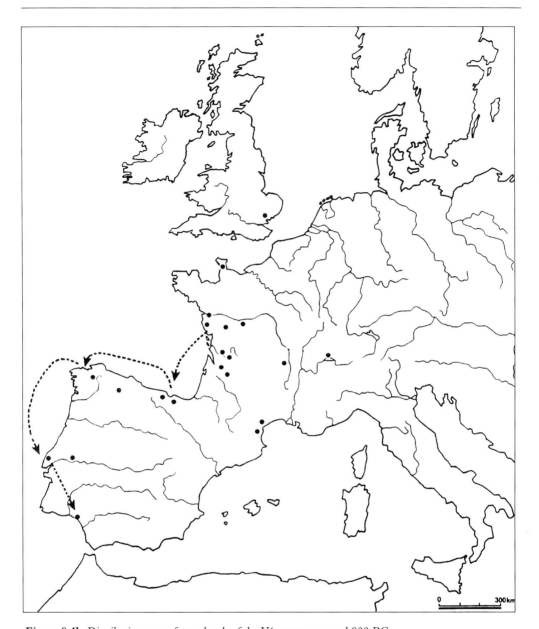

Figure 8.4b *Distribution map of spearheads of the Vénat type, around 800 BC*

had taken place at the same time, suggesting that some people had been killed deliberately in order to accompany others who had died. The grave goods were not those usually
found in Urnfields; there were no pottery services in any grave and the standard gifts were
reduced to one bronze pin and one very fine and delicate pottery vessel for each grave. The
chiefly graves, at the pinnacle of the social hierarchy, were the three with swords. These all

lay at the east end of the cemetery; two of them were double inhumations and the third was a triple inhumation. The date must be between 1330–1250 BC (Bronze D), judging by the rod-tanged swords and other metalwork. In addition to the unique burial customs and grave goods from Neckarsulm, there are important anthropological results from the preliminary autopsy. There are no children, juveniles or old people. The body size (calculated from the length of the skeletons in their graves) was remarkable too, and most were between 1.65 to over 1.8 m tall. Most are male and, despite their unusual height, they were not heavily mus-cled. Indeed, they all show an excellent level of health, nutrition and dental hygiene, with only one tooth in nine skeletons showing a sign of decay (Wahl 2001). It is perfectly rea-sonable to agree with Andrea Neth and interpret this cemetery as belonging to an upper stratum of Late Bronze Age society, well fed and cared for, physically larger and healthier than other people, who were the Urnfield warrior class. Neckarsulm is indeed one of the most important discoveries for understanding Bronze Age Europe, since it provides the clearest evidence for a warrior elite, of a kind compatible with a tribal society and serves to corroborate the idea of personal beauty and an exceptional physique. The sinister, multiple burials may indicate human sacrifice.

Warrior elites like this do not always leave such unambiguous traces. However, the ideals could be worked out in any number of combinations, with the reality of power dis-played through warrior images in Iberia, graves like those in southern Germany and Austria, or through ritualised depositions. The ideal of a warrior, represented through physical attributes and a notion of personal beauty, is entirely congruent with the pan-European weaponry and armour.

8.4   Invisible heroes

The warrior ideology is expressed through locally approved idioms, but nowhere can the person of a hero, or social institution connected with him, be recognised unambiguously in the Late Bronze Age. For years, writers on Bronze Age Europe have used the term 'hero' loosely, as a convenient synonym for almost any well-furnished warrior grave, or grand piece of equipment, so that by stages, the idea that there really was once a social institu-tion of the hero defined by status, deeds and myths, has become a commonplace. Bronze Age 'heroes' sound right and it seems wrong to challenge what is apparently obvious. But the idea of a hero, as known from Ugaritic, Aegean and finally Archaic Greek sources, is more complicated ideologically than this. The Greek hero cults make claims to connect the eighth century world with ancestors of great antiquity and it is plausible to view this as an aristocratic reaction to the foundation of the state in Attica, a deliberate invention of tra-ditions. The religious and mythical elements that attend the creation of a hero and serve to maintain his memory, need to feed on more than the martial spirit of a famous warrior (Whitley 1995, 2001:150–156; Shanks 1999). It is at this point that the documents from

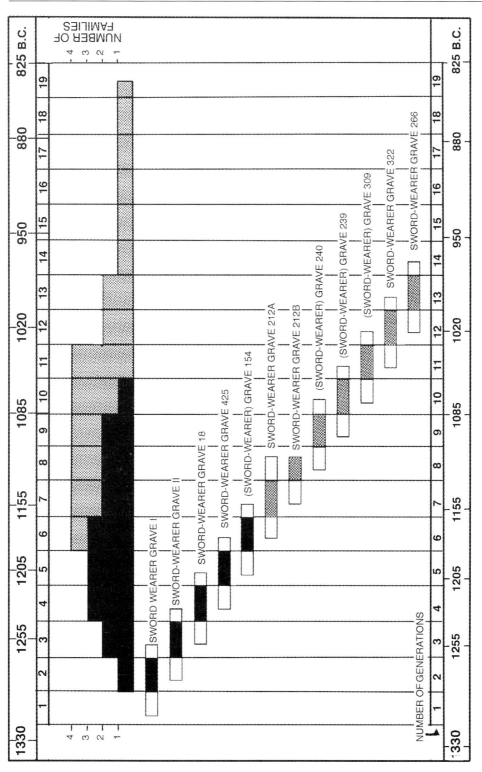

Figure 8.5 *Chronological chart of the graves of the sword-wearing elite, excavated from the cemetery of Volders. The chart has the calendar dates BC across the top. The vertical columns numbered 1–19 represent 19 successive generations of 'sword wearers' ('Schwertträger'), identified by their grave number in the Volders cemetery. (Modified after Sperber 1999: Abb 21)*

prehistoric Europe fail to authenticate the status of any warrior as a hero. There are many Scandinavian scenes showing rituals; sun cults are reasonably well known; and warrior elites existed everywhere. All this existed in embryo from the Early Bronze Age c 1700 BC; but none of it actually defines a hero. Despite the tantalising glimpses of regalia, of burials with accompanying human sacrifices and the horned figures on the stelae, it has to be accepted that ideologies identified with heroes, if they had ever existed, must have been generalised and lacking in materialisation.

In the Early Iron Age (Hallstatt D: 625–475/450 BC), the picture changes with a quantitative and qualitative evolution in the scale of sumptuary magnificence of the social elite. Their large fortified *Fürstensitze* and colossal burials, do seem to be the settings that are adequate for a heroic ideology to take root, much more so than in the relatively small-scale, tribal societies of the Late Bronze Age. At this point we leave the Bronze Age world entirely and enter that of the new archaic states, spectacular in both their expansion and decline.

9

Summary

The cognitive aspects of Bronze Age life, revealed through images made on stone stelae, are the subjects of this study. These engravings are graphic, using pictorial language to express social values held not just in Spain or Portugal, but also throughout much of the Mediterranean and Atlantic Europe. Their most unusual feature is that they are single pictures, dedicated to the memory of one individual, which gives them a coherent intellectual context and which allows exploration of the minds of their engravers and the people who viewed them. Rarely does such a treasure-trove of well-preserved ideas survive. Making the most of this opportunity, this study examined the manner in which they were engraved and considered how the compositions met challenges from their ideological rivals over time, and their likely meaning. The clues were in the images themselves, since any changes made on stone surfaces are almost indelible. Once the authority of the readings of individual compositions was established, they became intelligible as part of a larger ideological world.

A particular life-style develops in the European Bronze Age, one recognisable in its martial ideals and in the importance accorded to the role of individual men; the period is marked also by cycles of economic expansion and contraction, as competing chiefdoms grow, then fade. A barbarian world can be seen emerging in a recognisably self-conscious form, with an ideological code expressed symbolically in engravings of shields and armed men, supported by a panoply of luxuries like chariots and mirrors. The social processes behind this ideology express a world-view that was current throughout Europe and much of the Mediterranean in the second millennium BC and for almost a millennium resisted pressures to create the archaic states like those in the Aegean and Cyprus. Europe maintained complex chiefdoms for the whole of the Bronze Age. This study uses the contemporary Bronze Age images of weapons and warriors to propose an argument to explain how a particular ideology becomes dominant, moulding new life-styles to existing social practices. Understanding the nature of power, expressed through images as well as artefacts, the development of a specific iconic representation and the creation of an Atlantic Bronze Age world-view, are the purposes of this study.

It opens with a general discussion of Bronze Age Europe in Chapter 1, the rise of the individual life-style for leading men and the manner in which artefacts, like stelae and metal weapons and ornaments, were created in order to make it concrete. The act of materialising the ideology is essential for its maintenance and propagation. Setting up statues and stelae was a frequent practice between the fourth and first millennia BC. The human body was used to symbolise different meanings to different communities. The warrior stelae of the

Final Bronze Age are individual monuments erected between 1250–750 BC in southern Portugal and south-west Spain. They represent individual men and real objects; later on, some individuals may claim the status of a 'hero' through extraordinary attributes.

Chapter 2 places the warrior stelae in a wider archaeological setting and establishes them as defining a province of the Atlantic Bronze Age. The idea of the Atlantic Bronze Age as a linked network of independent communities stretching right across the British Isles, France and western Iberia is explained. The stelae are uniquely interesting since their pictorial compositions express the coded values common to all of it, not just one region, so the conclusions derived from their study should be widely applicable. Long distance exchanges between the eastern Mediterranean, Sardinia and Iberia on one hand and Europe as far as Ireland on the other, certainly existed from the thirteenth century BC. The absolute chronology followed here is based on the central European master sequence of tree-ring dates, expressed in calendar years. The entire cultural phenomenon is placed firmly in the Final Bronze Age and precedes the far-western Phoenician settlements of the ninth century BC.

Chapter 3 presents the geographical setting in which stelae are found and discusses the distinctive savanna landscape of Extremadura known as the *dehesa* and the extensive farming and ranching economies of the Bronze Age in this area. These distinctive landscapes are explained as cultural creations and perceptions. The Mediterranean climate, forest ecology and environmental evolution of south-west Iberia are explained through new data. There are modern arguments that stelae 'sign the landscape' and act as territorial markers of possession placed at boundaries, but after discussing these, it is clear that they are more complex and are actually pluri-vocal monuments. That is, they have multiple functions, including marking burials, identifying individuals with a landscape, organising territories, competing with neighbouring elites and perhaps making claims to 'heroic' status. Stelae developed from funerary markers and retain important elements of that symbolism until the end of their period of use. All these functions are linked by the shared ideology and world-view that evolves over the centuries. Originally, there must have been between one and two thousand stelae erected. They were not rarities in the cultural landscape.

Chapter 4 presents the stelae as artefacts. They cluster in four geographical zones: Zone I the Sierra de Gata; Zone II the Tagus Valley-Sierra de Montánchez; Zone III the Guadiana Valley and its tributary the Zújar river valley; Zone IV the Guadalquivir Valley. Very few stelae are in their original contexts and only eight have a prehistoric context at all. However, there is evidence for their use as grave markers in at least two cases and many were originally set upright in the ground. They are likely to represent dead individuals, whose bodies were consumed through exposure to natural processes, without leaving any trace, following similar customs at this time in western France and the British Isles.

One important novelty in this analysis derives from close observation of stelae. Many published descriptions are critically mistaken. From fresh examinations, it is evident that not all the stelae are pictures made at one moment and fixed forever in stone, but are monuments that were often re-cut, corrected, added to, engraved a second time, defaced, re-used in later grave settings and so on. In all, 27 of the 103 stelae in this study were modified. At least six stelae were re-cut; another eight have corrections to their motifs and five more had motifs added to them. This activity on 19 stelae took place in the Final Bronze Age. Transforming the original compositions was an important activity that goes beyond making corrections or performing acts of deliberate cultural vandalism; it goes to the heart of how stelae were seen and functioned as ideological markers in Bronze Age societies.

From these data, it is clear that embedded in the surface of the stelae is a physical stratigraphy that allows one to construct an accurate chronological sequence of motifs and compositions. In turn, this strongly supports an evolutionary model for the developing ideology over a period of at least 400 or 500 years, which covers all the Final Bronze Age in western Europe. The stelae bear compositions in which the motifs are arranged in a formal aesthetic that changes over time. There is a single code that evolves from basic compositions of shield, sword and spear, to ones with mirrors and chariots and finally to compositions dominated by human figures. A single process is at work, developing an iconic language of power based on actual Bronze Age artefacts. About 35 different types of object and human figure occur, and it is notable that new discoveries of stelae in the last 10 years provide further examples of motifs already known, but not wholly new classes. This suggests there is now a valid sample of the original motifs.

Weapons and the male image are the dominant themes. Striking are the subjects that are ignored completely, what is called here 'a code of exclusions'. Astonishingly, no female representations occur; there is no feasting equipment either, and entire classes of bronze artefacts like tools, and the domestic domain represented by fine garments and skins, are also missing. Even the imported ideas from the eastern Mediterranean world are strictly limited to a brooch, mirror, lyre and chariot. The iconographic themes also exclude the natural world, and that of animals, from any protagonism. These observations show that social closure operated at several levels and that the motifs on the stelae were explicitly selected to represent a narrow range of ideas that supported one world-view. Since the stelae had a commemorative and funerary role, it is likely that this distorts the world-view.

Working out the consequences of the evolving ideology is done in Chapter 5. This chapter discusses the anthropological theories of Timothy Earle in relation to the evolution of Bronze Age Europe and applies them specifically to the Atlantic Bronze Age and the commemorative stelae and demonstrates how a theory of materialisation accounts for the actual data on the ground. Stelae materialise a chiefly ideology and evolve to meet challenges to its authority. The re-cutting of stelae and the stylistic evolution of the compositions are probably a direct response to these challenges, using normative objects familiar to the Bronze Age observer.

Chapters 6 and 7 form a pair using complementary analytical approaches. The comparative method as a heuristic tool is explained. In Chapter 6, the composition sequence from basic to figurative scenes is explored systematically. First, the evolutionary sequence is established from internal evidence derived from the engravings and their re-cuttings, supported by a type-sequence where the compositions are arranged in order of ascending complexity. It is clear that the full compositions are developed in a piecemeal fashion, with elements being added one at a time, not in packages. This observation is important since it demonstrates that the evolution of the compositions follows the logic of a single, evolving code in which the decisions of what to include or exclude are being made by the social elites in Bronze Age Iberia. This eclecticism is maintained to the end of the Final Bronze Age. The full panoply develops gradually. Many elements are west European in origin, including all the early ones such as the round shields, simple spears and most of the sword types, from the Rosnoën and leaf-shaped ones, to the later Carp's Tongue weapons. Equally important are the eastern Mediterranean motifs, such as brooches, chariots, mirrors and musical instruments. It is clear that the lyre and mirror are the first motifs to be added to the basic compositions and that the chariot appears later. There are at least 25 chariots, 41 or 42 mirrors and five or six lyres. The chariots are types known in the Mycenaean world, with the prominent handles projecting from their bodies, and the mirrors vary from simple ones to elaborate shapes with handles and tassels. The horned men bear horns that emerge from their heads and do not appear to be part of helmets. One interpretation is that they may be 'heroes', or divinised ancestors, rather than deities, although the divine personality may not be excluded in all cases.

The oldest compositions are the basic ones with the warrior panoply and this has just three elements: a big shield in the centre and a spear and sword above and below it. Then a lyre or a mirror is added, followed by these artefacts in order of historical appearance: brooch and helmet, comb, chariot and the bow and arrow. This creates the fully panoply of weapons and dress ornaments. The figurative compositions with human beings evolve in four successive stages after this, and the warrior himself replaces the shield, which formerly dominated the composition. Stage I has the human figure as a marginal motif to the shield; Stage II has the human figure as a central motif but the shield is still present; Stage III has the human figure as the central motif without a shield and Stage IV has several compositions which may be contemporary, scenes with paired figures, horned figures, ones with headdresses (*diademadas*) and the warriors in narrative scenes.

The links with the east Mediterranean are through the islands of Sicily and Sardinia, to the Aegean, Cyprus and then to the Syrian coast. This linkage is physical, marked by trade and distribution of bronzes, and ideological in that a range of shared symbols and values exists. There are textual accounts from the thirteenth–twelfth centuries BC in Ugarit that describe the accoutrements of warriors, why they need and use chariots and what their roles are as 'heroes' and defenders of their tribes after death. The masculine iconographic code emerges swiftly, enriched by mirrors (perhaps acting as talismans) and toilet articles that express the life-style of the warrior and his need to be groomed and man-icured. 'Hero' cults arose in Syria in the third millennium BC and may well have been part of the ideological beliefs adopted in the far west, along with the chariots and horned human figures that may serve to define them.

Marshalling the archaeological evidence in Chapter 7 demonstrates that the objects carved on the stelae were real things, not imaginary objects of desire beyond the reach of Iberian chiefs. Of the 14 categories of objects, the commonest are the shields (71 exam-ples), mirrors (about 42) and swords (37). The results of this survey, which is illustrative rather than exhaustive, is to show that all the objects were known in the Final Bronze Age and that there is a broad, and at times quite close, correspondence between the engraved motif and the shape and decoration of the real object. It is now accepted that the shields depicted must be of leather or wood, like those from the Irish mires, and they can be traced back to Atlantic prototypes current by 1300 BC. The 71 shields are the largest single group of this armour in Bronze Age Europe. The sword typology includes recognisable types known in bronze, as well as several that are unique, or whose classification is impossible. It is notable that the commonest swords, with cross-shaped handles and related to the Carp's Tongue class, are rare in Iberia, although well known on Sardinia. Mirrors are known from an early date (at least by the thirteenth century BC) in Sicily and on the Balearic islands, but are not found in mainland Iberia until the eighth century BC. The chariots are all remarkably similar to one another in their depiction and technical details (there are no four-wheeled vehicles) and are probably based on the models current in the Aegean, from the thirteenth century. The lyres are poorly drawn, but the best one from Luna (C93) is related to the Mycenaean models, not the ones of later date. Combs are com-mon motifs (21) and a wide range of parallels for them can be found in the second millennium, in Iberia and across the Mediterranean.

Through the centuries, the human body is used as a social metaphor in different ways. In the Final Bronze Age, in Iberia just as in Ireland or France, burials are almost unknown and clearly the overwhelming majority of bodies were exposed to the elements until they were completely absorbed. It is therefore exceptionally interesting to note how rapidly this cultural practice was reversed in Iberia, beginning around 800–775 BC, when human bur-ial returned to fashion. After this date, almost no stelae were erected and the ideological focus moves from images of the body, to actual bodies placed in graves. The change is so swift and so complete that by 750 BC, almost everyone in the social elite used burial as the focus of their ideology and the fashion for large mounds over the richest graves returns. In my view, this ideological change does not signal a rupture with previous elite groups, but is more likely to reflect their desire to follow Mediterranean customs. From this time onwards the social pressures, visible in the Orientalising processes of capital accumulation and new trading monopolies, propelled the Bronze Age chiefdoms towards new political formations, which led eventually to the archaic states like Tartessos. Those processes were stimulated in large measure by contacts with the Phoenician world and led to the complete disappearance of the Bronze Age life-styles within a few generations.

The concluding Chapter 8 is a wide-ranging synthesis, integrating the stelae of Iberia in the wider picture of the Final Bronze Age in Europe. After explaining the main elements of the cultural geography of Europe around 1000 BC, there is an account of the interconnectivity of the continent, stressing the permeability of all areas to novel ideas and innovations and illustrating this point with new discoveries. One mechanism that promoted this interconnectivity was the shared ideal of what a warrior elite should be, how it should look, dress, feast, behave and fight. Warrior elites expressed themselves in different guises according to their own fashions, so these can be recognised in special suites of artefacts, graves of sword-wearers such as Neckarsulm and Volders, and monuments like the Iberian stelae. These values and mental templates imply that there was a significant degree of cultural affinity over great distances, as the Bronze Age elites shared ideas rather than objects. Iberia was not a marginalised region on the remote confines of western Europe, but an integrated participant in the principal cultural fashions and ideology of the time. Finally, it is recognised that the evidence for 'heroic' beliefs is ambiguous and at best diffuse and generalised.

Illustrated catalogue of stelae

C13 BROZAS, Ca, p 206
Photograph courtesy of F Marco Simón

10

Illustrated catalogue of stelae

All those warrior stelae known to me in May 2002 are included in this catalogue. For convenience, it follows the number sequence established by Celestino in 2001, with the prefix C to indicate an example in his list. The asterisk ★ indicates a stela seen and checked against the figure in the survey conducted in the years 2000–2002. Regions of Spain referred to in the catalogue are abbreviated as follows: Toledo, To; Badajoz, Ba; Córdoba, Co; Cáceres, Ca; Málaga, Ma; Lérida, Le; Sevilla, Se.

The descriptions try to present an unambiguous reading of the engraved motifs, but on many stelae this ideal is impossible to attain, because surfaces have eroded, or the original engraving was too light to leave clear traces, or because the motif itself was badly drawn and executed. Some coarse-grained rocks, like sandstone, gneiss or granite are difficult to engrave with any clarity and stelae made from them are always going to be hard to read; the examples of C17 Santa Ana and C19 Robledillo de Trujillo illustrate this problem. Modern damage also obscures fine details, as on the limestone stela from C80 Ategua. These add a margin of error to the work. Consequently, rather than adjudicate in every case between two or more different observations made on the same stela and present my reading as the best one, I chose to emphasise the divergence of views and for that reason show two, or even three, versions of the same stela on one figure (for example C71 Setefilla). This allows the reader to judge the difference and take a view as to which interpretation to use. However, my preferences are explained and I refer the reader to an accurate published photograph, or include a new one. Where a stela has been re-engraved, each stage of the engraving is shown separately and numbered.

The figures include the most accurate published ones, all modified for publication in this volume, and they are compared against the original stelae whenever this has been possible. References are given to the original illustrations. A total of 45 stelae were seen and compared directly with the published illustrations, so the sample comprises 48 per cent of the total 93 warrior stelae. A second drawing numbers the motifs for reference.

Engraving technique is an important characteristic, varying across regions and through time, so it must be shown on the drawings. The following conventions describe engraving techniques in all the figures:

- *background with a pale grey tone* indicates that the surface has been pecked evenly to a level finish before the motifs were engraved
- *background with dark tone* indicates that the surface has been pecked away, leaving the motifs standing above the level of the stela, in relief (only seen on the C4 Baraçal stela)
- *solid black motif* indicates the intaglio technique whereby the shape of the motif is pecked away to make it lie below the surface of the stela

- *pale grey tone in a motif* indicates that the surface of the motif was pecked all over to make a distinct texture, to accent its shape and volume
- *plain white motif* indicates a motif without any treatment of its interior
- *single line* indicates a single engraved line
- *double line* indicates an especially wide or deeply engraved line that may be emphasised by secondary smoothing, or (more rarely) a motif that has a double line of engraving to emphasise its outline.

There is no true surface polishing, nor traces of colour on any stela. The sample confirms about 80 per cent of the readings in the most complete stelae catalogue (Celestino 2001); the differences are chiefly in the specific detail of some motifs.

A few related stelae (X95–X98) are included for comparison, which do not belong to the series, but share elements with it. All these are prefixed with an X.

Seven other stelae are listed as known to exist, but are not yet published (X99–X105).

1 Catalogue number and findspot: **C1 SAN MARTÍN DE TREVEJO, Ca**

2 Circumstances of discovery, context and present location

The landowner found it in 1981 when clearing stones with a tractor. The stela was uncovered on a small knoll, which in turn lies in the foothills of the hill of La Manta, which rises to 865 m altitude. This area lies at a high altitude and the countryside of granite hills is suitable only for grazing and woodland.

Deposited in the bar called the 'Plaza de España', in the village of San Martín de Trevejo.

3 Stone type, size and condition of the monument

Granite, measuring 1.2 m high, 0.78 m wide and 0.21 m thick; complete. The surface has eroded and the area on the upper right has exfoliated, damaging the shield motif.

4 Composition and motifs

A basic composition of (1) spear, (2) shield (3) sword and (4) mirror. Motif 5 may be natural, or later scratches. The motifs were pecked first and polished afterwards for emphasis.

5 Commentary

The original drawing by García de Figuerola was published the wrong way round. The V-notched shield belongs to Type IA, with four concentric rings, a rectangular handle and no decoration. The sword is shown with a rectangular hilt, on which Celestino identifies four rivets, but these are invisible on the published photograph and not marked on Celestino's own drawing. The sword blade is a leaf-shaped one, belonging to Group A. The mirror is depicted in simple outline.

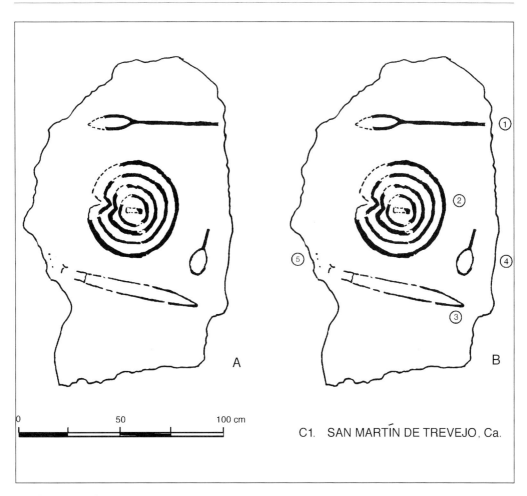

A

B

0   50   100 cm

C1. SAN MARTÍN DE TREVEJO, Ca.

6 Bibliography

See: Celestino 2001:324; García de Figuerola 1982 (figure 1, with poor photograph).

1 Catalogue number and findspot: **C2 HERNÁN PÉREZ, Ca**

2 Circumstances of discovery, context and present location

Almagro Basch (1972:91, 93) says the fragment of the warrior stela was found in 1971, piled up loosely with five other stelae, which were of the older anthropomorphic *Diademada* types of the third millennium BC (he numbered them III–VII). He did not believe that large stone slabs found nearby were from cists marked by stelae and he discounted the circumstantial account of discovery made by one workman who said most of them had been upright when they first saw them in the woodlands. A detailed site visit found everything so churned up and scattered by the deep ploughing that was done before planting saplings, that no signs of any cists or burials could be recognised.

The area is best thought of as an enormous natural amphitheatre with the Sierra de Gata behind it and in the foothills are the headwaters of a stream called Las Helechosas (the area of ferns). The actual findspot is in a hollow in a savanna landscape formerly reserved for cattle pastures that was being planted with pine trees.

Deposited in the Museo Arqueológico Nacional, Madrid.

3 Stone type, size and condition of the monument

Compact black slate, measuring 0.81 m high, 0.35 m wide on average, with an average thickness of 0.20 m. It is a fragment of a larger stela, conserving the lower third of its original surface. The rest has flaked away.

4 Description of the composition and motifs

It bears a simple composition of (1) shield and (2) sword. The motifs are engraved with deep, wide incisions.

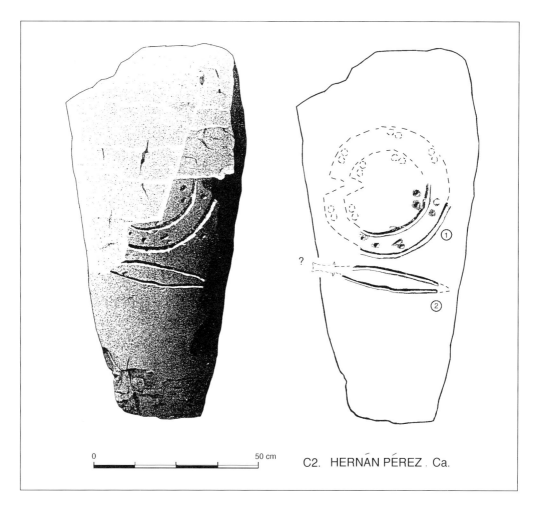

0   50 cm   C2. HERNÁN PÉREZ . Ca.

5 Commentary

Almagro devoted considerable attention to the question of context for this stela and the other seven Copper Age ones found with it and concluded, rather sadly, that any idea that they were once burials in rectangular cists was '... only hypothetical and very uncertain' (Almagro 1972:93). However, there are two fourth millennium BC megalithic tombs near-by and it seems probable that they are linked to the older images.

I suggest the shield was originally a V-notched one of Type IB, with at least two concentric rings and decorative bosses arranged in pairs (or perhaps a triplet alternating with a pair) evenly spaced on the inside of the shield. The handle is missing. The sword blade is wide and leaf shaped and belongs to Group B. The reconstruction is similar to the C4 Baraçal sword hilt. The composition lacks the typical spear, which was probably engraved above the shield.

6 Bibliography

See: Almagro Basch 1972, figure 10; 1974 (photograph on figure 13); Bueno-Ramirez 1995; Celestino 2001:325.

1 Catalogue number and findspot: **C3 MEIMÃO, Castelo Branco, Beira Baja, Portugal**

2 Circumstances of discovery, context and present location

This stela was a casual discovery during agricultural work, on a hill called the Cabeça Gorda, which is part of the Sierra de la Malcata. The abrupt landscape is formed of slate and schist, with notable deposits of copper and tin minerals nearby. The findspot is 9 km from the stela of C4 Baraçal.

Deposited in the Museu Diocesano, Porto.

3 Stone type, size and condition of the monument

The stela is made of badly preserved schist and measures 0.83 m high, 0.69 m wide and a maximum thickness of 0.18 m. It is broken and probably only half its original size.

4 Description of the composition and motifs

It bears a basic composition of shield, sword and spear. The engraver made shallow pecked outlines that were smoothed afterwards.

5 Commentary

I suggest the shield was originally a V-notched one of Type IB, with four concentric rings, decorative bosses arranged in groups of three inside the second and third rings and traces of a rectangular handle. The sword has a long, slightly triangular-shaped blade and belongs in Group A, of swords engraved in outline. The blade shape seems a very early one, probably of Middle Bronze Age date, similar to one from Tucela (Forcas, Orense). The

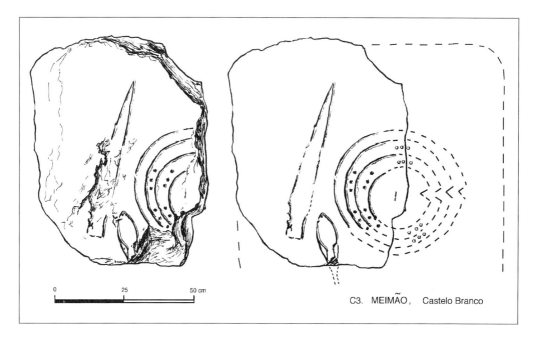

C3. MEIMÃO,   Castelo Branco

drawing is based on Almagro Basch's figure 32 and does not show the square sword hilt that Celestino describes, since it is not visible in his very clear photograph of this stela. The spearhead may have been re-cut, to replace an original large spearhead with a smaller, stubbier one.

6 Bibliography

See: Almagro Basch 1966 (figure 32 and Lám XXVII); Celestino 2001:326; Coffyn 1985 (Planche II/1 for the Forcas sword).

1 Catalogue number and findspot: **C4 BARAÇAL, Sabugal, Beira Alta, Portugal**

2 Circumstances of discovery, context and present location

The stela was found re-used to pave a lane outside the village. The findspot is 9 km from that of Meimão and only 2 km from the stela of C5 Fóios.

Deposited in the Museu Municipal, Sabugal.

3 Stone type, size and condition of the monument

It is made on a block of fine textured grey granite and measures 1.55 m high and a maximum of 0.83 m wide and an average thickness of 30 cm. The stela is complete and in good condition.

4 Description of the composition and motifs

It bears a simple composition of (1) spear, (2) shield and (3) sword. The motifs have been

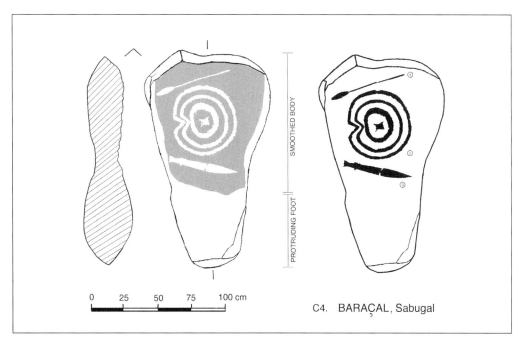

C4. BARAÇAL, Sabugal

carved in low relief by laboriously pecking away the background to make them stand out clearly. The shape of the stela enhances the composition by approximating the volume and outline of a human body, with a flat upper section for the decoration and a protruding foot to embed in the ground.

5 Commentary

This is an elegant monument that makes an immediate visual impact with its clear motifs and strong composition. The shield is a V-notched one of Type IA, with three rings (two with V notches) and a rectangular handle. The sword has a broad leaf-shaped blade and large rectangular hilt with clear guards. It belongs to Group B. The technique of relief carving is unique in the series of warrior stelae, but commonly used for decorating the older Middle Bronze Age stelae in the Alemtejo region of southern Portugal. This detail suggests that the early basic stelae developed from them.

6 Bibliography

See: Celestino 2001:327; Curado 1984 (figures 2 and 3, with photographs).

1 Catalogue number and findspot: **C5 FÓIOS, Sabugal, Beira Alta, Portugal**

2 Circumstances of discovery, context and present location

The stela was found in the 1930s buried in the ground on the estate called Las Eiras. The findspot is 2 km from Baraçal and 12 km to the east is the stela of C1 San Martín de Trevejo.

3 Stone type, size and condition of the monument

The stela is of well preserved, micaceous schist and measures 0.95 m high, 0.64 m average width and 0.08 m thick. Despite some edge damage and surface spalling it is substantially complete.

Deposited in the house of D Jose Ramos Pacheco, in the village of Fóios.

4 Description of the composition and motifs

It bears a simple composition of (1) spear, (2) shield and (3) sword, with (4) an unclear motif, or two natural scratches. The motifs were engraved using a fine point that made deep pecking marks, which gives a well-defined outline.

5 Commentary

The V-notched shield is of Type IA with four concentric rings, two of them with notches and a prominent rectangular handle. Note that this shield and the one from C83 Cordoba, are the only ones to show the handles perpendicular to the notch rather than parallel with it (see also figure 7.1). The sword had a long parallel-sided blade with four rivets set in a rectangle in the hilt; this form distinguishes the Rosnoën type of sword and is placed in Group A. The sword has attachments for a belt or a baldric (not shown on Celestino's drawing). The drawing is based on the figure in Curado (1986), since the details correspond closely to those visible on the photograph, but motif (4) seems to be later scratches, not a fourth object.

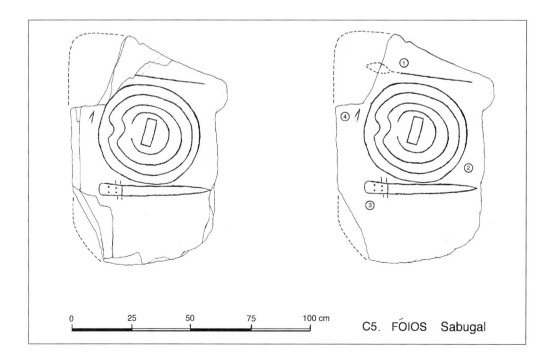

0   25   50   75   100 cm

C5. FÓIOS   Sabugal

The cluster of simple basic stelae C1 to C5 in this remote, hilly region with its grazing lands and copper and tin resources is noteworthy.

6 Bibliography

See: Celestino 2001:328; Curado 1986 (figure 1 and photograph on figure 2).

1 Catalogue number and findspot: **C6 TORREJÓN EL RUBIO I, Ca★**

2 Circumstances of discovery, context and present location

This stela, and a second one described in the next entry (C7), was discovered in 1949 on the estate of El Oreganal, 1.5 km north of the village of Torrejón el Rubio. The findspot lies near an important ford across the river Tagus, which is dangerous to cross since it runs swiftly in deep gorges for much of its course. Medieval drove-ways for sheep and modern main roads nearby indicate the strategic importance of the place as a good natural route between the Extremadura and the Meseta.

Deposited in the Museo Arqueológico Provincial de Cáceres.

3 Stone type, size and condition of the monument

The stela is of dark grey slate and measures 1.22 m high, 0.75 m wide and from 0.10 to 0.14 m thick. It is complete.

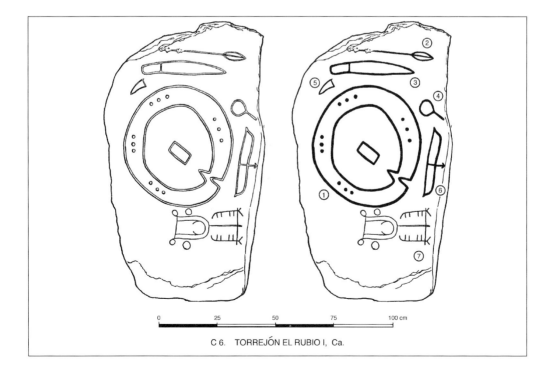

C 6.   TORREJÓN EL RUBIO I, Ca.

4 Description of the composition and motifs

It bears a basic composition, which focuses on the (1) shield, (2) spear and (3) sword, with four additional motifs. These are a (4) mirror, (5) brooch, (6) bow and arrow and (7) a chariot. All motifs, except the chariot, are deeply engraved in outline. The chariot is engraved with shallower and lighter incisions, as can be seen in the photograph published by Almagro Basch in 1966 and on the drawing.

5 Commentary

This is a striking and well-proportioned monument. The drawing is based on Almagro Basch's figure. The V-notched shield has two concentric notched rings, four triple boss ornaments evenly spaced and a big rectangular handle like Fóios. It is of Type IB. The sword has a broad leaf-shaped blade and a rectangular handle. The brooch is an elbow fibula in Group B; we could not see the spring that Celestino shows. The chariot is more lightly engraved than the other motifs and one possible reason for this is that it was engraved after the rest of the motifs had been completed. Adding motifs later is known from other stelae, such as C13 Brozas. Celestino depicts its wheels with spokes and an empty chariot body.

6 Bibliography

See: Almagro Basch 1966 (figure 26 and Lám XXI); Celestino 2001:329.

---

1 Catalogue number and findspot: **C7 TORREJÓN EL RUBIO II, Ca★**

2 Circumstances of discovery, context and present location

This stela was discovered in 1949 on the estate of El Oreganal, together with stela C6. The discovery details are identical.

Deposited in the Museo Arqueológico Provincial de Cáceres.

3 Stone type, size and condition of the monument

The stela is made on a dark grey slate or schist rock, measuring 0.89 m high, 0.48 m maximum width and 0.09 m thick. It is substantially intact, but the edges are heavily damaged and parts of the surface with motifs have flaked off.

4 Description of the composition and motifs

The human figure wears a striking headdress or diadem and the stela belongs to the class of figurative compositions with *Diademadas*. The composition centres on the human figure which is 0.69 m high, with a body shown with some volume (1) and wearing a decorated belt (4). Several lines were incised to get the required body shape and volume and these mistakes show as ghosts on the right hand side. The head is a large circle, with the face shown in its most basic form; the legs and arms curve away from the body; the hands are emphasised with each finger engraved separately, but the feet are not engraved (they may have been lost when the base of the stela was damaged). Spalling of the stone surface has removed most of the right hand. The headdress is clearly separate from the head and tied beneath the chin with two cords. This very large object has two identical layers to it and is divided into 27 equal rectangles. This compares well with a similar headdress on the C38 Capilla I stela where the headdress had 26 compartments. The other motifs are (2) a brooch and (3) a comb. There are no weapons and no shield.

The engraving technique of pecking then smoothing the motifs has left wide, shallow incisions.

5 Commentary

The headdress or diadem amplifies the human figure, but we do not know what it is, or represents. However, it is clearly detached from the head of the figure, which dominated the composition. Without the headdress, this figure shares many similarities with that on the third stela from C8 Torrejón el Rubio. Celestino's figure shows the body and brooch more accurately than Almagro Basch. The unique brooch is an antennae type. Motif 3 is a surely a comb, not a lyre. The drawing in version A is after Almagro Basch; version B is modified after Celestino.

A   B

0   25   50   75   100 cm

C7. TORREJÓN EL RUBIO II, Ca.

6 Bibliography

See: Almagro Basch 1966 (figure 27 and Lám XXII); Celestino 2001:331.

1 Catalogue number and findspot: **C8 TORREJÓN EL RUBIO III, Ca⋆**

2 Circumstances of discovery, context and present location

The stela was discovered in 1954 when a building in the outskirts of the village of Torrejón el Rubio was demolished.

   Deposited in the Museo Arqueológico Provincial de Cáceres.

3 Stone type, size and condition of the monument

The stela is made of a dark grey slate or schist, measuring 1.52 m high, 0.53 m wide and 0.13 m thick. The stela has conserved its original size and form, but the rock surface has been scratched, pitted and parts of the engraving have flaked away.

4 Description of the composition and motifs

The stela bears a composition dominated by the central figure (1) of a warrior, which is

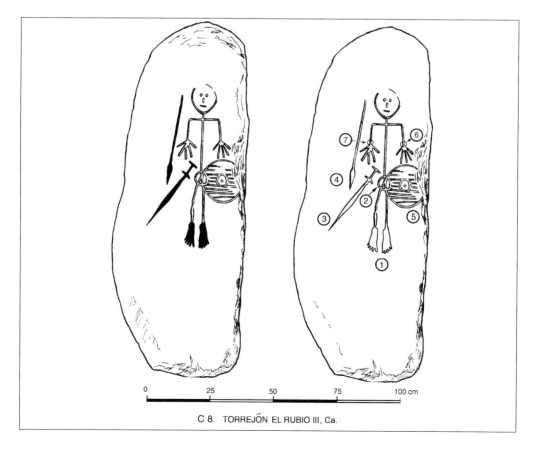

C 8. TORREJÓN EL RUBIO III, Ca.

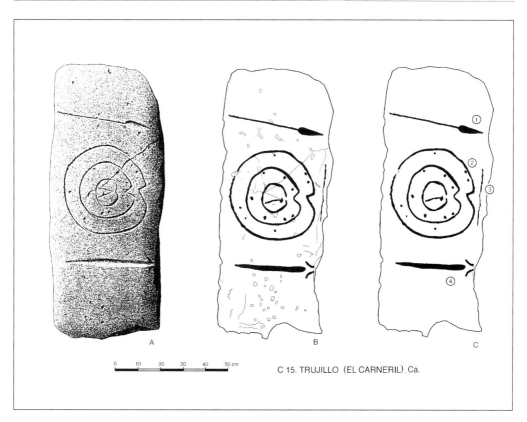

A   B   C

0 10 20 30 40 50 cm

C 15. TRUJILLO (EL CARNERIL), Ca.

4 Description of the composition and motifs

It is a perfectly symmetrical composition of the basic type. It has (2) a shield, (1) a spear and (4) a sword. Motif 3 appears to be a natural crack in the rock. The spearhead and sword were pecked then emphasised by intaglio engraving.

5 Commentary

The shield is of the V-notched Type IB, with three circles and decorated with bosses in pairs and as single ornaments. The handle is indistinct. The sword is best depicted by Almagro Basch and has a leaf-shaped blade and hilt guard, typical of the twelfth/eleventh centuries BC.

Note the contrast between the drawings of Almagro Basch (version A), Beltrán and Alcrudo (version B) and Celestino (version C). The differences between them show the difficulties of establishing an authoritative and exact reading of all the motifs. Our photographs suggest version B (with the sword modified by us) is the most accurate.

Celestino believes the symmetry of the composition and the lack of space below the design to allow for burial to set it upright, meant that it may have lain flat on the ground.

6 Bibliography

See: Almagro Basch 1974 (figure 10); Beltrán & Alcrudo 1973; Celestino 2001:341. There is no good published photograph.

---

1 Catalogue number and findspot: **C16 IBAHERNANDO, Ca★**

2 Circumstances of discovery, context and present location

It was found on the estate called Santa María de la Jara and utilised as a window lintel in a farm building, but had been removed from an irrigated plot of land nearby where a Roman cemetery was located. Its prehistoric location is not known.

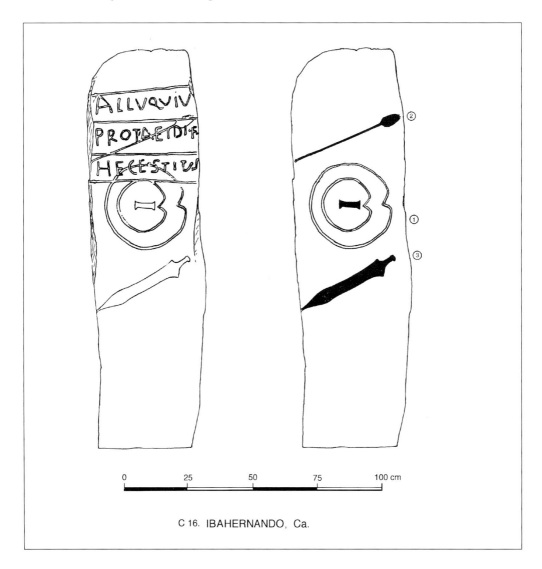

C 16. IBAHERNANDO, Ca.

It is deposited in the Museo Arqueológico Provincial de Cáceres.

3 Stone type, size and condition of the monument

The stela is of local hard granite and measures 1.63 m high, 0.50 m wide and 0.26 m thick. It is complete, but eroded and the Latin inscription is clearer than the Bronze Age motifs.

4 Description of the composition and motifs

This is a basic composition of (1) shield, (2) spear and (3) sword. The pecked decoration has been deepened by intaglio to emphasise the spearhead, shield handle and sword.

 The Latin inscription is complete, with the letters carved carefully between parallel lines in three rows and reads:

 ALLVQVIV
 PROTAEIDA . F
 HECE : STITVS

which transcribes more fully as; ALLUQUIU(s)/ PROTAEIDI.F (ilius) / HEC EST (s)ITUS. It can be translated literally as: 'Alluquius, son of Protaeidus, lies here'. The artisan did not properly measure the space to engrave the inscription and the final letter of the dead man's name lacks the letter S, well as the initial S of situs (with a nexum tû). The name Alluquius is attested mainly in Lusitania and also in Britannia, while the name Protaeidus is the only occurrence in Hispania, but it is attested in Britannia. Both seem clearly Celtic.

5 Commentary

The drawing is based on Almagro Basch 1966, whose details we corroborated in 2001. The shield is a simple V-notched Type IA with no bosses. Almagro Basch drew the sword accurately and it does have a broad leaf-shaped blade and narrow handle ending in a rounded pommel. It is probably a rod-tanged sword, perhaps shown in its scabbard, which would explain the lightly expanded end of the blade. The shield and sword should both date to the thirteenth–twelfth century BC.

6 Bibliography

See: Almagro Basch 1966 (figure 29 and Lam XXIV); Celestino 2001:342. Inscription discussed in HAE (Hispania Antiqua Epigraphica 1397, Sta María de la Jara).

1 Catalogue number and findspot: **C17 SANTA ANA DE TRUJILLO, Ca★**

2 Circumstances of discovery, context and present location

It was found in farming work, lying face down in the ground, in the place called La Cerca de La Cabeza, near Trujillo. Four other stelae were found in the same area; C19 Robledillo is 2 km to the south; C16 Ibahernando lies 3 km to the east; C18 Salvatierra lies 3 km to the east and finally that of C21 Zarza de Montánchez is 6 km to the south-west.

It is deposited in the Museo Arqueológico Provincial de Cáceres.

3 Stone type, size and condition of the monument

The stela is of coarse pinkish granite local to the area and measures 1.84 m high, 0.43 m wide and 0.20 m average thickness. It is complete.

4 Description of the composition and motifs

It bears a basic composition with two additional motifs. The (1) shield centres the field, with a (2) spear, (3) sword, (4) mirror and (5) crested helmet.

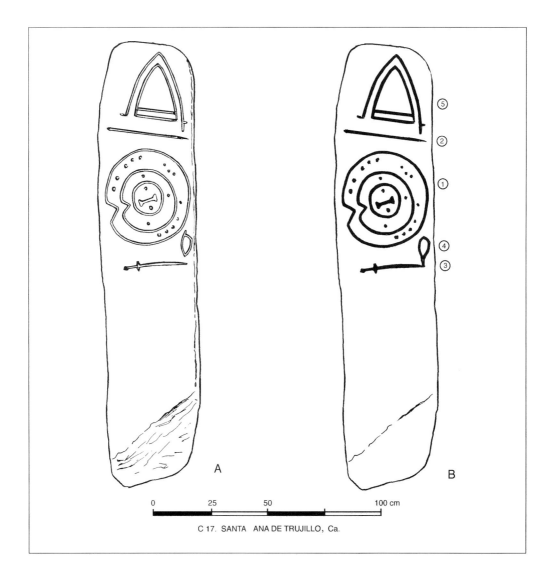

C 17. SANTA ANA DE TRUJILLO, Ca.

5 Commentary

The shield is a V-notched one with decorative bosses in singles, pairs and triplets, of Type IB. The sword has a rounded pommel and big hilt, with a long thin blade. The helmet is clearly a crested one with decorative rivets. Celestino is surely correct in interpreting motif 4 as a mirror. The drawing is based on Almagro Basch, with motif 4 modified to depict a mirror.

6 Bibliography

See: Almagro Basch 1966 (figure 20 and Lám XV); Celestino 2001:343.

1 Catalogue number and findspot: **C18 SALVATIERRA DE SANTIAGO, Ca**

2 Circumstances of discovery, context and present location

At present it forms the threshold to a house and nothing is known of its origins.

It is in the house of Doña Florencia Sánchez Méndez, C/Santo No 5, in the village of Salvatierra de Santiago.

3 Stone type, size and condition of the monument

It is of local, coarse pinkish granite, measuring approximately 1.2 m wide by 0.98 m tall. It is fragmentary and eroded.

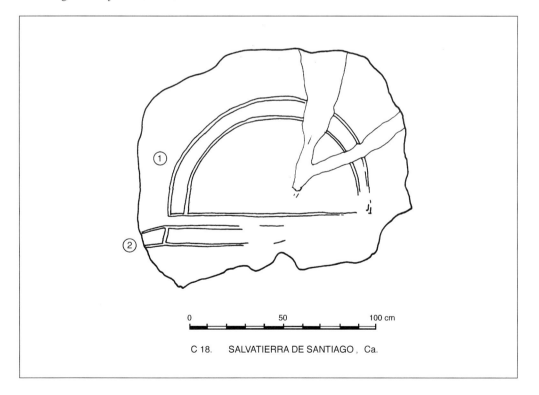

0   50   100 cm

C 18.   SALVATIERRA DE SANTIAGO , Ca.

4 Description of the composition and motifs

A (1) huge brooch and (2) a sword were recognised by Celestino.

5 Commentary

Motif 1 is apparently a giant arc or bow fibula as Celestino says and is certainly not a shield, as suggested by González and De Alvarado in 1989–1990. The sword is probably a leaf-shaped one since the hilt is D-shaped, like the weapon depicted on C6 Torrejón el Rubio I. The drawing follows the original publication (González Cordero and De Alvarado Gonzalo 1989–1990, figure 1).

6 Bibliography

See: Celestino 2001:344. Originally published by González Cordero and De Alvarado Gonzalo 1989-90, with a good photograph on Lám 1.

1 Catalogue number and findspot: **C19 ROBLEDILLO DE TRUJILLO, Ca★**

2 Circumstances of discovery, context and present location

The stela was found in 1947, when a well was enlarged on the farm called El Oreganal. The modern land use is for growing olives and grazing livestock.

It is deposited in the Museo Arqueológico Provincial de Cáceres.

3 Stone type, size and condition of the monument

The stela is of pale grey granite, eroded and coarse textured. It is substantially intact and measures 1.05 m high, 0.55 m wide and 0.12 m thick.

4 Description of the composition and motifs

The composition is a basic one, roughly incised, but with the spearhead and sword blade cut out in intaglio for emphasis. There is a (1) shield, with a (2) spear and (3) a sword.

5 Commentary

The shield is a version of the V-notched Type I A, with three simple incised circles and a peculiar design for the notches. The sword is unique and Celestino's drawing appears accurate. Its open handle is attached to a straight guard and the blade is a deep triangular one, with a marked central rib. No swords like this are known from western Europe. The spear blade is also unusual, with a large oval shape with a strong midrib.

The drawing is based on Almagro Basch, modified for motif 3.

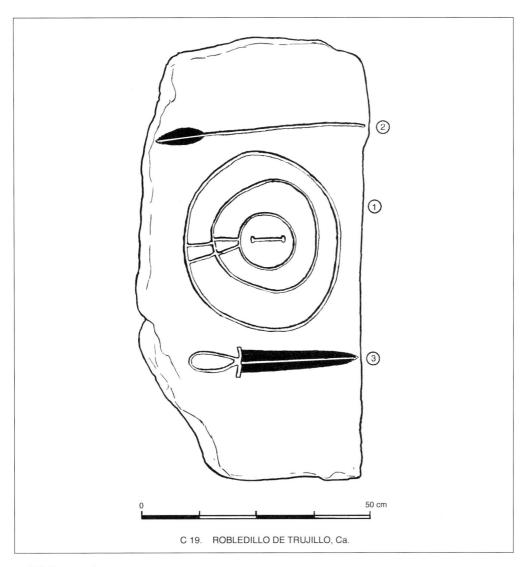

C 19.   ROBLEDILLO DE TRUJILLO, Ca.

6 Bibliography

See: Almagro Basch 1966 (figure 25 and Lám XX); Celestino 2001:345.

1 Catalogue number and findspot: **C20 ALMOHARÍN, Ca**

2 Circumstances of discovery, context and present location

No details are known of its discovery.

It is deposited in the Museo Arqueológico Provincial de Cáceres.

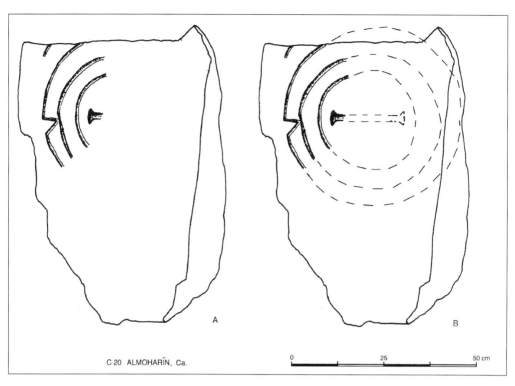

C 20 ALMOHARÍN, Ca.

3 Stone type, size and condition of the monument

Pale grey granite, the fragment measures 0.80 m high, 0.55 m wide and 0.17 m thick. It is an eroded fragment with one motif.

4 Description of the composition and motifs

The central motif is a V-notched shield, probably undecorated and belonging to Type IA. Only the outermost of the three concentric circles has a notch.

5 Commentary

In version B, we reconstruct the shield.

6 Bibliography

See: Celestino 2001:346. No good photograph is published.

1 Catalogue number and findspot: **C21 ZARZA DE MONTÁNCHEZ, Ca★**

2 Circumstances of discovery, context and present location

It was discovered lying by the country track called the Camino de la Sierra, where it had been known for many years before being identified as a stela. Rain washed its decoration clean. The findspot lies 3.5 km south of the town.

Deposited in the Museo Arqueológico Provincial de Cáceres.

3 Stone type, size and condition of the monument

The stela is of local granite, pale grey in colour and with an eroded surface. It measures 1.69 m high, 0.95 m wide and has an average thickness of 0.20 m. It is substantially complete.

4 Description of the composition and motifs

The composition centres on the shield, with the human figure introduced as a protagonist on one side. The motifs are (1) a shield, (2) a spear, (3) a sword, (4) a helmet, (5) a mirror, (6) a human figure and (7) a chariot. The lines are engraved deeply and intaglio carving emphasises the human figure, mirror and spearhead.

5 Commentary

The figure has two drawings: version A is that published originally by Almagro Gorbea and Sánchez Abal in 1978 and version B is that of Celestino in 2001. Our examination and photographs confirm all the details in Celestino's version, changing only the size of the stela and its main motifs.

This is a well-designed and carefully executed composition. The shield has three con-

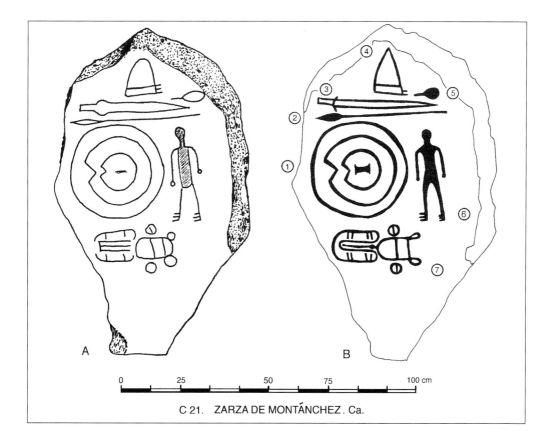

C 21.   ZARZA DE MONTÁNCHEZ, Ca.

centric circles and its V-notches place it in Type IA. The sword has a well-defined hilt and big guards and the long blade is parallel-sided, ending in a pronounced point. The crested helmet shows two decorative rivets. The human figure has significant details; the hands are not shown, but the feet are depicted clearly, each with three toes. This contrasts markedly with many other human figures having over-sized hands in grasping position. The body is also given some volume and made the same height as the shield. The chariot wheels have spokes inside them.

6 Bibliography

See: Almagro Gorbea 1977 (photograph on Lám XIX/1); Almagro Gorbea & Sánchez Abal 1978 (figure 2); Celestino 2001:347.

---

1 Catalogue number and findspot: **C22 SOLANA DE CABAÑAS, Ca★**

2 Circumstances of discovery, context and present location

The findspot lies 600 m north of some isolated farm buildings belonging to the district of Cabañas del Castillo, at an altitude of about 870 m. The terrain is stony, dry and full of abrupt faults in the Quaternary rocks. Various natural paths lead through the mountainous landscape, which is only suitable for rough grazing.

The publication in 1898 stated that the stela was found buried under a low mound of stones from clearing fields (called a *majano*) and when it was raised a grave cut into the earth was revealed (Roso de Luna 1898). The grave contained ashes, the impression of some decayed metal and a pot made of yellowish clay. This information was obtained several weeks after the discovery and Celestino (2001:348) doubts its relevance, since the real position of the decorated face of the stela was not mentioned and the pot is of a different type than the ones known for the Final Bronze Age. Almagro Basch (1966:27) believed it did mark a grave and noted Roso de Luna's comment that there were 'light (faint) ashes like a human skeleton', which could well mark the remains of an inhumation. Roso de Luna visited the site of the discovery and also excavated several other promising stone mounds, without finding anything further.

It is deposited in the Museo Arqueológico Nacional, Madrid.

3 Stone type, size and condition of the monument

The stela is of compact, calcareous slate and measures 1.29 m high, 0.67 m wide and an average thickness of 0.18 m. It has a naturally smooth, even surface. The bottom portion has broken away, perhaps losing 50 cm of the stela, but the composition is substantially intact.

4 Description of the composition and motifs

The composition centres on the shield with accompanying human figure, very like C21.

The motifs are (1) a shield, (2) a spear, (3) a sword, (4) a mirror, (5) an object of uncertain identification, (6) a human figure and (7) a chariot with re-cuttings. The engraving uses deep, clear incisions throughout, with intaglio to emphasise the volume of the spear, sword, mirror and human figure.

5 Commentary

The figure is based on Almagro Basch's drawing, with modifications. The composition is boldly laid out and despite obvious engraving errors on the chariot, it is highly effective visually.

The Herzsprung shield is a V-notched one of Type IB, decorated with pairs and triplets of bosses. The spear has a large, ogival blade like some British spearheads. The sword has a marked rectangular pommel, a narrow hilt, big guards and a prominent leaf-shaped blade ending in a sharp point. It appears to belong to the rod-tanged swords with leaf-shaped blades of the thirteenth/twelfth century BC. We do not know what motif 5 represents; it may be a conical helmet as Celestino suggests, or a large brooch, or even a drinking cup.

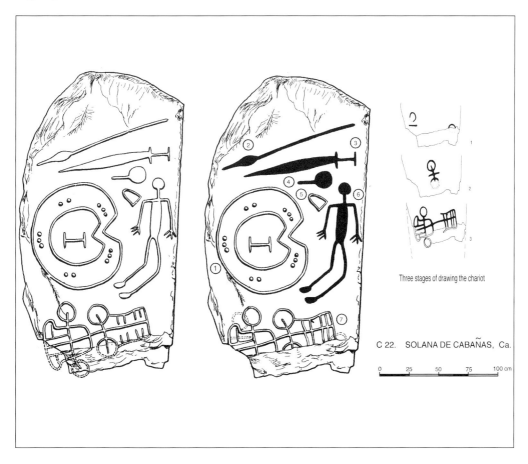

Three stages of drawing the chariot

C 22.   SOLANA DE CABAÑAS, Ca.

0   25   50   75   100 cm

The naked human figure is given volume by intaglio carving and the fingers are carefully exaggerated, while the feet are left poorly defined as clubs, as if they wore shoes. The emphasis on the fingers and toes is exactly the opposite of that on the C21 stela. Celestino suggests that the bent legs are due to the artist's desire to fit the figure into the reduced space; others see them as representing a dead person, with the legs bent unnaturally to convey this idea. In either case, the legs are disproportionately long.

The chariot caused the engraver much difficulty. We can detect two failed efforts to place the motif correctly, before the final position was chosen. The effect of the second error was to leave an extra pair of wheels in the motif, which make the chariot look like a four-wheeled cart, which it is not. Note that one horse is a stallion, since its penis is depicted. All these details appear on the photographs.

6 Bibliography

See: Almagro Basch 1966 (figure 2 and Lám I); Celestino 2001:348–349; Roso de Luna 1898.

---

1 Catalogue number and findspot: **C23 LOGROSÁN I, Ca**

2 Circumstances of discovery, context and present location

There are no details of the findspot.

It is deposited in the house of D Matías Rodríguez Pazos, in Cañamero, Cáceres.

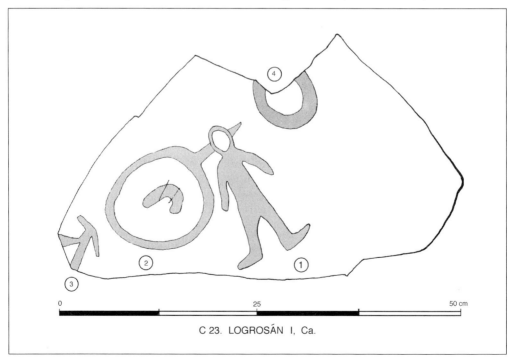

C 23. LOGROSÁN I, Ca.

3 Stone type, size and condition of the monument

A fragment of local slate, it measures 0.30 m high, 0.50 m wide and an average thickness of 0.23 m. It is a small fragment of a larger composition.

4 Description of the composition and motifs

There are four motifs: (1) a small human figure, apparently fully clothed, (2) a possible shield, (3) an angular motif and (4) a small circle. The engraving is rough pecking.

5 Commentary

The clothed figure is most unusual, since nearly all figures, large or small, are depicted naked. This is a secondary fragment from a larger composition.

6 Bibliography

See: Celestino 2001:350. There is no good published photograph.

1 Catalogue number and findspot: C24 LOGROSÁN II, Ca

2 Circumstances of discovery, context and present location

There are no details of the findspot.

It is deposited in the house of D Matías Rodríguez Pazos, in Cañamero, Cáceres.

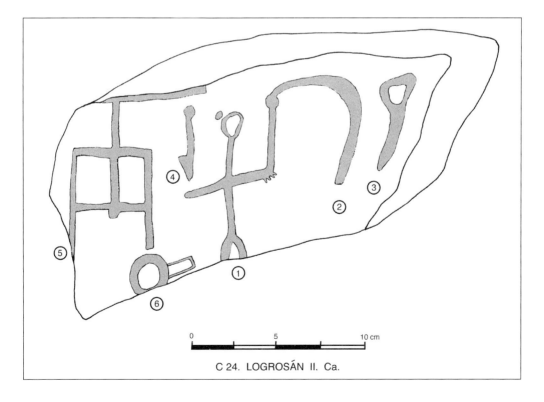

C 24. LOGROSÁN II. Ca.

3 Stone type, size and condition of the monument

A fragment of very hard local slate, it measures 0.25 m high and 0.47 m wide. It is a small fragment from a larger composition.

4 Description of the composition and motifs

Celestino suggested it might be a test piece where the engraver practised his technique. There are six separate motifs: (1) a stick-figure, (2) a curved object in the right hand, (3) a possible mirror, (4) an angular motif which may be an arm of the stick figure that was not finished, (5) a schematic chariot body and (6) a circular motif with handle, which may be a chariot wheel.

5 Commentary

None.

6 Bibliography

See: Celestino 2001:351. There is no good published photograph.

1 Catalogue number and findspot: **C25 LAS HERENCIAS I, To★**

2 Circumstances of discovery, context and present location

In 1981 the stela was re-discovered in the Barrioseco Alto, which lies 300 m from the left

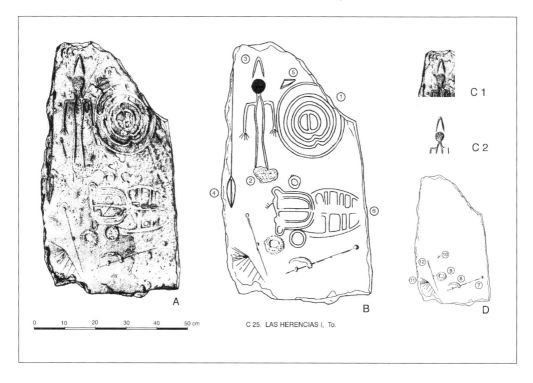

C 25. LAS HERENCIAS I, To.

bank of the Tagus river, near the village of Las Herencias. The landscape today is exploited by dry farming and grazing and although the surface geology is formed of Oligocene
sediments, the underlying rocks and those that outcrop commonly in the region, are of
granite and slate.

It is deposited in the Museo de Santa Cruz, Toledo.

3 Stone type, size and condition of the monument

The stela is a small plaque of dark grey sandstone from the Precambrian/Palaeozoic strata of the area, which comes to the surface at La Jara. Portela and Jiménez (1996:42) identified its distinctive petrology. It is not granite, as Fernández-Miranda says (1987:464). It
has lost the top right corner. The surface is worn and has many exfoliations. The vertical
edges of the block have been carefully trimmed by direct percussion to produce a rectangular shape that measures 0.75 m high, 0.42 m wide and an average thickness of 0.15 m.
The composition is substantially complete and the stela could not have been much larger
than it is now and could never have had a large base for burial in the earth.

4 Description of the composition and motifs

The whole surface had been pecked smooth before engraving, which was done in at least
four different techniques, all clearly visible.

The drawing is based on the exquisitely detailed one in *pointillé* technique, published
by Fernández Miranda (version A), with the motifs copied as outlines in the version B for
analytical clarity. The composition centres visually on a big shield (1). A human figure of
equal size is to the left, engraved in deep, wide lines like the shield and chariot. Note that
its fingers are carefully depicted with finely incised lines and the head emphasised by the
intaglio technique (2), thus using three different types of line to create the motif. The feet,
if there were any, have been lost in an exfoliation. Above the head is a crested helmet (3)
and on the left hand side a long spear (4), very lightly incised, like the fingers. Motif 5 is
probably a brooch and at the bottom of the stela is a large chariot (6).

The drawing also shows the motifs 7 to 12 separately (version D) from the main composition. Motifs 8 and 9 are pecked lightly and appear to be unsuccessful attempts at
depicting chariot wheels. All the other motifs are fine incised lines that are later in date,
or natural markings.

5 Commentary

This stela is not easy to study, but the excellent drawing in Fernández Miranda (1987) confirms our own observations that there is a real possibility that the composition was executed at two different periods, or might be the work by two different engravers. The ambiguity of the main human motif and the lack of a sword, as well as the variety of engraving
techniques, make this stela technically unique. Our hypothesis would reconstruct the two
engraving episodes as follows.

The first would include the shield, chariot and human figure (motifs 1, 6 and 2), all outlined in deep incisions that were polished for effect. The human figure is a most peculiar shape, and its size and volume are approximately that of a sword, and it is possible that a weapon was the original intention of the engraver, which then changed into a silhouette figure.

The second moment of composition could have strengthened the human figure, adding a head by making a deep pit at the tip and adding arms and lightly incised fingers to the body. The head is carved in intaglio and is the only motif on the stela to use it. The figure shows these details in versions C1 and C2 of the human figure. The helmet, spear and brooch (motifs 3–5) were added at this time; the spear is more lightly incised with finer lines than any other motif.

Finally, there are several lightly incised lines and illegible elements (motifs 7–12) and whose date we cannot determine. If our reading of the motifs is correct, this stela began as a simple composition, to be replaced by a more complex one.

It is notable that four different engraving techniques were used, more than on any other stela. Furthermore, the lack of a sword in the final composition is most unusual, since the weapon is the defining motif of the warrior series. For this reason, we think it likely that an original sword was transformed into a human figure in a second stage of engraving, with another peculiar result, that of a figure which appears to be clothed, not naked as is usually the case. Visually, the human figure has absorbed the shape of the sword into its own image, rather than keeping it separate or showing the sword worn at the warrior's waist. In this way the lack of a sword in the composition could be overcome by a clever use of an ambiguous motif, something that is extremely rare in these stelae. Both stages of engraving could have followed close to one another, perhaps even a matter of a few days.

The shield is of the V-notched Type IA without decoration. If the sword/human figure (2) had been a sword, then it would have had a leaf-shaped blade.

6 Bibliography

See: Celestino 2001:352–353; Fernández-Miranda 1987:476 (un-numbered figure and an adequate photograph).

1 Catalogue number and findspot: **C26 LAS HERENCIAS II, To**

2 Circumstances of discovery, context and present location

This stela was found in archaeological excavations in September 1990, in an Iron Age settlement at Arroyo Manzanas, which is on a terrace on the left bank of the Tagus river. It is 10 km south-west of Talavera de la Reina. The Oligocene geology and landscape is the same as that for stela C25. 'The stela had been placed in the interior of buildings made of daub resting on stone footings and of square plan, which correspond, according to the level in which they are found, to cultural material of Cogotas IIb' (Moreno Arrastio

1995:275–276). He continues, 'It was found, offering its engraved face upwards, resting on a fill of clay analogous in texture, colour and hardness to that which we found in other parts of the room' (Moreno Arrastio 1995:279).

Deposited in the Museo de Santa Cruz, Toledo, but could not be found in 2001.

3 Stone type, size and condition of the monument

The stela is of mottled grey slate. It measures 1.07 m high, 0.60 m wide and an average thickness of 0.15 m. It is damaged around the edges but the composition is intact.

4 Description of the composition and motifs

This composition has a horned 'hero' figure as protagonist. The horned figure is well-defined (1), with an irregular shield next to his left hand (2). The other motif (3) may be a spear. All motifs are incised with thin, scratchy lines.

5 Commentary

This is certainly a secondary re-use of the stela as a convenient piece of flat stone for a floor, in a period dating to the fourth–third centuries BC, as the pottery associated with the house shows. It is also likely that the stone was an imported rock, not native to this area, but which outcrops 17 km away, at the confluence of the river Gévalo with the Tagus.

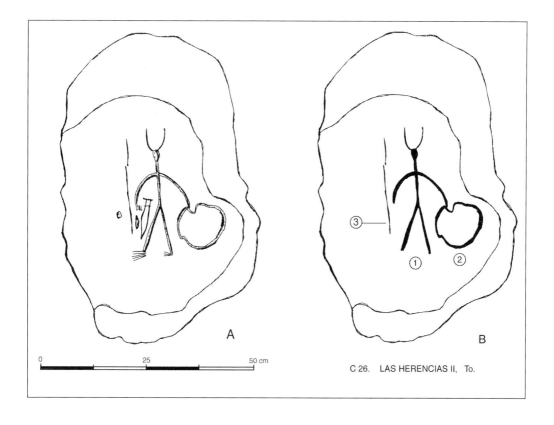

A

B

0   25   50 cm

C 26.   LAS HERENCIAS II, To.

(Portela & Jiménez 1996:42). Its original location is unknown.

The drawing offers two versions of this composition. Version A is the drawing by Celestino and includes fingers and toes on the figure, a sword and two other illegible motifs. Version B is the preferred interpretation, based on the published photograph by Moreno Arrastio, where none of the extra details appear. The scratched, pockmarked surface of the stela is quite apparent. Moreno specifically mentions the difficulty of identifying motifs on this eroded stone surface and does not mention the extra motifs of a sword and other objects in his original publication of the stela. I conclude they are erroneous interpretations of natural fissures (Dr Dirk Brandherm directed my attention to these details).

Note that the horns of the figure spring directly from the head of the figure and are not attached to any helmet or headdress. The shield is probably a V notched type but crudely rendered.

6 Bibliography

See: Celestino 2001:354; Moreno Arrastio 1995:294 (photograph).

1 Catalogue number and findspot: **C27 TALAVERA DE LA REINA, To⋆**

2 Circumstances of discovery, context and present location

The stela was discovered in April 1996 next to a country path in the 'Barraca del Águila', which is an area of low clay hills near the town of Talavera de la Reina, on the left bank of the Tagus river. Today the Oligocene clays and sandstones are fertile farming land. Its findspot is about 5 km away from the two stelae at Las Herencias.

It is deposited temporarily in the Museo Ruiz de Luna, Talavera de la Reina.

3 Stone type, size and condition of the monument

The stela is made of a fine-grained leuco-granite that does not occur in the locality, but outcrops in a specific area 25 km to the north-east. Its petrology is quite specific (Portela & Jiménez 1996:42). This means it has been transported at least that distance. It is cylindrical in form, tapering to a rounded head. It is of an oval section, measuring 1.42 m high, 0.51 m wide and averaging 0.33 m in thickness. The bottom part may have broken away and the engraved surface has suffered heavy erosion and exfoliation, but the stela is essentially complete.

4 Description of the composition and motifs

The stela is a reused statue menhir, probably of the third millennium BC. The shaping of the stone into a phallus with a human head is clear and the granite has been pecked then polished to a smooth surface on its upper quarter. The phallic shape was carefully made and the eyes and nose deeply incised into the surface to create a face. The shoulders are indicated and perhaps the ears.

It was engraved in the Final Bronze Age and the motifs respect the original monument to the extent that none deface it. The shield (1) and the human figure (2) wearing a sword and with outstretched hand displaying the fingers clearly, are the protagonists of the composition. The figure has one horn emerging from the head; the other has eroded. There is also (3) a mirror, (4) a chariot, (5) a possible spear and (6) an indistinct motif that is probably natural.

5 Commentary

The examination in 2001 corroborated the main motifs, although not all the detail described by Portela and Jiménez in 1996 was visible. For this reason the drawing has version A of the discoverers and our version B.

The strong composition centres on the horned 'hero' figure, with outstretched and over-sized hand ready to grasp the mirror. The horns are simple ones and do not curve or end in knobs. The shield is a V-notched one of Type IB, with decorative bosses in pairs and arranged singly. The V notch is obscured by an exfoliation, but visible in both outer circles of decoration in angled light. The mirror has a decorated handle. Cross-spoked wheels dis-

C 27.   TALAVERA DE LA REINA, To.

tinguish the chariot, which is actually depicted quite simply, with a strong geometry.

The intentional reuse of the monument is important, adding a powerful male message to the warrior composition and it is one of the very few stelae to be made of imported rock. Moving such a large and heavy menhir over 25 km would have been arduous, unless a raft was used on the river. It may have been moved in the third millennium BC, or later.

6 Bibliography

See: Celestino 2001:355; Portela Hernando & Jiménez Rodrigo 1996 (figure and photographs not numbered).

1 Catalogue number and findspot: C28 ALDEANUEVA DE SAN BARTOLOMÉ, To

2 Circumstances of discovery, context and present location

For decades this stela had been used as an outdoor seat at the entrance to a farm labourer's store known as 'El Portalillo', outside the village of Aldeanueva. It was saved when the building was demolished in 1995.

Deposited temporarily in the town hall of Aldeanueva de San Bartolomé.

3 Stone type, size and condition of the monument

It is made of grey slate and measures 1.40 m high, 0.60 m wide and has an average thickness of 0.15 m. The stone has been trimmed to a rough rectangular shape, with a narrow (but lopsided) foot. It has survived quite well, with some erosion of motifs, worn away when it was a seat, but appears complete. The undulating surface is natural.

4 Description of the composition and motifs

There are three separate phases of decoration. The first and most important one is the horned figure, surrounded by his panoply of weapons. This (1) is deeply incised and both hands have the fingers drawn clearly. The horns spring directly from the head and are twisted sharply at their tips. The other motifs are (2) a shield, (3) a sword, (4) a spear, (5) a possible brooch, (6) a chariot without any draught animals and (7) a separate animal that may be a dog, or a horse. Surface erosion has effaced part of the shield and chariot. The engravings are deeply pecked lines, smoothed to a wide profile. The second phase of decoration covered the back of the stela with over a dozen deep cup marks. The third phase contains a later motif in the name JESUS J J, engraved in cursive capital letters typical of the sixteenth–seventeenth centuries AD (8), and a few small pits above the figure's head (9).

5 Commentary

Version A is the drawing published by Pacheco et al in 1998. Versions B and C identify the discrepancies with the colour photographs and add extra motifs.

The 'hero' figure has exaggeratedly large horns springing directly from each side of the head; note the outstretched fingers of each hand. The shield is worn away, but probably

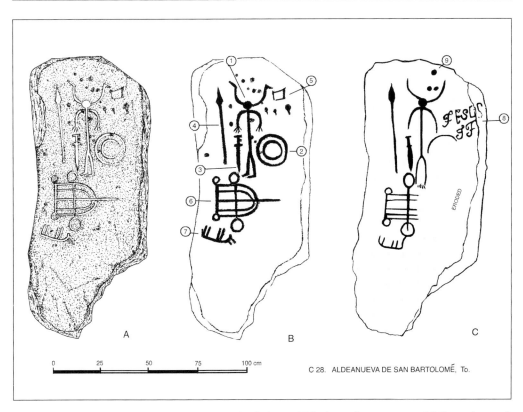

A

B

C

0   25   50   75   100 cm

C 28. ALDEANUEVA DE SAN BARTOLOMÉ, To.

belongs to the Type II. The sword has a leaf-shaped blade and pronounced hilt and guard and the photograph differs significantly from the original drawing. The sword may be a slashing weapon, not a Carp's Tongue type. Motif 5 is hard to identify certainly and may not exist at all. The mirror suggested by the discoverers is invisible, but there are dimples in the rock surface.

The stela may be reused, since the cup marks on the reverse face are known on other stelae associated with megalithic tombs in the Toledo area, dated to the Copper Age. Similar pits are cut over the face of an early stela from C82 Córdoba I and must be later than the engravings.

6 Bibliography

See: Celestino 2001:356; Pacheco et al 1998 (with five good colour photographs).

1 Catalogue number and findspot: **C29 SÃO MARTINHO I, Castelo Branco, Beira Baixa, Portugal**

2 Circumstances of discovery, context and present location

On 17 September 1903 the Portuguese archaeologist F Tavares de Proença excavated three stelae (C29–C31) from the lower slopes of the small hill of São Martinho, which is on the right bank of the river Mercoles, 3 km to the east of the modern city of Castelo Branco. Extensive excavations by Tavares de Proença on the site of the stelae in 1905 failed to uncover any more information about them. A Roman settlement and cemetery lies nearby (details on the map in Tavares de Proença 1903:23).

It is deposited in the Museu 'Francisco Tavares de Proença Júnior', in Castelo Branco.

3 Stone type, size and condition of the monument

The stela is of the local compact, pinkish granite and it measures 1.65 m high, 0.65 m wide and has an average thickness of 0.22 m, expanding to 0.33 m at the foot. The upper part is damaged and part of the composition lost. The block has been carefully trimmed to a rectangular shape and section, then pecked smooth for engraving.

4 Description of the composition and motifs

The composition belongs to the group of paired figures and is schematically portrayed. Decoration is in two zones. Zone 1 contains a figurative scene with two horned human figures (1 and 2) on each side of a central feature like a tree (3). Above each of them is an elongated motif (4 and 5) like a sword. Zone 2 fills the lower part of the stela with a horizontal band of dots (6) and a deep fringe of 16 vertical lines (7). The foot of the stela expands slightly at this point and thickens distinctly. The lines are deeply but irregularly engraved.

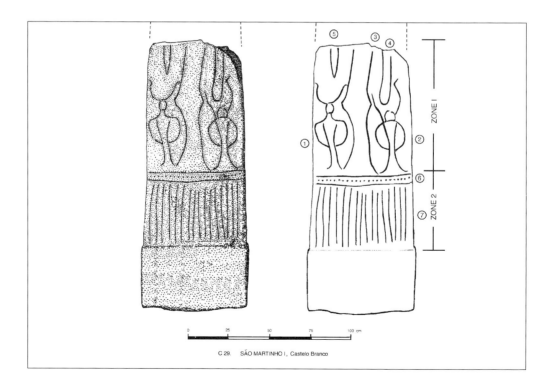

C 29.   SÃO MARTINHO I, Castelo Branco

5 Commentary

An exceptional feature of this stela and the other two from this site, is their rectangular shape and section, obtained after much work on the granite base, imparting a formality and refinement to them that is missing in other stelae. When they were intact and new, they would have been most impressive monuments. They are unique for this reason and may be older Copper Age stelae re-used in the Final Bronze Age. Probably, they were brought to the site from elsewhere and their present findspot is certainly not their original setting. They might have been building material for the Roman settlement.

The composition is difficult to describe, due to its advanced stylisation. However, it is not a unique composition (except in motif details) and belongs to a group of six sets of paired figures (figures 6.15–16). The drawings and photograph by Almagro Basch are faithful to the original and the analysis is based on them. Celestino's description of the context and the engravings on all three stelae, are confused.

The central image of a (3) tree, is hard to read at first sight, since the eye is deflected to the figures, rather than this feature. It is certainly not a symmetrical pair of flexed bows, as Almagro and Celestino say, but the vertical axis of the entire composition, to which the figures are related symmetrically. The pair of figures (1 and 2) clearly has big horns springing from their heads; note the distinctive twisted horn tips, just like those on the stela C28 from Aldeanueva de San Bartolomé. The next feature is visually ambiguous and admits variant readings; the figures may each stand in front of a round shield, or alternatively be portrayed with their arms akimbo, elbows outwards and hands on hips. The motifs 4 and 5 could be almost any object, even branches of a tree.

The motifs in zone 2 create the horizon for the composition, which is a unique feature in the stelae series. From the horizontal motif 6 springs the trunk of the tree (3). The scene may represent the heroisation of two warriors, or the epiphany of divine beings in warrior form.

There are no specific details to date any motif.

6 Bibliography

See: Almagro Basch 1966 (figure 4 and Lám II); Celestino 2001:357–358; Tavares de Proença 1903, 1905 (figures 1 and 2).

1 Catalogue number and findspot: **C30 SÃO MARTINHO II, Castelo Branco, Beira Baixa, Portugal**

2 Circumstances of discovery, context and present location

It was excavated by Tavares de Proença in 1903 a few metres away from stela C29, lying horizontally at a depth of 60 cm below the surface. Stela C31 was found nearby.

It is deposited in the Museu 'Francisco Tavares de Proença Júnior', in Castelo Branco.

3 Stone type, size and condition of the monument

The stela is of local granite like C29, with a well-preserved surface due to its burial. The menhir was carefully trimmed to a regular square cross section and all the faces smoothed before engraving. It measures 2.23 m high and is 0.40 m in width and thickness, making it among the biggest stela known. It is complete.

4 Description of the composition and motifs

The composition is unique. It presents a hunting scene with a warrior aiming his arrow at a stag in front of him. The hunter (1) draws his bow (2) and aims the arrow at the stag. Around the figure is the panoply of artefacts: a brooch (3), scabbard? (4), quiver for arrows (5), mirror (6) and a hunting dog (7). The motifs on the upper part of the stela are three stylised trees (9–11) in front of which stands a stag with elaborate antlers (8), pursued by a dog (12). The engraving is executed in firm, deep incisions.

5 Commentary

This monument was originally made as a statue-menhir in the shape of a phallus, which explains its shape and clearly marked glans at the top (13) and should belong to the Copper Age as Gomes and Monteiro said in 1977. The engravings were added to it later on. Despite being well illustrated by Almagro Basch in 1966, there is disagreement about the exact profile of the menhir and its motifs. Almagro Basch's drawing is in version A and what appear to be an accurate profile and sections; version B from Gomes and Monteiro

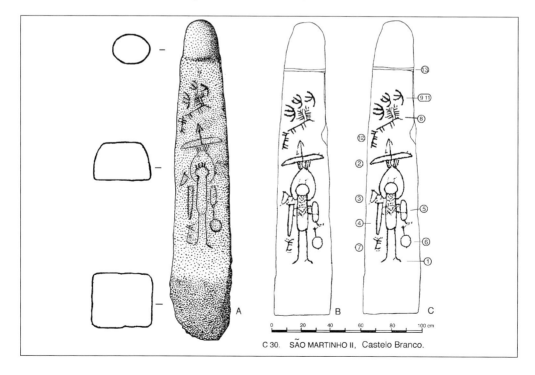

C 30.   SÃO MARTINHO II, Castelo Branco.

captures the motifs more accurately. Version C labels the motifs for reference. There is yet another version in Celestino (2001), which adds a comb motif next to the mirror (6), which was not seen by the other writers nor is visible in their photographs; therefore it is excluded. Observers also disagree on whether or not the warrior has spiky hair (Almagro Basch), or has a decorated tunic over his body (Gomes & Monteiro 1977). Celestino interprets the trees as birds.

The composition is firmly related to the other warrior stelae by virtue of its panoply, in the same way that the *Diademada* from C7 Torrejón el Rubio II is included. The mirror, brooch and scabbard are unmistakable. The lack of a shield is important.

The warrior's head and body are given volume (and perhaps some internal decoration) and the raised arms end in exaggerated fingers grasping the bow firmly, in a gesture so familiar on stelae of the series. The mirror is a simple one and the brooch appears to be an asymmetrical elbow fibula.

The scene is well composed and didactically clear in arraying the panoply around the warrior, even to the detail of showing two hunting dogs, one in each half of the composition. The unique thematic link between this stela and C29 is that both make use of trees, introducing the natural world in a way that is central to the composition.

6 Bibliography

See: Almagro Basch 1966 (figure 5 and Lám III); Celestino 2001:359–360; Gomes & Monteiro 1977 (figure 7); Tavares de Proença 1903, 1905 (figures 1 and 2).

1 Catalogue number and findspot: **C31 SÃO MARTINHO III, Castelo Branco, Beira Baixa, Portugal**

2 Circumstances of discovery, context and present location

This fragment was found in 1903 near C29 and C30, but not published until 1966 by Almagro Basch.

It is deposited in the Museu 'Francisco Tavares de Proença Júnior', in Castelo Branco.

3 Stone type, size and condition of the monument

A fragment of local granite like the other two stelae, which measures 0.9 m high, 0.32 m, wide and an average thickness of 0.26 m.

4 Description of the composition and motifs

It is impossible to reconstruct the original composition from this fragment, on which three separate motifs can be seen; a possible sword blade (1), a line (2) and a rectangular panel of seven lines (3). The lines are all deeply incised.

5 Commentary

Carefully worked all over, this fragment has a rectangular cross section like C29 and

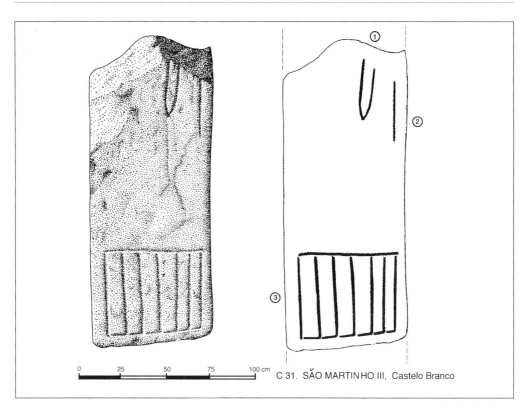

C 31. SÃO MARTINHO III, Castelo Branco

although broken, was originally a tall and symmetrical stela, which would have been most imposing. Its composition may have been like C29. It is probably an older Copper Age menhir that was re-engraved.

6 Bibliography

See: Almagro Basch 1966 (figure 6 and Lám IV); Celestino 2001:361.

1 Catalogue number and findspot: **C32 CABEZA DEL BUEY I, Ba**

2 Circumstances of discovery, context and present location

It was found in 1940 on a low hill on the estate of La Baileja, which lies 10 km north of the town of Cabeza del Buey. The landscape of Precambrian slate rocks is dry-farmed for cereals.

It is deposited in the house of Sr del Río y Martínez de la Mata, in the Paseo de San Vicente, in Cabeza del Buey.

3 Stone type, size and condition of the monument

The stela is grey calcareous slate, damaged at the top and broken at the base, measuring 1.12 m high, 0.85 m wide and an average thickness of 0.19 m. The natural face of the stone was not prepared before engraving.

4 Description of the composition and motifs

The composition centres on the shield, with the human figure introduced as a secondary theme. The motifs are: (1) a spear, (2) a shield, (3a) chariot that has an aborted earlier engraving beneath it (3b), (4) sword and (5) the human figure with exaggerated hands and fingers. Above the head is a feature that might be a diadem or a helmet; and two earrings are visible near the neck. A probable mirror with a square face (6) and a brooch (7) complete the panoply. Motifs 4–6 are emphasised in intaglio; all the other broad lines are pecked and smoothed. The composition appears to be complete despite the damage to the supporting block.

5 Commentary

Celestino is correct in noting that this is a composition of an early kind to which the chariot has been added as an extra motif, rather than integrated into the composition as a fundamental element. That is why it appears perched on the upper margin, rather than being placed below the warrior's feet.

The figure is based on the drawing in Almagro Basch. The V-notched shield is of Type IB with decorative bosses irregularly placed on it. The sword has a big hilt with round pommel and large guard, while the blade swells to a prominent leaf-shape. The square face of the mirror is unique; the brooch is an asymmetric elbow fibula. The chariot is well

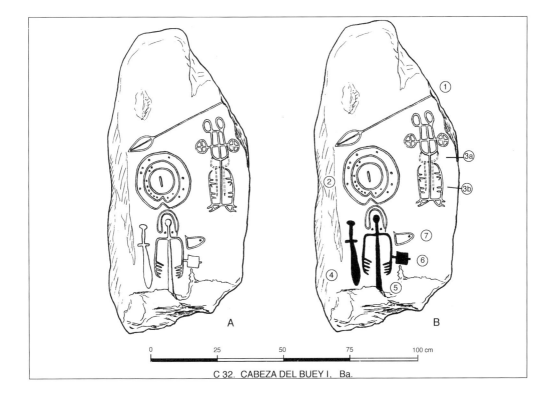

C 32. CABEZA DEL BUEY I, Ba.

drawn. The stallions drawing it have clear penises and the wheels are shown with four spokes each.

6 Bibliography

See: Almagro Basch 1966 (figure 21 and Lám XVI); Celestino 2001:362–363.

1 Catalogue number and findspot: **C33 CABEZA DEL BUEY II, Ba★**

2 Circumstances of discovery, context and present location

It was found on the farm called La Yuntilla Alta, which lies 15 km north of the town of Cabeza del Buey, between the left bank of the Cebolloso gully and the right bank of the Fraile gully. The freshwater spring of La Tiesa rises 500 m away and still flows. The undulating landscape of Precambrian slate is good grazing land.

The stela was found when working the land with a tractor and the discoverer reports that it was standing upright but completely buried in the ground. He noticed that no more than 20 metres away stones were piled into three or four circles that touched each other, so he ceased ploughing. Celestino visited the site afterwards and observed that there appeared to be plain stelae scattered over an area 30 metres square on a small earth mound that he thought was not natural. His excavation in 1992 produced no results of any kind.

It is deposited in the Museo Arqueológico Provincial de Badajoz.

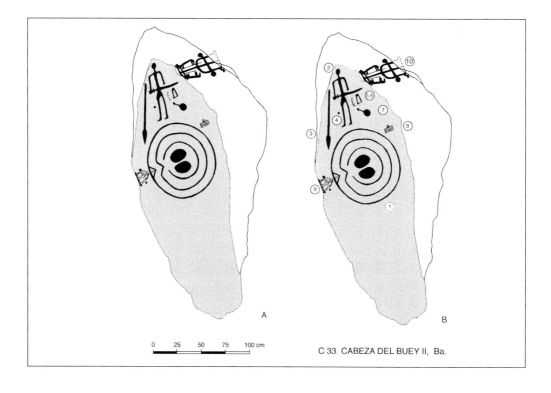

A

B

0   25   50   75   100 cm

C 33. CABEZA DEL BUEY II, Ba.

3 Stone type, size and condition of the monument

The stela is of hard calcareous slate, with the surface in very good condition due to its burial. It measures 1.71 m high, 0.85 m wide and has an average thickness of 0.24 m. It is complete and appears undamaged.

4 Description of the composition and motifs

The entire main face was carefully pecked smooth before engraving. The (1) shield is the centre of the composition. Above the shield, is (2) an armed warrior with his fingers just discernible, surrounded by his panoply of (3) spear, (4) dot, (5) dog and (6) an unidentified object, (7) mirror, (8) comb, (9) an incompletely engraved chariot and on the side facet of the stela (not smoothed like the main face), is a complete chariot (10).

The engravings are deeply pecked and smoothed, except the dog that is lightly incised. Intaglio emphasises the centre of the shield, the mirror and the big chariot.

5 Commentary

This is a confidently executed stela, even though the engraver mistook the position of the chariot and failed to leave enough room to distribute the motifs properly. The shield belongs to the V-notched Type IA; the comb is quite elaborate with a knob on its handle. The lightly incised dog (5) may be a later motif to the main composition.

The figure is based on Celestino's drawing, but the pectoral he shows on the warrior is invisible and therefore ignored and motif 6 is not a lyre.

6 Bibliography

See: Almagro Gorbea 1977 (Lám XIX/2 only shows the front clearly); Celestino 2001:364–365 with details of discovery and context.

1 Catalogue number and findspot: **C34 CABEZA DEL BUEY III, Ba★**

2 Circumstances of discovery, context and present location

It was found on the farm of El Corchito, which lies 9 km west of Cabeza del Buey, next to a minor road that leads to the town of Villanueva de la Serena.

It is deposited in the Museo Arqueológico Provincial de Badajoz.

3 Stone type, size and condition of the monument

The stone is calcareous slate and although the stela has been damaged on all sides, the main composition is well preserved. It measures 0.99 m high, 0.52 m wide and its average thickness is 0.21 m.

4 Description of the composition and motifs

The warrior dominates the composition. The motifs are: (1) a shield, (2) an armed warrior with exaggerated fingers, (3) comb and (4) large sword engraved over the body, (5) unidentified object, (6) mirror, (7) row of five dots, (8) another unidentified motif that may be a helmet and (9) a spear. The engravings are pecked in wide, shallow grooves and smoothed later. Intaglio emphasises the warrior, his sword and mirror.

5 Commentary

In this powerful composition the human figure is the protagonist. The drawing is based on the figure in Almagro Gorbea, with some changes. The shield is clearly of Type IIA with three concentric circles, no decoration and a big rectangular handle. The warrior figure not only has volume to give it authority, but might also be dressed in a long tunic and perhaps heavy footwear; this would break the usual pattern of showing warriors naked. The body was engraved first and then the arms and sword were cut across it. The sword has a big leaf-shaped blade and a large hilt with large pommel and guard. A grand weapon of this dimension and profile matches the leaf shaped swords of Atlantic type used for slashing and would date to the eleventh century BC; it is not a Carp's Tongue sword. There are two unidentifiable motifs, but Celestino calls them (5) a brooch and (8) a helmet.

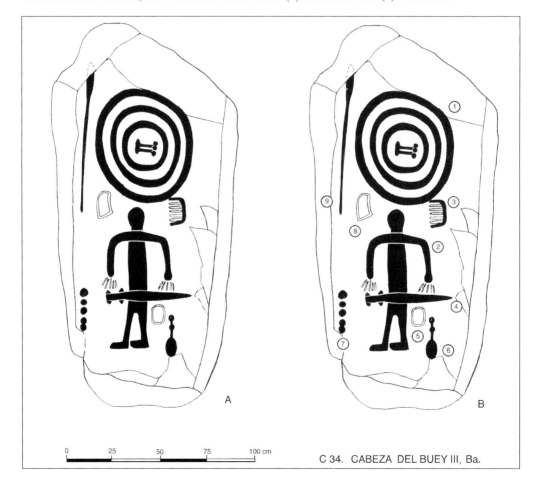

A

B

0   25   50   75   100 cm

C 34.   CABEZA DEL BUEY III, Ba.

6 Bibliography

See: Almagro Gorbea 1977 (figure 69/6 and Lám XIX/3); Celestino 2001:366-367.

1 Catalogue number and findspot: **C35 ESPARRAGOSA DE LARES I, Ba★**

2 Circumstances of discovery, context and present location

It was found casually in 1983 among the stones of a ruined building, in the area flooded by the dam of the river Zújar, on its right bank. The landscape is open and at 450 m altitude, based on Precambrian rocks, was suitable for grazing.

It is deposited in the Museo Arqueológico Provincial de Badajoz.

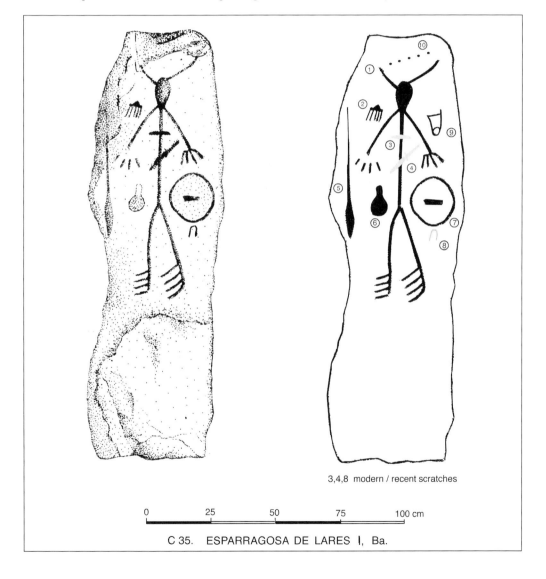

3,4,8 modern / recent scratches

0   25   50   75   100 cm

C 35.   ESPARRAGOSA DE LARES I, Ba.

3 Stone type, size and condition of the monument

The stone type is slate schist, with lateral damage and exfoliation at the top; 1.72 m high, 0.51 m wide and 0.16 m thick; complete.

4 Description of the composition and motifs

This stela bears a composition centred on a horned figure (1), probably naked, the body twisted back at a slight angle, with arms extended, showing the fingers and toes exaggerated. Recognisable motifs are: (2) a comb, (5) a spear with the point facing downwards near the right hand, (6) a mirror, (7) a shield, (9) a brooch and (10) row of five dots. The pecked engraving makes a broad, shallow line and intaglio emphasises the mirror.

5 Commentary

The stela has a prominent horned 'hero' figure. The brooch (9) and row of 5 dots (10) are shown by Celestino 2001, but missing from the original publication by Enríquez and Celestino 1984. Both motifs were visible in 2001. We disagree over the nature and detail of five others; three motifs (3, 4, 8) are actually modern scratches to the stela, not a pectoral and a dagger. Other details invisible to us are the crossbar on the mirror and the rectangular handle on the comb.

The shield is of Type IIA, which is a round outline with only the handle shown. The brooch is clearly drawn and might be an asymmetric elbow type. The lack of a sword is unusual.

6 Bibliography

See: Celestino 2001:368; Enríquez & Celestino 1984. No good photograph is published.

---

1 Catalogue number and findspot: **C36 ESPARRAGOSA DE LARES II, Ba**

2 Circumstances of discovery, context and present location

It was found in 1986 on the farm called La Barca, at the point where the river Guadalemar joins the river Zújar on its right bank, between the hills of Doña Maria and Masatrigo.

It is deposited in the Museo Arqueológico Provincial de Badajoz.

3 Stone type, size and condition of the monument

The stela is an irregular schist slab, broken at the sides and base and which measures 0.84 m high, 0.56 m wide and has an average thickness of 0.12 m. We are uncertain if it is complete, or not.

4 Description of the composition and motifs

The stela was apparently engraved on two separate occasions. In each case the composition was the same, with a stylised warrior in the centre. The first engravings were later rubbed out by heavy pecking, but their outlines remain visible (1–4). Motifs 1 and 2 are unidentifiable; motif 3 is a human figure with an arc over its head and motif 4 is a set of five dots.

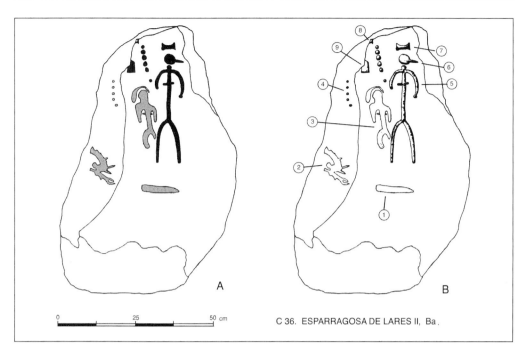

A

B

0   25   50 cm

C 36. ESPARRAGOSA DE LARES II, Ba.

The second engravings are (5) a stick figure, (6) a mirror, (7) an unidentified object, (8) a set of five dots plus an extra one and (9) another unidentified motif.

5 Commentary

Celestino is the only published source for this stela and its drawing. It is another example showing the technical limitations of the engravers and the problems they had in making even simple compositions. The lack of any weapons or shield indicates a later date in the series.

6 Bibliography

See: Celestino 2001:369. There is no published photograph.

1 Catalogue number and findspot: **C37 NAVALVILLAR DE PELA (COGOLLUDO), Ba**

2 Circumstances of discovery, context and present location

This stela was found at Cogolludo, on the right bank of the river Guadiana, 8 km north-west of the town of Orellana. It appeared when drought lowered the water level of the lake behind the dam of Orellana.

It is deposited in the garden of the public school of Orellana la Vieja, Badajoz.

3 Stone type, size and condition of the monument

It is of slate-schist that has been broken and partly exfoliated. It measures 1.1 m high, 0.60 m wide and 0.21m thick.

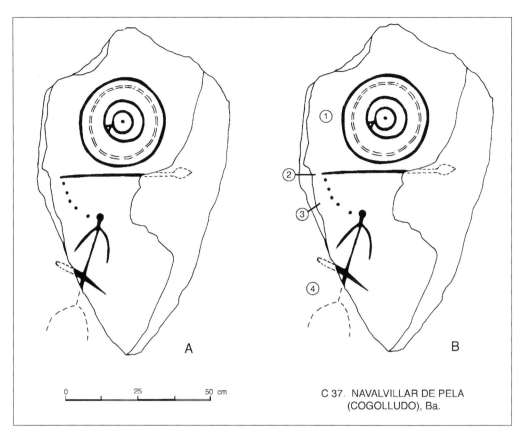

A

B

0   25   50 cm

C 37. NAVALVILLAR DE PELA
(COGOLLUDO), Ba.

4 Description of the composition and motifs

The composition figures a prominent shield and a stick figure below it. The motifs are (1) a shield, (2) a spear, (3) a row of five dots and (4) a stick figure of a warrior with a stylised sword at his waist. The engravings are pecked and smoothed.

5 Commentary

The drawing is based on Celestino, with modifications. Perhaps this shield was intended to be a V-notched one of Type IC since one ring has a tiny notch and has an incomplete circle of decoration (shown as a dotted line). However, it actually fits better with the shields in Type IIC, which are like simple bull's-eyes. We cannot be certain if the human figure has a pectoral ornament as Celestino indicates, or not.

6 Bibliography

See: Celestino 2001:370. There is no good published photograph that shows the motifs clearly.

1 Catalogue number and findspot: **C38 CAPILLA I, Ba★**

2 Circumstances of discovery, context and present location

It was found on the right bank of the river Guadalmez, 2 km before it joins the river Zújar. The findspot is known as La Moraleja, on the estate called Berrocal y Santa Piedra, in Capilla, belonging to the township of Cabeza del Buey. The abrupt landscape is difficult to traverse except by the streams and riverbeds; a ford over the river lies close by. The findspot is just 500 m away from that of C39 Capilla II and less than 1 km distant from C40 Capilla III. Over the provincial border in Córdoba less than 5 km away, in the municipality of El Viso, is another concentration of six stelae.

It is deposited in the Museo Arqueológico Provincial de Badajoz.

3 Stone type, size and condition of the monument

The stela is on an irregular slab of quartzite. It measures 0.80 m high, 0.47 m wide and 0.17 m thick. Although the main motif is complete, it is uncertain if the stela was originally larger.

4 Description of the composition and motifs

The composition is that of a *Diademada* with four motifs. They are (1) a stick figure in the

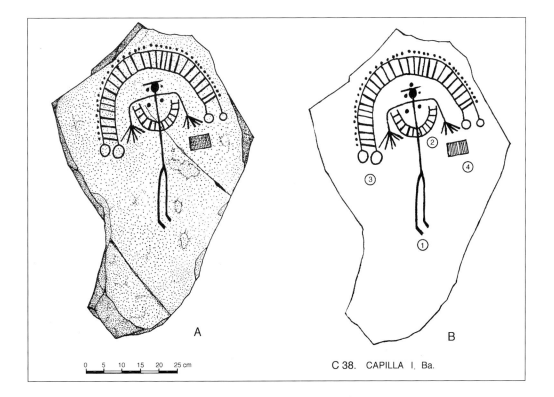

A

0   5   10   15   20   25 cm

C 38.   CAPILLA I, Ba.

centre with (2) five dots symmetrically place around the head and torso, a curved object that may be a belt or chest ornament, (3) an enormous headdress above the figure and (4) a comb. The engraved lines are deep and clear.

5 Commentary

The drawing of version A is based on that in Enríquez and Celestino, incorporating our observations in version B. Motif 4 is probably a comb, not a lyre. There is certainly an artificial dot made above the head of the figure.

The scene is notable for the protagonism of the huge headdress (3), which dwarfs the stick figure at the centre of the composition. It has 26 equal compartments (exactly the same number as the headdress on C7 Torrejón el Rubio II) and ends in two pairs of loops; above it is an arc of 39 deep dots. The figure has outstretched hands and huge grasping fingers, six on the right hand and five on the left; there is nothing to show its sex and no obvious female sexual signs. The head has a flat line across it, as if to depict a hat.

Similar headdresses on two other stelae (C7 and C60) are so alike that they may represent an image of a warrior in heroised form; in this case materialised not with horns but with the headdress and belt. The fantastic headdress would also explain why the grasping hands on both stelae reach out towards a comb. The lack of weapons and shield is notable, too.

6 Bibliography

See: Celestino 2001:371–372; Enríquez & Celestino 1981/2 (Láms I and II).

---

1 Catalogue number and findspot: **C39 CAPILLA II, Ba★**

2 Circumstances of discovery, context and present location

The stela was found on the right bank of the river Guadalmez, in a heap of stones from

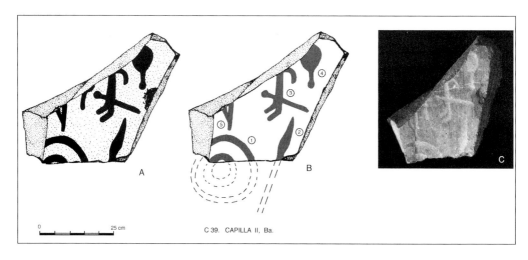

C 39. CAPILLA II, Ba.

field clearance, 500 m away from stela C38.

It is deposited in the Museo Arqueológico Provincial de Badajoz.

3 Stone type, size and condition of the monument

This stela is made of quartzite and measures 0.50 m high, 0.38 m wide and has an average thickness of 0.15 m. It is a small fragment from a larger scene.

4 Description of the composition and motifs

There are five motifs: (1) a shield with two concentric circles, (2) a spear head, (3) a small warrior figure wearing a sword, (4) a mirror and (5) an unidentifiable motif that may be a bow or a fibula. The motifs are pecked in wide, clear lines, highlighted by intaglio.

5 Commentary

We observed no fingers on the hand of the warrior, who is essentially a stick figure. It is impossible to know the original composition accurately, but version B reconstructs the existing motifs.

6 Bibliography

See: Celestino 2001:373; Enríquez & Celestino 1984 (figure 2a and photograph on Lám I/3).

---

1 Catalogue number and findspot: **C40 CAPILLA III, Ba★**

2 Circumstances of discovery, context and present location

The stela was found casually, before 1974, on the right bank of the river Guadalmez, on the estate known as Las Yuncas.

It is deposited in the Museo Arqueológico Provincial de Badajoz.

3 Stone type, size and condition of the monument

The stela is of quartzite like the two others from this area and measures 1.35 m high, 0.44 m wide and has an average thickness of 0.33 m. It is substantially complete.

4 Description of the composition and motifs

The composition centres around the (1) warrior figure, which has outstretched hands with the fingers shown and an aureole of small pits around the head, like a large coiffure. The other motifs are (2) a sword, (3) unidentifiable motif, (4) bow and arrow, (5) another unidentifiable motif, (6) a mirror, (7) a head of a spear and (8) a comb. The pecking is clear and quite deep, almost an intaglio technique.

5 Commentary

There are two versions of the stela; version A follows Enríquez and Celestino (1984 figure

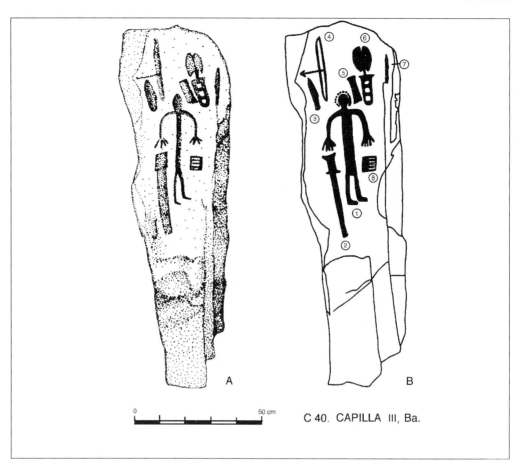

C 40. CAPILLA III, Ba.

2b) and version B is after Celestino 2001, with changes. Our observations and photographs confirm version B is accurate, including the important details of the figure.

The warrior wears a long tunic, like C34 Cabeza del Buey III. The aureole is unlikely to represent a helmet or a diadem and may be an attempt to show a special style of hair arrangement, perhaps plaited in braids and pulled back from the face, like that on the stela from X95 Lantejuela. The sword has an exceptionally big hilt and exaggerated guards and, from its slender profile ending in an expanded tip, appears to have a thin blade that is sheathed, showing the sword in its scabbard. These details would fit the style of Carp's Tongue sword known from Sardinia, which have especially big hilts. The motif 3 could be a quiver for arrows; and Celestino suggests (5) could be a dagger.

Motif 6 is unique and in prominence rises above any other object in the panoply, even the sword. Celestino says it is a razor, but it is more likely to be an oval mirror with an openwork handle, like the ones from Sardinia, or the bronze handle from Baiões. At the warrior's left hand is a comb (not a lyre) and coupled with the interest in the mirror and tunic, they confirm the special attention paid to the warrior's physical appearance and dress, reducing that of the weapons. Note there is no shield in this composition.

6 Bibliography

See: Celestino 2001:374–375; Enríquez & Celestino 1984 (Lám I/2).

---

1 Catalogue number and findspot: **C41 CAPILLA IV, Ba**

2 Circumstances of discovery, context and present location

The stela was discovered in the Vega de San Miguel, on the right bank of the river Zújar. It appeared after the land was ploughed. Three kilometres north-west are the other stelae from Capilla and the two from El Viso I and IV are 2 km to the south.

   It was exhibited in the Museo Arqueológico Provincial de Badajoz, but has returned to private possession.

3 Stone type, size and condition of the monument

The stela is of soft quartzite with slate-like laminations, which exfoliates easily. It meas-

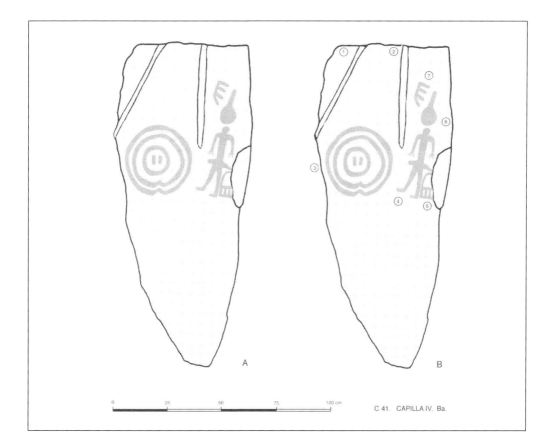

C 41. CAPILLA IV, Ba.

ures 1.45 m high, 0.65 m wide and has an average thickness of 0.17 m. The top portion is missing; about two-thirds of it are preserved.

4 Description of the composition and motifs

The composition gives equal importance to the (3) shield and (4) the warrior, whose fingers are outstretched and who wears a sword at his waist. There is a lyre (5), a mirror (6) and a comb (7). Motifs 1 and 2 are probably modern and not connected with the composition. The engraving is wide and had deep pecking.

5 Commentary

The shield is of the V-notched Type IA with three concentric rings. Little can be said of the other motifs given their schematic depiction. The figure is after Celestino.

6 Bibliography

First published by Celestino 2001:376–377.

1 Catalogue number and findspot: **C42 CAPILLA V, Ba**

2 Circumstances of discovery, context and present location

It was found casually on the farm called El Tejadillo, on the right bank of the river Zújar, 4 km east of the town of Capilla. The area is suitable for dry farming.

It is deposited in the Museo Arqueológico Provincial de Badajoz.

3 Stone type, size and condition of the monument

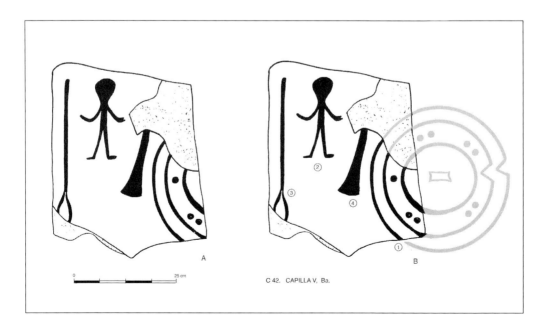

C 42. CAPILLA V, Ba.

The stela is of soft quartzite like C41. It measures 0.46 m high, 0.36 m wide and 0.15 m thick. It is a small fragment from a much larger stela.

4 Description of the composition and motifs

The composition is dominated by the remains of (1) a large decorated shield and seems to include secondary elements. The motifs include (2) a small figure, (3) a spear and (4) what may be the scabbard tip of a large sword. All motifs are deeply pecked and in intaglio.

5 Commentary

The shield is a probably a V-notched one of Type IB and would have had an original diameter of more than 35 cm. The small figure has an enlarged head and assumes an attitude of supplication or submission, not grasping with big fingers, like the main figures do. The drawing is modified after Celestino 2001.

6 Bibliography

First published by Celestino 2001:378. There is no published photograph.

---

1 Catalogue number and findspot: **C43 CAPILLA VI, Ba**

2 Circumstances of discovery, context and present location

The find circumstances and findspot are the same as for C42.

   It is deposited in the Museo Arqueológico Provincial de Badajoz.

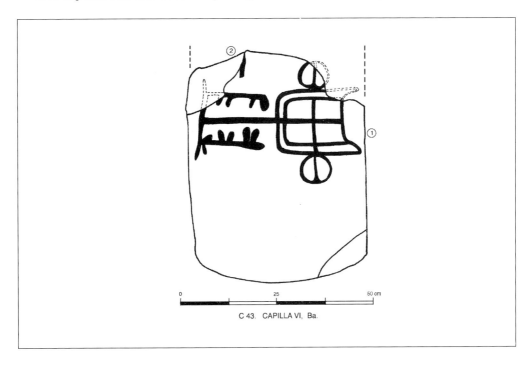

C 43. CAPILLA VI, Ba.

3 Stone type, size and condition of the monument

It is carved on local reddish quartzite and it measures 0.58 m high, 0.45 m wide and 0.12 m thick. It is a fragment, perhaps only one quarter, of a large stela.

4 Description of the composition and motifs

The main motif is a chariot with spoked wheels (1) and an indecipherable mark (2). The engraving is careful but shallow.

5 Commentary

The drawing is modified after Celestino 2001, who notes an important detail, namely that all three sides of the stela have been very carefully prepared and smoothed to a fine edge. This means that the stela must have been quite slender in shape and that the chariot motif would have figured very prominently on it.

6 Bibliography

First published by Celestino 2001:379. There is no published photograph.

---

1 Catalogue number and findspot: **C44 ZARZA CAPILLA I, Ba★**

2 Circumstances of discovery, context and present location

Although it was recorded as found on the estate known as Los Llanos within the district of Zarza Capilla la Nueva, the stela actually comes from a savanna owned by the town of Zarza Capilla, where the findspot is reported as being at the foot of the cemetery, 1 km south of the town. Stones from this area were transported to Los Llanos for modern buildings and it seems this stela must have been one of them.

It is deposited in the Museo Arqueológico Provincial de Badajoz.

3 Stone type, size and condition of the monument

The stela is of reddish quartzite, made of a regular block that has one naturally smooth face and is exceptionally thick. It measures 1.23m high, 0.40m wide and a thickness of 0.34 m. It is complete.

4 Description of the composition and motifs

The composition is centred on the armed warrior. The motifs are (1) an unidentified object, (2) a row of five dots, (3) horizontal spear, (4) shield, (5) mirror, (6) lyre, (7) warrior with sword at his waist and 'leggings' on his thighs, (8) chariot, (9) brooch and (10) a bow and arrow (later obliterated). The carving is clear but shallow pecking throughout.

5 Commentary

The drawing (Version A) is based on Celestino 2001, but with many modifications, based on our photographs of it.

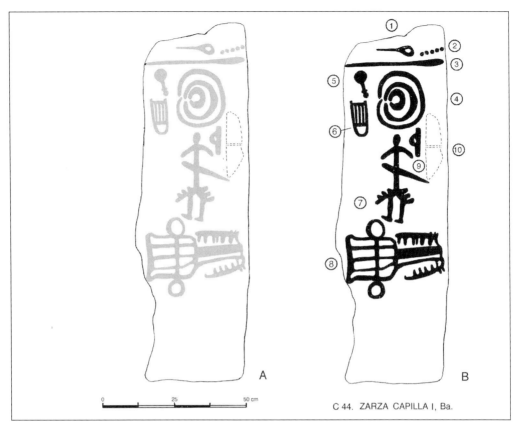

C 44. ZARZA CAPILLA I, Ba.

The shield is a V-notched one of Type IC, with no handle shown. The mirror has an elaborate handle with at least two ornaments on it; the lyre has three strings and is well drawn; the brooch is clumsily depicted. Of especial interest is the skirt or 'leggings' on the warrior, a feature that has been compared to that on the warrior from C65 Olivenza, but which appears quite different to us. The chariot is excellently drawn in contrast and has a complete vehicle drawn by two harnessed animals that are yoked.

The obliteration of motif 10 is important, since it suggests that the engraver made corrections, or alternatively, that the motif was damaged later on, intentionally.

6 Bibliography

See: Celestino 2001:380–383; Enríquez & Celestino 1984 (Lám I/1).

---

1 Catalogue number and findspot: **C45 ZARZA CAPILLA II, Ba★**

2 Circumstances of discovery, context and present location.

It was found in the same place as C44.

It is deposited in the Museo Arqueológico Provincial de Badajoz.

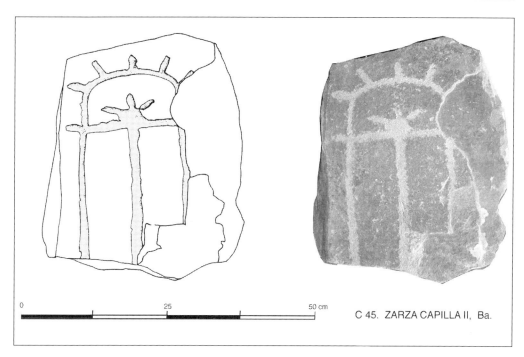

C 45. ZARZA CAPILLA II, Ba.

3 Stone type, size and condition of the monument

The stela is of reddish quartzite and measures 0.42 m high, 0.32 m wide and an average thickness of 0.13 m. It is broken and only the upper part survives.

4 Description of the composition and motifs

There is one motif of a schematic human figure that may have a simplified headdress above it.

5 Commentary

It is not certain this stela belongs to the warrior series.

6 Bibliography

First published by Celestino 2001:382. There is no good published photograph.

1 Catalogue number and findspot: C46 ZARZA CAPILLA III, Ba★

2 Circumstances of discovery, context and present location

It was found only 100 m from the centre of the settlement of Zarza Capilla la Vieja, in a rubbish heap next to a trackway that separates the road into the village from the cattle pastures.

It is deposited in the Museo Arqueológico Provincial de Badajoz.

3 Stone type, size and condition of the monument

The fragment is of hard reddish quartzite like C44 and C45 from this area and measures 0.88 m high, 0.35m wide and an average thickness of 0.13 m.

4 Description of the composition and motifs

Although only a fragment from a complex scene, the composition is similar to Ategua, with at least two zones. In Zone 1, the central motif is a poorly drawn and confused depiction of a chariot (1), with a small human figure, recumbent with arms outstretched, above it (2), then what may be the legs of a second small figure (3), a possible sword scabbard (4) and unidentified motif (5), a deep dot (6) and a probable lyre with the splayed frame, but no strings (7). In Zone 2, three naked male figures link arms at shoulder height, legs forward as if dancing, and each one has a headdress or helmet above his head (8–10). In between figures 8 and 9 is a clearly engraved mirror (11). All motifs are pecked in wide, shallow lines.

5 Commentary

The figure is based on Celestino, with modifications. Originally this was a big and very impressive stela, since what remains is almost a metre high. The complexity of the

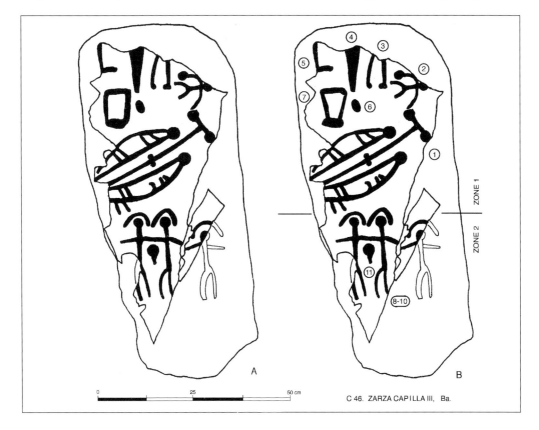

C 46. ZARZA CAPILLA III, Ba.

composition makes it probable that the original scene would have been like the one depicted on the C80 Ategua stela, narrating a story of the life, death and apotheosis of the 'hero'.

6 Bibliography

First published by Celestino 2001:383–384. There is no good published photograph.

---

1 Catalogue number and findspot: **C47 BENQUERENCIA DE LA SERENA, Ba★**

2 Circumstances of discovery, context and present location

Only the name of the large estate where it was found is known.

It is deposited in the Museo Arqueológico Provincial de Badajoz.

3 Stone type, size and condition of the monument

The fragment is of greenish slate that exfoliates easily. It measures 0.76 m high, 0.71 m wide and has an average thickness of 0.07 m. Three sides have been carefully worked and the face has been pecked smooth before engraving. The bottom part has broken away.

4 Description of the composition and motifs

The composition centres around the large shield (1), with a warrior wearing a sword depicted as a stick figure (2), accompanied by (3) a mirror, (4) an upright spear and (5) a short row of five dots. All the engraving is shallow pecking.

5 Commentary

The shield is a V-notched one of Type II, with three concentric circles and no decorative

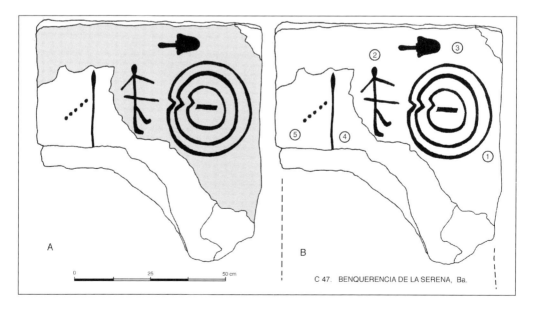

C 47. BENQUERENCIA DE LA SERENA, Ba.

bosses. The mirror (if that is what motif 3 is intended to depict) is a large and peculiarly shaped one, with a bell shaped face. The drawing is after Celestino.

6 Bibliography

See: Celestino 2001:385. There is no good published photograph.

1 Catalogue number and findspot: **C48 MAGACELA, Ba★**

2 Circumstances of discovery, context and present location

In the 1940s, it was found built into a field wall of clay bricks, near the village well.

It is deposited in the Museo Arqueológico Nacional, Madrid.

3 Stone type, size and condition of the monument

It is a fine-grained sedimentary rock, of dark grey green colour. It measures 1.43 m high, 0.35 m wide and has an average thickness of 0.33 m. It is complete.

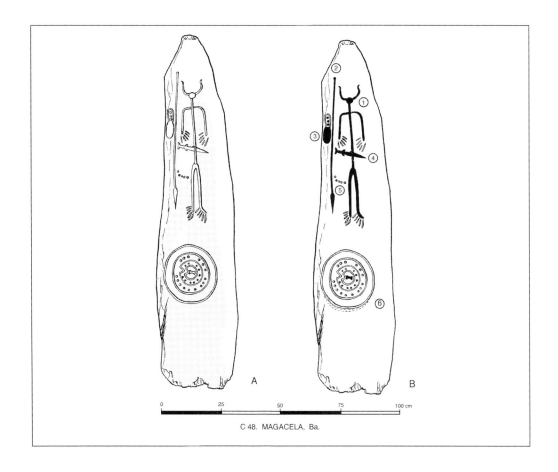

C 48. MAGACELA, Ba.

4 Description of the composition and motifs

The stela has the shape and profile of a menhir and the engraved face was previously smoothed. The composition is strikingly vertical and focused on the large figure of a horned warrior surrounded by his panoply (1). The digits on the feet and hands are clearly engraved and the horns emerge from the side of the head before twisting outwards at their tips. The panoply includes (2) a spear with a rounded metal butt, (3) a large mirror with decorated handle, (4) a sword with a big symmetrical handle worn at the waist, (5) a set of five dots and below everything else, (6) a large shield.

5 Commentary

The drawing is based on Almagro Basch 1966, modified. This commanding composition is among the most confident and well-executed warrior stelae and the engraver has achieved a balanced scene that is aesthetically pleasing and easy to read. The human figure has many details in common with that from Esparragosa de Lares I (C35), such as the extended digits, horned head and stick figure body. The sword is shown in great detail and the fine hilt has a big disc-shaped pommel and large curved guards; the blade is short and slightly leaf-shaped. The mirror has a unique handle. The spear clearly shows the rounded metal butt on the end, like C83 Córdoba II. The shield is a V-notched one of Type IB, with four concentric circles; the innermost ring has the pairs of bosses and the next ring has them in triples. This is a pattern found on other shields of this type. The engraver corrected the shield motif (shown on version B). This ghostly line is visible in Almagro Basch's photograph.

6 Bibliography

See: Almagro Basch 1966 (figure 24 and Lám XIX); Celestino 2001:386.

1 Catalogue number and findspot: **C49 CANCHO ROANO, ZALAMEA DE LA SERENA, Ba**

2 Circumstances of discovery, context and present location

Archaeological excavations at the palace-sanctuary of Cancho Roano discovered this stela in 1990, embedded with the engraved face upwards, as the second step in the staircase that ascends to the patio from the principal entrance. The staircase was constructed in the fifth century BC.

It remains in its archaeological context, at the site museum of Cancho Roano, Badajoz.

3 Stone type, size and condition of the monument

The stone is granite but it erodes easily. It measures 2.0 m high, 0.60 m wide and has a variable thickness from 0.20 to 0.45 m. Its shape is a pointed menhir, rounded completely and well finished, but eroded by use on the staircase.

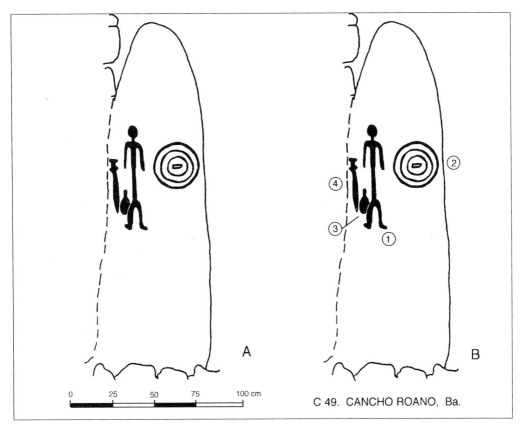

C 49. CANCHO ROANO, Ba.

4 Description of the composition and motifs

The human figure dominates the simple composition (1). The panoply includes (2) a shield, (3) a mirror and (4) a sword.

5 Commentary

Our drawing is based on Celestino 2001. All the motifs are eroded and therefore not easily copied. The human figure is schematic, but the head is in intaglio. The shield is a simple one of Type IIA with three concentric circles and horizontal handle. The sword is unsheathed and its big hilt, guards and leaf-shaped blade are clear on the drawing. Celestino (1992:29) says other motifs can be detected 'intuitively' such as a spear, comb and brooch. We can see none of them.

6 Bibliography

First published by Celestino 1992 (photograph on Tav VI/3) and again in 2001:387.

1 Catalogue number and findspot: **C50 QUINTANA DE LA SERENA, Ba**

2 Circumstances of discovery, context and present location

Found in 1977 with other large stones of similar size when ploughing a low rise called Cuatro Pies, on the estate of Las Reyertas, which adjoins that of Cancho Roano. The countryside is flat oak savanna today.

   The stela is at present in the house of D Braulio Nogales, which is next to the estate, in the township of Zalamea de la Serena.

3 Stone type, size and condition of the monument

It is of granite and measures 1.04 m high, 0.85 m wide and an average thickness of 0.14 m. The top is slightly damaged and the engraved face is badly eroded. It is substantially complete.

4 Description of the composition and motifs

Celestino says that the motifs are difficult to see and are of uncertain identification. He recognises (1) a shield in the centre, (2) a sword, (3) a possible spear, (4) a brooch and (5) the body of a chariot. The engraving is broad and shallow and the sword has been smoothed.

5 Commentary

We can see only the shield, sword and chariot. The shield is clearly engraved and has V-notches, so it is probably type IA. Suárez and Ortiz report that the shield is partly pecked

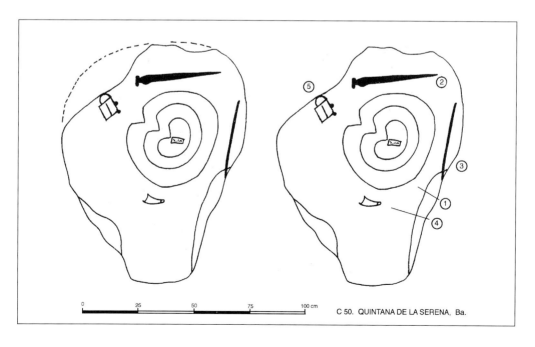

C 50. QUINTANA DE LA SERENA, Ba.

in low relief (like C4 Baraçal). This is possibly a basic composition with an additional motif (the chariot). The triangular base of the stela was intentionally prepared.

The drawing follows Celestino, with changes.

6 Bibliography

See: Celestino 2001:388; Suárez de Venegas & Ortiz Romero 1994:55 (photograph).

---

1 Catalogue number and findspot: **C51 VALDETORRES I, Ba★**

2 Circumstances of discovery, context and present location

It was found during building works to the cellar of a house, located at the Cerro del Santo, buried in the farmyard. The district of Valdetorres is on the left bank of the river Guadalmez, 5 km from its confluence with the Guadiana. The area is dry farmed today.

It is deposited in the Museo Arqueológico Provincial de Badajoz.

3 Stone type, size and condition of the monument

The stela is of reddish quartzite with white veins. It measures 1.24 m high, 0.54 m wide

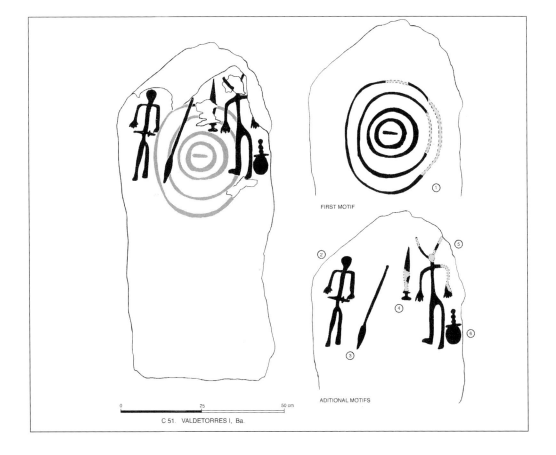

FIRST MOTIF

ADITIONAL MOTIFS

C 51. VALDETORRES I, Ba.

and a maximum thickness of 0.26 m. It is damaged on the sides and splintered on the top and is incomplete.

4 Description of the composition and motifs

The stone surface was not smoothed before engraving and the subsequent damage and exfoliation makes the motifs difficult to read. There are clearly two phases of engraving. The first motif is a very big shield (1), over which a second composition is added. This consists of a paired warrior scene, with a naked figure on the left (2), a spear (3), sword (4), a horned figure on the right (5) and a motif difficult to determine that may be a mirror (6). The engravings are wide shallow lines pecked into the surface.

5 Commentary

This is a very important example of a stela being re-cut and the composition changed. The first composition centres on the shield, which is a simple design of four concentric circles and of Type IIC. The second composition of the paired warriors with their panoply is ideologically more advanced and probably represents one warrior with 'heroic' attributes. The 'hero' figure (5) has clearly incised fingers and is the primary figure in the composition, since the sword and mirror are close to his hands. The scene is similar to that on C53 Alamillo.

The drawing differs from Celestino's and includes only the motifs visible to us. The warrior (2) does not have a sword or wear a pectoral. The mirror and its elaborate handle were most indistinct. The sword has a clear pommel and guard, but the blade is eroded; it may be leaf-shaped and unsheathed.

6 Bibliography

See: Celestino 2001:389–90. There is no good published photograph.

1 Catalogue number and findspot: **C52 VALDETORRES II, Ba**

2 Circumstances of discovery, context and present location

Not known. Only a drawing, in a letter dated October 1902, mentions the existence of this monument.

The stela is lost.

3 Stone type, size and condition of the monument

The stela is of granite and measures approximately 1.0 m high, 0.70 m wide and 0.12 m thick. It is fragmentary.

4 Description of the composition and motifs

There is (1) a chariot, (2) a dot (possibly natural) and (3) a circular shield of Type IIC.

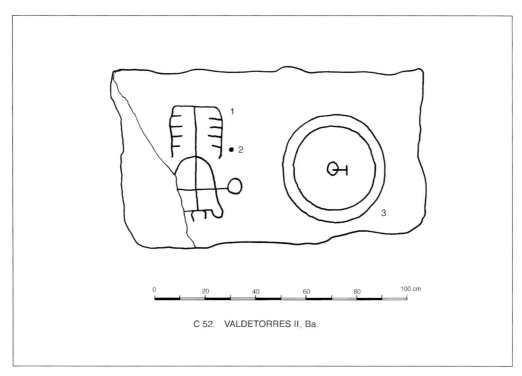

C 52.   VALDETORRES II, Ba.

5 Commentary

It is possible that one day, this stela will appear again. It is one of the first to be described and the manuscript is clear and precise about the stela and its main motifs.

6 Bibliography

See: Celestino 2001:391. First published, with copy of the manuscript showing the stela as a small sketch, by González Cordero & De Alvarado Gonzalo 1989–1990, figure 2.

1 Catalogue number and findspot: **C53 ALAMILLO, Ciudad Real**

2 Circumstances of discovery, context and present location

It was found casually in 1980, on a meander of the left bank of the river Alcudia, in the area known as the Dehesa de Castilseras. The river runs in an east-west direction and provides an easy route through the area. Today this is savanna.

   It is deposited in the Museo de Ciudad Real.

3 Stone type, size and condition of the monument

The stela is of quartzite, with a naturally smooth face suitable for engraving. It has been damaged and the left side and base have broken off. It measures 0.46 m high, 0.56 m wide and has an average thickness of 0.21 m. It must be considered a fragment.

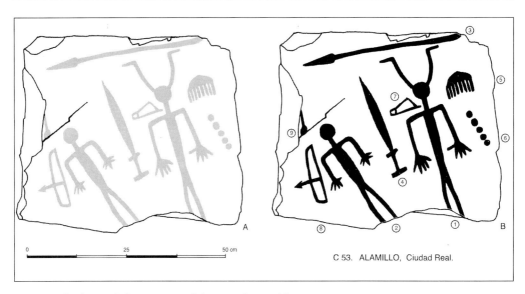

C 53. ALAMILLO, Ciudad Real.

4 Description of the composition and motifs

The scene centres on two naked warriors with outstretched hands. The larger figure has horns emerging from his head (1), with a panoply around him of (3) a spear, (4) a sword, (5) a comb, (6) a row of five dots and (7) a brooch. The second naked figure (2) has a bow and arrow (8) and an unidentified object (9). The motifs are all executed in shallow pecking.

5 Commentary

The paired composition is like several others, notably C51 Valdetorres I. The horned figure is larger than the other, distinguished by the horns emerging from his head as well as the panoply around him. Note the horns twist outwards at the tips. The sword is well depicted and has a big handle, with horizontal pommel and guards and a leaf-shaped blade. The brooch is an asymmetric elbow fibula.

6 Bibliography

First published by Celestino 2001:392–393. There is no published photograph.

---

1 Catalogue number and findspot: **C54 EL VISO I, Co★**

2 Circumstances of discovery, context and present location

Nothing is known of the find circumstances, except that the stone was caught in the tines of a harrow and left at the edge of a farm.
    Deposited in the Museo Arqueológico Nacional, Madrid.

3 Stone type, size and condition of the monument

The stela is of dark brown quartzite and measures 1.21m high, 0.39 m wide and has an average thickness of 0.20 m. It is substantially complete.

4 Description of the composition and motifs

The stone has been carefully trimmed on all sides and the pointed shape is probably intentional. The face is naturally smooth.

Dominating the composition is a large horned warrior with outstretched hands and extended fingers and an erect penis (1). The warrior wears earrings. Around him is a complete panoply, with a large decorated shield (2), a comb (3), a mirror (4), an unidentified object (5), a spear pointing downwards (6), and two swords (7, 8). There is a bow and arrow (9), a brooch (10), a stallion with a mare, pulling a chariot (11), and a dog below them (12). The engraving has wide, shallow lines. We show the deeper motifs in a darker tone.

5 Commentary

Our drawing is based on Almagro Gorbea 1977, with changes.

The scene portrays the horned warrior in his glory, surrounded by one of the largest panoplies recorded. Many details are remarkable; the warrior's sex is unambiguous; the horns and earrings are larger than life, too. The unique shield of Type III has 10 compartments, each with a boss. There is a brooch whose type is impossible to determine and a simple chariot, where the sex of one stallion is shown clearly. It is rare to find two swords

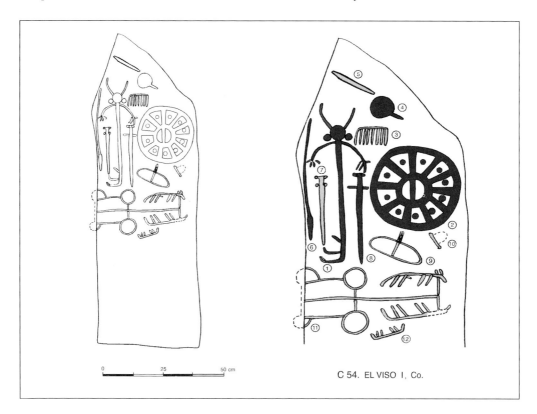

0   25   50 cm

C 54. EL VISO I, Co.

specifically reserved for the use of one warrior, as if the warrior 'hero' was able to fight with both swords at once. They are Carp's Tongue swords with big guards, horizontal pommels and long parallel-sided blades.

The technical ability of the engraver failed to match his ambition to document every object faithfully and the crowded composition shows his weak sense of design. The theme is that of a warrior 'hero' with all his attributes; and the pair of swords may reflect a widespread European custom of burying two swords together as an offering.

6 Bibliography

See: Almagro Gorbea 1977 (figure 70/6 and Lám XIX/4); Celestino 2001:394–395.

---

1 Catalogue number and findspot: **C55 EL VISO II, Co**

2 Circumstances of discovery, context and present location

The stela was found after ploughing a narrow strip of land near the riverbank on the left bank of the river Zújar, at a place known as Las Mangadas. Not far away is a ford over the river and a modern provincial road. Other stelae have been found nearby, in similar riverbank locations. The abrupt geography means the rivers and fords are important for moving around the landscape. Today it is savanna.

It is deposited in the Casa de Cultura, in the town of Cabeza del Buey, Prov Badajoz.

3 Stone type, size and condition of the monument

The stela is of quartzite, rectangular in shape and measuring 0.76 m high, 0.68 m wide and with an average thickness of 0.18 m. Apart from some damage to one edge, it appears complete.

4 Description of the composition and motifs

The composition presents a large shield and warrior as the twin focal points. The main motifs are clear: (1) shield, (2) a warrior wearing a sword at his waist, with a panoply of (3) a mirror, (4) a spear pointing upright and (5) a chariot above the shield. The engravings

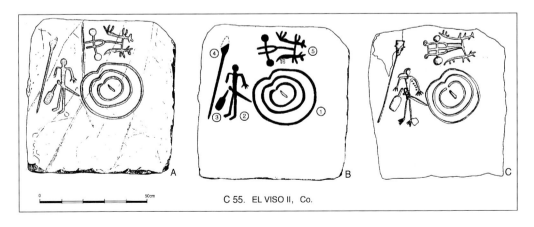

C 55. EL VISO II, Co.

are shallow and wide, on the naturally flat face of the rock.

5 Commentary

There are many differences of detail between the drawing published by Bendala et al in 1979/1980 (versions A and B) and that in Celestino 2001 (version C). We do not know if the extra details, such as the warrior's digits, a possible helmet, lyre and row of five dots really exist and can be seen. The shield is a V-notched one of Type IA, with three concentric circles.

6 Bibliography

See: Bendala et al 1979/1980; Celestino 2001:396–397; Vazquerizo 1989:31 (poor photograph).

---

1 Catalogue number and findspot: **C56 EL VISO III, Co★**

2 Circumstances of discovery, context and present location

It was found after ploughing, at a place only 300 m from the river Zújar and just 1 km from where stela C55 was discovered.

It is deposited in the Museo Arqueológico Provincial de Córdoba.

3 Stone type, size and condition of the monument

A large water-worn block of very hard quartzite, dark brown in colour, was chosen for the stela and it measures 0.96 m high, 0.77 m wide and has a maximum thickness of 0.35 m. The upper part has been lost, but the composition appears complete.

4 Description of the composition and motifs

The scene comprises three human figures and two shields. The central figure has short legs and has the head and upper body concealed in a voluminous garment and headdress (1).

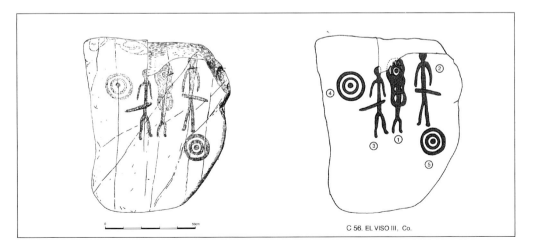

C 56. EL VISO III, Co.

On each side is a naked warrior, depicted identically with a sword at the waist and arms pointing downwards (2 and 3). A simple shield accompanies each figure (4 and 5). The engraving is by shallow pecking.

5 Commentary

This elegant composition is unique; although other paired scenes are known. The engraver has used an exquisite economy of line and symmetrical placing of the motifs to convey the message of a ritual scene, where two warriors escort a shrouded central figure, either a 'hero' or a divinity. After close study of the engravings, we are convinced this figure is not a female and has no breasts. Its head is clearly visible, surrounded by a headdress indicated by five gaps in the engraving and the arms are held close to the body. The area of the body has four small reserved areas in it, probably representing a pectoral ornament or a cuirass. The shields are of Type IIC, like simple bull's eyes and much more regular in shape than on Celestino's drawing.

The importance of this scene is that it is an advanced composition, historically late in the series and may be part of the heroisation of the warrior elite.

The drawing is based on that in Bendala et al 1979/1980, with changes.

6 Bibliography

See: Bendala et al 1979/1980 (figure 3); Celestino 2001:398; Iglesias Gil 1980:255 (a clear photograph).

1 Catalogue number and findspot: **C57 EL VISO IV, Co★**

2 Circumstances of discovery, context and present location

It was found when quarrying gravel in 1978, on the estate known as La Solanilla. The findspot lies between a minor local road and a gully that feeds into the right bank of the river Zújar, some 2 km to the west. The landscape is like the other settings for the El Viso stelae.

It is deposited in the Museo Arqueológico Provincial de Badajoz.

3 Stone type, size and condition of the monument

The stela is of hard quartzite with slate-like laminations, dark brown in colour, on a natural boulder with rounded edges. It measures 1.20 m high, 0.90 m wide and has an average thickness of 0.30 m. It is complete.

4 Description of the composition and motifs

The entire face of the stone has been pecked to make it suitable for engraving, leaving five fairly smooth facets as a result. The motifs respect these facets. The composition centres on the dual protagonism of (1) a warrior figure with a huge sword and (2) a shield. The

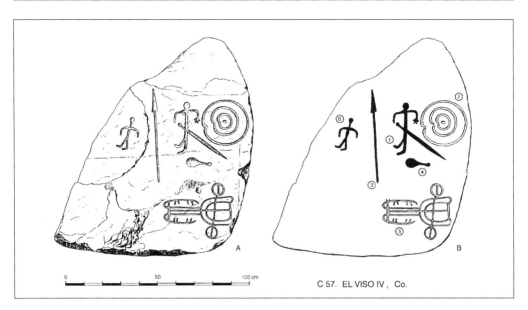

C 57. EL VISO IV, Co.

panoply includes: (3) a spear set with its point upright, (4) a mirror, (5) a chariot and (6) a small human figure in a secondary position. Celestino remarks on the two different engraving techniques employed, with motifs 2 and 5 more lightly engraved with a finer chisel than the rest.

5 Commentary

The main figure wears a sword that looks like a phallus-substitute and which from the shape of its blade would be a Carp's Tongue sword. The shield is a V-notched one of Type IC, with three concentric circles of decoration and a round umbo.

The drawings show version A (after Bendala et al 1979/1980), modified according to our observations in version B.

6 Bibliography

See: Bendala et al 1979/1980 (figure 4); Celestino 2001:399–400. There is no good published photograph.

1 Catalogue number and findspot: **C58 EL VISO V, Co**

2 Circumstances of discovery, context and present location

In 1982 farm workers found this stela on the estate called Befilla (or Adelfilla), just 500 m south of the findspot of the stela El Viso IV.

It is deposited in the private house of D José Domínguez Exojo, C/Carrera No. 28, in the town of Villanueva de la Serena.

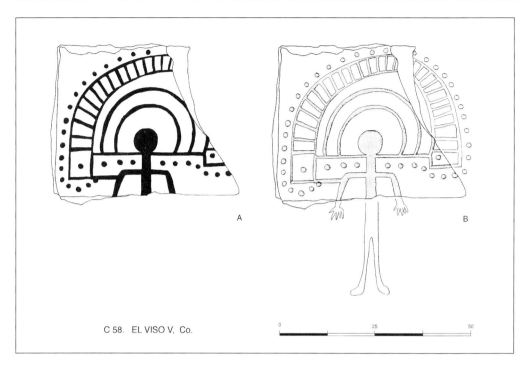

C 58. EL VISO V, Co.

3 Stone type, size and condition of the monument

The fragment of a small stela is on a thin slab of pale coloured quartzite that measures 0.36 m high, 0.50 m wide and has a thickness of 0.12 m.

4 Description of the composition and motifs

There is only one motif, namely a schematic human figure with an enormous headdress or aureole above it. The headdress is composed on a semicircular frame that has two inner arcs, then a broad segmented band above that and finally a line of large dots. The engraving is shallow but clear pecking.

5 Commentary

This stela probably belongs to the *Diademada* group and represents a 'hero' or divinity, whose special attributes are identified by the headdress. Of all the known headdresses, this is the largest and most elaborate. Its size alone makes it difficult to imagine as a real object and it may be an attribute of the divinity or 'hero' that is expressed in this extraordinary form. The drawing A is based on Celestino and in version B we reconstruct the complete headdress.

6 Bibliography

See: Celestino 2001:401. There is no good published photograph.

1 Catalogue number and findspot: **C59 EL VISO VI, Co**★

2 Circumstances of discovery, context and present location

It was discovered after ploughing and its findspot is between the two stelae just described (El Viso II and III), no more than 300 m from them.

   It is deposited in the Museo Arqueológico Provincial de Córdoba.

3 Stone type, size and condition of the monument

The stela is of dark brown quartzite, irregular in shape and damaged on all sides. It measures 0.79m high, 0.82 m wide and 0.18 m thick. The composition is probably complete.

4 Description of the composition and motifs

Dominating the scene are two naked male warriors, one with horns emerging directly from his head (2), the other damaged, but equal in size (1), at whose right hand is a sword (3). The rest of the panoply includes: (4) a comb, (5) bow and arrow, (6) a mirror, (7) a brooch and (8) a dog. The engraving is shallow pecking.

5 Commentary

This is an important paired scene with a horned warrior 'hero' clearly depicted; the horns emerge from the head in such a manner that they cannot belong to a helmet. Observing

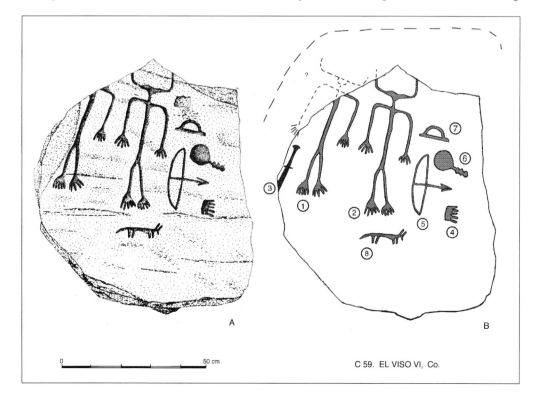

A

B

0   50 cm

C 59. EL VISO VI, Co.

closely, one can see the head is not human at all, but simply two swollen roots for the horns. Exaggerated hands and feet stress the grasping power of the figures. The mirror has an elaborate handle with three knobs on it; the brooch is impossible to classify. Note that there is neither chariot nor shield in the composition. This is a stylistically late composition, probably towards the end of the series, in the tenth/ninth century BC. It may show a warrior in the form of a 'hero'.

The drawings show version A (after Ruiz Lara 1986, figure 2) which reproduces the surface texture of the stela well, but failed to record the sword and has inaccurate details. Version B includes our changes; we could not see the sex of the dog, nor the extra motif above the brooch that Celestino describes.

6 Bibliography

See: Celestino 2001:402; Ruiz Lara 1986; Vazquerizo 1989:33 (photograph).

1 Catalogue number and findspot: **C60 BELALCÁZAR, Co★**

2 Circumstances of discovery, context and present location

This stela was found lying on the surface after being pulled up from the ground during ploughing, on the estate called El Mato. The findspot is about 500 m from an important

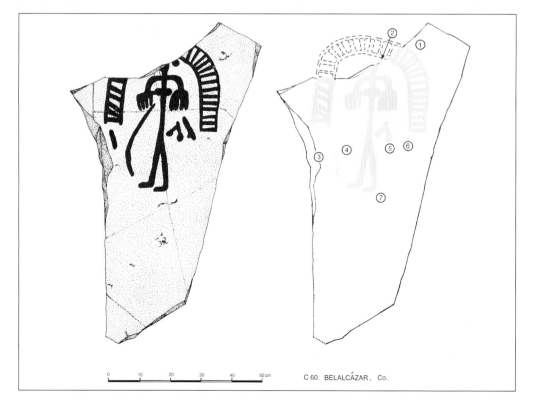

C 60. BELALCÁZAR, Co.

ford that allows the river Zújar to be crossed easily, known as the Vado de Junta. The stelae of El Viso II, III and VI were found 3 km to the east of this place.

It is deposited in the Museo Arqueológico Provincial de Badajoz.

3 Stone type, size and condition of the monument

The stone is of rose-coloured quartzite, naturally flat and even, which measures 1.0 m high, 0.55 m wide and 0.12 m average thickness. The top quarter has broken off but the composition, and the trapezoidal shape of the stela, is substantially complete.

4 Description of the composition and motifs

The scene depicted is simply that of a naked warrior with huge hands (1), with an enormous headdress above him (2). The motif 3, shown as a dot by Celestino, was invisible to us, and is probably not an original motif. The other motifs seem to be modern scratches (4–7). The engraving is by shallow pecking.

5 Commentary

The composition is that of a *Diademada*, a figure wearing a spectacular headdress, to show his divine or 'heroic' status. The schematic figure has exceptionally large hands and fingers and a motif on the chest that is probably a pectoral ornament, although this is uncertain. The other motifs identified by Celestino seem to be later damage, probably caused when the stela was ploughed up and thrown aside in the field. The headdress has the numerous small compartments that distinguish it from all other motifs.

The drawing shows the original figure from Enríquez and Celestino (1984, figure 5) in version A and in version B we reconstruct the headdress and include our observations.

6 Bibliography

See: Celestino 2001:403–404; Enríquez & Celestino 1984 (Lám I/4. This photograph is inaccurate since the motifs were retouched with chalk or similar material to make them stand out).

1 Catalogue number and findspot: **C61 CHILLÓN, Ciudad Real**

2 Circumstances of discovery, context and present location

It was found in 1990, while ploughing on the estate called Llano de los Roncos, in a place where three other inscribed Roman tombstones were found. The findspot is near the 7 km milestone on the road from Chillón to Siruela.

It is deposited in the Museo Arqueológico Provincial de Ciudad Real.

3 Stone type, size and condition of the monument

The stela is of pale coloured quartzite and measures 1.44 m high, 0.51 m wide and has an average thickness of 0.21 m. It is complete.

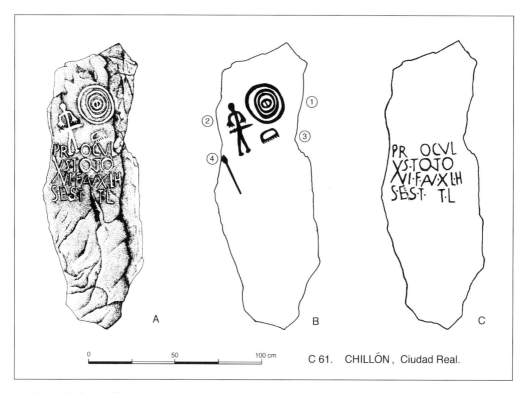

C 61.   CHILLÓN , Ciudad Real.

4 Description of the composition and motifs

The stone is largely unmodified and the motifs were engraved on a poorly prepared surface (and the Latin inscription was also engraved on a rough face). The composition is
probably complete and the shield (1) and the armed warrior (2) are the main elements.
There is (3) a comb and (4) a spear. The engraving is coarse, deep and clear.

5 Commentary

The engraver seems to have had little ability and failed to smooth the working surface, or
plan the composition carefully. The warrior has exaggerated hands and wears a sword at
his waist. The shield is of Type IIA, with four circles irregularly drawn. The stela was re-
used in the Roman period, like C16 Ibahernando.

   The Latin inscription drawn in version C reads:
        PROCVL
        VS . TOVTO
        NI . F . AN . XL . H
        S . E . S . T . T . L.
   When fully transcribed, it should read: PROCUL / US. TOUTO / NI. F(ilius).
AN(norum). XL. H(ic) / S(itus). E(st). S(it). T(ibi). T(erra). L(evis). This translates liter-
ally as; 'Proculus, son of Toutonus, aged 40, lies here. May the earth be light to you'
(Nexum ân). The spear is used cleverly to form part of the letters V and N. Toutonus is

clearly Celtic (the same root as Teutates, for example) and Proculus is a well-known Latin cognomen in Hispania. An alternative reading of TOVTO is TOTONI (Abascal 1994:247).

The drawing in version A is after Fernández Ochoa and Zarzalejos 1995, with modifications.

6 Bibliography

See: Abascal 1994; Celestino 2001:405; Fernández Ochoa & Zarzalejos Prieto 1994:267. There is no good published photograph.

---

1 Catalogue number and findspot: **C62 HERRERA DEL DUQUE (QUINTERÍAS), Ba**

2 Circumstances of discovery, context and present location

This stela was found thrown up on the surface of the ground, in the area known as Las Quinterías within an extensive tract of common land, 7 km north-west of the town of Herrera del Duque.

It is concealed privately and believed to be near Herrera del Duque.

3 Stone type, size and condition of the monument

The incomplete stela is of dark brown quartzite and measures 0.33 m high, 0.27 m wide and with an average thickness of 0.16 m. It is a small fragment of a larger stela, which was broken in two by the discoverers, who discarded the other part, which was undecorated.

4 Description of the composition and motifs

The warrior with a sword at his waist (1) dominates the composition. His panoply

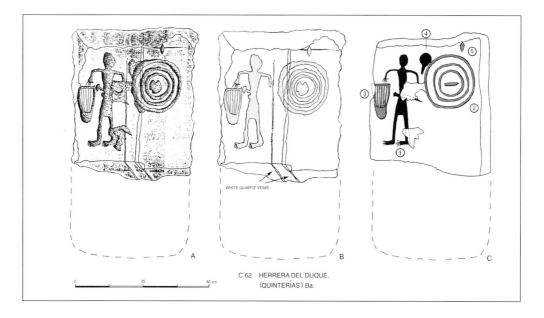

C 62. HERRERA DEL DUQUE, (QUINTERÍAS) Ba.

includes: (2) a shield, (3) a lyre, (4) a mirror and (5) an unidentified motif. The engraving is by wide shallow pecking, and intaglio for motifs 1 and 4.

5 Commentary

The surface is damaged and the motifs are difficult to observe. The drawings include the original version (A) by Vazquerizo Gil (1989:29) and a line drawing made from it (version B), but the figure from Celestino (version C) is probably the most accurate. The exfoliations damage all the motifs.

The warrior is remarkable for appearing dressed in a long skirt or kilt (or perhaps in a tunic that covers the body as well; the detail is unclear at this point), the fingers and toes are clear and the sword at his waist has a big domed pommel. The shield is a simple round one of Type IIA, with three irregular circles and horizontal handle. In contrast to these, the lyre is well drawn so that the strings and sound box are obvious.

6 Bibliography

See: Celestino 2001:406; Vazquerizo 1989:33. There is no good published photograph.

1 Catalogue number and findspot: **C63 ALMENDRALEJO (ARROYO BONAVAL), Ba**

2 Circumstances of discovery, context and present location

Although recorded as found on the banks of the Bonaval gully, in the district of Almendralejo, it is more likely (as Celestino argues) that it comes originally from Alange, where this particular type of crystalline limestone is found.

It was formerly in the collection of the Marqués de Monsalud but has since been lost.

3 Stone type, size and condition of the monument

The stela is made on a block of distinctive crystalline limestone, which outcrops in the Sierra de Las Peñas Blancas, close to the confluence of the river Matachel with the Guadiana, in the township of Alange. It measures 0.75 m high, 0.75 m wide and has a thickness of about 0.35 m. It is probably fragmentary.

4 Description of the composition and motifs

The simple composition consists of a (1) shield, (2) sword and (3) spear. They are all deeply incised.

5 Commentary

The drawing is after Almagro Basch 1966 (figure 3). The shield is a V-notched type IA with just two circles incised and no decoration. The sword has a blade that seems leaf-shaped, with a large hilt and big guards.

The interest of the stela lies in its possible proximity to the large Final Bronze Age set-

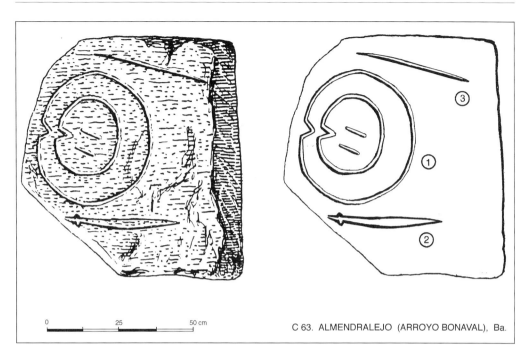

0   25   50 cm

C 63. ALMENDRALEJO (ARROYO BONAVAL), Ba.

tlement site of Alange, dominating this fertile area.

6 Bibliography

See: Almagro Basch 1966 (figure 3 and poor photograph on Lám XI/1); Celestino 2001:407.

1 Catalogue number and findspot: **C64 BADAJOZ (GRANJA DE CÉSPEDES), Ba⋆**

2 Circumstances of discovery, context and present location

In 1950, the stela was found lying flat above an inhumation burial without grave goods. The site is located 3.5 km west of the city of Badajoz, on the estate called the Granja de Céspedes. The findspot is 200 m from the small river Caya and the Guadiana river is 2 km away. There is a famous ford over the Guadiana only 3 km to the east.

   It is deposited in the Museo Arqueológico Nacional, Madrid.

3 Stone type, size and condition of the monument

The stela is of sandstone (not granite as Almagro Basch says) with a good proportion of quartzite, so it erodes quite easily. It measures 1.12 m high, 0.57 m wide and has an average thickness of 0.18 m. It has been trimmed to a regular rectangle, but the surface is badly eroded. It is complete.

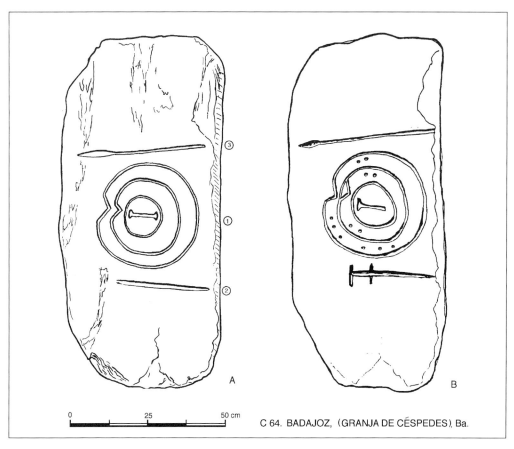

A

B

0   25   50 cm

C 64. BADAJOZ, (GRANJA DE CÉSPEDES), Ba.

4 Description of the composition and motifs

A simple composition has three motifs: (1) a shield, (2) a sword below it and (3) a spear above. All are deeply incised.

5 Commentary

This stela does seem to be associated with a human burial and the details provided by Almagro Basch in 1962 seem coherent. Celestino is sceptical and does not accept them. Almagro Basch (1962, 1966:105–106) was unequivocal about the association, writing:

> The stela from the Granja de Céspedes was found with all certainty covering an inhumation burial. It could have been upright and then would have fallen on the body, buried there, crushing it over time, since at the moment of being discovered and the monument recovered, the remains of a body, now very decomposed, were found below it. No other grave good appeared with the bones, the remains of which, conserved in a little box and wrapped in papers, were given to us. They do not have any anthropological value, since they were such scanty fragments, all very broken and decomposed, but one saw they belonged to some long bones and some scraps of cranium, all this, as we said, very decomposed and smashed up.

It is a great pity that the human remains were not studied.

Almagro Basch and Celestino saw different things on this stela, so we reproduce both drawings on our figure. Version A is after Almagro Basch; version B is after Celestino. Our observations confirm version A.

The shield is a V-notched one of type IA with three concentric circles and no decorative bosses. The sword hilt may be just visible, but this is uncertain.

6 Bibliography

See: Almagro Basch 1962, 1966 (figure 34 and Lám XXIX); Celestino 2001:408.

1 Catalogue number and findspot: **C65 OLIVENZA, Ba**

2 Circumstances of discovery, context and present location

Agricultural work revealed this stela on the estate called Monte Blanco, on the north side of the gully of San Benito. The area has many tributary streams draining into the Guadiana river and is savanna and dry farmland today.

The stela is deposited in the Museo Etnográfico Municipal 'González Santana', in the town of Olivenza.

3 Stone type, size and condition of the monument

The stela is of dark brown limestone, very soft and easy to engrave and measures 1.12 m high, 0.83 m wide and with a thickness of 0.22 m. The stone outcrops within 3 km of the findspot. It is incomplete although most of the composition has survived.

4 Description of the composition and motifs

The surface was smoothed before engraving and the lines are shallow and wide. The motifs are complicated and confused, since many have been re-engraved and corrected. Celestino thoroughly corrects the original drawing, which was full of errors, and we follow his account. However, Dirk Brandherm saw the stela in 2002 and notes that details of the sword, brooch and human figure are uncertain (information *in lit* to R Harrison). The figure shows version A following Bueno and Piñón and version B after Celestino, with changes.

A dramatically large warrior figure with outstretched hands dominates the composition (1). Around him is the panoply of (2) a shield, (3) a sword worn at the waist, (4) a spear placed horizontally above his head, (5) a chariot, of which only the wagon half survives and (6) attempts at an earlier drawing of the chariot below it. Celestino indicates (7) a brooch, (8) a horned helmet and earrings on the figure, (9) bow and arrow overlaying the lower legs, (10) a line of 10 dots, (10a) an isolated dot, (11) an arc of eight dots of which three are on the warrior's waist, (12) a ring on the warrior's finger, (13) a mirror, (14 and 15) two unidentified motifs, (16) a circle that may be an early attempt to draw a shield and (17) a line that marks a lower horizon to the composition.

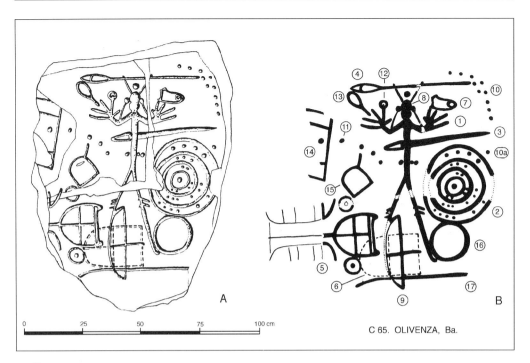

A

B

0   25   50   75   100 cm

C 65. OLIVENZA, Ba.

5 Commentary

The repeated re-engravings of several motifs appear to be due to the lack of skill on the part of the engraver, who failed to space them out properly on the stone face, with the confused result we have today. In particular, the chariot (once again) is the motif that was troublesome to place properly. This is not a monument that was corrected for its ideological content.

That said, the luxury of the panoply is remarkable and, despite the jumbled composition and amateurish execution, the stela impresses the viewer for the vigour of the warrior. This figure is enormous and his huge hands have five objects close by. He has some peculiar attachments to his legs, like leggings, but they may be an engraver's error and be the toes for a figure that was originally shorter than the present one, which was later enlarged. They are not at all similar to the skirt or leggings depicted on C44 Zarza Capilla I. The headdress or horned helmet with its earrings is unique. A few details emerge from the other motifs; the shield (2) is probably a V-notched one of type IC, since it has decorative bosses and a round centre, but has lost the V-notches in an exfoliation. The bosses have an interesting regularity to them, since the innermost ring has pairs, the next ring triples and the outer ring groups of four. A pattern like this has the effect of making the shield larger, since it seems to grow from the centre outwards. Other shields show the same design. The brooch may be a type of asymmetric elbow fibula.

6 Bibliography

See: Celestino 2001:409–410. There is no good published photograph, which is why the inaccurate drawing in Bueno & Piñón (1985) persisted for so long.

1 Catalogue number and findspot: **C66 ALDEA DEL REY I, Ciudad Real**

2 Circumstances of discovery, context and present location

In 1976, a tractor driver ploughing a field turned up this stela, in the area known as El Chiquero, 5.5 km north of the village of Aldea del Rey. The findspot was on the slopes of a low hill, overlooking the left bank of the river Jabalón, just 300 m away.

It is deposited in the Museo Arqueológico Provincial de Ciudad Real.

3 Stone type, size and condition of the monument

The stela is made of dark grey basalt, which occurs locally, and measures 0.96 m high, 0.51 m wide and 0.14m in average thickness. The upper portion, probably at least a third of the original stela, has been broken off and lost.

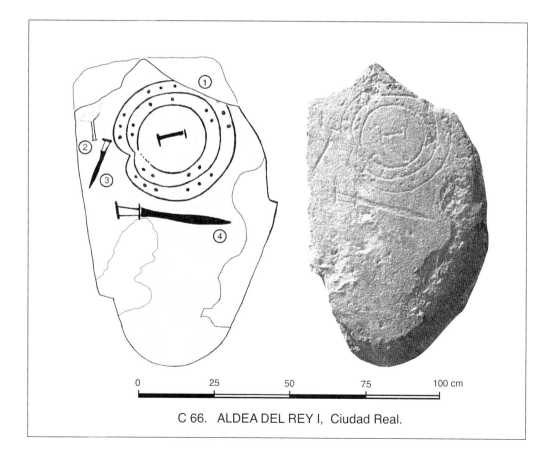

C 66. ALDEA DEL REY I, Ciudad Real.

4 Description of the composition and motifs

The surface was carefully pecked smooth before engraving. The composition centres on (1) a large shield, with (4) a sword, (3) a dagger and (2) the handle for a mirror is visible. The blades of the sword and dagger are emphasised by intaglio. Fine engraving marks the rest of the motifs.

5 Commentary

The composition may have been a basic one with additional motifs. The engraving is exceptionally clear and the shield is a V-notched one of Type IB. Its decorative bosses are arranged in pairs on the inner band and triplets on the outer band. The sword has a leaf-shaped blade, but the flat pommel and big guards on the hilt are typical of the Carp's Tongue weapons. The dagger is identical in design and engraving.

The drawing is based on the original one in Valiente and Prado.

6 Bibliography

See: Celestino 2001:411; Valiente & Prado 1978 (figure 1 with photograph).

1 Catalogue number and findspot: **C67 ALDEA DEL REY II, Ciudad Real**

2 Circumstances of discovery, context and present location

Farming work in 1976 revealed this stela, on the right bank of the river Jabalón. The findspot is in the area known as La Minilla, next to an abandoned mine and is 1.5 km north of stela C66.

It is deposited in the yard of the house belonging to the estate of Hurdillas, which is 3 km outside the village of Aldea del Rey.

3 Stone type, size and condition of the monument

The stela is a small fragment of slate with quartzite inclusions, grey in colour, measuring 0.53 m high, 0.37 m wide and with an average thickness of 0.18 m. It is a damaged fragment in rather poor condition.

4 Description of the composition and motifs

The motifs indicate that the stela was engraved on at least two separate occasions, each time with a different orientation. We propose the following reading of the composition; the *first motifs* were (1) a shield, (2) a stick figure of a man and (3) an unidentified motif. Subsequently, the stela was turned upside down and new motifs engraved on it, ignoring the previous ones. These *second motifs* are (4) a larger stick figure (with only the legs surviving), (5) a spear pointing to the ground, (6) a single dot and (7) an unidentified motif that may be the fingers of the larger figure.

5 Commentary

The re-engraving is the most important feature of this fragment and it was recognised first

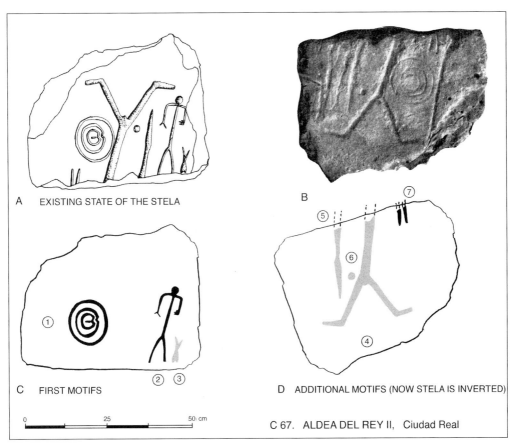

A   EXISTING STATE OF THE STELA

B

C   FIRST MOTIFS

D   ADDITIONAL MOTIFS (NOW STELA IS INVERTED)

0   25   50 cm

C 67.   ALDEA DEL REY II,   Ciudad Real

by Celestino. The shield is a V-notched one of Type IA, with three concentric circles and a horizontal handle. There are modern scratches on the surface, too.

The drawings are based on the published figures and photograph of Valiente and Prado.

6 Bibliography

See: Celestino 2001:412; Valiente & Prado 1978 (figure 3 with photograph).

1 Catalogue number and findspot: **C68 ALDEA DEL REY III, Ciudad Real**

2 Circumstances of discovery, context and present location

It appeared casually on a field just 200 m away from stela C66, on the left bank of the river Jabalón.

It is deposited in the yard of the house belonging to the estate of Hurdillas, which is 3 km outside the village of Aldea del Rey.

3 Stone type, size and condition of the monument

The stela is of local sandstone, which is poorly preserved. It measures 0.91 m high, 0.75 m

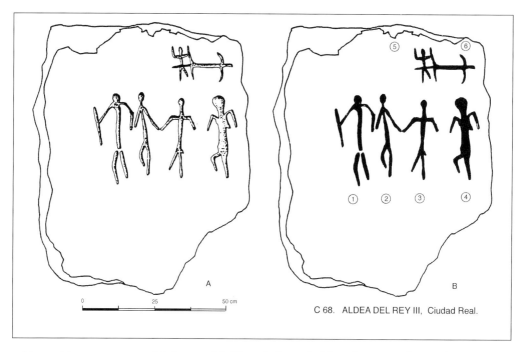

C 68. ALDEA DEL REY III, Ciudad Real.

wide and has an average thickness of 0.20 m. It is probably a fragment from a larger stela.

4 Description of the composition and motifs

The motifs are difficult to see due to the erosion of the stone surface and the technique of fine, shallow engraving. There appears to be a group of four stick figures holding hands and dancing (1–4), while above them are another two figures, one of which has raised arms (5–6).

5 Commentary

Since the motifs are so uncertain, it is prudent to recognise that this scene has a general similarity to those secondary compositions of dancing figures on the stela from C46 Zarza Capilla III and C80 Ategua. An alternative reading of the motifs could be that they show a human figure with a sword standing before a quadruped (instead of two humans with different positions), in which case the scene might be that of the taming of an animal.

6 Bibliography

See: Celestino 2001:413. There is no good published photograph.

1 Catalogue number and findspot: **C69 TOYA (PEAL DE BECERRO), Jaén**

2 Circumstances of discovery, context and present location

This stela was excavated in 1944 and properly recorded on the settlement site of Haza de Trillo, near Toya, as its excavator describes:

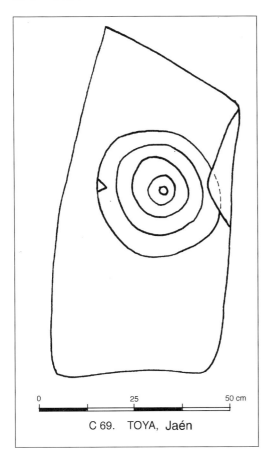

C 69. TOYA, Jaén

... and at a depth of 1.20 (metres) we found a bed of large smooth cobbles and stones packed into a pit, a metre square and 1.10 (metres) deep, which closely supported a great slab set up on the NE side. This appeared upright. ... Once the stone was extracted, we noticed it used to cover the entrance to a cavity and we saw that its interior face showed four badly drawn concentric circles – Some other motif below these circles could be detected but was confused and indistinct. The cavity – was explored carefully. It formed an almost circular space 1.5 (metres) across by 1.35 deep with a roof in the form of a domed oven. ... (It was a) collective grave in which were made two inhumation burials, then another three later ... The height of the cavity from the base to the roof was 0.80 (metres). Our grave reveals a special interest since it is not abundant in our Peninsula – it could correspond to the final period of the Bronze Age (Mergelina 1944).

This stela has been lost since the 1940s.

3 Stone type, size and condition of the monument

The description and a rather poor photograph are all the details known.

4 Description of the composition and motifs

There is certainly a shield and the excavator noted other vague marks (perhaps poorly engraved motifs).

5 Commentary

Celestino is certainly correct to include this stela in the series and to remind us of its real importance. Its exclusion by Almagro Basch can only be explained by his desire to date these monuments to a late period and the fact that no other basic stelae were known in Andalusia. As an early example and a geographical outlier, it appeared unconvincing to him and its physical loss served his purpose further, since the only record was Cayteno de Mergelina's account, buried in a short excavation report published in the aftermath of the Civil War. This story shows how fragile our control of archaeological data and their contexts can be and how academic authority works in practice.

The shield is a V-notched one of Type IC, with four concentric circles, a central umbo and no decoration. Only the outer circle has a V-notch. The grave goods included two or three small copper or bronze awls, which could be of any date in the second millennium BC.

Its importance derives from two contextual observations; first, it was definitely used to seal a tomb and so has a funerary use; and secondly, the tomb was a collective one, for two inhumations. The tomb was opened on at least one later occasion to receive three more inhumations, but Mergelina gives no more details. This stela was used as a grave marker and its decoration faced into the tomb, not displayed outside it, as one would expect. This detail makes one wonder if the stela was re-used as a closing stone? The composition is one of the simplest and its date could be in the middle of the second millennium BC.

However one argues about the possible date or cultural affiliations of the stela, its funerary context is unassailable, like that of C70 Setefilla.

6 Bibliography
See: Almagro Basch 1966:15; Celestino 2001:414; Mergelina 1944 (figure 7 and Lám XI).

1 Catalogue number and findspot: **C70 CARMONA (CUATRO CASAS), Se★**

2 Circumstances of discovery, context and present location
Found casually in 1960 in the area called the Haza de Villaos (or Billaos), which is part of the estate known as Cuatro Casas. Celestino believes it may have been found near the banks of the river Corbones, which runs through the estate at this point. The land is today part of the fertile campiña, noted for its olives and cereals.

Deposited in the Museo Arqueológico Provincial de Sevilla.

3 Stone type, size and condition of the monument
The stela is a large slab of sandstone, dark brown in colour, measuring 1.15 m high, 1.03 m wide with an average thickness of 0.18 m. It is complete.

4 Description of the composition and motifs
The composition centres on the large stick figure of a warrior (1), surrounded by his panoply, with (2) a shield, (3) a sword, (4) a chariot with (5) a set of three dots inside it, (6) bow and arrow and (7) a small secondary figure below the chariot. All motifs are engraved deeply, except motif 7 that is shallower and broader. The face of the stela is irregular and has not been pecked smooth before engraving.

5 Commentary
Note that the warrior has an open right hand, towards the sword. The shield is a simple one of three concentric circles with no handle or umbo, of Type IIC. The sword has a big hilt and rounded pommel and the straight blade suggested to Almagro Basch that it was

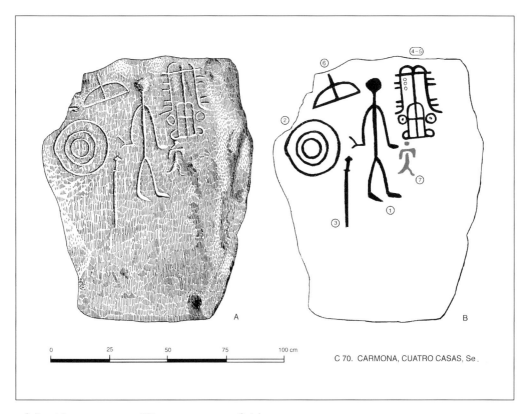

C 70. CARMONA, CUATRO CASAS, Se.

of the Alconetar type. We are not sure of this.

The drawing by Almagro Basch (version A) conveys the surface texture accurately; version B incorporates our observations and Celestino's more accurate rendering of the chariot and motif 5. All the details are visible in the excellent photograph in Almagro Basch.

6 Bibliography

See: Almagro Basch 1966 (figure 33 and Lám XXVIII); Celestino 2001:415–416.

1 Catalogue number and findspot: **C71 SETEFILLA, Se★**

2 Circumstances of discovery, context and present location

In 1997, Maria Eugenia Aubet described the circumstances of discovery minutely. Bonsor and Thouvenot excavated the stela in 1927 in the cemetery of Setefilla, the graves of which are dated to the seventh–sixth centuries BC. It was found re-used as the covering slab for a simple grave that lay just below the surface of the ground and which contained two burials, one a cremation and the other an inhumation orientated on a N–S axis. Alongside this was a pit dug into the ground with another inhumation burial. Nothing is known of the grave goods, if there were any, from these burials.

This grave lay equidistant between the two large, prominent tumuli called G and I by Bonsor, which contained early Iron Age finds. The entire Iron Age cemetery, and not just the grave with the stela covering it, was located deliberately in an area already used as a cemetery from the Middle Bronze Age, but the deficient excavation in 1926–1927 failed to make this clear and mixed graves and finds of different periods. Perfunctory publication further obscured important details. The slab was briefly published in 1928 and disappeared until discovered again by Aubet in the precinct of the swimming pool at the town of Lora del Río in 1973 and shortly afterwards taken to the Museo Arqueológico de Sevilla by its director, Dra Fernández Chicarro y de Dios. Aubet explains why the fanciful account of the rediscovery by Almagro Basch in 1974 is mistaken.

Deposited in the Museo Arqueológico Provincial de Sevilla.

3 Stone type, size and condition of the monument

It is made of laminated sandstone, 1.7 m high, 0.5 m wide and from 0.45 to 0.22 m thick, making a powerful trapezoidal shape inclining to a point at the top. It is complete. When discovered, the lower quarter of the stela was a paler colour than the rest, suggesting it had been buried upright in the earth and not lying flat.

4 Description of the composition and motifs

The stela bears a figurative composition with the human figure as the central motif. Version D of the stela on our figure is the one we prefer, since it matches the photograph closely. It derives from the drawings published by Almagro Basch and Aubet. The motifs are (1) a crested helmet, (2) a spear borne horizontally on the shoulders, (3) a sword worn at the waist and (4) the naked human figure with arms and legs outstretched, feet shown as if in motion. The human is a stick figure with the head depicted with more volume.

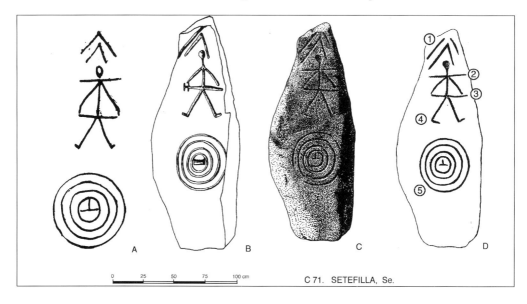

C 71. SETEFILLA, Se.

Below this is the shield (5). The whole face of the stela was pecked smooth before engraving, which is done in wide, shallow pecked lines, making the detail difficult to discern.

5 Commentary

We show the four different versions of this stela; A is the original drawing from Bonsor and Thouvenot (1928); B is from Celestino (2001) and C is from Aubet (1997), whose figure derives from Almagro Basch (1974, figure 5). We observed the spear (3) clearly when we examined the stela in 2001 and we failed to see any details of the sword hilt (4), depicted on version B by Celestino. The excellent photograph of the stela in the open air at Lora del Río published by Almagro Basch (1974, figure 6) makes this clear.

The shield belongs to the Type IIA shields with four concentric circles and a handle of T- shape (not a horizontal bar as Celestino depicts). The crested helmet is sketchily shown by four incisions, clear on photographs, but deficiently drawn in Celestino's figure.

Aubet states firmly that the context of the stela is not connected to the strategic location of Setefilla on commercial routes, drove ways or frontier zones, but rather it is linked to the funerary world. Aubet notes that Bonsor and Thouvenot found other stelae, without decorations, placed vertically, or on top of Middle Bronze Age graves and her excavations identified the same phenomenon when no less than 10 plain stelae of the same type of stone were recovered below the mass of Tumulus A, marking the edge of an older cemetery covered by it. Tumulus B had one stela near its edge. In total 16 plain stelae have been found so far at Setefilla. The conclusion is that these stelae (the Bronze Age warrior stelae and the later plain ones of the Early Iron Age) marked a sacred space dedicated to the collective, communal memory of the Tartessian group who lived nearby.

6 Bibliography

See: Almagro Basch 1974 (figure 5 and photograph on figure 6); Aubet 1997; Bonsor & Thouvenot 1928; Celestino 2001:417–418.

---

1 Catalogue number and findspot: **C72 BURGUILLOS, Se★**

2 Circumstances of discovery, context and present location

Discovered in 1981 by a tractor driver working fields on the estate called La Nea, which is 1 km south-east of the town of Burguillos. The landscape changes from the fertile campiña to the foothills of the Sierra Morena at this point.

It is deposited in the Museo Arqueológico Provincial de Sevilla.

3 Stone type, size and condition of the monument

The stela is of local granite and measures 1.33 m high, 0.67 m wide and has an average thickness of 0.33–0.34 m. It is damaged all around the edges and part of the face has exfoliated. The composition is substantially complete.

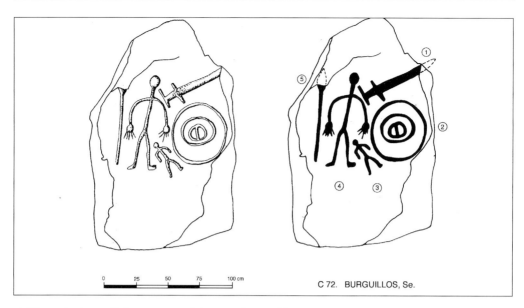

C 72. BURGUILLOS, Se.

4 Description of the composition and motifs

The scene is composed around a warrior figure (4), with hands and well-marked fingers. The panoply includes (2) a shield, (1) a large sword and (5) a spear. At his feet, lying almost horizontally, lies a smaller human figure (3). The engraving is fine and shallow and the surface was scratched deeply by the steel ploughshare, leading to confusion about the original motifs.

5 Commentary

This dominant warrior is crudely drawn and apparently naked. The shield has three concentric circles and is of Type IIA. The very large hilt with big cruciform guards and pommel distinguishes the sword as a Carp's Tongue type.

Celestino's drawing is clearly more accurate than the one published in 1983.

6 Bibliography

See: Celestino 2001:419; Rodríguez Hidalgo (1983, figure 2). There is no good published photograph.

1 Catalogue number and findspot: **C73 LOS PALACIOS, Se★**

2 Circumstances of discovery, context and present location

The stela was known for many years and had been buried in the surface of a track, at a place known as Torres Alocaz, which is about 20 km south of Sevilla.

It is deposited in the Museo Arqueológico Provincial de Sevilla.

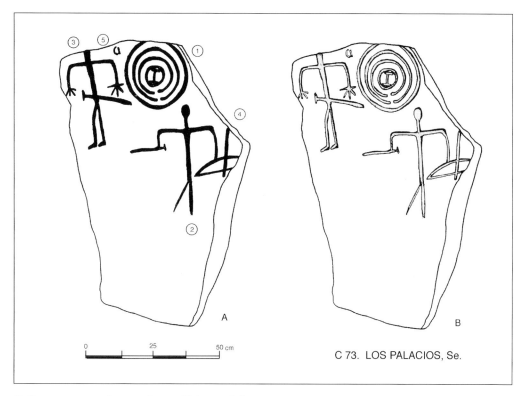

A

B

0   25   50 cm

C 73. LOS PALACIOS, Se.

3 Stone type, size and condition of the monument

The stela is an irregular slab of pale grey limestone, which measures 0.99 m high, 0.60 m wide and has an average thickness of 0. 14 m. Its surface is eroded. The top has been broken and some motifs probably lost.

4 Description of the composition and motifs

A shield (1) occupies the centre of the composition, flanked by two armed warriors, one with a sword in his right hand (2), the other wearing the weapon at his waist (3). There is a bow and arrow (4), an unidentified motif (5) and vague impressions that observers see as other motifs that we cannot recognise as anything definite. The engravings were originally wider and deeper before eroding to their present condition and the motifs are difficult to observe.

5 Commentary

The scene is important for its protagonism of two figures, which is a theme repeated on at least six stelae. Figure one grasps a sword and bow and arrow and adopts a dynamic posture. Figure two has his arms and hands stretched out, with his sword sheathed at his waist. Both give the impression of movement and action. Between them is a shield that is probably a V-notched one of Type IA, of four concentric circles and a big vertical handle.

6 Bibliography

See: Celestino 2001:420-1; Oliva & Chasco 1976:397 (photograph).

1 Catalogue number and findspot: **C74 ÉCIJA I, Se★**

2 Circumstances of discovery, context and present location

The stela was discovered on the slopes of the Cerro Perea, which lies 10km north-west of the city of Écija and right next to the main Madrid-Cádiz highway. Stela C75 was found 2 km to the south.

It is deposited in the Museo Arqueológico Provincial de Sevilla.

3 Stone type, size and condition of the monument

The stela is of dark brown limestone, of rectangular shape, measuring 0.60m high, 0.40m wide and 0.12m average thickness. The base is broken off and it is not certain that the composition is complete.

4 Description of the composition and motifs

The figure of the warrior totally dominates this composition, with his big hands and long fingers (1). He is surrounded by the panoply of (6) a sword, (4) an upright spear, (3) a mirror, (5) a comb and (7) a shield. The engravings are deeply pecked lines and the figure and the mirror are both emphasised in intaglio.

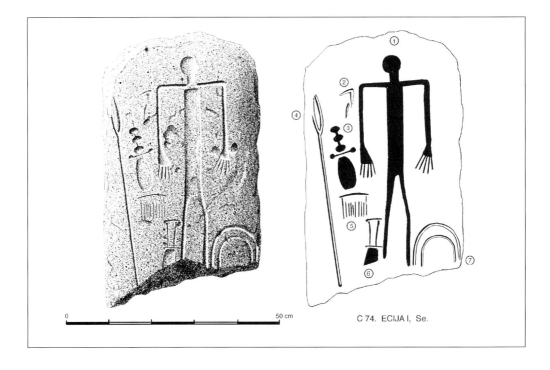

0   50 cm   C 74. ECIJA I, Se.

5 Commentary

Although only a small stela (the original height was probably no more than double the present size, perhaps 1.20 m), the image is striking and impressive. The hulking figure of the warrior exudes menace, an effect achieved by carefully placing the objects near his right hand and at his feet, leaving the body in a clear field. Intaglio carving further emphasised it.

The mirror is a splendidly baroque object, drawn in detail to show off its handle and bulbous ornaments; the comb and spear are depicted effectively. The shield is a simple one of two circular rings (there is no handle inside it). The sword blade and hilt are incised. Other motifs shown by Celestino were invisible to us.

The drawing shows Almagro Basch's version (A), with our modified one as version B.

6 Bibliography

See: Almagro Basch 1974 (figure 3, photograph on figure 4); Celestino 2001:422–423.

---

1 Catalogue number and findspot: **C75 ÉCIJA II, Se**

2 Circumstances of discovery, context and present location

Ploughing in the late 1970s brought this stela to the surface in a place called the Atalaya de la Moranilla, which is next to the Cerro de Los Mochales, from which stela C77 comes. A large settlement of the Final Bronze Age overlooks the right bank of the river Genil and fertile farmland surrounds it. It is about 2 km from the findspot of C74.

It is deposited in the Town Hall of Écija.

3 Stone type, size and condition of the monument

The stela is of limestone and measures 0.85 m high, 0.71 m wide and has an average thickness of 0.15 m. It is a very irregular block of stone and the surface is also rough and not prepared for engraving. The composition appears complete, although the stone has been broken.

4 Description of the composition and motifs

The central figure of a horned warrior with no fingers on his right hand, but five incised on his left, dominates the scene (1). His panoply includes (2) a shield, (3) possible bow, (4) a sword and (5) a mirror. Intaglio emphasises motifs 1, 4 and 5.

5 Commentary

The warrior 'hero' dominates the composition, which is symmetrical and well designed. The warrior's horns emerge directly from the side of his head; and he may have lost the fingers of his right hand, given the specific depiction of them on his left. The shield is a simple one with two concentric circles and a big handle, of Type IIA. The sword has a long

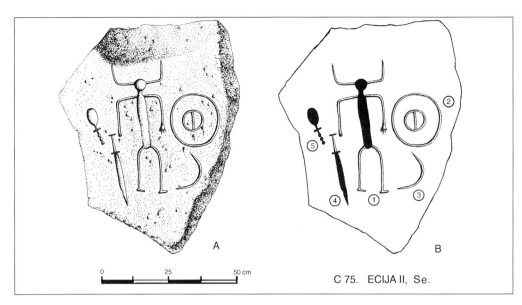

C 75. ECIJA II, Se.

handle with cruciform pommel and guards and a leaf-shaped blade. The mirror is an elaborate one, like that depicted on C74 and has identical decorations.

   The drawing includes the original one of Rodríguez and Núñez in version A and our
version B next to it.

6 Bibliography

See: Celestino 2001:424; Rodríguez & Núñez 1983/4 (figure 1). There is no good published
photograph.

1 Catalogue number and findspot: **C76 ÉCIJA III, Se**

2 Circumstances of discovery, context and present location

This stela was discovered by chance in 1984, on the estate called the Molino de Rojas,
which is 6 km south-west of Écija. The findspot is by the road which links Écija and
Marchena.

   It is deposited in the Town Hall of Écija.

3 Stone type, size and condition of the monument

The stela is on coarse, soft sandstone called molasa and measures 0.58 m high, 0.81 m wide
and has an average thickness of 0.12 m. It is broken on all sides and eroded. The composition appears to be complete.

4 Description of the composition and motifs

The composition has a large horned warrior figure at the centre (1), with outstretched

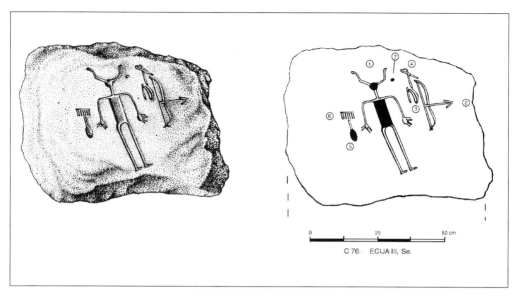

C 76.   ECIJA III, Se.

hands and a corpulent body. The horns have twisted tips. The motifs around him include (2) a bow and arrow, (3 and 4) two unidentified objects, (5) a small mirror, (6) a comb and (7) a single dot near the warrior's head. All motifs are engraved deeply, with the warrior and mirror emphasised by intaglio.

5 Commentary

This is another instance where a horned figure dominates the scene but it is very surprising to see there are no weapons and no shield or chariot. Celestino adds further details on his drawing, showing the comb with a triangular handle and a set of four dots next to the warrior's right hand.

Our drawing includes the original figure of Rodríguez and Núñez as version A and version B with further details.

6 Bibliography

See: Celestino 2001:425–426; Rodríguez & Núñez 1985 (figure 1). There is no good published photograph.

1 Catalogue number and findspot: **C77 ÉCIJA IV, Se**

2 Circumstances of discovery, context and present location

This stela was found in a stone heap on the east side of the hill known as the Atalaya de la Morenilla, which overlooks the right bank of the river Genil. In the Final Bronze Age a large settlement (probably fortified) flourished on this hill. Stela C75, and perhaps also C76, was found nearby.

Deposited in the Museo Arqueológico Provincial de Sevilla.

3 Stone type, size and condition of the monument

The stela is of sandstone and measures 1.12 m high, 0.35 m wide and has an average thickness of 0.19 m. The upper part is damaged and the composition is fragmentary.

4 Description of the composition and motifs

Filling the centre of the composition is a warrior (1). Other motifs are (2) a shield, (3) unidentifiable object, (4) a very long sword and (5) a possible brooch. The engravings were pecked and then smoothed for emphasis.

5 Commentary

The drawing lacks the detail required for our analysis. The shield is a simple one of Type IIA, but the sword is unique for its peculiar hilt and immensely long, thin blade. We think it is a corrected engraving and that the hilt was drawn first as simple one, then a cruciform design was imposed on it but left incomplete. That would explain the lopsided guard and

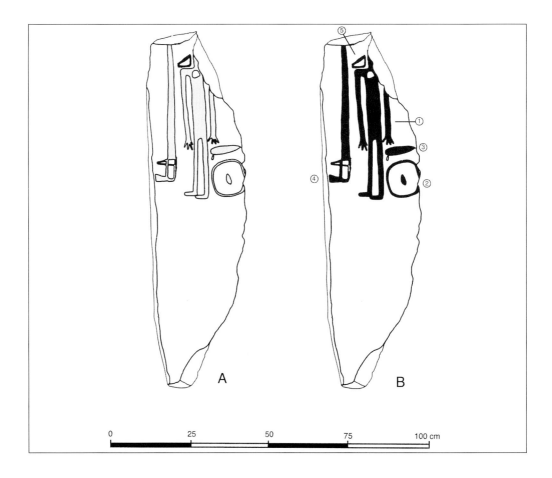

pommel. As it stands, it depicts a weapon wholly unknown in the Atlantic or western Mediterranean worlds.

Recent surveys show the settlement at Atalaya de la Morenilla was an important regional centre during the Final Bronze Age.

6 Bibliography

See: Celestino 2001:427; Tejera Gaspar et al 1995 (figure 1 and an indistinct photograph on Lám I).

---

1 Catalogue number and findspot: **C78 ÉCIJA V, Se**

2 Circumstances of discovery, context and present location

This stela was discovered next to a gully called El Berraco on the estate of the same name and taken to a boundary wall where it was examined. Villages and settlements of the Final Bronze Age are common in the landscape and at least 11 are known within two hours' walk of the estate.

The stela disappeared from the estate soon after discovery and its whereabouts is unknown.

3 Stone type, size and condition of the monument

The stela is of limestone, in good condition, measuring 1.49 m high, 0.82 m wide and 0.22m average thickness. It is damaged at the edges, but the composition is complete.

4 Description of the composition and motifs

This is a warrior stela dominated by a horned warrior in the centre, hands outstretched and fingers visible (1). Around him is the panoply of (2) a comb, (3) a shield, (4) complete chariot, (5) a possible dog?, (6) an uncertain motif that may be a dagger, (7) spear pointing downwards, (8) a sword and (9) an uncertain motif that may be a brooch. The engraving is shallow and of U-section, while the large motifs are intaglio.

5 Commentary

This is a fine stela of trapezoidal shape, dominated by the warrior 'hero', whose bull-like horns emerge from the side of his head, twisting at their tips for emphasis. It is an impressive stela for its size and its symmetrical composition and the 'hero' gains prominence from his central position, huge grasping hands and large size in the composition; he stands almost one metre tall. Confidently laid out, this is the grandest of all the monuments from Écija and the only one with a chariot.

The shield is of Type IIA with three concentric circles. The sword is clearly engraved and has a long hilt with simple pommel and triangular guards. The blade has a pronounced leaf-shape. The sword is an Atlantic type current between 1150–950 BC, which should be the date of the stela.

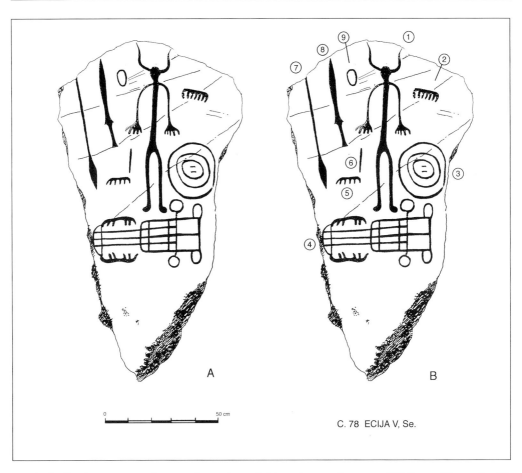

A
B

0 ———————— 50 cm

C. 78 ECIJA V, Se.

A similar bronze sword comes from the neighbouring settlement of El Santo Siervo (or El Salto del Ciervo) and there is a complete Carp's Tongue sword and spearhead from the village of Los Castellares, a few kilometres upriver on the Genil (Padilla Monge & Valderrama Juan 1994:284). The chariot is drawn confidently and with attention to symmetry.

The drawing is based on that of Eduardo Valderrama Juan.

6 Bibliography

See: Celestino 2001:428; Padilla Monge & Valderrama Juan 1994 (figure 3). There is no published photograph.

---

1 Catalogue number and findspot: **C79 MONTEMOLÍN (MARCHENA), Se**

2 Circumstances of discovery, context and present location

The discovery was made in 1981 on the estate called the Cortijo de Montemolín, within the township of Marchena. The findspot was in a stone heap, of materials dragged from the nearby hill, which is an important proto-historical settlement site. The area is fertile farming land today.

It stands in the garden of the owner of the estate, Sr López Marín.

3 Stone type, size and condition of the monument

The stela is on a block of sandstone, roughly trimmed to shape all around by heavy blows with a hard hammer, and measures 1.35 m high, 0.36 m wide and has an average thickness of 0.27 m. It is apparently complete.

4 Description of the composition and motifs

The surface is rough and not prepared for engraving. The composition features a figure with detailed fingers and toes (1), with a huge mirror next to him (2), a bow and arrow (3) and a comb (4). The motifs are engraved lightly and the mirror and the head of the figure are emphasised in intaglio.

5 Commentary

An excellent photograph allows one to examine the engraved details and interpret the composition. The warrior is notable for his very large hands and feet, dramatically out of scale. The mirror is also very big, but we could only see one knob on its handle. The bow is lightly engraved but clear in outline. However, the comb is almost invisible and

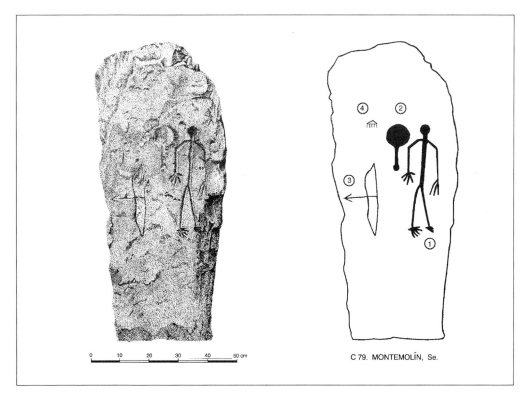

0   10   20   30   40   50 cm

C 79. MONTEMOLÍN, Se.

engraved as an afterthought, with very delicate incisions. Is it a later addition to the monument? It is just visible on the photograph in Chaves and Bandera.

The composition is notable, like stela C76 from Écija, for its lack of weapons or chariot. For these reasons it is likely to date to the ninth, or even eighth century BC, at the end of the series. The arrangement of the motifs is poor, with no skill in engraving them.

Version A is the drawing by Chaves and De la Bandera, which conveys the texture of the rock excellently, and version B is our reading of the motifs.

6 Bibliography

See: Celestino 2001:429; Chaves & De la Bandera 1982 (figure 3 with a photograph in figure 1).

---

1 Catalogue number and findspot: **C80 ATEGUA, Co★**

2 Circumstances of discovery, context and present location

In April 1968, agricultural workers found the stela and took it on their tractor to the nearby estate of Gamarrillas, thinking it might be suitable for building stone. When they saw the engravings, they notified the archaeological team then excavating at Ategua, who came over and identified the monument correctly. Blanco et al (1969) clearly state that the findspot is at the base of a defensive wall that encircled much of the hilltop and which dates to the proto-historic fortification of the early first millennium BC.

Ategua itself is an isolated hill, set in land famed for growing good cereal crops, that was repeatedly fortified and enlarged until it became an Iberian city. It lies on the right bank of the Guadajoz river and is about 32 km north-west of Córdoba.

It is deposited in the Museo Arqueológico Provincial de Córdoba.

3 Stone type, size and condition of the monument

The stela is made of limestone, a rock that is not native to the area and which must have been transported a distance of at least 25 km. Limestone is especially suitable for delicate engraving and given the extraordinary complexity of the scenes engraved on this monument, it was an excellent choice. The stela measures 1.70 m high, 0.70 m wide and has a maximum thickness of 0.20–0.30 m, which increases towards the base. Despite some damage to the top, the stela is substantially intact.

One side has been worked to a straight edge and the entire carved face has been pecked smooth before engraving. However, there is substantial modern damage to the engraved face on both edges, caused by the tractor in 1968. These grooves and heavy scratches have obscured some motifs and removed others entirely. Until it was cleaned recently, the surface was further obscured by lime carbonates and ingrained dirt. The composition can be considered complete.

4 Description of the composition and motifs

Celestino drew the cleaned stela. We offer three versions to convey the detailed iconogra-

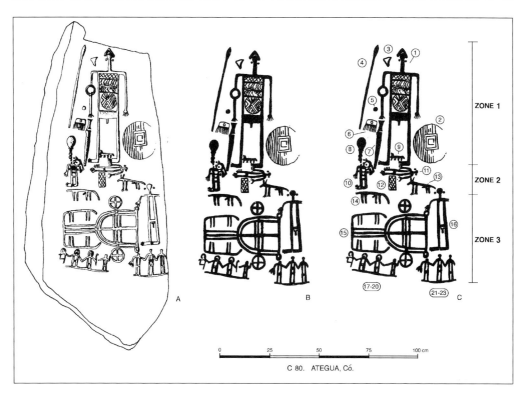

C 80.   ATEGUA, Có.

phy; version A is the Celestino 2001 drawing; version B presents all the motifs in black for contrast; version C numbers the motifs to help in their description.

The composition extends over three successive zones, starting with Zone 1, dominated by a huge warrior figure, with outstretched hands and penis indicated (1). The warrior wears a bracelet on one arm, earrings and a helmet. A decorated tunic or plates of armour, with bands of geometric decoration above and a circular motif below cover his body. He is surrounded by a panoply which includes (2) a shield, (3) brooch, (4) spear with its point upright, (5) a single dot that may be a ring, (6) a comb with a decorated handle, (7) a sword in its sheath, (8) a decorated mirror and (9) a dog between his feet.

Zone 2 motifs show a scene of mourning. A small figure (10) at the end of the sword may be a female, with one hand raised to the head. Its fingers and toes are clear and its body has volume. Lying horizontally at the feet of the warrior is another small figure (11), naked except for a pair of earrings, with hands and feet extended and the digits stretched out straight. Next to it is a rectangular motif filled with cross-hatching that may be a carpet or blanket (12). Two animals, perhaps dogs, look on the scene, one from each side and both male (13 and 14).

The scene in Zone 3 is focused on the chariot (15), drawn in very deep lines and with attention to detail. The naked charioteer, with a large phallus and wearing only earrings (16) stands behind the chariot with right hand outstretched, as if about to step up into the vehicle. Below, in the lowest position of all, is a line of small figures arranged in two groups, all holding hands. One group (17–20) has four figures, one separate from the others and three of them with a headdress or large coiffure. The other group (21–23) has only three figures (there was never a fourth since there is no room for it on the stela), also holding hands, but with their heads uncovered. The hand of figure 21 has all five fingers extended. Both groups have a ground line engraved below them.

The warrior (1), chariot (15) and charioteer (16) are more deeply engraved than other motifs.

5 Commentary

Our observations differ at some points from Celestino. We could not see the helmet or the phallus on the main warrior, nor the ring (5), nor the dog between his feet (9). Figure 10 seems to us to be wearing a diadem or tall hat; figure 19 does not hold a stick; this is a modern scratch. All the figures in both groups (17–23) wear belts. The typology of the artefacts reveals little extra information, given their stylisation.

More interesting is the narrative embedded in the composition, first described by Bendala Galán in 1977, when he suggested it was a prothesis, like the ones in Dark Age Greece, showing the warrior alive and powerful in Zone 1; then in Zone 2 he dies and is mourned and finally his apotheosis and ascent to the heavenly realms, in the chariot of the immortals, in Zone 3.

The identity and role of the small figures 17–23 is harder to explain. They may be dancers at the funeral, or the sons and daughters of the dead warrior.

6 Bibliography

See: Bendala Galán 1977; Blanco et al 1969 (three excellent photographs of the stela before cleaning, in natural light. Láms XIV–XV); Celestino 2001:430–432.

---

1 Catalogue number and findspot: **C81 PEDRO ABAD (ALCORRUCÉN), Co**

2 Circumstances of discovery, context and present location

The stela was discovered casually when working the land in the savanna known as Alcorrucén. It lies close to a meander in the river Guadalquivir, on its left bank, which can be crossed at this point on foot.

3 Stone type, size and condition of the monument

The stela is a block of soft sandstone, cut to a rectangular shape and its face smoothed before engraving. It measures 0.87 m high, 0.52 m wide and has an average thickness of 0.19 m. The bottom has broken off and motifs lost. It must be considered a fragmentary composition.

It is in private hands, on an estate in the Alcorrucén area.

4 Description of the composition and motifs

The scene gives equal prominence to a warrior figure and shield. The warrior (1) has a large body, perhaps intended to represent a tunic, and all the fingers and toes are prominent. The panoply around him includes (2) a shield, (3) a spear, (4) a comb, (5) a sword, (6) probably a sheathed dagger, (7) a pair of dots, (8 and 9) two isolated single dots, (10) an arc of six dots, (11) a secondary figure with outstretched hands and fingers and (12 and 13) two unidentified motifs that belong to elements lost at the bottom of the composition. The motifs are engraved deeply and then smoothed flat, giving an intaglio effect to the engraving.

5 Commentary

The drawings show the original figure by Bendala et al 1994, since it conveys a good impression of the surface and nature of the stela (version A) and the motifs in version B. The illustration by Celestino 2001 differs in several details and after examining the published photographs, we cannot see the arc of five dots above the warrior's head, nor the mirror where motif 8 is situated, nor what may be a shield or a chariot element next to the secondary figure (motif 11). Motif 7 may be an initial attempt to engrave the sword, which was placed lower down in a second attempt.

The shield is of Type IIA, with three concentric circles and large handle. The sword has a big handle and cruciform pommel and guards, like Carp's Tongue types.

Evidently, this composition lacks balance and symmetry, but its subject matter and sword type indicates it is probably of the tenth century BC.

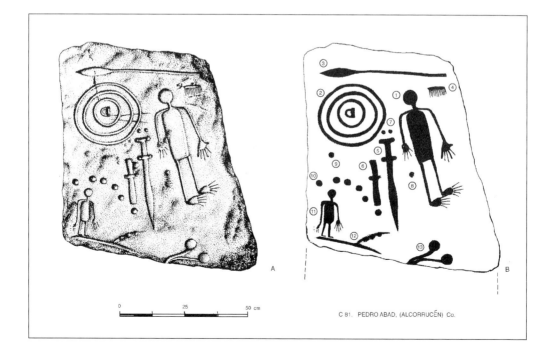

A

B

0   25   50 cm

C 81. PEDRO ABAD, (ALCORRUCÉN) Co.

6 Bibliography

See: Bendala Galán et al 1994 (figure 1 and Láms I and II); Celestino 2001:433–434.

1 Catalogue number and findspot: **C82 CÓRDOBA I, Co**

2 Circumstances of discovery, context and present location

In 1986 a tractor driver dislodged this stela from his harrow, in the estate known as the Cortijo de la Vega, near a modern industrial estate, about 10 km north of the city of Córdoba. The area is flat and until recently was fertile farmland. Nearby is an important and well-known ford over the river Guadalquivir at Alcolea. Stela C83 was found a short distance away.

It is deposited in the Biblioteca Municipal de Vilafranca de Córdoba.

3 Stone type, size and condition of the monument

The stela is of soft sandstone, pale in colour, which measures 1.02 m high, 0.65 m wide and has an average thickness of 0.14 m. Before engraving the surface was pecked smooth. The bottom portion has broken away, so it is about half or two-thirds complete.

4 Description of the composition and motifs

The composition is a simple one, centred on a shield (2), with a spear above it (1). A later period of engraving was probably responsible for the 33 irregular pits that were then made all over the surface (3–35), which nevertheless respected the motifs and did not actually cut into them.

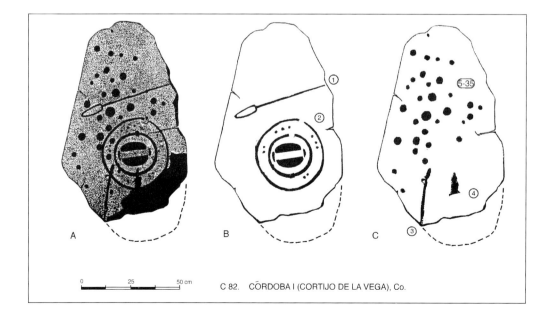

C 82.   CÓRDOBA I (CORTIJO DE LA VEGA), Co.

5 Commentary

The composition is an early one. The shield is of Type IIB, decorated with an inner ring of bosses arranged in triplets and has a very prominent handle; however, it lacks the characteristic V-notch and is unique for this reason. The irregular pits are like those on the back of the stela from C28 Aldeanueva de San Bartolomé in Toledo.

The drawing in version A follows Morena and Muñoz and versions B and C show the two periods of engraving.

6 Bibliography

See: Celestino 2001:435–436; Morena López & Muñoz Muñoz 1990:14–15

1 Catalogue number and findspot: **C83 CÓRDOBA II, Co**

2 Circumstances of discovery, context and present location

It was found in the Cortijo de la Ribera Alta (Córdoba), on the right bank of the river Guadalquivir, at the confluence with the tributary known as the Guadalmellato.

It is held privately in the district of Cerro Muriano, in Córdoba.

3 Stone type, size and condition of the monument

It is of pale grey limestone and measures 0.97 m high, 0.48 m wide and has an average thickness of 0.26 m. It has been roughly trimmed to shape and the main face pecked smooth. It is complete.

4 Description of the composition and motifs

The basic composition is of the simplest type. The shield (1) centres the composition, with a sword (2) below and a spear (3) above. The engravings are shallow lines.

5 Commentary

The context is the most important aspect of this find and it could have been a sepulchral slab, perhaps intended to lie flat on the surface, as Celestino believes, like the one reported from C64 Badajoz. The actual findspot is of interest, since Celestino (2001:437) records first hand accounts that the stelae was found 40 cm below ground, decorated face upwards and below it a stain (*mancha*) of black, ashy earth. The stain contained no artefacts. The natural subsoil is reddish gravel and clay, so this discolouration would be quite obvious. It is not clear what this stain was and there is no certainty it was related in any way to the stela. However, the coincidence between the ashy stain and the horizontal stela is suggestive, to me, that they are elements connected to one another.

The shield belongs to the V-notched Type IB, with three circles of decoration, the outer two decorated with single bosses. The sword has a rectangular handle and pommel, but big guards and a long parallel-sided blade. It is not certain if it belongs to the Rosnoën type of sword, or not. The spear may have a metal butt, like the one on C48 Magacela.

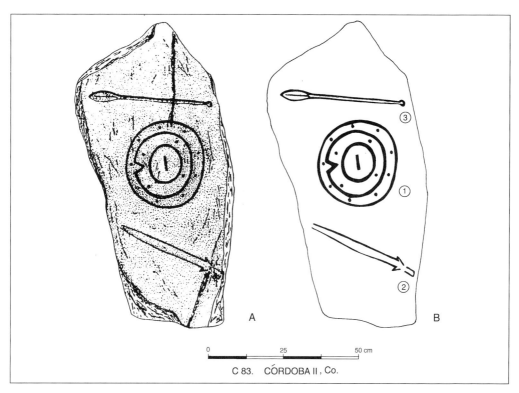

A   B

0   25   50 cm

C 83.   CÓRDOBA II , Co.

The drawings (versions A and B) are based on the figure published by Celestino.

6 Bibliography

See: Celestino 2001:437. There is no good published photograph.

1 Catalogue number and findspot: **C84 ALMARGEN, Ma**

2 Circumstances of discovery, context and present location

It was found by the roadside, within the boundaries of the town of Almargen, which is on the border with the province of Córdoba and lies in the northern foothills of the Sierra de Ronda.

It is deposited in the town hall of Almargen.

3 Stone type, size and condition of the monument

The stela is of soft stone, damaged at the edges but substantially complete. It measures 1.0 m high, 0.60 m wide and has an average thickness of 0.17 m.

4 Description of the composition and motifs

The composition is a simple one and the shield (1) and the warrior figure (2) are its protagonists. The warrior has huge outstretched hands and wears a crested helmet (3). Other motifs are (4) a spear arranged horizontally and (5) a brooch. The engraving is deep and assured.

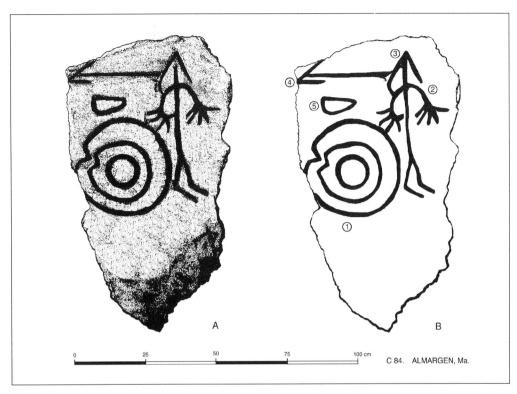

C 84.   ALMARGEN, Ma.

5 Commentary

The drawing modifies that published in Villaseca 1995. The shield is a V-notched one of Type IC, with three concentric circles. The brooch is schematic but may be an asymmetric elbow fibula. The helmet occupies the place where the head of the figure should be.

6 Bibliography

See: Celestino 2001:438; Villaseca Díaz 1995 (Lám 2). There is no published photograph.

1 Catalogue number and findspot: **C85 FUENTE DE CANTOS, Ba★**

2 Circumstances of discovery, context and present location

It was uncovered by a tractor driver in 1965 while ploughing a field in the estate called El Risco, which lies 3 km south of the town of Fuente de Cantos. The estate lies on an important medieval communications route, with the main drove way (La Cañada Real Leonesa) passing nearby, which suggests the area was important for winter pastures.

Deposited in the Museo Arqueológico Nacional, Madrid.

3 Stone type, size and condition of the monument

The stela is of local granite and measures 2.31m high, 0.79 m wide and has an average thickness of 0.46 m. It is complete and the largest stela known.

4 Description of the composition and motifs

This huge block of granite was trimmed to shape all down its right hand side. The horned figure (1) dominates the composition, with panoply of (2) a comb, (3) sword, (4) single dot (a possible ring), (5) a spear, (6) a mirror, (7) a shield, (8) a chariot and (9) a group of eight small pits. All are deeply engraved.

5 Commentary

This assured composition features a warrior 'hero', in the centre. His large size and clear details of horns with twisted tips, big fingers and toes, makes him a forceful figure. The shield is of Type IIC, with four concentric rings and a round umbo in the centre. The sword is distinctive, with a heavy pommel and large guards, but a rapier-like blade; Celestino draws it with more width. We could not see the brooch that Celestino includes.

The drawings are based on the figure in Almagro Basch.

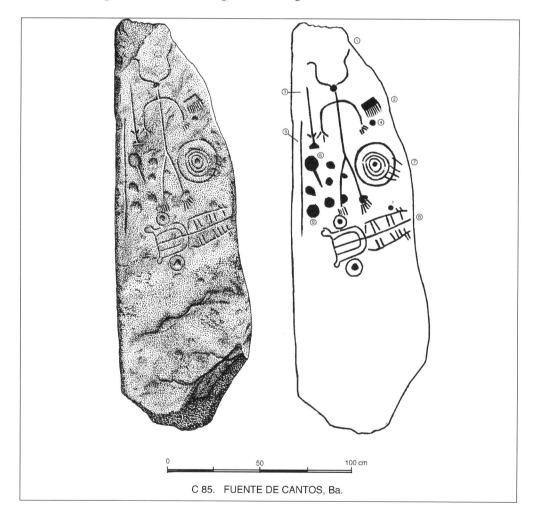

0   50   100 cm

C 85. FUENTE DE CANTOS, Ba.

6 Bibliography

See: Almagro Basch 1966 (figure 42 and Lám XXXVII); Celestino 2001:439–440.

1 Catalogue number and findspot: **C86 CAPOTE (HIGUERA LA REAL), Ba★**

2 Circumstances of discovery, context and present location

It was found in 1984, re-used as a lintel in a rough farm building, on the estate called El Capote. This lies 7.5 km north of the town of Higuera la Real, in a very hilly and inaccessible area.

It is deposited in the Museo Arqueológico Provincial de Badajoz.

3 Stone type, size and condition of the monument

The stela is of slate and measures 0.97 m high, 0.47 m wide and has an average thickness of 0.16 m. It is a fragment.

4 Description of the composition and motifs

The stela has three periods of carving and use. The oldest is of the Final Bronze Age and includes motifs 1–5. These appear to represent a small human figure (1) at the head of a pair of draught animals that were once part of a chariot team (2). Below are confused motifs that Celestino interprets (correctly, in our opinion) as (3) a mirror and (4) a large lyre. Motif 5 is a natural crack. The later periods of use are when the stela was cut down to a smaller size and used as a gravestone, with two inscriptions (motifs 6 and 7). The engraving is clear, but Celestino suggests motif 1 may be a later addition, since it is more lightly engraved.

5 Commentary

The drawings in versions A and B are after Berrocal (1987) who first published it and version C follows Celestino's (2001) interpretation that became possible after the surface was cleaned.

Although only a fragment from a much larger composition, this stela is important for its context and for its secondary utilisation as a funerary monument, complete with inscriptions, in the Tartessian Period (Early Iron Age, seventh century BC). In the same area as the stela was found, there are many large cairns, which suggests a Tartessian cemetery.

The inscriptions were transcribed by Berrocal to read phonetically (motif 6). 'i . ke e. (n/i').' (= Keeni). This is possibly an element from a ritual formula, repeated on other southwest inscriptions. Motif 7 reads from right to left as: o . s . o . r . e . r . Ta . a . (u . na). This is similar to an inscription from Siruela and probably spells out a name of a person, place or ethnic group. The different letter shapes suggest two different engravers cut the inscriptions. Motif 6 is shallower than motif 7, which is deeper, more elegant and confident.

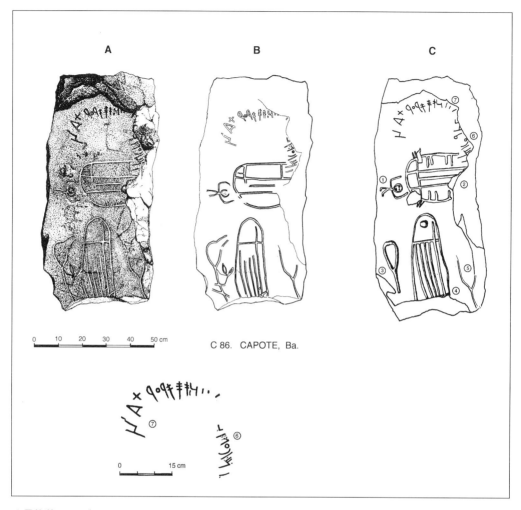

C 86. CAPOTE, Ba.

6 Bibliography

See: Berrocal 1987 (figs. 1–3); Celestino 2001:441–442. There is no good published photograph.

1 Catalogue number and findspot: **C87 FIGUEIRA (ALGARVE), Portugal**

2 Circumstances of discovery, context and present location

This stela was found in the village of Figueira, only a short distance away from Cape St Vincent. Confused accounts of the discovery make it impossible to be certain of anything more than the fact that the stela was found upright, with the lower third buried in the ground (Almagro 1966:72).

   It is deposited in the Museu de Lagos, Portugal.

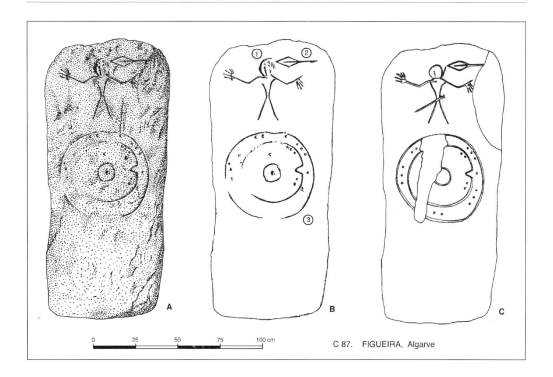

C 87. FIGUEIRA, Algarve

3 Stone type, size and condition of the monument

The stela is of hard reddish sandstone, measuring 1.67 m high, 0.70 m wide and with an average thickness of 0.20 m. It is eroded, but complete.

4 Description of the composition and motifs

The stone was trimmed to a neat rectangular shape before engraving, but the face was not pecked smooth. The pitted and cracked surface makes it hard to ascertain the motifs accurately. The motifs are (3) a dominant shield, (1) a human figure above it with outstretched hands and (2) a horizontal spear. The lines are deeply but finely engraved.

5 Commentary

Almagro Basch describes the considerable confusion surrounding early notices of its discovery. His drawings (versions A and B) differ somewhat from Celestino's (version C), which includes details of motifs that are probably natural cracks in the rock surface. The shield is a V-notched one of Type IC, with pairs of bosses on the inner ring of decoration and triples on the outside one.

6 Bibliography

See: Almagro Basch 1966 (figure 22 and Lám XVII); Celestino 2001:443–444.

1 Catalogue number and findspot: **C88 GOMES AIRES (ALMODOVAR), Baixo Alemtejo, Portugal**

2 Circumstances of discovery, context and present location

It was discovered in 1971 when ploughing dislodged the stela, which was face down, covering a grave. This consisted of a pit, with a large jar filled with ashes from a cremation. The findspot is on a hillock, on the estate of Abóbada and appears to be one grave in a cemetery where others are known, also with stelae.

It is deposited in the Museu Regional de Beja, Portugal.

3 Stone type, size and condition of the monument

The stela is of hard schist and measures 0.90 m high, 0.60 m wide and has an average thickness of 0.08m. It is complete.

4 Description of the composition and motifs

There is a schematic figure in the centre. Dressed in bulky garments or armour, he carries a spear in one hand and unidentified objects in the other. Around him is an inscription in the south-west Tartessian script.

5 Commentary

This is not really a warrior stela at all, but it illustrates an important Tartessian stela in an undisputed funerary context and can be dated to the seventh century BC. It is therefore the immediate successor in style and iconographic content to the Final Bronze Age examples and demonstrates the clear link these monuments have with the world of the dead.

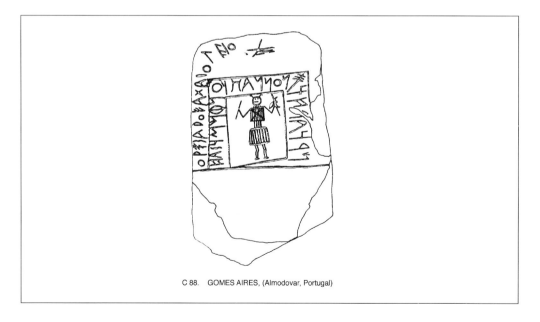

C 88.   GOMES AIRES, (Almodovar, Portugal)

6 Bibliography

See: Alves Dias & Coelho 1971 (figure 1); Celestino 2001:445–446.

1 Catalogue number and findspot: **C89 ERVIDEL II (ALJUSTREL), Baixo Alemtejo, Portugal**

2 Circumstances of discovery, context and present location

In 1976 the Portuguese archaeologists Mario Varela Gomes and J Pinho Monteiro found the stela lying face down, embedded in the soil, in the middle of an older Middle Bronze Age cemetery. This belongs to the estate known as the Herdade do Pomar and is on a small hillock with a freshwater spring nearby. Ervidel is the nearest village and gives its name to several stelae from the area.

It is deposited in the Museu Regional de Beja, Portugal.

3 Stone type, size and condition of the monument

The stela measures 1.77 m high, 0.55 m wide and has an average thickness of 0.20 m. It is complete and in good condition.

4 Description of the composition and motifs

The stela was roughly shaped, one face completely pecked smooth before engraving. Two narrative zones make up the composition. Zone 1 has a large warrior figure (1) with huge hands, a prominent phallus and a big sword worn at his waist. Below are (2) a shield, (3) a spear, (4) a brooch, (5) a motif hard to interpret but which may be a pair of tweezers or a razor (5), (6) a mirror, (7) a comb, (8) a dog and (9) a deep dot. In Zone 2, there are two recumbent figures, both with huge hands. One has a phallus (10), the other not (11). Around them are three deep dots (12–14) marking three corners of a square, as if to separate the scene from the action of Zone 1 above it. Motif 15 is an engraving error or incomplete element.

All the motifs are clearly engraved, then smoothed for emphasis.

5 Commentary

A story unfolds as a narrative on this stela, rather like that on C80 Ategua. In Zone 1, the naked warrior is alive and powerful, his large figure striding forward, with his status symbols around him. In Zone 2 there is a scene of death; it may be either the warrior after his life is over, or it may represent his triumph over enemies, two of whom are shown defeated and killed, naked without any weapons or other attributes of power.

The composition is excellently designed and conceived, with a rare aesthetic equilibrium achieved between the warrior and the objects. The space on the stone is fully exploited without any sense that the carvings are crowded together, or that the engraver was uncertain of where to place an item, or how to depict it. Technically impressive, this stela must rank with

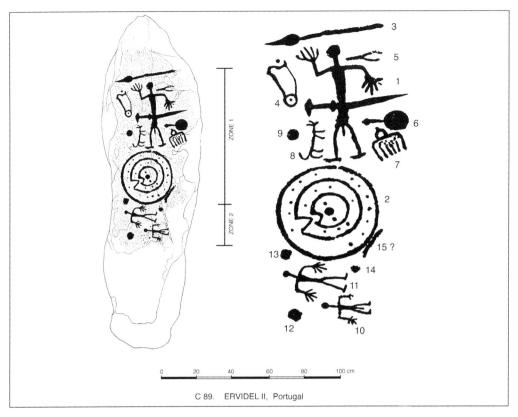

C 89.   ERVIDEL II, Portugal

C48 Magacela and C85 Fuente de Cantos as the finest composition of any warrior stela and which succeeds in its aim to inform, impress, record and commemorate, all in one monument.

The motifs are engraved with great realism. The shield is a V-notched one of Type IC, with three circles of decoration and a round umbo. The decorative bosses are arranged singly. The sword worn by the warrior has a big handle with solid pommel and large guards. A Carp's Tongue weapon is indicated by the parallel-sided blade and long point. The spearhead has a distinctive ogival shape. The brooch is an asymmetric elbow fibula realistically drawn, of the same type as on the C65 Olivenza stela.

The drawing is modified after Gomes and Monteiro.

6 Bibliography

See: Celestino 2001:447–448; Gomes & Monteiro 1977 (figure 4 and Láms VI–VIII).

1 Catalogue number and findspot: **C90 SUBSTANTION (MONTPELLIER), Herault, France**

2 Circumstances of discovery, context and present location

In 1916, the stela appeared in archaeological excavations on the Iron Age and Iberian *oppidum* of Substantion, which lies 3.5 km north-east of the city of Montpellier. The details of the find-spot are that at a depth of 1.10 metres, in a heap of stones, pottery and ashes, the excavator found the stela, apparently discarded and no longer in its original position (Soutou 1962:30).

It is deposited in the Museé de la Société Archéologique de Montpellier.

3 Stone type, size and condition of the monument

The stela is of limestone and measures 0.91 m high, 0.50 m wide and has an average thickness of 0.15 m. It is substantially complete.

4 Description of the composition and motifs

The stela is a well-dressed block, with recognisable motifs on three sides. It is important to state that there are two different engraving techniques employed; the motifs on the sides

C 90.   SUBSTANTION, Montpellier, France

(1–7) are deeply engraved lines, while the main motifs on the face are in low relief, with the background pecked away.

The motifs on one edge are (1) a geometric lozenge, (2) a 'spectacle' motif and (3) a band of 12 multiple chevrons. On the other edge are (4 and 5) two rectangular ornaments with repeated rectangles nesting inside them and two bands of inverted chevrons, one with three bands (6) and one with four bands (7); a reverse chevron lies below this.

The composition on the main face consists of three wheels, each with four spokes and hubs (8–10), a large spearhead placed horizontally (11), two shapes that may be water birds (12 and 13) and the largest motif of all, a shield (14). It is the shield which organises the composition and dominates it.

5 Commentary

There appear to be two periods of decoration on this stela and that it was originally a Copper Age monument that was re-used in the Final Bronze Age, like some Spanish and Portuguese ones. The differences in engraving technique, motif choice and symbol composition all support this suggestion, which has not been proposed before.

In this interpretation, the oldest motifs are those stark geometric ones engraved on the sides. Their style connects with Copper Age decorations on pottery and on megalithic monuments and stelae of the third millennium BC, which were used throughout the western Mediterranean and Atlantic regions. Local stelae bearing these motifs are actually known from Basse-Languedoc and in Basse-Provence (Soutou 1962:546). They have nothing in common with any motifs in use in the Final Bronze Age, either on pottery or metalwork. There are also technical points to consider, which indicate that the back face of the stela has been cut down to produce a more regular shaped block of stone and in doing so has damaged the symmetry and proportion of the older motifs; this is obvious in motifs 2 and 3, which have lost at least half of their original size. Such damage is not due to the edge being struck, or exfoliated after years of weathering; this is deliberate damage caused by a later engraver as he levelled the rear face, which must have happened in the Final Bronze Age. Motifs 4–7 were also damaged on the other edge. Soutou (1962:522) quotes the earlier comments of E Bonnet in 1924, who published the excavations of 1916, that there are traces of more engravings on the back, but he does not describe them further; and the back of the stela is inaccessible since it is mounted on a wall in the museum.

The Final Bronze Age carving is quite different. A careful composition balances four elements, with an attention to symmetry and executed in a different engraving technique for emphasis. Low relief carving is slower and more laborious work than simple engraving and this face took many hours to complete. All the elements are known in the iconography of the Urnfield societies in the west Alpine region; and they fit perfectly with those used to decorate metal work, such as shields, wine mixing bowls and some helmets. The wheels are usually interpreted as solar symbols and are found from Scandinavia to Italy. So, too, are the water birds, perhaps identifying the underworld. The shield and spear are the common elements that link this composition to the south-west Iberian stelae and the great V-notched shield is a fine example of Type IC. Spoked wheels and shields are associated together on the gold hats discussed earlier and shields bear water birds (one from Nackhälle in Sweden is a fine example), so this iconography is part of the Final Bronze Age world flourishing from 1250–1000 BC. This should be the date of the stela, too.

The weapons, and especially the shield, link these religious expressions to the world of warriors, exactly as J Déchelette proposed in 1924 (Vol II, 426–444).

The drawing is based on published oblique photographs, which are corrected for perspective, so that all the motifs can be seen without distortion.

6 Bibliography

See: Almagro Basch 1966 (Lám XXXVIII); Celestino 2001:449–450; Soutou 1962 (photographs on Figures 1 and 3).

---

1 Catalogue number and findspot: **C91 BUOUX I (VAUCLUSE), Provence, France**

2 Circumstances of discovery, context and present location

This stela lay flat on the ground, decoration hidden, in a farm called Salen, which is 1 km from Buoux. An inhumation grave was found very close by.

It is in the house of the owner of the farm, M Dekester.

3 Stone type, size and condition of the monument

It is of soft sandstone and measures 1.53 m high, 0.68 m wide and has an average thickness of 0.18 m. Its composition is probably complete.

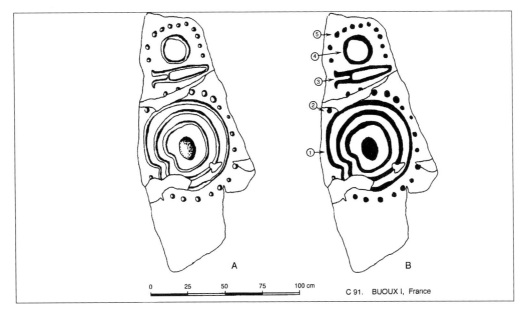

A   B

0   25   50   75   100 cm

C 91. BUOUX I, France

4 Description of the composition and motifs

The stone was pecked smooth before engraving. The composition is basic and focuses on (1) the large shield that is surrounded by (2) a ring of pits. Above is (3) a dagger, (4) a plain circle (perhaps another shield), also surrounded by (5) an arc of pits.

5 Commentary

The discovery of a burial very nearby, with human bones in a pot, suggests that this stela may have been a grave marker, like some of those from Spain and Portugal.

The motifs are familiar, but executed in an idiosyncratic manner. The shield is a V-notched one of Type IC, like Substantion.

6 Bibliography

See: Celestino 2001:451. There is no good published photograph.

1 Catalogue number and findspot: **C92 BUOUX II (VAUCLUSE), Provence, France**

2 Circumstances of discovery, context and present location

It was found while ploughing, on the farm called Bremonde, which is 400 m away from where Buoux I (C91) was found.

It is in the possession of the farm owners, M and Mme Chazine, of Bremonde.

3 Stone type, size and condition of the monument

It is of soft sandstone and its size is not known. It is a fragment.

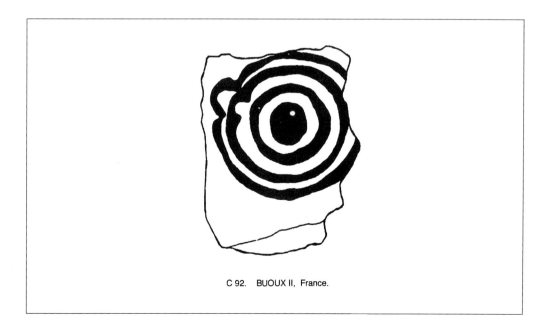

C 92.   BUOUX II, France.

4 Description of the composition and motifs

A poorly engraved shield, with three deep circles, two of them with what may be V-notches.

5 Commentary

The stela is very like Buoux I and must be of the same Final Bronze Age date.

6 Bibliography

See: Celestino 2001:452. There is no proper drawing, nor any published photograph.

---

1 Catalogue number and findspot: **C93 LUNA, Zaragoza**⋆

2 Circumstances of discovery, context and present location

The stela was discovered while ploughing in an area known as La Tiñica, in the municipality of Luna. The area is moderately fertile for dry farming.

    Deposited in the Museo Arqueológico Provincial de Zaragoza.

3 Stone type, size and condition of the monument

The stela is of soft local Tertiary sandstone and measures 1.35 high, 0.67 m wide and has an average thickness of 0.16 m in the upper part and 0.40 m in the lower. It has lost the head and is broken in two, but the motifs are complete.

4 Description of the composition and motifs

It is a stela shaped to look like a human torso, with the sides and front carefully smoothed to a uniform finish. The back is not worked, retaining its original rough state. The motifs are a huge decorated shield (1) and an equally large lyre (2) below it. There is a fine incised line on the neck, perhaps part of a human face or necklace (3).

5 Commentary

This is a remarkable monument for its decoration. The shield is a V-notched one of Type IC, with a band of zigzags on the outer ring. The lyre is depicted in astonishing detail. It has a decorated body and sound box, with ornamental cords on each side of the strings used to make the notes. These are nine in all and attached to a bridge. Across the top is a tension bar, with adjustment lugs visible. Lyres of this type originate in the Aegean world and this may depict an instrument from a Mycenaean or even Minoan workshop.

    The photograph is from the Museo de Zaragoza and the drawing is derived from that and corrected for perspective.

6 Bibliography

See: Celestino 2001:454–455; Fatás 1975.

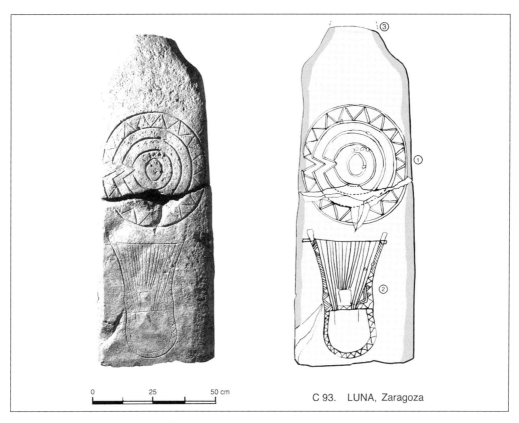

0   25   50 cm

C 93.   LUNA, Zaragoza

1 Catalogue number and findspot: **X94 EL CORONIL, Se★**

2 Circumstances of discovery, context and present location

In 1994, this stela was found lying face upwards on the right bank of the gully of Las Aguzaderas, where it is crossed by the drove way known as the Vereda de Churriana. There is a large prehistoric settlement nearby, on a hill overlooking the gully at Las Aguzaderas. It is in the township of El Coronil.

Deposited in the Museo Arqueológico Provincial de Sevilla.

3 Stone type, size and condition of the monument

The stela is of sandstone and measures 1.86 m high, 1.10 m wide and has a thickness of 0.18 m. The triangular shape is typical of many stelae, but this stone has a natural hole through it and has not had the face pecked smooth for engraving. Erosion has blurred the motifs. It is complete.

4 Description of the composition and motifs

The huge figure of a horned warrior 'hero' with enormous hands (1) dominates the com-

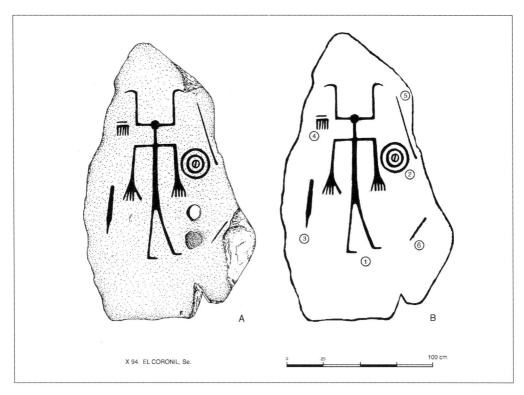

X 94. EL CORONIL, Se.

0   25   100 cm

position. Around him is panoply of (2) a shield, (3) a sword, (4) a comb, (5) a spear and (6) an unidentified motif. The engraving was pecked and rubbed smoothed.

5 Commentary

This is an impressive warrior 'hero', perhaps divine. The rigid geometry of the figure is exceptional, as is his size at over 1 metre tall. The shield is of Type II, but erosion has removed any typological features from the remaining motifs. The drawings are based on the figure published by Izquierdo and López.

6 Bibliography

See: Izquierdo de Montes & López Jurado 1998 (figure 2). There is no published photograph.

1 Catalogue number and findspot: **X95 LA LANTEJUELA, Se★**

2 Circumstances of discovery, context and present location

Its find place and context are unknown.

Deposited in the Museo Arqueológico Provincial de Sevilla.

3 Stone type, size and condition of the monument

It is of soft, dark brown sandstone, with the carved face cut smooth. It measures 0.62 m high, 0.21 m wide and has a thickness of 0.22 m. It is complete.

4 Description of the composition and motifs

The figure occupies the entire face of the stela. The head and face are emphasised by the rebate cut out around them, setting the plaited hair (or diadem?) in relief. From the shoulders down the figure is engraved, to show motifs that include an ornament for the chest, a band of shoulder decoration and a belt. The figure itself is notable for its large hands and feet and what may be intended to be a breast on the left side of the torso, carved in low relief. The surface has spalled in places. Three cross sections show the shallow carving compared to the thickness of the matrix.

5 Commentary

Although not strictly a warrior stela, this anthropomorphic monument is included since its iconography shares features with the *Diademada* figures and it is discussed with them (Galán 1993). Its size, technique of execution and choice of motifs, set it apart from the main series.

The drawings are modified from Oliva Alonso's figure 2.

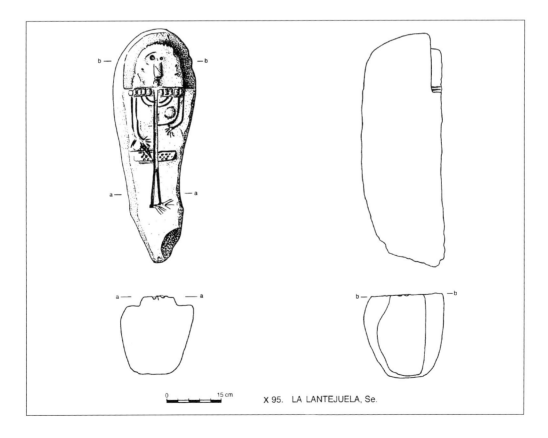

X 95.   LA LANTEJUELA, Se.

6 Bibliography

See: Oliva Alonso 1983 (figure 2 and Lám I).

1 Catalogue number and findspot: **X96 PREIXANA, Le**

2 Circumstances of discovery, context and present location

This stela was found casually in 1970 and afterwards used to mark the edge of a field in the village of Preixana, near Cervera. However, its original position was close to the Canal de Urgel, whose excavation cast it aside earlier.

Deposited in the Museo de Cervera, Lérida.

3 Stone type, size and condition of the monument

It is of soft local Tertiary sandstone and measures 1.15 m high, 0.70 m wide and has an average thickness of 0.17 m. It is substantially complete.

4 Description of the composition and motifs

The stone was carefully shaped to a neat rectangle and smoothed before engraving. The

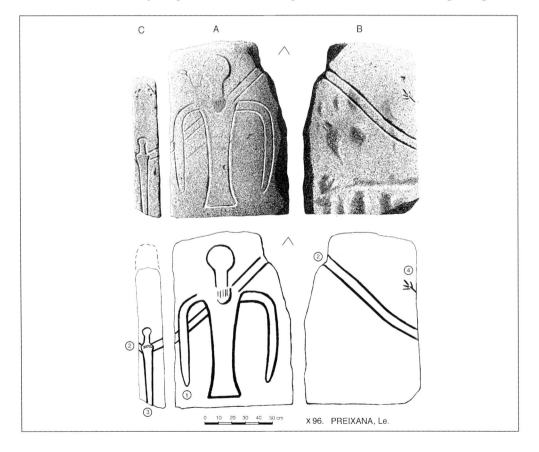

X 96. PREIXANA, Le.

composition uses the entire volume of the block to create an expressive monument. The central figure is of a warrior dressed in a long tunic and wearing an ornament at his throat (1). Across his shoulders hangs a long baldric, (2), with the sword hanging from it on the side panel (3). There is an illegible motif on the back (4). The baldric is engraved right round the stela. The engraving is firm and clear.

5 Commentary

Its geographical position and style set it apart from other stelae. The schematised warrior wears a tunic like that on the Longroiva stela (X97) and both it, and the distinctive shape of the sword hilt and pommel, indicate a date around 1800–1500 BC.

The drawings are modified from Almagro Basch's illustrations.

6 Bibliography

See: Almagro Basch 1974 (figures 14–17, with photographs)

1 Catalogue number and findspot: **X97 LONGROIVA (GUARDA), Beira Alta, Portugal**

2 Circumstances of discovery, context and present location

It was found in 1965 in Longroiva, near the city of Guarda, without further details of its discovery being recorded.

It is deposited in the Museu da Guarda, Portugal.

3 Stone type, size and condition of the monument

The stela is of coarse granite and measures 2.40 m high, 1.30 m wide and has an average thickness of 0.28 m. The main face was pecked roughly before engraving. It is complete.

4 Description of the composition and motifs

A fully dressed and armed warrior dominates the composition. Motifs overlap one another, showing at least two phases of decoration (or modifications) took place. To highlight this feature, the first carvings are shown in black and the later ones in a grey tone.

The warrior faces the viewer, with a neatly trimmed beard and an ornament on his chest (1). He wears a long tunic that reaches to his lower legs (2). He carries a huge halberd on his right side, with its thick stave (3) and heavy binding for the metal blade (5). The five lines of motif 4 may be his right hand grasping the weapon. Motifs 6 and 7 are impossible to identify. On his left side is a longbow (8), with a triangular dagger or short sword in its sheath (9). Engraved over this are indistinct motifs (10 and 11), that may represent the warrior's left arm and hand.

5 Commentary

Size alone makes this an impressive monument, with the human figure over 1.40 metres

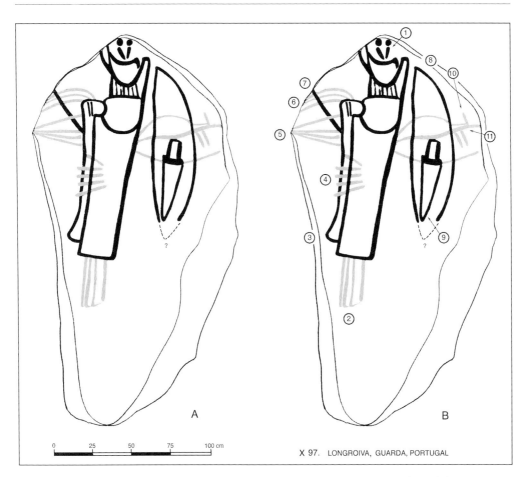

A   B

0   25   50   75   100 cm

X 97. LONGROIVA, GUARDA, PORTUGAL

tall. The style of the halberd and dagger are unmistakeable and place this stela in the Early Bronze Age, probably between 2200–1900 BC. The halberd blade has a big central rib and is a truly massive weapon, with a thick shaft ending in a rounded butt. Especially interesting are the dress and beard of the warrior, both features that are conspicuously different from the Final Bronze Age stelae, where warriors are nearly always shown naked and clean-shaven.

Despite the clumsy engraving, and corrections made to the motifs during carving, they were probably made at the same time.

The drawing is based on Almagro Basch's figure and photographs.

6 Bibliography

See: Almagro Basch 1966 (figure 35 and Lám XXX).

1 Catalogue number and findspot: **X98 BENACCI-CAPRARA Grave 63,
Bologna, Italy**

2 Circumstances of discovery, context and present location

The stela was excavated in Grave 63 at the proto-historic cemetery of Benacci-Caprara,
where there are rich male graves with horse harnesses, sword and bronze vessels.

3 Stone type, size and condition of the monument

The stela is broken in two but substantially complete. Its exact dimensions are not given.

4 Description of the composition and motifs

The scene features two large spoked wheels in the upper register (1 and 2) which dominate
the composition. Below them are the warrior and his panoply. The motifs are (3) a shield,
(4) a horse, (5) the warrior wearing a long tunic and helmet and carrying (6) a mirror in
his left hand and a (7) spear in his right. A second horse faces him (8). The entire composition rests on a ground line (9).

5 Commentary

The scene recalls the sun wheels on Substantion (C90), while the panoply of shield, spear
and mirror is similar to many Iberian stelae. The main difference is the addition of two
horses. Especially remarkable is the mirror that the warrior holds in his hand, since it is
clearly shown. The date of the stela is around 700 BC.

The longevity of the theme of the warrior with his panoply and religious attributes like
the solar wheels, as well as its dispersal right across the western Mediterranean, indicates
the shared values and world-views of these social elites. The same symbols recur time and

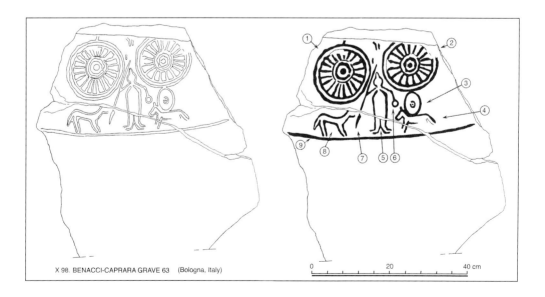

X 98. BENACCI-CAPRARA GRAVE 63   (Bologna, Italy)

0   20   40 cm

again, linking the world of the living warrior to that of the dead 'hero'.

The drawing is modified after Kossack's figure.

6 Bibliography

See: Kossack 1999 (Abb 31).

The following list includes stelae known to exist, but which have not been published fully, or have been concealed by their owners.

X99 Pocito Chico (Bahía de Cádiz), Cádiz

The upper part of a stela depicts a horned figure. It was found inside an unusual building, which radiocarbon dates show can be no later than eighth century BC (Celestino 2001:320).

X100 Logrosán, Cáceres

The stela is known to exist but is unavailable for study (Celestino 2001:350).

X101 and X102 Lacipo, Málaga

Two stelae are known from the Iberian-Roman city of Lacipo in Málaga, which has a Final Bronze Age occupation. No further details are available (Villaseca 1994:72 and note 6).

X103 Baños de San Cristóbal, (Pozuelo de Calatrava), Ciudad Real

The stela fragment was found in a stone heap and carries a V-notched shield of Class IB and possibly a sword motif. Catalogued by Galán as his stela 53, but not drawn by him (Galán 1993:105).

X104 and X105 La Serena, Badajoz

Two new stelae were discovered in 2002 during an archaeological survey. One is eroded and has a human figure next to a big shield, a chariot and weapons. The other is well preserved and has two figures bearing swords, a shield, spear and bow and arrow. Their discoverers will publish them.

Bibliography

Abascal Palazón, JM 1994. *Los nombres personales en las inscripciones latinas de Hispania*. Murcia: Universidad de Murcia.

Almagro Basch, M 1940. El hallazgo de la Ría de Huelva y el final de la Edad del Bronce en el Occidente de Europa. *Ampurias* II, 85–143.

Almagro Basch, M 1962. Una nueva estela grabada extremeña. Valor cultural y cronológico de estos monumentos. *Munibe XIV* 3/4:285–296.

Almagro Basch, M 1966. *Las estelas decoradas del suroeste peninsular*. Bibliotheca Praehistorica Hispana, Vol VIII. Madrid.

Almagro Basch, M 1972. Los ídolos y la estela decorada de Hernán Pérez (Cáceres) y el ídolo estela de Tabuyo del Monte (León). *Trabajos de Prehistoria* 29:83–124.

Almagro Basch, M 1974. Nuevas estelas decoradas de la Península Ibérica. *Miscelánea Arqueológica I, XXV Aniversario de los Cursos Internacionales de Prehistoría y Arqueología de Ampurias (1947–1971)*: 5–39.

Almagro Gorbea, M 1977. *El Bronce Final y el Período Orientalizante en Extremadura*. Bibliotheca Praehistorica Hispana, Vol XIV. Madrid.

Almagro Gorbea, M & Sánchez Abal, JL 1978. La estela decorada de Zarza de Montánchez, Cáceres. *Trabajos de Prehistoria* 35:417–422.

Alves Dias, MM & Coelho, L 1971. Notável lápide proto-histórica da Herdade da Abóbada - Almodóvar. *O Arqueologo Português Ser* III 5:181–190.

Anlen, L & Padiou, R 1989. *Les miroirs du Bronze Anciens. Symbolisme et tradition*. Paris: Éditions Guy Trédaniel.

Anthony, DW 1995. Horse, wagon and chariot: Indo-European languages and archaeology. *Antiquity* 69:554–565.

Antonaccio, C 1995. *An archaeology of ancestors. Tomb cult and hero cult in early Greece*. Lanham MD: Rownham and Littlefield.

Armbruster, BR 1998. Zu den technologischen Aspekten bronzener Fleischhaken und Bratspiessen der Atlantischen Spätbronzezeit. In Mordant, C, Pernot, M, and Rychner, V (eds) *L'Atelier du Bronzier en Europe du XXe au VIIIe siècle avant notre ère*, tII: 183–192.

Armbruster, BR 2001. *Goldschmiedekunst und Bronzetechnik. Studien zum Metallhandwerk der Atlantischen Bronzezeit auf der Iberischen Halbinsel*. Éditions Monique Mergoil. Monographies Instrumentum 15. Montagnac.

Assmann, J 1992. *Das kulturelle Gedächtnis. Schrift, Erinnerung und politische Identität in frühen Hochkulturen*. München: Beck.

Atchity, JK 1977. *Homer's Iliad: the shield of memory*. Carbondale: Southern Illinois University Press.

Aubet Semmler, Ma E 1997. A propósito de una vieja estela. *Saguntum* 30:163–172.

Aubet Semmler, Ma E 1989. (Coordinator). *Tartessos. Arqueología protohistórica del bajo Guadalquivir*. Sabadell: Editorial AUSA.

Baillie, MGL 1996. The chronology of the Bronze Age 2354 BC to 431 BC. In Randsborg, K (ed) *Absolute Chronology: Archaeological Europe 2500–500 BC. Acta Archaeologica* (Copenhagen) 67 (*Acta Archaeologica Supplementa* 1). Copenhagen: Munksgaard:291–298.

Balmuth, M (ed) 1986. *Studies in Sardinian archaeology, Vol II: Sardinia and the Mediterranean*. Ann Arbor: University of Michigan Press.

Barceló, JA 1988. Introducción al razonamiento estadístico aplicado a la Arqueología: Un análisis de las estelas antropomorfas de la Península Ibérica. *Trabajos de Prehistoria* 45:51–85.

Barceló, JA 1989. Las estelas decoradas del sudoeste de la Península Ibérica. In Aubet Semmler, Ma. E (Coordinator) Tartessos. *Arqueología protohistórica del bajo Guadalquivir*. Sabadell: Editorial. AUSA:189–208.

Barnett, RD 1975. The Sea Peoples. In Edwards, IES, Gadd, CJ, Hammond, NGL & Sollberger, E (eds) *The Cambridge Ancient History*, Vol II (2), 3rd edn. Cambridge: Cambridge University Press:359–378.

Barfield, LH 1995. The context of statue-menhirs. In Casini, S, de Marinis, RC and Pedrotti, A (eds) *Statue-Stele e Massi Incisi nell–Europa dell–Età del Rame. Notizie Archeologiche Bergomensi* Vol 3. Bergamo: Civico Museo Archeologico de Bergamo:11–20.

Bartelheim, M & Heyd, V 2001. Cult after burial: Patterns of post-funeral treatment in the Bronze and Iron Ages of Central Europe. In Biehl, PF, Bertemes, F and Meller, H (eds) *The archaeology of cult and religion*. Archaeolingua 13. Budapest: Archaeolingua Alapítvány:261–276.

Beltrán, M & Alcrudo, C 1973. Noticia de dos nuevas estelas decoradas del Museo de Cáceres. *Estudios del Seminario de Prehistoría, Arqueolgía e Historía Antigua de la Facultad de Filosofía y Letras de Zaragoza* II, 81–93.

Bendala Galán, M 1977. Notas sobre las estelas decoradas del Suroeste y los orígenes de Tartessos. *Habis* 8:177–205.

Bendala Galán, M, Hurtado, V & Amores, F 1979/1980. Tres nuevas estelas de guerrero en la Provincia de Córdoba. *Habis* 10/11:381–390.

Bendala Galán, M, Rodríguez Temiño, I & Núñez Pariente de León, E 1994. Una nueva estela de guerrero tartésico de la Provincia de Córdoba. In Mangas, J and Alvar, J (eds) *Homenaje a José Maria Blázquez*. Madrid: Ediciones Clásicas:26–35.

Bernabò Brea, L & Cavalier, M 1980. *Meligunìs-Lipára IV. L'acropoli di Lipari nella preistoria*. Palermo: Flaccovio.

Berrocal, L 1987. La losa de Capote (Higuera la Real). *Archivo Español de Arqueología* 60:195–207.

Biehl, PF, Bertemes, F & Meller, H (eds) 2001. *The archaeology of cult and religion*. Archaeolingua 13. Budapest: Archaeolingua Alapítvány.

Black, J & Green, A 1992. *Gods, demons and symbols of ancient Mesopotamia*. London: British Museum Press.

Blanco Freijeiro, A, Luzón Nogué, JM & Ruiz Mata, D 1969. Panorama tartésico en Andalucía Oriental. *Tartessos y sus Problemas. V Symposium Internacional de Prehistoría Peninsular. Jérez de la Frontera, Septiembre 1968*. Barcelona: Universidad de Barcelona, Publicaciones Eventuales No 13:119–162.

Blázquez Martínez, JM 1983. Las liras de las estelas hispanas de finales de la Edad del Bronce. *Archivo Español de Arqueología* 56:213–228.

Boos, A 1999. The chieftain's grave of Hagenau and related warrior graves. In Demakopoulou, K, Eluere, C, Jensen, J, Jockenhövel, A and Mohen, J-P (eds) *Gods and heroes of the European Bronze Age. Catalogue of the exhibition Gods and Heroes of the Bronze Age Europe at the time of Ulysses*. London: Thames and Hudson:106–107.

Bonsor, GE & Thouvenot, R 1928. *Nécropole ibérique de Setefilla, Lora del Río (Sevilla)*. Bibliothèque de L'École des Hautes Études Ibériques, fasc. XIV. Bordeaux, Paris.

Borges, JL 1953. 'Les Miroirs' in *L'Auteur et autres textes*. Paris: Gallimard.

Boura, F, Faye, O, Gebus, L, Klag, Th, Lambert, G & Lavier, G 1995. Le gisement de Vandières-Les Grandes Corvées (Meurthe-et-Moselle). In: *Un monde villageois. Habitat et milieu naturel en Europe de 2000 à 500 av*. J.-C. Colloque Lons-le-Saunier 1990:73–82.

Bouzek, J 1985. *The Aegean, Anatolia and Europe: Cultural interrelations in the Second Millennium BC*. Studies in Mediterranean Archaeology, Vol XXIX. Prague: Paul Åströms Förlag and Prague Academia (Publishing House of the Czechoslovak Academy of Sciences).

Bradley, R 1990. *The passage of arms*. Cambridge: Cambridge University Press.

Bradley, R 1997. *Rock art and the prehistory of Atlantic Europe. Signing the land*. London and New York: Routledge.

Brandherm, D & Ruiz-Gálvez Priego, M 2003. *Las espadas del Bronce Final en la Península Ibérica y Baleares*. Prähistorische Bronzefunde, Abteilung IV.

Brelich, A 1960. *Gli eroi greci: un problema storico-religioso*. Rome: Dell'Ateneo.

Briard, J 1965. *Les Dépôts Bretons et l'Âge du Bronze Atlantique*. Rennes: Travaux du Laboratoire d'Anthropologie Préhistorique.

Brun, P 1991. Le Bronze Atlantique et ses subdivisions culturelles: essai de définition. In Chevillot, C and Coffyn, A (eds) *L'Âge du Bronze Atlantique*. Beynac-et-Cazen: Association des Musées du Sarladais:11–23.

Bueno-Ramirez, P 1995. Megalitismo, estatuas y estelas en España. In Casini, S, de Marinis, RC and Pedrotti, A (eds) *Statue-Stele e Massi Incisi nell'Europa dell'Età del Rame. Notizie Archeologiche Bergomensi* Vol 3. Bergamo: Civico Museo Archeologico de Bergamo:77–129.

Bueno Ramirez, P & Piñón Ramirez, F 1985. La estela de Monte Blanco, Olivenza (Badajoz). *Estudios de Arqueología Extremeña (Homenaje a Cánovas Pessini)*, Badajoz: 37–43.

Burgess, C 2001. Swords, warfare and Sea Peoples: the end of the Late Bronze Age in the East Mediterranean. In Le Roux, C-T (ed) *Du monde des chasseurs à celui des métallurgistes: hommages à Jean L'Huelgouach et Jacques Briard*. Revue Archéologique de l'Ouest, Supplement 9:277–287.

Cabré Aguilo, J 1923. Losas sepulcrales del suroeste de la Península, pertenecientes a la Edad del Bronce, con bajorrelieves y grabados de armas. *Revista de Coleccionismo*, XI 125/126:49.

Cardoso, JL 1996. Bases de subsistência em povoades do Bronze Final e da Idade do Ferro do território Português. O testemunho dos mamíferos. In (various authors), *De Ulisses a Viriato*:160–170.

Carneiro, R 1970. A theory of the origin of the state. *Science* 169:733–738.

Casini, S, de Marinis, RC & Pedrotti, A (eds) 1995. *Statue-Stele e Massi Incisi nell'Europa dell'Età del Rame. Notizie Archeologiche Bergomensi* Vol 3. Bergamo: Civico Museo Archeologico de Bergamo.

Castelo Ruano, R 1990. Aproximación a la danza en la antigüedad hispana. Manos entre-lazadas. *Espacio, Tiempo y Forma, Serie II, Historía Antigua*, t 3:19–42.

Celestino Pérez, S 1990. Las estelas decoradas del suroeste. La Cultura Tartésica y Extremadura. *Cuadernos Emeritenses* 2:45–62.

Celestino Pérez, S 1992. Cancho Roano. Un centro comercial de carácter político-religioso e influencia oriental. *Rivista di Studi Fenici* XX-1:19–46.

Celestino Pérez, S 2001. *Estelas de guerrero y estelas diademadas. La precolonización y formación del mundo tartésico*. Barcelona: Edicions Bellaterra.

Chaves, F & De la Bandera, ML 1982. Estela decorada de Montemolín (Marchena, Sevilla). *Archivo Español de Arqueología* 55:136–139.

Chevillot, C & Coffyn, A (eds) 1991. *L'Âge du Bronze Atlantique*. Beynac-et-Cazen: Association des Musées du Sarladais.

Cirio, AM 2001. Nuovi dati sul culto degli eroi: una interpretazione di Alceo, 140 V. In Ribichini, S, Rocchi, M and Xella, P (eds) *La cuestione delle influenze vicinoorientali sulla religione greca*. Rome: CNR:299–305.

Coffyn, A 1985. *Le Bronze Final Atlantique dans la Péninsule Ibérique*. Publications du Centre Pierre Paris 11. Paris: Diffusion de Boccard.

Coles, J 1962. European Bronze Age shields. *Proceedings of the Prehistoric Society* 28:156–190.

Coles, JM 2001. Bronze Age rock carvings at Häljesta, Västmanland, Sweden: domination by isolation. *Germania* 79(2):237–271.

Coles, JM 2002. Chariots of the Gods? Landscape and imagery at Frännarp, Sweden. *Proceedings of the Prehistoric Society* 68:215–246.

Crouwel, JH 1981. *Chariots and other means of land transport in Bronze Age Greece*. Allard Pierson Series Vol 3; Amsterdam: Allard Pierson.

Crouwel, JH 1992. *Chariots and other wheeled vehicles in Iron Age Greece*. Allard Pierson Series Vol 9; Amsterdam: Allard Pierson.

Cunliffe, B 2001. *Facing the ocean. The Atlantic and its peoples*. Oxford: Oxford University Press.

Curado, FP 1984. Uma nova estela do Bronze Final na Beira Alta (Baraçal, Sabugal-Guarda). *Arqueologia (Porto)* 9:81–84.

Curado, FP 1986. Mais uma estela do Bronze Final na Beira Alta (Fóios, Sabugal-Guarda). *Arqueologia (Porto)* 14:103–109.

D'Anna, A, Gutherz, X & Jallot, L 1995. Les stèles anthropomorphiques et les statues-menhires néolithiques du Sud de la France. In Casini, S, de Marinis, RC and Pedrotti, A (eds) *Statue-Stele e Massi Incisi nell'Europa dell'Età del Rame. Notizie Archeologiche Bergomensi* Vol 3. Bergamo: Civico Museo Archeologico de Bergamo:143–165.

Déchelette, J 1924. *Manuel d'Archéologie Préhistorique, t II*. Paris: Auguste Picard.

Della Casa, P & Fischer, C 1997. Argumente für den Beginn der Spätbronzezeit im 14.

Jahrhundert v. Chr. *Prähistorische Zeitschrift* 72:195–233.

Demakopoulou, K, Eluere, C, Jensen, J, Jockenhövel, A & Mohen, J-P (eds) 1999. *Gods and heroes of the European Bronze Age. Catalogue of the Exhibition Gods and Heroes of the Bronze Age Europe at the time of Ulysses*. London: Thames and Hudson.

De Marrais, E, Castillo, J & Earle, T 1996. Ideology, materialization and power strategies. *Current Anthropology* 37:15–31.

Derrida, J 1976. *Of grammatology*. London: The Johns Hopkins University Press.

Derrida, J 1978. *Writing and difference*. London: Routledge.

Domergue, C 1988. *Catalogue des mines et fonderies antiques de la Péninsule Ibérique*. 2 Vols + portfolio of maps. Madrid: Casa de Velazquez; Diffusion de Boccard.

Echt, R 2000. *Das Fürstinnengrab von Reinheim. Studien zur Kulturgeschichte der Früh-La-Tène-Zeit*. Saarbrücker Beiträge zur Altertumskunde 69. Bonn: Habelt.

Eco, U 1990. *The limits of interpretation*. Bloomington: Indiana University Press.

Earle, T (ed) 1991. *Chiefdoms: power, economy and ideology*. New directions in archaeology series. Cambridge: Cambridge University Press.

Earle, T 1997. *How chiefs come to power. The political economy in prehistory*. Stanford: Stanford University Press.

Egg, M & Tomedi, G 2002. Ein Bronzehelm aus dem Mittelbronzezeitlichen Depotfund vom Pillar, Gemeinde Fleiss, in Nordtirol. *Archäologisches Korrespondenzblatt* 32:543-560.

Eiwanger, J 1989. Talanton. Ein bronzezeitlicher Goldstandard zwischen Ägäis und Mitteleuropa. *Germania* 67(2):443–518.

Enríquez, JJ 1982. Dos nuevas estelas de guerrero en el Museo Arqueológico Provincial de Badajoz. *Museos* 1:65–68.

Enríquez, JJ & Celestino, S 1981/1982. La estela de Capilla (Badajoz). *Pyrenae* 17/18:203–210.

Enríquez, JJ & Celestino, S 1984. Nuevas estelas decoradas en la Cuenca del Guadiana. *Trabajos de Prehistoria* 41:237–251.

Eogan, G 1990. Possible connections between Britain and Ireland and the east Mediterranean region during the Bronze Age. *Orientalisch-Ägäische Einflüsse in der Europäischen Bronzezeit. Ergebnisse eines Kolloquiums*. (Monographien des Römisch-Germanischen Zentralmuseums 15). Bonn: Habelt:155–163.

Eogan, G 1994. *The accomplished art. Gold and gold-working in Britain and Ireland during the Bronze Age* (c. 2300–650 BC) Oxford: Oxford University Committee for Archaeology Monograph 42.

Evans, AJ 1905. The prehistoric tombs of Knossos. *Archaeologia* 59:391–562.

Fadda, MA & Lo Schiavo, F 1992. *Su Tempiesu di Orune: Fonte Sacra Nuragica.* Soprintendenza ai Beni Archeologici per le province di Sassari e Nuoro. Ozieri: *Quaderni* 18:61–128.

Fatás Cabeza, G 1975. Una estela de guerrero con escotadura en V aparecida en las Cinco Villas de Aragón. *Pyrenae* 11:165–169.

Fernández Miranda, M 1987. La estela de las Herencias (Toledo). *Estudios en Homenaje a A. Beltrán.* Zaragoza: Boletín del Museo de Zaragoza: 463–476.

Fernández Miranda, M & Olmos, R 1986. *Las ruedas de Toya y el orígen del carro en la Península Ibérica.* Museo Arqueológico Nacional Catálogos y Monografías 9, Madrid: Ministerio de Cultura.

Fernández Ochoa, C & Zarzalejos Prieto, M 1994. La estela de Chillón (Ciudad Real). Algunas consideraciones acerca de la funcionalidad de las 'estelas de guerrero' del Bronce Final y su reutilización en época Romana. *V Congreso Internacional de Estelas Funerarias; Actas del Congreso (Soria, 28 de abril a 1 de mayo de 1993)*: 263–272.

Ferrer Albelda, E & Mancebo Davalos, J 1991. Nuevos elementos de carros orientalizantes en la alta Andalucia. Algunas precisiones en torno a su función, significado y distribución. *Cuadernos de Prehistoría y Arqueología de la Universidad Autónoma de Madrid* 18:113–148.

Fittschen, K 1973. *Der Schild des Achilles.* Archaeologia Homerica II, Kap. N, Teil 1. Göttingen: Vandenhoeck and Ruprecht.

Foster, ILL & Alcock, L (eds) 1963. *Culture and environment. Essays in honour of Sir Cyril Fox.* London: Routledge and Kegan Paul.

Foucault, M 1972. *The archaeology of knowledge.* London: Tavistock.

Frankenstein, S & Rowlands, M 1978. The internal structure and regional context of Early Iron Age society in south-western Germany. *Bulletin of the Institute of Archaeology* 15:73–112.

Frizell, BS 1991. *Arte militare e architettura nuragica. Nuragic architecture in its military, territorial and socio-economic context.* Proceedings of the First International Colloquium on Nuragic Architecture at the Swedish Institute in Rome, 7–9 December, 1989. Skrifter Utgivna av Svenska Institut i Rom, 4°. XLVIII. Stockholm: Paul Åströms Förlag.

Furmanek, V & Horst, F (eds) 1982. *Beiträge zum bronzezeitlichen Burgenbau in Mitteleuropa.* Berlin and Nitra: Zentralinstitut-für Alte Geschichte und Archäeologie, Nitra: Archeologicky Ustav Slovenskej Akademie Vied.

Furmanek, V & Horst, F (eds) 1990. *Beiträge zur Geschichte und Kultur der*

Mitteleuropäischen Bronzezeit. Berlin and Nitra: Zentralinstitut für Alte Geschichte und Archäeologie, Nitra: Archeologicky Ustav Slovenskej Akademie Vied.

Galán Domingo, E 1993. *Estelas, paisaje y territorio en el Bronce Final del suroeste de la Península Ibérica*. Complutum Extra No. 3, Madrid: Universidad Complutense de Madrid.

Gallay, A & Chaix, L 1984. *Le dolmen M XI: texte et planches, documents annexes*, 2 vols., Lausanne. Bibliothèque historique vaudoise (*Le site préhistorique du Petit-Chasseur (Sion, Valais)*; 5, 6. Cahiers d'Archéologie Romande. Genève: Document du Département d'Anthropologie de l'Université de Genève:31, 32.

García-Bellido, Ma. P 1999. Sistemas metrológicos, monedas y desarrollo económico. *IV Symposio sobre Celtíberos*, Zaragoza:363–385.

García de Figuerola, M 1982. Nueva estela del tipo II en San Martín de Trevejo (Cáceres). *Zephyrus* 35:173–180.

Gebhard, R, with a contribution from M Moosauer 1999. Der Goldfund von Bernstorf bei Kranzberg. *Bayerische Vorgeschichtsblatter 64*:1–18 (Taf. 1–8).

Gebhard, R & Rieder, K-H 2002. Zwei bronzezeitliche Bernsteinobjekte mit Bild- und Schriftzeichen aus Bernstorf (Lkr. Freising). *Germania* 80:115–133.

Gerloff, S 1986. Bronze Age Class A cauldrons: typology, origins and chronology. *Journal of the Royal Society of Antiquaries of Ireland* 116:84–115.

Giardino, C 1995. *Il Mediterraneo occidentale fra XIV ed VIII secolo a. C. Cerchie minerarie e metallurgiche. The West Mediterranean between the 14th and 8th Centuries B.C. Mining and metallurgical spheres*. Oxford: British Archaeological Reports International Series S-612.

Giardino, C 2000. Sicilian hoards and protohistoric metal trade in the Central West Mediterranean. In Pare, C (ed) *Metals Make the World Go Round. The supply and circulation of metals in Bronze Age Europe*. Oxford: Oxbow Books:99–107.

Gomes, M. Varela & Monteiro, J. Pinho 1977. Las estelas decoradas do Pomar (Beja, Portugal). Estudio comparado. *Trabajos de Prehistoria* 34:165–214.

González Cordero, A. & De Alvarado Gonzalo, M 1989/90. Nuevas estelas decoradas en Extremadura. *Norba, (Revista de Historía)* 10:59–66.

Gran atlas de España. Vol 4. Castilla y León/Extremadura 1989. Barcelona: Planeta.

Gräslund, B 1967. The Herzsprung shield type and its origin. *Acta Archaeologica (Copenhagen)* 38:59–71.

Gregory, R 1996. *Mirrors in mind*. Oxford, New York, Heidelberg: WH Freeman/Spektrum.

Grove, AT & Rackham, O 2001. *The nature of Mediterranean Europe: an ecological history*.

New Haven: Yale University Press.

Harding, AF 1984. *The Mycenaeans and Europe*. London: Academic Press.

Harding, AF 2000. *European societies in the Bronze Age*. Cambridge: Cambridge University Press.

Harris, DR (ed) 1996. *The origins and spread of agriculture and pastoralism in Eurasia*. London: UCL Press.

Harrison, RJ 1985. The 'Policultivo Ganadero' or Secondary Products Revolution in Spanish agriculture 5000–1000 BC. *Proceedings of the Prehistoric Society* 51:75–102.

Harrison, RJ 1993. La intensificación económica y la integración del modo pastoril durante la Edad del Bronce. *Trabalhos de Antropolgia e Etnologia Vol 33 (3–4), 1 Congresso de Arqueologia Peninsular, Porto. Actas* II: 293–299.

Harrison, RJ 1994. The Bronze Age in Northern and Northeastern Spain 2000–800 B.C. In Stoddart, S and Mathers, C (eds) *Development and decline in the Mediterranean Bronze Age*. Sheffield: University of Sheffield Press:73–97.

Harrison, RJ 1996. Arboriculture in Southwest Europe: dehesas as managed woodlands. In Harris, DR (ed) *The origins and spread of agriculture and pastoralism in Eurasia*. London: UCL Press:363–367.

Harrison, RJ, Moreno López, G & Legge, AJ 1994. *Moncín; un poblado de la Edad del Bronce (Borja, Zaragoza)*. Colección Arqueología No. 16. Zaragoza: Cometa.

Harrison RJ & Mederos Martín, A 2000. Patronage and clientship; a model for the Atlantic Final Bronze Age in the Iberian Peninsula. In Pare, C (ed) *Metals Make the World Go Round. The supply and circulation of metals in Bronze Age Europe*. Oxford: Oxbow Books: 133-150.

Hedges, REM, Housley, RA, Bronck, CR & Van Klinken, GJ 1991. Radiocarbon dates from the Oxford AMS System: Archaeometry datelist 12. *Archaeometry* 33(1):121–134.

Hedges, REM, Housley, RA, Bronck, CR & Van Klinken, GJ 1993. Radiocarbon dates from the Oxford AMS System: Archaeometry datelist 17. *Archaeometry* 35(2):305–326.

Helms, MW 1988. *Ulysses Sail: an ethnographic odyssey of power, knowledge, and geographical distance*. Princeton NJ: Princeton University Press.

Hencken, HO'N 1950. Herzsprung shields and Greek trade. *American Journal of Archaeology* LIV(4):295–309.

Hencken, HO'N 1971. *The earliest European helmets. Bronze Age and Iron Age*. American School of Prehistoric Research, Peabody Museum. Cambridge, MA: Harvard University, Bulletin 28.

Hernando Gonzalo, A 1989. Inicios de la orfebreria en la Península Ibérica. In *El oro en la España Preromana. Revista de Arqueología*, 32–45. Madrid: Zugarto.

Hill, JD 2002. Wetwang chariot burial. *Current Archaeology* 178:410–412.

Hodder, I 1990. *The domestication of Europe*. Oxford: Blackwell.

Hodder, I 1996. Comment on De Marrais et al. *Current Anthropology* 37:57–59.

Höckmann, U 1982. *Die Bronzen aus dem Fürstengrab von Castel San Mariano bei Perugia* Munich: Staatliche Antikensammlungen München, Katalog der Bronzen, 1. Munich.

Huth, C 2000. Metal circulation, communication and traditions of craftsmanship in Late Bronze Age and Early Iron Age Europe. In Pare, CFE (ed) *Metals Make the World Go Round. The supply and circulation of metals in Bronze Age Europe*. Oxford: Oxbow Books:176–193.

Iglesias Gil, JM 1980. Estela inédita hallada en El Viso. *Archivo Español de Arqueología* 53:189–191.

Izquierdo, I & Arasa, F, 1999. La imagen de la memoria. Antecedentes, tipología e iconografía de las estelas de época ibérica. *Archivo de Prehistoria Levantina XXIII*, 259–300.

Izquierdo de Montes, R & López Jurado, S 1998. Estela de Guerrero de El Coronil (Sevilla). *SPAL* 7:177–182.

Jockenhövel, A 1990. Bronzezeitlicher Burgenbau in Mitteleuropa. Untersuchungen zur Struktur frühmetallzeitlicher Gesellschaften. In *Orientalisch-Ägäische Einflüsse in der Europäischen Bronzezeit. Ergebnisse eines Kolloquiums.* (Monographien des Römisch-Germanischen Zentralmuseums 15). Bonn: Habelt: 209ff.

Jorge, SO (ed) 1998. *Existe uma Idade do Bronze Atlântico?* Trabalhos de Arqueologia 10. Lisboa: Instituto Português de Arqueologia.

Karageorghis, V 1973–1974. *Excavations in the necropolis of Salamis III*, Nicosia, Volume 5 in 3 parts: (Text 1973, Department of Antiquities, Cyprus. Zavallis Press Ltd., Nicosia) (Plates, Folding Plans and Sections, 1974, Enschede; Haarlem). Cyprus: Department of Antiquities.

Kaul, F 1998. *Ships on bronzes. A study in Bronze Age religion and iconography*. Publications from the National Museum Studies in Archaeology & History Vol 3. Copenhagen: National Museum of Denmark.

Kossack, G 1999. *Religiöses Denken in dinglicher und bildlicher Überlieferung Alteuropas aus der Spätbronze- und Frühen Eisenzeit (9–6. Jahrhundert v. Chr. Geb.)* Bayerische Akademie der Wissenschaften, Phil.-Hist. Kl., Abhandlungen NF, 116. München: Verlag der Bayerischen Akademie der Wissenschaften.

Krzyszkowska, OH 1992. A 'new' mirror handle from Cyprus. *Annual of the British School of Archaeology in Athens* 87:237–242.

Kristiansen, K 1993. From Villanova to Seddin. The reconstruction of an elite exchange network during the eighth century BC. In Scarre C and Healy F (eds) *Trade and exchange*. Oxford: Oxbow books:143–151.

Kristiansen, K 1998. *Europe before history*. Cambridge: Cambridge University Press.

Kristiansen, K 2002. The tale of the sword – swords and swordfighters in Bronze Age Europe. *Oxford Journal of Archaeology* 21(4):319–332.

Laffineur, R (ed) 1999. *Polemos: le contexte guerrier en Égée à l'Âge du Bronze*. Actes de la 7eme recontre égéenne internationale Université de Liège, 14–17 avril 1998. Vol 1. Austin TX: Université de Liège and University of Texas.

Lanfranchi, F & Weiss, MC (eds) 1997. *L'aventure humaine préhistorique en Corse*. Ajaccio, Corsica: Editions Albiana.

Lautensach, H 1964. *Iberische halbinsel: Geographische handbücher*. Munich.

Laurens, A & Lissarrague, F 1992. Entre dieux. *Metis* 5 (1990):53–73.

Layton, RH 2001. Intersubjectivity and understanding rock art. In Biehl, PF, Bertemes, F and Meller, H (eds) *The archaeology of cult and religion*. Archaeolingua 13. Budapest: Archaeolingua Alapítvány:27–36.

Le Roux, C-T 2001 (ed) *Du monde des chasseurs à celui des métallurgistes: hommages à Jean L'Huelgouach et Jacques Briard*. Revue Archéologique de l'Ouest, Supplement 9.

Leach, E 1976. *Culture and communication: the logic by which symbols are connected*. Cambridge: Cambridge University Press.

Leighton, R 1999. *Sicily before history. An archaeological survey from the Palaeolithic to the Iron Age*. London: Duckworth.

Lilliu, G 1966. *Sculture delle Sardegna nuragica*. Mondadori, Verona: 'La Zattera'.

Lilyquist, C 1979. *Ancient Egyptian mirrors from the earliest times through the Middle Kingdom*. Münchner Ägyptologische Studien 27. Munich, Berlin: Deutscher Kunstverlag.

Littauer, MA & Crouwel, JH 1979. *Wheeled vehicles and ridden animals in the Ancient Near East*. Handbuch der Orientalistik. Leiden/Cologne: EJ Brill.

Lloyd, S 1984. *The archaeology of Mesopotamia* (revised edn). London: Thames and Hudson.

Lo Schiavo, F 1997. La Sardaigne de L'Âge du Bronze Final et du Premier Âge du Fer. In Lanfranchi, F and Weiss, MC (eds) *L'aventure humaine préhistorique en Corse*. Ajaccio, Corsica: Editions Albiana:418–434.

Lo Schiavo, F 1999. The Nuragic Bronze Statuettes. In Demakopoulou, K, Eluere, C, Jensen, J, Jockenhövel, A and Mohen, J-P (eds) *Gods and heroes of the European Bronze Age. Catalogue of the Exhibition Gods and Heroes of the Bronze Age Europe at the time of Ulysses*. London: Thames and Hudson:123–124.

Lo Schiavo, F 2000. Sea and Sardinia; Nuragic bronze boats. In Ridgway, D, Serra Ridgway, FR, Pearce, M, Herring, M, Whitehouse, RD and Wilkins, JB (eds) *Ancient Italy in its Mediterranean setting. Studies in honour of Ellen Macnamara*. Accordia Specialist Studies on the Mediterranean, Vol 4. London: University of London:141–158.

Lo Schiavo, F, Macnamara, E & Vagnetti, L 1985. Late Cypriot imports to Italy and their influence on local Bronzework. *Papers of the British School at Rome* 53:1–71.

Lo Schiavo, F & Manconi, F 2001. Animals in Nuragic Sardinia: *Accordia Research Institute 8:101–132*. Accordia Research Papers, University of London.

Mangas, J & Alvar, J (eds) 1993. *Homenaje a José María Blázquez*. Madrid: Ed Clásicas.

Mayer-Prokop, I 1967. *Die gravierten etruskischen Griffspiegel archaischen Stils*. Mitteilungen des Deutschen Archäologischen Instituts, Römischen Abt, Ergänzungsheft. Heidelberg: Kerle.

Mederos Martín, A 1996a. La conexión Levantino-Chipriota. Indícios de comercio atlántico con el Mediterráneo Oriental durante el Bronce Final (1150–950 AC). *Trabajos de Prehistoria* 53(2):95–115.

Mederos Martín, A 1996b. Representaciones de liras en las estelas decoradas del Bronce Final de la Península Ibérica. *Cuadernos de Prehistoría y Arqueología de la Universidad Autónoma de Madrid* 23:114–123.

Mederos Martín, A 1997. Nueva cronología del Bronce Final en el occidente de Europa. *Complutum* 8:73–96.

Mederos Martín, A 1999. Ex occidente lux. El comercio Micénico en el Mediterráneo Central y Occidental (1625–1100 AC). *Complutum* 10:229–266.

Mederos, A & Harrison, RJ 1996. 'Placer de Dioses'. Incensarios en soportes con ruedas del Bronce Final de la Península Ibérica. *Homenaje al Profesor Manuel Fernández Miranda. Complutum Extra* 6, Madrid: Universidad Complutense:Vol 1, 237–253.

Mederos, A & Lamberg-Karlovsky, CC 2001. Converting currencies in the Old World. *Nature* 411:437.

Megaw, JVS (ed) 1976. *To illustrate the monuments*. London and New York: Thames and Hudson.

Melchior-Bonnet, S 2001. *The mirror. A history*. (Trans. KH Jewett) New York and London: Routledge.

Menghin, W 1999. The Berlin gold hat: a ceremonial headdress of the Late Bronze Age. In Demakopoulou, K, Eluere, C, Jensen, J, Jockenhövel, A and Mohen, J-P (eds) *Gods and heroes of the European Bronze Age. Catalogue of the Exhibition Gods and Heroes of the Bronze Age Europe at the time of Ulysses*. London: Thames and Hudson:172–175.

Mergelina, C de 1944. Tugia. Reseña de unos trabajos. *Boletín del Seminario de Arte y Arqueología de Valladolid* X:27–30.

Merideth, C 1998. *An archaeometallurgical survey for ancient tin mines and smelting sites in Spain and Portugal*. British Archaeological Reports S714. Oxford: Hadrian Books.

Merlo, P & Xella, P 2001. Da Erwin Rohde ai Rapiuma ugaritici: antecedenti vicino-orientali degli eroi greci', In Ribichini, S, Rocchi, M and Xella, P (eds) *La cuestione delle influenze vicinoorientali sulla religione greca*. Rome: CNR:281–297.

Mezzena, F 1998. Les stèles anthropomorphes en Europe. In *Dieux de pierre. La grande statuaire anthropomorphe en Europe au IIIème millénaire avant J.C.* Geneva-Milan: Skira:15–89.

Miller, DA 2000. *The epic hero*. Baltimore: Johns Hopkins University Press.

Montoya Oliver, JM 1983. *Pastoralismo mediterráneo*. Ministerio de Agricultura, Pesca y Alimentación, ICONA Monografía NE25. Madrid.

Montoya Oliver, JM 1988a. *Encinas y encinares*. Ediciones Mundi-Prensa; Madrid.

Montoya Oliver, JM 1988b. *Los alcornocales*, 2nd edn. Madrid: Ministerio de Agricultura.

Mordant, C, Pernot, M & Rychner, V (eds) 1998. *L'Atelier du Bronzier en Europe du XXe au VIIIe siècle avant notre ère*. Actes du Colloque International 'Bronze '96' Neuchâtel et Dijon, 1996, 3 vols. Paris: Comité des Travaux Historiques et Scientifiques.

Morena López, JA & Muñoz Muñoz, JF 1990. Nueva estela de guerrero del Bronce Final hallada en Córdoba. *Revista de Arqueolgia* 115:14–15.

Moreno Arrastio, FJ 1995. La estela de Arroyo Manzanas (Las Herencias II. Toledo). *Gerión* 13:275–294.

Morgan, I 1991. The archaeology of the ancestors: The Saxel Goldstein hypothesis revisited. *Cambridge Archaeological Journal* I:147–169.

Morris, I 1992. *Death-ritual and social structure in classical antiquity*. Cambridge: Cambridge University Press.

Müller-Karpe, H 1959. *Beiträge zur Chronologie der Urnenfelderzeit nördlich und südlich der Alpen*. Römisch-Germanische Forschungen 22. Berlin: De Gruyter.

Needham, S 1979. Two recent British shield finds and their continental parallels. *Proceedings of the Prehistoric Society* 45:87–93.

Needham, S, Bronk Ramsey, C, Coombs, D, Cartwright, C & Pettitt, P 1997. An independent chronology for British Bronze Age metalwork. *Archaeological Journal* 154:55–107.

Neth, A 2001. Ein aussergewöhnlicher Friedhof der Urnenfelderzeit in Neckarsulm, Kreis Heilbronn. *Archäologische Ausgrabungen in Baden-Württemberg 2001*. Stuttgart: Theiss:51–55.

Nocete, F 2001. *Tercer milenio antes de nuestra era. Relaciones y contradicciones centro/periferia en el Valle del Guadalquivir*. Barcelona: Ediciones Bellaterra.

Norling-Christensen, H 1946. The Viksø helmets. A bronze votive find from Zealand. *Acta Archaeologica (Copenhagen)* 17:99–115.

Oliva Alonso, D 1983. Una nueva estela antropomorfa del Bronce Final en la Provincia de Sevilla. *Homenaje al Prof. Almagro Basch*. Vol II, Madrid: Ministerio de Cultura:131–140.

Oliva Alonso, D & Chasco, R 1976. Una estela funeraria con escudo de escotadura en U en la provincia de Sevilla. *Trabajos de Prehistoria* 33:387–397.

Olmos, R (ed) 1996. *Al otro lado del espejo. Aproximación a la imagen ibérica*. Madrid.

Orsi, P 1899. Pantalica e Cassibile. *Monumenti Antichi dei Lincei* 9:33–146.

Osgood, R, & Monks, S, with Toms, J 2000. *Bronze Age warfare*. Oxford: Oxbow books.

Pacheco, C, Moraleda, A & Alonso, M 1998. Una nueva estela de guerrero en Toledo. La estela de Aldeanueva de San Bartolomé. *Revista de Arqueología* 213:6–11.

Pader, EJ 1982. *Symbolism, social relations and the interpretation of mortuary remains*. Oxford: British Archaeological Reports, International Series 131.

Padilla Monge, A & Valderrama Juan, E 1994. Estela del Bronce Final hallada en el término de Écija (Sevilla). *SPAL* 3:283–290.

Pare, CFE 1992. *Wagons and wagon-graves of the Early Iron Age in central Europe*. Oxford: Oxford University Committee for Archaeology Monograph 35.

Pare, CFE 1998. Beiträge zum Übergang von der Bronze- zur Eisenzeit in Mitteleuropa. Teil 1: Grundzüge der Chronologie im östlichen Mitteleuropa (11.-8. Jahrhundert v. Chr.). *Jahrbuch des Römisch-Germanischen Zentralmuseums (Mainz)* 45(1):293–433.

Pare, CFE 1999. Weights and weighing in Bronze Age Central Europe. *Eliten in der Bronzezeit. Ergebnisse zweier Kolloquien in Mainz und Athen*. Mainz: Monographien des Römisch-Germanischen Zentralmuseums 43:421–514.

Pare, CFE (ed) 2000. *Metals Make the World Go Round. The supply and circulation of metals in Bronze Age Europe*. Oxford: Oxbow Books.

Parsons, JJ 1962. The acorn-hog economy of the oak woodlands of southwestern Spain. *Geographical Review* 52:211–235.

Patay, P 1968. Urnenfelderzeitliche Bronzeschilde im Karpatenbecken. *Germania* 46:241–248.

Pavón Soldevila, I 1998. *El tránsito del II al I milenio a.C. en las cuencas medias de los ríos Tajo y Guadiana: la Edad del Bronce*. Cáceres: Universidad de Extremadura.

Petrovic, N 2001. The 'Smiting God' and religious syncretism in the Late Bronze Age Aegean. In Biehl, PF, Bertemes, F and Meller, H (eds) *The archaeology of cult and religion*. Archaeolingua 13. Budapest: Archaeolingua Alapítvány:107–120.

Piette, J 1998. Les pectoreaux du Bronze Final: les découvertes récentes de La Saulsotte (Aube, France). In Mordant, C, Pernot, M and Rychner, V (eds) *L'Atelier du Bronzier en Europe du XXe au VIIIe siècle avant notre ère*. Actes du Colloque International 'Bronze '96' Neuchâtel et Dijon, 1996, 3 vols. Paris: Comité des Travaux Historiques et Scientifiques:129–140.

Piggott, S 1983. *The earliest wheeled transport from the Atlantic coast to the Caspian sea*. London and New York: Thames and Hudson.

Pingel, V 1992. *Die vorgeschichtlichen Goldfunde der Iberischen Halbinsel. Eine archäologische Untersuchung zur Auswertung der Spektralanalysen*. Madrider Forschungen 17. Berlin and New York: De Gruyter.

Polomé, EC 1997. Animals in Indo European cult and religion. *Studies in honour of M. Gimbutas II*, Washington DC: Institute for the Study of Man:258–265.

Portela Hernando, D & Jiménez Rodrigo, JC 1996. Una nueva estela de guerrero. La estatua-menhir-estela de guerrero de Talavera de la Reina. *Revista de Arqueología 188*:36–43.

Powell, TGE 1963. Some implications of chariotry. In Foster, ILL and Alcock, L (eds) *Culture and environment. Essays in honour of Sir Cyril Fox*. London: Routledge and Kegan Paul:153–169.

Powell, TGE 1976. South-west peninsula chariot stelae. In Megaw, JVS (ed) *To illustrate the monuments*. London and New York: Thames and Hudson:164–169.

Primas, M & Pernicka, E 1998. Der Depotfund von Oberwilfingen. Neue Ergebnisse zur Zirkulation von Metallbarren. *Germania* 76(1):25–65.

Pryor, F 1991. *Flag Fen. Prehistoric fenland centre*. London: Batsford and English Heritage.

Pulak, C 2000. The balance weights from the Late Bronze Age shipwreck at Uluburun. In Pare, CFE (ed) *Metals make the world go round. The supply and circulation of metals in Bronze Age Europe*. Oxford: Oxbow Books:247–266.

Puhvel, J 1987. *Comparative mythology*. Baltimore & London: The Johns Hopkins University Press.

Quesada, F 1994. Datos para una filiación egea de los carros grabados en las 'Estelas del Suroeste'. In De la Casa, C. (ed) *V Congreso Internacional de Estelas Funerarias. Soria, 28 de abril al 1 de Mayo de 1993. Actas del Congreso* I:179–187.

Randsborg, K (ed) 1996. *Absolute chronology: Archaeological Europe 2500–500 BC. Acta Archaeologica (Copenhagen) 67 (=Acta Archaeologica Supplementa 1)*. Copenhagen: Munksgaard.

Rank, O 1914 (1971 edn). *The double: a psychoanalytical study*. (H Tucker, trans and ed). Chapel Hill: University of North Carolina Press.

Raulwing, P 2000. *Horses, chariots and Indo-Europeans. Foundations and methods of chariotry research from the viewpoint of comparative Indo-European linguistics*. Archaeolingua, Series Minor, 13. Budapest: Archaeolingua Alapítvány.

Renfrew, C 1982. Socio-economic change in ranked society. In Renfrew, C and Shennan, S (eds) *Ranking, resources and exchange*. New Directions in Archaeology series, Cambridge: Cambridge University Press:1–9.

Renfrew, C & Shennan, S (eds) 1982. *Ranking, resources and exchange*. New Directions in Archaeology series, Cambridge: Cambridge University Press.

Ribichini, S, Rocchi, M & Xella, P (eds) 2001. *La cuestione delle influenze vicinoorientali sulla religione greca*. Rome: CNR.

Rice, M 1998. *The power of the bull*. London: Routledge.

Ridgway, D, Serra Ridgway, FR, Pearce, M, Herring, M, Whitehouse, RD & Wilkins, JB (eds) 2000. *Ancient Italy in its Mediterranean setting. Studies in honour of Ellen Macnamara*. Accordia Specialist Studies on the Mediterranean, vol 4. London: University of London.

Risch, R, Lull, V, Micó, R & Rihuete Hernanda, C 2001. Neue Entdeckungen zur Vorgeschichte von Menorca. In Ulbert, T (ed) *Hispania Antiqua. Denkmäler der Frühzeit. 2* vols. Deutsches Archäologisches Institut, Madrid. Mainz: VonZabern:153–170.

Rodríguez Diaz, A, Pavón Soldevila, I, Merideth, C & Juan i Tresserras, J 2001. El Cerro de San Cristóbal, Logrosán, Extremadura, Spain. *The archaeometallurgical excavation of a Late Bronze Age tin-mining and metalworking site. First season excavation 1998*. British Archaeological Reports, International Series 922. Oxford: Archaeopress.

Rodríguez Hidalgo, JM 1983. Nueva estela decorada en Burguillos (Sevilla). *Archivo Español de Arqueología* 56:229–231.

Rodríguez Temiño, I & Núñez Pariente de León, E 1983/4. Una segunda estela del Bronce Final hallada en Écija. *Pyrenae* 19/20:289–294.

Rodríguez Temiño, I & Núñez Pariente de León, E 1985. La tercera estela del Bronce Final hallada en Écija. *Habis* 16:481–485.

Roso de Luna, M 1898. Lápida sepulcral de Solana de Cabañas, en el Partido de Logrosán. *Boletín de la Real Academia de la Historia* XXXII-XXXIII: 179–182.

Rowlands, M 1993. The role of memory in the transmission of culture. *World Archaeology* 25(2):141–151.

Ruiz-Gálvez Priego, M 1986. Navegación e comercio entre el Atlántico y el Mediterráneo a fines de la Edad del Bronce. *Trabajos de Prehistoria* 43:9–42.

Ruiz-Gálvez Priego, M 1991. Songs of the Wayfaring Lad. Late Bronze Age Atlantic exchange and the building of the regional identity of the west Iberian peninsula. *Oxford Journal of Archaeology* 10(3):277–306.

Ruiz-Gálvez Priego, M (ed) 1995. *Ritos de paso y puntos de paso. La Ría de Huelva en el mundo del Bronce Final Europeo*. Complutum Extra No. 5, Madrid: Universidad Complutense de Madrid.

Ruiz-Gálvez Priego, ML 1998. *La europa atlántica en la Edad del Bronce. Un viaje a las raíces de la Europa occidental*. Barcelona: Critica.

Ruiz-Gálvez Priego, M 2000. Weight systems and exchange networks in Bronze Age Europe. In Pare, CFE (ed) 2000. *Metals Make the World Go Round. The supply and circulation of metals in Bronze Age Europe*. Oxford: Oxbow Books:267–279.

Ruiz-Gálvez Priego, M & Galán, E 1991. Las estelas del suroeste como hitos de vías ganaderas y rutas comerciales. *Trabajos de Prehistoria* 48:257–273.

Ruiz Lara, D 1986. Nueva estela decorada en el Valle del Zújar. *Estudios de Prehistoria Cordobesa* 3:43–52.

Scarre, C & Healy, F 1993. *Trade and exchange in prehistoric Europe: proceedings of a conference held at the University of Bristol, April 1992*. (Oxbow Monograph 33). Oxford: Oxbow Books.

Schäfer, J 1958. Elfenbeinspiegelgriffe des zweiten Jahrtausends. *Athenische Mitteilungen* 73:73–87.

Schauer, P 1971. *Die Schwerter in Süddeutschland, Österreich und der Schweiz I (Griffplatten-, Griffangel- und Griffzungenschwerter)*. Prähistorische Bronzefunde IV, 2. Munich: Beck.

Schauer, P 1975. Die Bewaffnung der 'Adelskrieger' während der späten Bronze- und frühen Eisenzeit. *Ausgrabungen in Deutschland 1960–1975*. (Monographien des Römisch-Germanischen Zentralmuseums 1/III): 305–311, plus 3 fold outs.

Schauer, P 1978. Die urnenfelderzeitlichen Bronzepanzer von Fillinges, Dep. Haute-

Savoie, Frankreich. *Jahrbuch des Römisch-Germanischen Zentralmuseums (Mainz)* 25:92–130.

Schauer, P 1980. Der Rundschild der Bronze- und frühen Eisenzeit. *Jahrbuch des Römisch-Germanischen Zentralmuseums (Mainz)* 27:196–248.

Schauer, P 1983. Orient im spätbronze- und früheisenzeitlichen Occident. Kulturbeziehungen zwischen der Iberischen Halbinsel und dem Vorderen Orient während des späten 2. und des ersten Drittels des 1. Jahrtausends v. Chr. *Jahrbuch des Römisch-Germanischen Zentralmuseums (Mainz)* 30:175–194.

Schauer, P 1984. Spuren minoisch-mykenischen und orientalischen Einflusses im atlantischen Westeuropa. *Jahrbuch des Römisch-Germanischen Zentralmuseums (Mainz)* 31:137–186.

Schauer, P 1985. Spuren orientalischen und ägäischen Einflusses im bronzezeitlichen Nordischen Kreis. *Jahrbuch des Römisch-Germanischen Zentralmuseums Mainz* 32:123–195.

Schauer, P 1986. *Die Goldblechkegel der Bronzezeit. Ein Beitrag zur Kulturverbindung zwischen Orient und Mitteleuropa.* (Monographien des Römisch-Germanischen Zentralmuseums Mainz 8). Bonn: Habelt.

Schauer, P 1990. Schutz- und Angriffswaffen bronzezeitlicher Krieger im Spiegel ausgewählter Grabfunde Mitteleuropas. In Furmanek, V and Horst, F (eds) *Beiträge zur Geschichte und Kultur der Mitteleuropäischen Bronzezeit*. Berlin and Nitra: Zentralinstitut für Alte Geschichte und Archäologie, Nitra: Archeologicky Ustav Slovenskej Akademie Vied.

Scott Littleton, C 1982. *The new comparative mythology: anthropological assessment of the theories of Georges Dumézil*, 3rd edn. Berkeley, CA: University of California Press.

Shanks, M 1999. *Art and the early Greek state. An interpretive archaeology*. Cambridge: Cambridge University Press.

Sherratt, S 2000. Circulation of metals and the end of the Bronze Age in the Eastern Mediterranean. In Pare, CFE (ed) 2000. *Metals Make the World Go Round. The supply and circulation of metals in Bronze Age Europe*. Oxford: Oxbow Books:82–98.

Smith, JR 1977. *Tree crops: a permanent agriculture*. 4th edn. New York: Devin-Adair.

Smith, JZ 1987. *To take place. Towards a theory in ritual*. Chicago & London: University of Chicago Press.

Snodgrass, A 1998. *Homer and the artists. Text and picture in early Greek art*. Cambridge and London: Cambridge University Press.

Sorabji, R 1993. *Animal minds and human morals: The origins of the Western debate*. London: Duckworth.

Soutou, A 1962. La stèle au bouclier à échancrures en V de Substantion (Castelnau-le-Lez, Hérault). *Ogam* XIV(6):521–546.

Sørensen, MLS 1998. The Atlantic Bronze Age and the construction of meaning. In Jorge, SO (ed) 1998. *Existe uma Idade do Bronze Atlântico?* Trabalhos de Arqueologia 10. Lisboa: Instituto Português de Arqueologia:255–266.

Sørensen, ML & Thomas, R (eds) 1989. *The Bronze-Iron Age transition in Europe. Aspects of community and change in european societies c.1200 to 500 B.C.* Oxford: BAR International Series 483.

Spenccr, N (cd) 1997. *Time, tradition and society in greek archaeology: bridging the 'Great Divide'.* London: Routledge.

Sperber, D 1982. *Le savoir des anthropologues.* Paris:Hermann.

Sperber, L 1999. Zu den Schwertträgern im Westlichenkreis der Urnenfelderkultur: Profane und Religiöse Aspekte. *Eliten in der Bronzezeit. Ergebnisse zweier Kolloquien in Mainz und Athen.* Mainz: Monographien des Römisch-Germanischen Zentralmuseums 43:625–659.

Spindler, K & Veiga Ferreira, O da 1973. Der spätbronzezeitliche Kuppelbau von der Roça do Casal do Meio in Portugal. *Madrider Mitteilungen* 14:60–108.

Springer, T 1999. The golden cone of Ezelsdorf-Buch: a masterpiece of the goldsmith's art from the Bronze Age. In Demakopoulou, K, Eluere, C, Jensen, J, Jockenhövel, A and Mohen, J-P (eds) *Gods and Heroes of the European Bronze Age. Catalogue of the Exhibition Gods and Heroes of the Bronze Age Europe at the Time of Ulysses.* London: Thames and Hudson:176–181.

Sprockhoff, E 1930. *Zur Handelsgeschichte der germanischen Bronzezeit.* Vorgeschichtliche Forschungen 7. Berlin: De Gruyter.

Spruytte, J 1977. *Études experimentales sur l'attelage.* Paris: Crépin-Leblond. (trans Littauer, MA 1983 Early Harness Systems. London: JA Allen.)

Stary, P 1991. Arms and armour of the Nuraghic Warrior-Statuettes. In Frizell, BS (ed), *Arte militare e architettura nuragica. Nuragic architecture in its military, territorial and socio-economic context.* Proceedings of the First International Colloquium on Nuragic Architecture at the Swedish Institute in Rome, 7–9 December, 1989. Skrifter Utgivna av Svenska Institut i Rom, 4°. XLVIII. Stockholm: Paul Åströms Förlag: 119–142.

Stead, I 1965. *The La Tène cultures of eastern Yorkshire.* York. The Yorkshire Philosophical Society; Hull: Brown and Sons.

Stevenson, A & Harrison, RJ 1992. Ancient Forests in Spain. A model for land-use and dry forest management in South-West Spain from 4000 BC to 1900 AD. *Proceedings of the Prehistoric Society* 58:227–247.

Stoddart, S & Mathers, C (eds) 1994. *Development and decline in the Mediterranean Bronze Age*. Sheffield: University of Sheffield Press.

Stokes, W 1987. *The tripartite life of Pâtrick with other documents relating to that saint*. 2 vols. London.

Suárez de Venegas, J & Ortiz Romero, P 1994. La estela decorada de Quintana de la Serena. *Revista de Arqueología* 161:54–56.

Taplin, O 1980. The shield of Achilles within the Illiad. *Greece and Rome* 27(1):1–21.

Tavares de Proença Júnior, F 1903. *Antiguidades. I. Explorações feitas nos arredores de Castello Branco em Setembro e Outoubro de 1903*. Coimbra: França Amado.

Tavares de Proença Júnior, F 1905. *Notice sur deux monuments épigraphiques*. França Amado: Coimbra.

Tejera Gaspar, A, Jorge Godoy, S & Quintana Montesceoca (Montesdeoca sic), R 1995. La estela IV de 'La Atalaya de la Morenilla' (Écija, Sevilla). *SPAL* 4:251–255.

Terés Landeta, J, Valero Sáez, A & Pérez Figueras, C 1995. *Extremadura. Cuadernos de la Trashumancia* 15. Madrid: ICONA, Ministerio de Agricultura, Pesca y Alimentación.

Thrane, H 1966. Dänische funde fremde Bronzegefässe der jüngeren Bronzezeit (Periode IV). *Acta Archaeologica (Copenhagen)* 49:1–35.

Thrane, H 1990. The Mycenaean fascination: a Northerner's view. *Orientalisch-Ägäische Einflüsse in der Europäischen Bronzezeit. Ergebnisse eines Kolloquiums.* (Monographien des Römisch-Germanischen Zentralmuseums 15) Bonn: Habelt: 165–179.

Torres Ortiz, M 1999. *Sociedad y mundo funerario en Tartessos*. Bibliotheca Archaeologica Hispana 3, Madrid: Real Academia de la Historia.

Tranoy, A 1988. Du heros au chef. L'image du guerrier dans les sociétés indigènes du nord-ouest de la péninsule ibèrique (IIème siècle avant J.-C. - Ier. siècle après J.-C.), in *Actes du Colloque 'Le Monde des Images en Gaule et dans les provinces voisines, Sèvres 16–17 mai 1987', Caesarodunum XXIII*: 219–227.

Treherne, P 1995. The warrior's beauty: the masculine body and self-identity in Bronze-Age Europe. *Journal of European Archaeology* 3(1):105–144.

Tronchetti, CN 1986. Nuraghic statuary from Monte Prama. In Balmuth, M. (ed) *Studies in Sardinian Archaeology, Vol II: Sardinia and the Mediterranean*. Ann Arbor: University of Michigan Press:41–59.

Ulbert, T (ed) 2001. *Hispania Antiqua. Denkmäler der Frühzeit*. 2 vols. Deutsches Archäologisches Institut, Madrid. Mainz: Von Zabern.

Valiente Malla, J & Prado Toledano, S 1978. Estelas decoradas de Aldea del Rey (Ciudad Real). *Archivo Español de Arqueología* 50/51:375–379.

van Dommelen, P 1998. *On colonial grounds. A comparative study of colonialism and rural settlement in first millennium BC in west central Sardinia*. Leiden: Archaeological Studies, Leiden University.

Various authors 1996. *De Ulisses a Viriato. O primeiro milénio a.C.* Lisbon: Ministerio de Cultura.

Vazquerizo Gil, D 1989. 'Estelas de guerreros' en la protohistoría Peninsular. *Revista de Arqueología* 99:29–38.

Velasco López, MH 1999. Loegaire y los muertos armados. In Alonso Dávila, Crespo Ortiz de Zátate S & Garabito Gómez, T (eds) *Homenaje al profesor Montenegro. Estudios de Historia Antigua*, Valladolid: 773–789.

Verlaeckt, K 1993. The Kivik Petrographs. A reassessment of different opinions. *Germania* 71(1):1–29.

Verlaeckt, K 2000. Hoarding and the circulation of metalwork in Late Bronze Age Denmark: quantification and beyond. In Pare, CFE (ed) *Metals make the world go round. The supply and circulation of metals in Bronze Age Europe*. Oxford: Oxbow Books:194–208.

Vernant, J-P 1991. In the mirror of Medusa. In Zeitlin, FI (ed) *Mortals and immortals. Collected essays*. Princeton NJ: Princeton University Press:141–150.

Vilaça, R 1995. *Aspectos do Povoamento da Beira Interior (Centro e Sul) nos Finais da Idade do Bronze*. Trabalhos de Arqueologia 9, 2 vols. Lisboa: IPPAR.

Villaseca Díaz, F 1995. Las estelas decoradas del Bronce Final en Málaga. Nuevas aportaciones para su estudio. *V Congreso Internacional de Estelas Funerarias; Actas del Congreso (Soria, 28 de abril a 1 de mayo de 1993)*, 71–75.

Waddell, J 1998. *The prehistoric archaeology of Ireland*. Dublin: Galway University Press Ltd.

Wahl, J 2001. Nur Männer 'im besten Alter'. Erste anthropologische Erkenntnisse zum urnenfelderzeitlichen Friedhof von Neckarsulm, Kreis Heilbronn. *Archäologische Ausgrabungen in Baden-Württemberg 2001*, Theiss: 55–56.

Wallerstein, I 1974. *The modern world system. Capitalist agriculture and the origins of the European world-economy in the sixteenth century*. New York: Academic Press.

Ward, BE 1979. Not merely players: drama, art and ritual in traditional China. *Man* (NS) 14(1):18–39.